B. E. Harrell-Bond

Modern Marriage in Sierra Leone

A study of the professional group

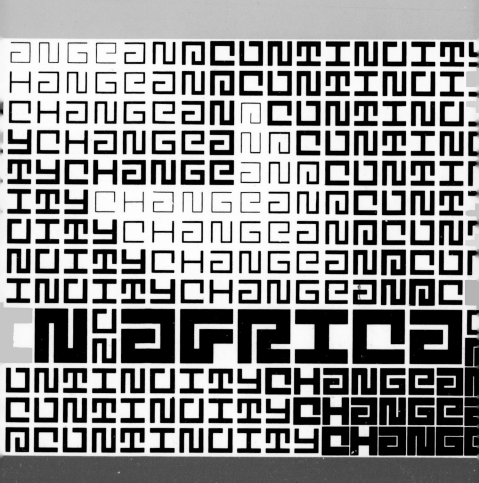

Mouton

Modern Marriage in Sierra Leone

CHANGE AND CONTINUITY IN AFRICA

MOUTON · THE HAGUE · PARIS

BARBARA E. HARRELL-BOND

Modern Marriage in Sierra Leone

A Study of the Professional Group

MOUTON · THE HAGUE · PARIS

ISBN 90 279 7871 9

Cover design by Jurriaan Schrofer

© 1975, Mouton & Co. B.V., Herderstraat 5, The Hague, The Netherlands

Printed in the Netherlands

To Stephen, Deborah, David

Foreword

Concerning the Congo (now Zaire), a Belgian offical once remarked, 'We used to think that the African mind was an empty vessel and all that we had to do was to pour European civilization into it'. Barbara Harrell-Bond's opening chapter reminds us that what became the Sierra Leone Colony served for much of the nineteenth century as a veritable laboratory for an attempted operation of this kind.

A sheer accident of history brought to the Colony's shores boat-loads of Africans, liberated from slave ships. They spoke a hundred or more different languages and dialects and for obvious reasons they pos-sessed no common culture. Thus there was – to use contemporary jargon – an immense problem of 'rehabilitation'. It was constructively tackled, and among the Creoles was developed a solid sense of community, with Christian evangelism and education being the principal instruments. Thanks in particular to the missionaries' zeal, these Creoles not only grew in prosperity but became themselves a major 'civilizing' force. By the indigenous population upcountry they were regarded as 'black Europeans', and they did in fact constitute little oases of westernized civilization in the other West African territories to which they them-selves moved as traders, evangelists, and educators. Indeed, in the Anglophone countries as a whole it was the members of these 'old' families living in or emanating from Freetown who were looked upon as the principal arbiters of civilized manners.

Dr. Harrell-Bond's book is concerned with marital relationships and their effect on family organization among both Creole and Provincial professional people in Sierra Leone. The term 'Provincial' refers to people descended from the former Protectorate's indigenous inhabi-tants, and I have recalled the historical antecendents for two inter-related reasons. First, despite all the European civilization 'poured' into the liberated Africans, it failed signally to bring about a complete cultural metamorphosis. In other words, the Creole community that emerged did not in fact become simply 'black Europeans'. On the contrary, it developed both a language and a culture of its own.

In consequence, unlike most studies involving 'culture-contact' what Dr. Harrell-Bond had to deal with was the inter-play not of two, but of three fairly distinctive traditions, as well as a measure of Islam. This is methodologically important because investigations into marriage involve questions of social status and mobility and so must naturally pay regard to the role of reference groups. Unlike some contemporary studies of African urbanization, Dr. Harrell-Bond's information was gained mainly by participant-observation. The intensive method of fieldwork is still the distinctive hallmark of social anthropology, but it is idle to pretend that one can deal adequately with urban phenomena by personal contact alone. Case studies have to be brought together in terms of a conceptual framework wide enough to encompass factors extrinsic to the fieldwork situation itself. It is, therefore, greatly to Dr. Harrell-Bond's credit that she provides the requisite perspective in language that is as straightforward as the description of everyday events.

Dr. Harrell-Bond uses her fieldwork material effectively to illustrate the causes of marital disharmony. She explains that in the traditional system great importance is attached to the procreation of children, and to have a large number of wives and many children is a mark of male prestige. The modern view, in which many professional men as well as the wives concur, is that polygyny is a backward practice. Nevertheless, although both parties consequently regard monogamy as the right type of marriage, this does not stop many husbands having extra-marital affairs and fathering 'outside' children. When wives object to this practice, the resulting quarrel, nowadays, is increasingly personal to the husband and wife alone. Harrell-Bond, however, draws attention to the context of this marital conflict. She analyses it in terms of the difference between traditional and Western values. This enables her to show that the conjugal relationship concerned is largely a reflection of the clash between traditional and Western culture.

Outwardly, at least, a good deal more was familiar than was strange in the society studied by Dr. Harrell Bond. It consisted largely of Africans who had resided overseas, in some cases for many years. Dr. Harrell-Bond herself raises by implication some interesting prospects for the future of African marriage. She writes:

'Today ideas about the husband's role in monogamous marriage require men to support the household, relieving wives, in theory at least of economic responsibility. A 'good husband' will not rely on the fact that his wife is contributing to the maintenance of the home, but will make it clear that she is free to spend her own earnings as she chooses. However, since most men spend money on their relatives, on women outside the marriage, and incur financial obligations for the support of illegitimate children, wives often feel it is necessary to insure their own security by investing their money outside the marriage, in their own families, or by saving it.'

This passage is worth pondering because there is evidence from other countries as well as Sierra Leone of women being prepared 'to go it alone'. In fact, almost all African women want a husband and so I am not referring here to spinsterhood. What I do mean is that women have an increasing desire to be economically independent; that they deliberately make this decision and try to equip themselves for money-earning. In other words, the women's attitude is pragmatic. Those who are 'westernized' may marry for 'love'; but they have also emotional reservations and have made their practical preparations in the event of 'love' turning sour.

In the West, there are many advocates of the so-called companionate type of union. Ideally, husband and wife should share each other's interests and take part in joint activities. This, as explained, is the aim as well of some of the Freetown elite; but, as yet, such a view is not widely held. The African traditional society divides men from women and this has been regarded as the basis of male domination. Does this mean that despite all the advance Sierra Leonean women have made in the professions, their matrimonial status may remain as it is?

The answer depends largely on whether the wife has an income of her own, because the traditional separation of man and wife is not disadvantageous in itself. At the cultural level of society where it applies, there are well-known cases of women traders doing well enough to build themselves fine houses, provide young relatives with a university education, and even take over family affairs. One of the reasons is that these almost illiterate women have in fact more room for manoeuvre than an educated wife whose conjugal relationship, though 'joint', is only so in a nominal sense.

A good deal also depends on the husbands' attitudes. In opting through monogamy for the conjugally-based nuclear family, they have secured a better springboard for individual achievement than the traditional family provides. This is the case because in professional circles a man's prestige requires that his household should be kept up to date, his guests appropriately entertained, etc. An educated wife can perform these functions, but what does a husband do if she is economically in a position to please herself? He may have to make greater concessions than he had bargained for in order to gain his wife's co-operation.

What Barbara Harrell-Bond does is to explain a complicated matrimonial situation in simple language. True, in the facts given, there may be nothing new to people already familiar with Freetown and Sierra Leone. However, if they study carefully what she has written, they will perceive that this is not the whole story. For what Dr. Harrell-Bond does, metaphorically speaking, is to thrust her hand into the existing picture of a jig-saw puzzle, to sort out the individual pieces and to show that a different picture might be created if the pieces were re-fitted in a different order.

It is for these reasons that I hope Dr. Harrell-Bond's book will reach a wider public than anthropologists and sociologists alone. For these members of her own profession it provides an invaluable piece of documentation for comparative purposes. But in the unindustrialized countries today, there are also almost countless agencies at work on 'social development'. These social administrators and community developers, too, are in need of first-hand information. Dr. Harrell-Bond's book may provide not only this, but insight into Third World social problems in general.

Kenneth Little

Preface

This study was part of a project originally designed by members of the Department of Anthropology, University of Edinburgh. The project included three separate studies of marriage relationships among professionals and their spouses in Ghana, Sierra Leone and Scotland.[1] For these studies 'professionals' were defined as those persons who had earned a university degree or equivalent professional qualification and their spouses.[2] I was employed to conduct the research in Sierra Leone. Although it was intended that the findings of the three studies would be comparable, each investigator was given considerable scope to adapt the research design during the course of the fieldwork. My own early observations led me to believe that the most useful approach in Sierra Leone would be to conduct an exploratory study of marriage among the professional group relying mainly on the traditional method of the anthropologist, as the participant-observer. In addition, a survey was made of the entire professional group in Sierra Leone. These interviews provided additional information on the composition and social background of the professionals and their marriage relationships as well as checking on the reliability of the information obtained through observations. I also conducted a survey of the university students.[3] The methods employed in collecting these and other kinds of data are described in Appendix A.

1. The Ghana study is reported in Oppong (1973).
2. Other defining criteria for the population to be studied were also laid down in the initial design. These included salary level, position of the family in terms of the developmental cycle (Goody 1966), etc. Why the Sierra Leone situation made it impractical to limit the focus of the study to the original design is discussed in Chapter One and Appendix A.
3. See Harrell-Bond (1972) for a discussion on some methodological issues raised by these surveys.

While the freedom to adapt the focus of the research and the methods used doubtless enhanced the results of the separate studies, the aim to collect strictly comparative data was not achieved. Campbell and Levine (1970) have recently discussed this problem of comparison, a perennial concern of anthropologists. They note that attempts to use the comparative method in social anthropology have mainly depended either on enumerative cross-cultural surveys like those of Murdock (1949) and Whiting and Child (1953) or upon ethnographic reports which have attempted to describe all aspects of a culture. Today, as they note, the trend is towards more specialized fieldwork which produces publication on a much narrower range of data. They also point to the shift away from descriptive ethnography to the newer goal of attempting to test hypotheses. 'Ironically', as they put it, 'the attempt to be scientific in this manner sometimes reduces the scientific values of the end-product'. Data collected for such narrowly specified purposes do not provide material for comparisons and, moreover, the potential for collecting data for comparative analysis on unanticipated topics is diminished. While comparison has always been a basic aim of anthropological research, perhaps studies of marriage and the family are especially prone to dangers of premature attempts to collect comparable data. Certainly, the relatively few studies of urban marriage relationships and family life in West Africa suggest that the need for detailed ethnographic studies should take precedence (Gutkind, 1962, p. 166).

The fieldwork in Sierra Leone was carried out over fourteen months in 1967-68. Although the majority of the professionals live in Freetown, the capital of the country, many are working in towns scattered over the country. During the course of the research I had opportunity to travel widely in the country, which greatly aided my understanding of the society. Since completing this research I returned to Sierra Leone for an additional eighteen months to conduct a study of family law.[4] This book has benefited greatly from the additional research experience in Sierra Leone.

Sierra Leone, according to the 1963 Census, has a population of 2,180,335.[5] This population is made up of eighteen indigenous tribes and the Creoles, descendants of the liberated African slaves who were

4. This study was supported by the Afrika-Studiecentrum, Leiden, Holland.
5. This and the other population figures are from *1963 Population Census of Sierra Leone*, Central Statistics Office, Freetown, 1965, Vol. I and II.

settled in the colony of Freetown on the peninsula in the eighteenth century.[6] Of the 60,000 or so persons on the peninsula who are non-Sierra Leonean, about 4,000 are from the United States, the United Kingdom, Europe or other western countries, and 3,000 from Lebanon or Syria,[7] the rest from nearby African countries.

Freetown, the capital, had, in 1963, a population of 127,907 and it is the largest city in the country. There are twelve other towns which have populations of over 5,000. Most of the Sierra Leoneans, however, continue to live in small villages of less than 1,000 inhabitants.

Sierra Leone has an extensive network of roads, many miles of which are paved, and the road system is constantly being extended. People travel by numerous privately-owned lorries and 'poda-podas' (small vans fitted out as buses) as well as by private motor cars. In addition, since the turn of the century Sierra Leone has had a railway connecting the south and parts of the north with Freetown.[8] Besides an international airport at Lungi, there are eight landing strips in the country accommodating small planes, with regular scheduled flight services. Telephones connect almost all main towns.

The climate of Sierra Leone is tropical. Only a few areas average less than 80 inches of rainfall is each year and in most parts of the country the mean annual rainfall over 100 inches. The Western Area and parts of the south average over 140 inches of rain every year. The rains come during the period from May to October.

The fieldwork for the research reported here was initially supported by the Department of Anthropology, University of Edinburgh. I wish to express my thanks to the members of this department, particularly Professor Kenneth Little, Professor James Littlejohn, and Dr. Mary Noble, who encouraged me and offered many helpful suggestions. I would like to acknowledge with gratitude the assistance of the Institute of Mental Health, Bethesda, Maryland (National Institute of Mental

---

6. The composition of the indigenous population of Sierra Leone is complex, several groups having migrated there more recently than others.

7. In Sierra Leone white people are referred to by Africans (and by themselves) as either 'Europeans' or 'expatriates'. The former term is perhaps more common and it makes a distinction between people of strictly European origin and other white people living in Sierra Leone who come from India, the Lebanon and Syria.

8. The railway is narrow gauge and is in need of such extensive repairs as to warrant a recent government programme to phase it out progressively with the expansion of the road network.

Health Fellowship No. 1 F03 MH 34, 176-01 [CUAN]), the American Association of University Women, Washington D.C., the Department of Anthropology, University of Illinois, Urbana, Illinois, and the Afrika-Studiecentrum, Leiden, Holland, all of whom provided support at various stages of the writing of this book.

I also want to express my thanks to several other persons who contributed intellectually to the study: Professor John Beattie, now of Leiden University, Mr. Edwin Ardener and Dr. Alan Milner of Oxford University, Professor Adam Podgorécki, Warsaw University, Mr. G. W. Grootenhuis, Director of the Afrika-Studiecentrum, Dr. William Young, late of Fourah Bay College, Dr. Jerry Windham, then lecturing in sociology at Njala University College; Dr. James Spradley, Macalester College; and Professor Edward Bruner, University of Illinois, Urbana, Illinois. Appreciation goes to several others who helped me in particular ways: Dr. A. K. Turay, a linguist from Njala University College who assisted me with the orthography and shared most generously many insights drawn from his own research; Mr. Peter Gorbach, Department of Social Medicine, Oxford, who served as statistical consultant; Dr. Joe Kennedy, a social psychologist who directed the Peace Corps in Sierra Leone, for spending many hours advising me on the construction and testing of the questionnaires; Dr. H. M. Joko Smart, Fourah Bay College, who spent much time discussing his own research on the law of inheritance; Mr. Albert Metzger, then a member of the Judicial Department, who gave most generously of his time to teach me about the law in Sierra Leone and later read drafts of Chapters Five and Six, giving me many helpful criticisms; Roy Kennedy who served as editor; Gillian Ball who typed the manuscript; and Peter MacIntyre who prepared the index.

It is impossible to name and thank properly all those in Sierra Leone who gave assistance, but some must be singled out: Dr. Edward Blyden III, then the director of the Institute of African Studies, who appointed me Visiting Research Fellow at Fourah Bay College and provided housing, office facilities and every other necessary assistance during my stay; Mr. Jonathan Hyde, who spent much time discussing the research; Mr. Jim Blair who helped in innumerable ways during my fieldwork and Mr. Samuel Clarke, my assistant. I also wish to thank the administrations of both University Colleges for permitting the administering of the questionnaires to the students. The staff of the Ministry of Social Welfare must be especially recognized for their dedicated support throughout my stays in Sierra Leone. Other Ministries also gave much-needed assistance: the Ministries of Health, the Interior, Education and Public Works. I also want to thank Omari Golley, Dr. and Mrs. Davidson Nicol, Mr. Joe Kowa, Mr. R. B. Kowa, Paramount Chief Foday Kai, Dyke Harding, Victor Kanu and John Labor for giving me generous help of various kinds while I was in Sierra Leone. I made a film during my fieldwork and many people were involved in this project. I especially thank the staff of the Film Unit of the Ministry of Information and the persons who took part in the actual filming. The residents of the village of Juhun, Jaima Bongor Chiefdom, where most filming was done, deserve special thanks.

My greatest debt is to the many people, necessarily anonymous, who co-operated by permitting me to question them about their own experiences, attitudes and opinions in the most intimate areas of their lives, their marriage and family relationships. The extent to which this book accurately reports the situation as regards marriage among the professionals is a testimony to their patience, tolerance and the sincerity with which they admitted me into their confidences.

The experience of conducting research in a foreign culture necessarily has a profound impact on the personal life of the anthropologist. Certainly the lives of my children and myself have been greatly enriched by our knowledge of family life in Sierra Leone. Having spent so much time there, we will always look on Sierra Leone as a second home. It is just not possible to convey the warmth of hospitality which Sierra Leoneans extended to us, but may I especially thank Mr. Augustine Sandi who was the first of many to invite me to join his family at their table to share their food.

Table of contents

Foreword by Kenneth Little   VII

Preface   XI

List of tabels   XXI

1. Introduction   1

2. The historical background   21
    The founding of the Colony   21
    The establishment of the Protectorate   25
    Independence   30

3. The composition and social background of the
    professional group   35
    Tribal composition and education   35
    Age and birthplace   36
    Marital status   37
    Religious affiliation   39
    Education   40
    Occupation and social status   48
    Social status in the village and in town   51
    Monogamy and social status   54
    The households of the married professionals   56

4. Stereotypes of traditional and western marriage
    and family life   61
    *Stereotypes of traditional and western marriage
    and family life*   66

Choice of a marriage partner, courtship and
    marriage ceremonies   67
Marriage relationships   71
The role of the wife   75
Children and family relationships within the home   76
Relationships between married couples and their relatives   79
Summary   81

5. The legal setting of marriage   84
    Marriage law   86
    Divorce law   97
    Property settlement and child custody   104
    Inheritance law   107
    Maintenance law   114
    Adoption   118

6. The status of children born out of wedlock   124
    The scope of the problem: how many children are born
        out of wedlock?   125
    The social position of the child born out of wedlock   130
    Attitudes towards husbands' extra-marital affairs   139
    The legal status of children born out of wedlock   144
    The attempt to eliminate illegitimacy   149

7. Choosing a marriage partner   157
    Criteria for selecting a spouse   159
    Relations between the unmarried: courtship   174
    Engagement   187
    Marriage ceremonies   192

8. The organization of domestic life and family relationships   196
    The organization of domestic work   197
    The organization of family finances   206
    Financial obligations to relatives   208
    The segregation of financial matters   218

9. Marital conflicts and their resolution   223
    Relatives   234
    The role of the wife and the authority of the husband   240
    Resolving conflicts   244

10. Attitudes towards sex, family limitation and the use
    of contraceptives   250
    Attitudes towards limiting the size of the family   250
    The use of contraceptives   254
    Beliefs and attitudes influencing the use of contraceptives   256
    Attitudes towards women's sexuality and their
        influence over men   264
    Attitudes of men towards sexuality   270

11. Prospects for marriage among the professional group   279
    Does the nuclear family 'fit' Sierra Leone Society?   289

Appendix A: Methods   296
    Learning the language   298
    Use of local resources   300
    Data collected   301
    Questionnaires administered to university students   306
    Questionnaires administered to the professionals   307
    Questionnaires administered to primary-aged children   310
    Essays by secondary school pupils   310
    Attitude scale   311
    Interviews with experts   311
    Official records and other statistical data   312

Appendix B: Questionnaires administered to samples of
    students and professionals   314

References   333

Index   341

List of tables

1. Sex and marital status of professionals   37
2. Level of western education of fathers of professional group and university students by tribal affiliation   41
3. Level of western education of mothers of professional group and university students by tribal affiliation   42
4. Occupations of wives of professional men   48
5. Occupational status and employment of married couples   49
6. 'What do you think it is that determines status and prestige in the city and the village?'   52
7. Attributes which students indicated as describing their father's family   53
8. Type of marriage of parents of professionals and students by tribal affiliation   54
9. 'How many half-brothers and sisters do you have on your father's side?'   56
10. Average number of persons per household   57
11. Age distribution of persons residing in professionals' households in the Western area   58
12. Marital status of males and females at time of marriage by type of marriage annually (1961-68)   96
13. Number of divorce petitions filed annually and decrees granted (1961-68)   97
14. The number of maintenance cases tried annually in Freetown (1961-68)   114
15. Number of children born out of wedlock in Western area (1961-68)   127
16. 'If a marriage does not produce children a wife should be understanding and allow her husband to have children outside'   144

17. 'A man's inheritance should be divided equally between all his children born within the marriage or outside'   152
18. The importance of love and parental approval in the choice of a spouse   172
19. Husband's assistance in household tasks   201
20. 'When I am old I expect my children to provide financial assistance for me'   211
21. 'The fear of my mother's curse is something I feel very deeply'   214
22. 'Which of these relatives do you expect to assist financially when you leave university?'   215
23. Students ranking of possible sources of conflict between married couples   223
24. Topics over which professional couples sometimes argue   224
25. Ideal number of children   251
26. 'What would you say was the best/worst thing about having a large family?'   253
27. Methods of contraception ever used   255
28. Methods of contraception currently used   256
29. Composition of the university sample   307
30. Sex and marital status of persons selected for interviews   308
31. Reasons for replacing persons included in the sample   309

Introduction

It is well-known that marriage and family organization in Africa have undergone a considerable transformation since the onset of the colonial era. The general trend towards monogamous marriage and the nuclear family among urban Africans has been amply documented.[1] It is assumed that these changes are connected with the growth of urban centres, the spread of western education and Christian religious ideas, and the modernization of the economic sphere. New symbols of prestige and status have emerged in urban Africa and the western type of marriage is a central one.

However, some writers, noting the problems and dissatisfactions of monogamously married couples, have reflected on the lack of 'fit' of western marriage practices in the African setting.[2] Others have commented with alarm on the disintegration of the traditional family, the central institution of African society.[3] One Sierra Leonean professional women put it this way: 'African marriage is at a crossroads, some people have the western form of marriage, some have the native, but many have neither. There is really no society. The old forms are gone but there is nothing to take their place, no morality, no principles upon which the individual can base anything.'[4] On the other hand, other observers have pointed to considerable evidence that, despite the many stresses, the African family has adapted itself to the urban

---

1. Baker and Bird 1959; Little and Price 1967, 1974; Little 1959, 1973, all bring together a number of studies of marriage in Africa which document this trend.
2. Little 1959; Noble 1968; Longmore 1959, pp. 15-16; Wilson 1942, 64.
3. For example, see Phillips and Morris 1971, p. 1; Balandier 1955, p. 262; Chin 1959 as quoted by Gutkind 1962; and Longmore 1959, pp. 103-104, 106.
4. These comments were made in an interview.

situation while retaining numerous rural characteristics.[5]

This book presents a description of marriage and family life among the professionals in Sierra Leone. In this introductory chapter I shall consider, in the light of relevant literature, some of the broad problems involved in a study of this kind, especially in the African (and particularly the West African) context. The topic of marriage among professionals, however, has not yet been extensively investigated in other African societies, so that this study has not been able to draw widely on such relevant materials. Hence it was felt necessary to present a relatively large body of description to offer a basis for future comparative work.

Although this study is about marriage relationships the emphasis will be on the behaviour of individuals, men and women: the role of husband or wife is only one of the many roles each plays in society. This emphasis upon the individual is in some contrast to many studies of this topic where the married couple or the nuclear family, rather than the individual, is taken as the unit of investigation. It is often assumed that in traditional societies it is the wider or extended family which provides the link or bridge between the members of the nuclear family and the larger society. Young and Willmott describe the approach of their own studies of the family in Britain in this way:

> 'We have . . . moved successively outwards from the married couple to the extended family, from the extended family to the kinship network, and from there to certain relations between the family and the outside world' (1957, p. 104).

With the assumed breakdown of the wider or extended family in modern, urban societies, it is also assumed that the nuclear family stands alone as an isolated, autonomous system, with an internal structure unaffected by outside influences. Elias and Scotson refer to this 'family-centred theoretical framework' as bearing a resemblance to 'early geocentric concepts of the universe according to which the earth was the kernel and the heavens the outer shell' (1965, p. 183). However, one may observe that the activities of persons who are part of a household are spread over a wide variety of social spheres, and conjugal role behaviour is just one aspect (although perhaps the most important aspect) of their lives.[6] Thus, to understand the nature of

5. Gutkind 1962.
6. For a discussion of this question see Harrell-Bond 1967, p. 430.

relationships between husband and wives and their attitudes towards their marital roles it is essential to examine the social environment in which they live. In Sierra Leone it became necessary to explore aspects of the society which at first glance might seem quite remote from the immediate relationships between husbands and wives.

Of course, taking the view that the form of the family and marriage relationships are somehow a product of the type of wider society in which they are embedded makes it difficult to decide at what point to limit the scope of the study. Dennis, Henriques and Slaughter, in their study of family life in a coal mining community in England, emphasize this difficulty:

'... phenomena like the relations between husband and wife, or the nature of leisure activities are viewed primarily from the standpoint of grasping their interrelations with the forms of activity and social relationships imposed by the coalmining work upon which the community is based. This emphasis will tend to obscure the fact that each of these particular sets of relationships is extended beyond the community, in both space and time. By itself, the community-study technique provides no way of measuring the significance of its findings against what may be crudely described as these "external factors" ' (1957, p. 7).

In Sierra Leone the difficulty of limiting the scope of the study is compounded by the fact that many profound influences on marriage relationships stem from the effects of the imposition of colonial rule and the accompanying intrusion of foreign institution, ideas and values. For example, discrediting the traditional polygamous form of marriage and upholding the ideals of Christian monogamous marriage was a fundamental missionary emphasis. Monogamous marriage continues to be very closely identified with the notions of progress and 'being civilized'. Although today the status of the professional depends on many attributes, it is hard to imagine that anyone could publicly flaunt at least the appearance of observing this practice and retain his social standing.

Balandier has developed the concept of the 'colonial situation', and this, he contends, must include more than a concern with ideological influences upon colonized societies. He argues for attention to the *totality* of the social situation, a concern which for anthropologists has been the tradition since Durkheim and Mauss. However, Balandier accuses anthropologists who are concerned with the phenomena of social change of having so far ignored the need to take account of the 'colonial situation' in the sense of considering it as a '. . . special combination of circumstances giving a specific orientation to the agents and process of change' (1970, p. 21). He notes that they have tended to treat these processes in isolation, looking at such things as the introduction of a monetary economy and a wage-earning class, the extension of education, or the efforts of missionary enterprises, without regarding them as '. . . comprising a single entity that provides the basis for a new and autonomous society' (1970). In order to have a comprehensive account of the situation created by colonial expansion, Balandier points out that it is necessary to go much further than is possible by using such notions as the 'clash of civilizations' or culture contact. He reminds us that in the case of these dependent people, these clashes or contacts occurred under very special conditions and it is this totality of conditions to which he refers as the colonial situation:

> 'This may be defined if we bear in mind the most general and obvious of these conditions: the domination imposed by a foreign minority, "racially" and culturally distinct, upon a materially inferior autochthonous majority, in the name of a dogmatically asserted racial (or ethnic) and cultural superiority; the bringing into relation of two heterogeneous civilizations, one technologically advanced, economically powerful, swift moving and Christian by origin, the other without complex techniques, economically backward, slow moving and fundamentally "non-Christian"; the antagonistic nature of the relations between the two societies, owing to the instrumental role to which the subject society is condemned; and the need for the dominant society, if it is to maintain its position, to rely not only upon "force", but also upon a whole range of pseudo-justifications and stereotyped patterns of behaviour, etc.' (1970, p. 52).

This study does not pretend to take complete account of the 'colonial situation' as Balandier defines it. It does, however, attempt to consider what seem to be the most important external factors which influence marriage and family relations – factors which reflect the special conditions of colonialism.

There is an enormous amount of literature, sociological, anthropological, and psychological, in the field of family and marriage. Mogey (1971) has compiled a comprehensive bibliography of the sociological literature in this area. Stephens (1963) is one example of an attempt to draw together a number of anthropological studies of the family and make some cross-cultural comparisons. For Africa, Mair (1969) has surveyed the anthropological literature on family and marriage. Little and Price (1967, 1974) brought together most of the studies of marriage in West Africa. Little (1973) discusses the role of urban African women and has referred to several more recent studies of marriage patterns in Africa. This study of marriage in Sierra Leone concentrates, however, on understanding marriage in this setting among a particular social group, the professionals. There are very few strictly comparable studies, although the relative absence of comparative references should not be taken to imply that marriage patterns among professionals in Sierra Leone are necessarily unique.

Although the study falls under the general rubric of 'elite' studies in Africa, the professionals do not include all those persons living in the country who could be considered part of the 'elite'. However, the use of professional level educational qualifications as one criterion of elite status in Africa is fully justified. While education is generally a means of social mobility, a university degree (or a 'B.A.' as Sierra Leoneans refer to it) has almost magical qualities which afford its recipient immediate access to the highest social positions in the society. Others have commented on this phenomenon in Africa of the status assigned to university degrees. Discussing recruitment to well-paid positions in the bureaucratic systems of government, Lloyd says:

'Rank at entry depends almost entirely on an educational qualification. Furthermore, ... it is not the content of education which is important but its standard. For many a young man his struggle to achieve ends with his entry to a university – the university will ensure that most of its students will graduate. Graduation is, of course, an achievement; but henceforth it becomes virtually an ascribed status, as promotion by seniority tends to prevail' (1966, p. 19).

Lloyd continues by noting that it is impossible to understand the characteristics of the modern elite in Africa without knowing something about the educational system which '. . . determines how open is recruitment to the elite and . . . the degree of corporate feeling among the elite' (1966). Kilson (1966) remarking on the importance of education in African social change, notes that normally education could be obtained by Africans '... without conjuring up fear among Europeans that its attainment would necessarily jeopardize their colonial prerogatives' (p. 38). He observes that education invariably altered the African's social position and way of life and so '... as a factor of social change, education necessarily contributed to the rise of a new system of social stratification' (p. 39).

The more general theoretical question of social stratification arises from this consideration of the exclusiveness and power of the professionals and of their relationships to the rest of the society, particularly in terms of the question of their influence on future change. I have already used the term 'elite' for the segment of society which includes the professionals, but Goldthorpe (1961) has quite rightly pointed out the limitations of this term. Lloyd (1966) considering this problem of terminology when describing the western-educated and wealthy men of contemporary African societies compares the components of both class terminology and the concept of the 'elite'. He concludes that while neither is completely satisfactory we must have some term, and 'elite' is probably less objectionable than most. As he says, 'Our search is for deeper understanding of the so-called elite and the trends in its development – not merely for the most appropriate label' (1966, p. 62).

The 'standard-setting' role or influence of the elite has been questioned by some who have looked at the problem of social stratification in urban Africa. Sinclair (1971) inquired into the perceptions of social stratification among the sub-elite in Sierra Leone whom he defined as including teachers, clerks, and other bureaucratic employees in middle grade posts which required a western education, but not up to university standard. From this research he suggests that it may well be more useful to consider the behaviour of these sub-elites rather than the elite themselves if one is interested in predicting trends throughout the society. He mentions that for West Africa others have also pointed out that the sub-elite may be an even more important reference group for the masses than the elite itself (Lloyd 1966; Krapf-Askari 1969).

In Sierra Leone education, particularly university education, has been closely linked with opportunity for social mobility since the beginnings of the Colony, much earlier than in most African colonies. Kilson traces this development historically:

> 'Law and medicine were the first liberal professions in which Sierra Leone Africans received full formal training. A Sierra

Leonean lawyer secured admission to the English Bar in 1854, and by 1890 twelve of his compatriots had done likewise. With the establishment of Fourah Bay College as an affiliated institution of Durham University in 1876, a major opportunity for the schooling of professionals opened up. The register of the College shows that before 1900 some nineteen African students studied law, and between 1900 and 1949 at least twenty-five graduates of the college became lawyers. Close to one hundred African lawyers were to be found in 1960 in Sierra Leone and a much larger number were studying law in Britain.

African doctors, clergymen, teachers, and senior civil servants have also been known in Sierra Leone for a considerable time. The first Sierra Leonean qualified in medicine in 1858 after training at St. Andrews University, Scotland. From 1858 to 1901 some twenty-five Sierra Leoneans (all Creoles) qualified as doctors; and from 1905 to 1956 some sixty-three qualified, all but five of whom were Creoles. About fifty Sierra Leonean doctors were practicing in 1960, and about one hundred students were training overseas in medicine' (1966, pp. 79-80).

Moreover, for a long time, economic position has been associated with the achievement of professional qualifications, and this association has been strengthened since the turn of the century when Sierra Leoneans began to be discouraged from attempting to compete in the commercial world, as will be described in Chapter Two. Women in Sierra Leone also had opportunities for higher education. Mrs. Hyde Forster, one of the first women to graduate from Fourah Bay College, received her degree in 1938. Individuals make enormous personal sacrifices to achieve an education and the prestige associated with it.

A speech by a young man who had just graduated made in 1968 at a lavish party in honour of the occasion illustrated these attitudes towards higher education. He wore his black academic gown and white fur-trimmed hood and held his cap in his hand as he gave the speech. Nor did he remove his gown during the entire evening, even when dancing. Most of the guests were young people who had left school and were working. Most likely none of them would ever attend university. Although he consoled them by saying that everyone could make a worthwhile contribution, whatever his education, his patronizing tone made it amply clear that his achievements had set him far above them.

'Master of Ceremonies, Distinguished Guests, I am very pleased to see so many of you here this evening. I am particularly delighted to see many female faces, charming, but alas tantalizing. It is with humility mingled with elation that I speak to you. Humility because when I compare my life a few years ago with my present position I can only feel humble by the side of the Almighty who has enabled me.

My sense of pride does not arise from the fatuous notion that the achievement of a B.A. is something extraordinary. I maintain that a B.A. is nothing unique or *sui generis*. Indeed it can be attained by anyone of average intelligence coupled, of course, with hard work, industry and assiduity. My feelings of elation derive from this: a few years ago, when my future seemed in doubt, when my whole career seemed hopelessly precarious, I became an object of ridicule, the target of humiliating gossips and contumely! I survived all this and, by Divine Dispensation, I am today what you already know I am. What is left, Ladies and Gentlemen, is for me to demonstrate that spiritual resilience which has enabled me to survive the onslaught of the past, and with my faith in God I am sanguine of success.

These are moments, you will appreciate, when one is inclined to be emotional but I assure you that I shall restrain myself. Indeed it is not the heights to which a man climbs but the depths from whence he came. And it is against this background that this rather elaborate activity has been designed.

... Remember that all of us cannot be Lawyers nor can all be Doctors; all of us cannot be B.A.s nor can all of us be Ph.D.s, all of us cannot be S. B. Joneses [a reference to a very prominent judge in Sierra Leone] nor can all of us be Davidson Nicols [at that time, Principal of Fourah Bay College]. But, we can make up our minds so serve our country well and to be thoroughly proficient in our various vocations. Now, Ladies and Gentlemen, let us lift up our heads from that depth of obscurity and ascend marvellously to heights of fame and achievement. Good sailing to us all.'

Since the data for this research derive from such a narrow segment of the society it is evidently not possible to extrapolate the results to the wider population. However, a more fundamental theoretical matter is raised by elite studies. One of the assumptions often made in such studies of elites is that the patterns which are found to occur among them are predictive of trends in the society as a whole. In Nadel's terms, the assumption is that the elites are the 'standard-setting group' (1956). In Sierra Leone, as far as marriage and family relationships are concerned, I suggest that the direction of change generally in the society cannot be predicted so simply. One reason for this is related to the special characteristics of the present-day professional group.

Many professionals come from established Creole families for whose ancestors the Colony was founded. As will be shown in Chapter Two, the Colony was organized around western and Christian values. Those professionals who originate from the Provinces were exposed to years of indoctrination in missionary-run boarding schools or as wards in Creole households. Most of them lived abroad for many years while they were being educated. They were achieving their professional qualifications during the period of colonial rule, and during this period it was very much in their interest to conform to the patterns upheld by their colonizers as representing western civilization. After all, an African could only hope for educational or economic advance if he could demonstrate to his white masters that he had absorbed (or had the potential to absorb) their culture. The early missionaries placed great stress on Christian monogamous marriage and education, and religious and educational institutions were provided from the beginning of the Colony. It is understandable that Africans associated the achievement of the white man's culture with the adoption of the values of education and religion, the practice of monogamous marriage being the hallmark of conversion.[7]

Today, however, as a result of the pressure from the indigenous population, who are in the majority, a new group of persons is being prepared to join the professionally qualified elite. In this study these are represented by the university students. Many of these new recruits have had considerably more experience of traditional village life than have the present group of professionals. A significant proportion of them come from Muslim rather than Christian backgrounds. Moreover,

---

7. Today the role of Christianity in the suppression of the colonized is often remarked upon. One of my informants told me he remembered standing in the church singing a hymn which included the line, 'Take my silver and my gold, naught from thee would I withhold'. Over the sounds of the congregation singing he could hear the sirens of the ships in the harbour as the gold and diamonds of his country were indeed being taken away! See Beetham 1967, p. 42, for a general statement of missionary policy in Africa.

many attended secular as well as religious schools and were taught by African rather than by European teachers. In some cases they are even receiving most or all of their higher education within Sierra Leone, so fewer will have the experience of living abroad for several years. Further, these young people are being trained to enter professional (and, therefore, influential) occupations and positions of authority in the country during a period of world history when Africans have become more self-confident. The proliferation of African literature and the greater interest today in African studies may suggest to these young people that African traditional culture, too, has an intrinsic value. One need not, however, disagree totally with Turnbull when he says that it is '. . . obvious that the old [in the sense of the traditional] has gone for good and in the cities the Africans have come to look upon it with shame, so that it is no longer even a source of pride, let alone of moral or spiritual strength' (1963, p. 181). As we shall see, university and other young people who are aspiring to professional occupations express overwhelming preference for the pattern of marriage and family life which they see as modern or western and 'anti-traditional'. Nevertheless, as will be shown, many traditional attitudes which influence behaviour persist. Young people are often not fully aware of these, and therefore these attitudes are not so open to correction in the light of modern ideas. It seems likely that these new recruits to the professionals will have a profound impact upon the general character of marriage relationships among them, in the direction of re-emphasizing aspects of the traditional.

The patterns of marriage relationships and attitudes towards them which exist today among the professionals developed, especially among the Creoles, under the special conditions of colonialism. In the absence of at least some of these special external circumstances, these patterns may never occur again in quite the same way. This argument is, however, weakened when one considers how exclusive these educated people of high status have become and how they have managed to make acceptance into their ranks contingent upon almost the same criteria as in the case of their colonial rulers. This was demonstrated in the incidents following an attempt to revise the law relating to children born out of wedlock, which are described in Chapter Six. The opposition appealed to the Christian ideals of monogamous marriage to defeat the law, in order to retain their exclusiveness and control of power.

One of the general problems of research in social behaviour is the tendency to impose theoretical concepts and categories which do not fit the data. Anthropologists have hoped to avoid this tendency since their research is usually conducted in a foreign culture where the relevant domains and categories have to be discovered by intensive participation and observation. However, despite the advantages of such a precaution, interpretations of ethnographic data frequently reveal the bias of the investigator. Studies of marriage and family life are perhaps most in danger of this pitfall. Birdwhistell, referring to psychological and sociological studies of the family, has observed that with very few exceptions these studies have accepted what he terms the 'sentimental model' of family life:

'Statistics are made of units derived of this model; anecdotes are collected; and formalistic abstractions are derived from it. There is no reason to be particularly surprised about this. Family processes and structures are camouflaged in depth by sanctions that idealize them. Unfortunately, these processes are further obscured by studies, which, while focusing upon the family's pathologies, serve to *reinforce the sentimental model of the family by the assumption that the pathologyless family has the shape of the sentimental model*' (author's italics) (1966).

Cohen (1971) comments on this problem in his study of marital instability among the Kanuri where he considers the value judgements which lie behind most studies of divorce:

'Unspoken yet present in the sociological material is a view of human nature, or at the very least, of the Western individual and his social psychological needs and dispositions. He and she are happier, more rewarded, less punished, less fearful, etc., if interpersonal relations in marriage can be maintained without serious disruption, breakage, and hostility. This presumption is so strong that one of the theoretical models used to explain marital relations equates husband-wife conflict to the escalation of hostilities preceding the outbreak of open warfare between nations' (p. 9).[8]

Cohen asks what would happen if everyone in a society divorced, not just once but several times. The material on Kanuri marriage presents such a high divorce society and, according to Cohen, it has been like

---

8. Esther Goody makes the same point in her discussion of the Sonja (1962).

this for quite a long time, and has prospered. If a Kanuri were writing about family life in American society, Cohen suggests, he would take quite an opposite point of view from the western observer. The Kanuri would ask how it is that the husbands and wives who fight, dislike each other, and who are attracted to other mates, remain married while the Kanuri simply break things off. Cohen points out that observers of both societies would be asking the same question, '... how does this unfamiliar human experience compare with my own? How can I explain these differences ... ?' So although it is almost impossible to write about marriage and family life and avoid making comparisons with categories and concepts drawn from our own cultural experience, perhaps we may usefully borrow Cohen's analogy that such a study serves, among other things, as a mirror in which to see ourselves.

In Sierra Leone monogamous Christian marriage has been a symbol of high status among the western-educated for a very long time. The several studies cited above raise a number of questions about urban African marriage. For example, is the present trend of marriage and family life among urban Africans predictive of the future of family life in Africa? Are the attempts of urban Africans to follow the western model of monogamous marriage as unsuccessful as some writers have suggested? If they are, do we conclude that the problems observed are simply an indication of a transitional phase of urban life in Africa, which in time will settle down to some satisfactory established pattern? And, if, as some have concluded, western patterns are so ill-adapted to the African situation, how do we explain that they have been adopted as such a significant symbol of prestige? In addition to being ethnographic, this book attempts to comment on the basic problem which underlies all these questions: just what are the chances in Sierra Leone for the emergence of the conjugally-based or nuclear family as a domestic unit in its own right?

There were found to be 754 persons in Sierra Leone who held professional qualifications. A sample of 160 was drawn for the interviews by means of a random number table. Among this sample there were 125 extant unions from which the data regarding marriage relationships were drawn. When I refer to the 'professionals' or 'professional group' I refer to all 754.[9] Since the sampling frame was

9. I use the term 'group' in its loosest sense, as defined in the *Concise Oxford*

complete (as will be discussed in Appendix A) and the sample was drawn with attention to statistical procedures, the results may be taken to refer to all the professionals. However, in this study, I have used statistical procedures at a very low level of sophistication. The weight has been placed upon descriptive statistics. More elaborate statistical procedures of analysis such as those involving tests of significance are inappropriate to such a study. There would be no sense in scattering the book with significance tests since those differences to which I refer as significant are so wide that their statistical significance may be assumed.

The terms, 'traditional' and 'western', which are used in this study, require some explanation. I use the term 'traditional' to describe an attribute which has characterized the society for a considerable length of time. I more closely restrict the term to refer to a pattern of social relations, attitudes, practices, and organization of family life which may be observed in Sierra Leone today. While by no means confined to them, it ismost completely represented by the non-literate indigenous peoples living in the rural areas of Sierra Leone.[10] Professionals and other western-educated people, when discussing this way of life, refer to it either as the 'traditional' or 'native' way of life. The behaviour of professional married couples is very much influenced by traditional attitudes and practices.

As for the term, 'western', it has been widely used in the literature about family life to refer to the new form of monogamous companionate marriage which urban Africans are adopting. The problems of accurately defining either 'western marriage patterns' or 'companionate monogamous marriage' are so obvious as to require no comment.

Dictionary. However, it might be argued that the professionals have some characteristics of a group in the narrower, sociological sense. Although they are not all personally acquainted with one another, they almost all know *about* one another. They have, to some degree, a sense of unity, common goals and shared norms.

10. It should be noted that when references are made in this book to such concepts as 'non-literate' or 'educated', it is in relation to western education that they are used. Islam has had a far-reaching impact in Sierra Leone. All over the country children are being taught to read Arabic. This teaching has been discounted by the western-educated elite as having no practical value, only a religious function. However, in my later research in Sierra Leone (1971-1973), I learned that a very large proportion of the so-called non-literate people of Sierra Leone were writing their indigenous languages in Arabic script.

However, educated Sierra Leoneans themselves describe their marriages and pattern of family life as 'western'. In Chapter Four these so-called western marriage practices, as perceived by educated Sierra Leoneans, are discussed in some detail. As will be shown there, when referring to marriage and family life, the terms, 'western' and 'traditional', have been dichotomized; all that is progressive and modern is associated with being 'western'. Throughout the book then, when mention is made of a 'traditional' practice, I will be referring to a phenomenon which is a general part of indigenous culture and is observable in practice today. However, at times I will use the term to refer to the *stereotypes* of that mode of family life, and these cases will be specified. When the term 'western' is employed it will be used in the sense of the popular stereotypes of companionate monogamous marriage as perceived by Sierra Leoneans.

This problem of imposing idealized concepts of the family and of marriage behaviour became apparent from the outset of this study. In the Preface it has been noted that the original design of this study in Sierra Leone was intended to be part of a comparative study of marriage among professionals in three countries. With this consideration in mind, the design laid out the defining criteria for 'professionals' on the basis of educational level and income.[11] It was also planned that the samples of couples investigated would be chosen in terms of their position in the development cycle of their family. This required that some couples would be included who had no children. (It was stipulated that these couples must have been married less than two years, as previous knowledge of marriage in West Africa suggested that marriage of any longer duration which had not produced children would already be 'in danger'.) The remaining number would be couples having children under thirteen years of age. The notion of the developmental cycle and its implications for understanding family behaviour has been developed by Goody (1966). It was hoped that the three studies could examine the extent to which factors relating to the development cycle of family life affect the division of labour between husbands and wives.

My initial inquiries did not lead to couples who conformed to these requirements for inclusion, i.e. extant unions with no children in their

11. As noted in the Preface, 'professionals' were defined as persons who hold university degrees, or equivalent professional level qualifications, and their spouses.

first two years of marriage and those with children under thirteen years of age. I conducted intensive interviews with a pilot group of couples during the first five months of fieldwork and although these couples, at first sight, *appeared* to conform to these criteria, more careful examination revealed complexities. Husbands were often supporting one or more children born to them before they contracted the present marriage. Other couples had cohabited for some time before marriage and had had children during this period. A large number of married couples had not actually lived together for periods of several years, although they would not admit to being estranged. Many husbands maintained more or less permanent relationships with women other than their wives, although their official residence was with their wives. The wide variations in family types and conjugal relationships which I encountered early in the fieldwork made it obvious that it was crucial to drop the original defining criteria for inclusion. I decided to interview a sample of the entire professional group without prejudging the nature of their conjugal relationships. However, had I been able to find families for the pilot study who conformed to the model presribed, the research might well have continued without my encountering the wide variations in marriage types which are practised. After all, professionals have strong vested interests in preserving the myth that their marriages conform to the 'sentimental model' of western monogamous companionate marriage.

While this book is about marriage among the professional group, data were drawn from several other sources besides married couples. Some of these additional sources helped to build up the picture of the position of the professional in relation to the wider society. Other data provided more depth of insight into family organization by examining it from another perspective. For example, I compared the views of the roles of parents as held by primary-aged children of professionals with my own observations and with statements made about these roles by married men and women. Again, the case materials from the files of the Department of Social Welfare dealing with family disputes, together with discussions with specialists in the nature of family life, such as lawyers, family case workers, teachers and clergymen, yielded information about the nature of conflicts which occur between married couples. This topic is a very difficult one to investigate through first-hand observation. A number of essays were collected from students in the upper forms of secondary school, and these essays were a rich source of information about the images or stereotypes of African and western marriage patterns.

The most important of these additional sources of data were the interviews with a sample of university students from Njala and Fourah Bay University Colleges. I lived on the campus of Fourah Bay College and so it was with the students that I became acquainted first. My informal discussions with them convinced me that including them would be extremely valuable. The professionals were defined as persons with university degrees or equivalent professional qualifications, and the students were just about to enter this group. While most of the students were unmarried, marriage is a topic with which they were very much concerned and about which they held very definite opinions. I learned a great deal from the students which helped me to frame questions for interviews with married couples. More important, I was interested in exploring the differences between their attitudes towards marriage and the actual behavior I was observing among married couples. Moreover, certain important differences were found between the social background and experiences of the students and the professionals. These, together with the divergences between the attitudes both groups expressed and between the expectations of the students and the behaviour I observed among the married couples, do suggest some important trends in marriage relations.

Of course, we cannot assume a direct relation between attitudes or expectations about marriage and behaviour either now or in the future. Nevertheless, it is fairly obvious that behaviour and values do interact and that where large discrepancies exist some modification of either behaviour or values or of both will occur. Only a later study, after they are married, can establish the relations between the attitudes or values these students expressed and their behaviour as married men and women.

Understanding the relation between attitudes or values and behaviour among the professionals is a complex problem. For a start, we cannot be sure that the attitudes expressed by professionals actually represent their values, since a personal interview with a white foreigner hardly constitutes a completely neutral situation. On the other hand, if we assume that the attitudes professional men and women expressed *do* represent their values about marriage and family relations, how are these people dealing with the disparity between their values and their behaviour? This problem is especially complicated when trying to understand the wives of professionals. The status of these women is inextricably bound up with the role of the wife in a monogamous union. Their values regarding marriage are even more westernized than those expressed by their husbands. To retain her position in society as well as within her own family, it is absolutely imperative for the wife of the professional to make a success of her marriage. At the same time, however, numerous forces within the society impinge on marriage relationships, and render her task extremely difficult. How does she reconcile the difference between her values about marriage and the situation in which she finds herself? This matter will be taken up again in the final chapter.

Reporting the results of research in such a sensitive area as marriage relationships places a heavy responsibility upon the investigator to conceal the identity of his informants. I have presented a considerable number of case studies, material from local newspapers and verbatim statements made by informants. [12] In this way I have tried to convey a more intimate picture of the lives of the people concerned than would have resulted from a bare report of the findings together with some statistical tables. In all instances I have changed the names and sometimes even the occupations of persons in the material used. However, the professionals in Sierra Leone are a very close-knit group and they know a great deal about one another and so, despite such precautions, it was often necessary to drop certain illustrative material to protect the anonymity of individuals.

Anthropologists are often asked how they can know if their informants are telling them the truth. Sometimes Sierra Leoneans implied that it would be impossible to do such a study since they knew informants would deliberately attempt to mislead. It is possible to build a number of checks for consistency into questionnaires but it is never possible for an anthropologist completely to win the confidence of every informant (even if that in itself were an assurance of reliable information). Knowing what areas of the inquiry people are likely to misrepresent (whether deliberately or not) is useful, and provides insight into their values. Discovering these areas requires that the

12. The reader may think that some of these case materials and verbatim accounts are unduly long. However, they have been selected because they illustrate the complexities of various matters better than other forms of description could.

anthropologist should have considerable familiarity with the culture. Sometimes one discovers such misrepresentations through simple good fortune. For example, in an interview one woman reported the two children in the household as her own by birth. By chance the very next day I happened to interview her husband's illegitimate son and he told me that his father's wife had never had children of her own but had reared her sister's two daughters. From other sources I found this information was general knowledge in the community. Nevertheless this woman found it difficult to admit it to me, an outsider. This also points to another important consideration. The investigator must, in addition to being familiar with the values of the society, have a deep awareness of the perception others have of him as an outsider conducting research. It is, for example, almost impossible completely to eliminate the tendency for the informants to give the answers they think will please the interviewer. And, of course, there is the fundamental problem of the subjectivity of the observer himself. As Dollard long ago pointed out, 'Since this self or ego is formed by society it is obviously impossible to liberate it totally from the biased view of the world transmitted by that society . . .' (1937, p. 39). He emphasized the vital need for the investigator to sharpen his awareness of himself. In addition to encountering problems which are general in anthropological research, this study was conducted during a period of extreme political tension. The field work was begun during a period of military rule and a *coup* occurred during the first five months of research. It was not possible to measure or control the effects of these special circumstances on the research.

The reader may wish to begin by turning to Appendix A where the methods employed in this research and the kinds of data collected are described. In Chapter Two a brief sketch of the history of Sierra Leone since it first came under the influence of Europeans is presented. Here we see how the establishment of the Colony for freed slaves as an attempt at a unique social experiment, together with the changing social policy of the colonial government towards the indigenous population of Sierra Leone over the years, led to the present composition of the professional group. We shall see how this historical development laid the foundation for the intense political rivalry we find today. The composition and social background of the professional group are described in Chapter Three.

In Chapter Four I discuss the social images or 'representations' which Sierra Leoneans hold of both the traditional African patterns and of the western style of marriage. As will be shown, most professionals seem to reject traditional African patterns of marriage and family life and favour an idealized version of the western model. The situation in Sierra Leone is much as Henriques found in his research in Jamaica when he observed that 'The essential contradiction of a society in which 90 per cent of the population is of non-European origin yet which models itself on a European ideal is as powerful as ever' (1968, p. 173).

The legal setting of marriage is discussed in Chapter Five. As is shown there, part of the legacy of colonial rule is a legal system based upon British law, which exists side by side with Muslim law and the legal systems of the various tribal groups in Sierra Leone. Marriage does not change the individual's personal law with respect to certain issues, e.g. inheritance, and so marriage across tribal lines creates certain conflicts of law. Most people are unaware of the possibility of such problems. They think that once they have married either in the church or the registrar's office they come under the jurisdiction of the legal system which is based on the British model. In Chapter Six I take up the matter of the social and legal status of children born out of wedlock, a problem central to understanding the nature of relationships between husbands and wives. I was led to investigate this problem through intensive interviews with married couples where I found that illegitimate children were a major source of marital discord. This problem ramifies in several directions affecting the economics of the household, inheritance, the status of the married woman, even the acceptance of the idea of birth control and the use of contraceptives.

The case study of an attempt to pass a law eliminating the concept of illegitimacy illuminates our understanding even more, for this struggle over the law reveals the manner in which a tiny minority group utilize legal machinery (together with the general respect for western values) to protect their position of power within the society. Although the proposed law seems to have reflected the consensus of the majority of the population, it was never passed. In fact, it never reached the vote. This case provides an opportunity to look at the relationship between law and social practice. Even more interesting is the fact that professionals think the law *has* been passed. This erroneous belief has had some important effects upon conjugal relationships. Tracing these effects allows us to speculate on the social consequences of certain law reforms as well as giving insight into the conflicting interests of husbands and wives.

After considering these aspects of the social setting of marriage, I move on in Chapters Seven, Eight and Nine to describe courtship practices and marriage and family relationships among the professionals. In Chapter Ten aspects of sexual behaviour are considered through exploring attitudes towards family limitation and the use of contraceptives. Acceptance of such an idea as artificially limiting the number of children born is in dramatic contradiction with traditional values. The way in which professionals manage such conflicts and the patterns of behaviour they assume support the argument that it is vital to consider the general social background of marriage and to explore the dialectic relationship between traditional and modern, western-based, stereotypes or representations.

2

The historical background

The founding of the Colony

The Portuguese had made prolonged contact with the coastal regions of Sierra Leone as early as the mid-fifteenth century, and they are credited with naming the country (Kup 1961; Fyfe 1962a). The trading activities of the Spanish, Dutch, French, and British up and down the coast of West Africa over the following three centuries brought the population of Sierra Leone into frequent contact with the western world. British manufactured products were imported, chiefly in return for slaves. There were also attempts to convert the indigenous population to Christianity, although, 'As Bishop Thomas Wilson observed . . . the intelligent heathen were bound to be repelled by discrepancies between Christian precept and practice' (Fyfe 1962a, p. 11). However, western education was found useful by the indigenous population in their dealings with foreign traders.

'Following European example, men took to wearing coats and trousers. Chiefs bought gorgeous footman's liveries, resplendent with gold lace, and sat on chairs. Friendly ship's-captains sometimes took them to visit England. Settled traders would send their children by their African wives to school there, and encourage chiefs to do the same, employing them as agents on their return. There were said to be about fifty, boys and girls, in Liverpool in 1789, others in London and Bristol.

Education was chiefly prized as a means to outwit European business rivals. Once back in Africa, apart from outward elegancies, the educated tended to assimilate themselves to their own – or if traders' children their mothers' – people again.' (Fyfe 1962a, p. 11).

Malaria and the other health hazards of the West African tropics ensured that Europeans who came to this part of the world rarely considered establishing a permanent settlement for themselves. However, in 1787 the British founded a colony on the western peninsula of Sierra Leone for the resettlement of freed slaves. Land for this colony, which eventually came to be called Freetown, was obtained through negotiations with the local population. However, it is quite probable that the local people did not understand the significance that the founders of the Colony attached to the small amount of trading goods which was handed over to them or to the paper to which they fixed their marks (Fyfe 1962a, p. 20; Collier 1970, p. 8). The idea of selling land was foreign, although it would have been regarded as only proper for temporary residents to offer gifts to their hosts.[1]

The first people settled in the Colony were freed slaves who had been repatriated from the United States, Canada, the West Indies and England. Later, others were brought to Freetown after being rescued from slave ships captured on the high seas. The first group were referred to as 'settlers' and the later arrivals as 'liberated Africans'. The different background and experiences of these people preceding their arrival influenced the structure of colonial society. Those who had served as slaves in the West had been exposed to western culture. They assumed a role of superiority towards those who came to Freetown directly from the slave ships (Porter 1963). We can get some idea of the extreme heterogeneity of the early population of the Colony by noting that Koelle, a German sent by the Church Missionary Society to teach at Fourah Bay College, recorded over one hundred different African tribal languages spoken in Freetown (Koelle 1851). All these people of diverse background came to be called 'Creoles'. While this term has different meanings in different societies, in Sierra Leone it came to be attached to '... the descendants of Settlers and Liberated Africans ... and to others who had come to accept their way of living' (Porter 1963, p. 3).

The Colony, as it was organized through the efforts of philanthropists and missionaries, emphasized the superiority of western education and religion. Although the settlers had originated from various parts of West Africa, they had been cut off from their own traditions and they

1. This misunderstanding of the intent of the founders doubtless set the stage for tension between indigenous groups and the settlers which resulted in a series of violent attempts to drive the settlers out (Petersen 1969, pp. 33-37).

were made aware that it was very much in their interest to adopt western ways.[2] Referring to the assimilation of the several groups who arrived in Freetown at various times, Porter says:

'Freetown became a cultural melting pot. Faced with western patterns as interpreted by the New World Settlers ... which patterns were reinforced by the patronage and favour of the European administration and other ancillary agencies like the missionary societies, the Liberated Africans, as this fourth group of immigrants came to be known, began to copy these patterns which soon became the high prestige culture for all groups in the territory' (1963, p. 12).

Relationships between the white settlers and administrators and the Creoles were remarkably good in the early period of the Colony. Equal treatment of white and black was even assured by legislation (Porter 1963, p. 24). In establishing the Colony its founders ambitiously aimed at developing a kind of utopian community based upon Christian ideals. They hoped the new colony would '... prove an agency for the spiritual and social regeneration of the whole African world' (Porter 1963, p. 48).

The Creoles did participate in missionary activities as well as trading in the hinterland of Sierra Leone. However, they were much more concerned with personal advancement defined by the values of the western world than they were in improving the lives of the indigenous population. As Collier notes:

'In their personal lives they aspired to European bourgeois standards, with their dinners, balls, fairs, and horse races. In their cultural lives, with amateur theatricals and literary, religious, scientific, and philosophic societies, they demonstrated the extent to which they had successfully imbibed western European value standards. The majority were self-centered, property-owning individuals, fully aware of their civil and property rights. With the assimilation of some of the finest values from western European civilization came also some of the worst excesses and by-products of that civilization, as exemplified by the Europeans who lived among them' (1970, p. 47).

2. It should be noted that there was always a significant group of liberated Africans who followed Islam. However, the prejudices of the colonial administration led to policies which served to frustrate their attempts to integrate themselves in the mainstream of Freetown society.

From the beginning relationships between the settlers and the local tribal groups were strained. During the early years the Temne had attempted more than once to get rid of the Colony by burning the town. Similarly, on occasion the Creoles resisted the migration of country people into Freetown by destroying their houses. As the Creoles' society became more established it assumed a position of superiority and patronage over the people in the country. The tribal population in Freetown served as the labour force and often its children were employed as household servants. Creoles were increasingly active in trade in the hinterland and also acted as government agents. They were regarded with continued suspicion by the tribal people and there were frequent outbreaks of violence against Creoles travelling in the hinterland. These were always ruthlessly suppressed by the British (Collier 1970, p. 49).

Activities aimed at development and improvement were concentrated in the Colony and were primarily for the benefit of the settlers, while the hinterland was mainly viewed in terms of its trading potential. A few mission schools existed in the country but most schools were concentrated in Freetown. Fourah Bay College was founded in 1827 and was the only institution of higher learning in West Africa until the 1940s (Nicol 1966). The Creoles achieved a level of education and sophistication in the western sense, which was indeed remarkable (Porter 1963, p. 14). Some persons from the indigenous tribes also managed to get an education either through missionary efforts or as wards in Creole households. However, in order to obtain employment such persons found it necessary to identify themselves with the Creoles and to take an English name. Many who grew up as wards were absorbed into the family of their foster-parents and assumed their name. As Banton notes, their acquisition of educational skills did nothing to resolve the social divisions between the Creoles and the various tribal groups:

> 'The possession of educational skills was at that time regarded as an attribute of Creoles and foreign to the Temne and other tribes. It was the possession of these skills that was the departure from the norm, not the passing into the Creole group and forsaking of the tribe, which was only its consequence. Since there was no recognized place for young literates in the existing tribal system, they were not hindered from turning Creole, and when they had done so they were renounced by their fellow tribesmen. The

exclusion of young literates helped to maintain intact the tribal group with its illiterate elders' (1957, p. 22).

This practice of 'passing' as Creoles continued throughout the history of Sierra Leone until the 1950s when the increase in the political power ot the indigenous groups made identification with Creole society less important. Since that time some 'Creoles' have reassumed their tribal names. However, even today, many of the professional group who call themselves Creoles have grandparents whose first language is one of the various tribal languages of the hinterland. And, in addition, many children, offspring of unions between settlers and indigenous persons, have been reared as part of Creole society.

During the nineteenth century many Creoles obtained higher educational qualifications in Britain and entered such professions as law, medicine, and the church. They were also permitted a large share in the administration of the Colony and to a great extent manned the civil service. However, the thriving economy of the Colony was primarily based upon trade both within Sierra Leone and up and down the coast (Porter 1963, p. 112).

The depression in Europe during the 1880s had an unfortunate impact on the economy of the Colony. About this time the number of immigrants from the hinterland to Freetown was greatly increasing. Further, indigenous people began to compete with the Creoles in trade. This trading competition, which was accompanied by more violence against Creole traders, together with the results of the depression, led the Creoles to attribute their adversities to the advance of the people of the hinterland. They urged the British to extend their control over the entire territory (Porter 1963, p. 58). Efforts were made to curb the movement of tribal people into the peninsula and legislation allowed forcible deportation of any who were unemployed ('An ordinance to promote a System of Administration by Tribal Authority among the settled in Freetown', 31 July, 1905).

The establishment of the Protectorate

On August 31st, 1896 the entire area of the hinterland was declared a British Protectorate. Although a number of treaties had been signed with some individual chiefs, the extension of British rule was declared without the consent of most of the native leaders of the territory. The imposition of a 'Hut Tax' in 1898 resulted in open rebellion on the part of chiefs all over the country. Penetration into the northern part of the country had never been as successful as into the south. This was partly the result of the strength of Muslim resistance to attempts by missionaries to convert the population to Christianity. In the most famous of the wars following the imposition of the 'Hut Tax', organized by Bai Bureh, a Temne chief from the north, a number of missionaries and Creoles were killed (Fyfe 1962b, p. 142). This and various other confrontations with British soldiers in the south produced general panic in Freetown. It was imagined that the Mende from the south were planning to invade Freetown itself. More troops were ordered to the Protectorate to deal with the uprisings.

Once the rebellions in the Protectorate had been thoroughly suppressed the British began to administer the entire area. Although District Commissioners were empowered to decide certain cases according to British law, in effect the Protectorate and the Colony were governed by two separate legal systems. Through their policy of indirect rule, the British administered the area through the leadership of certain co-operative chiefs whose authority was extended and legitimized under the British government. The Protectorate was opened up for more extensive trade through the building of a railway, begun in 1899 and completed in 1914.

Educational opportunities were also extended in the Protectorate during the period following the wars. Most schools were concentrated in the south where the indigenous population has been most receptive to missionary activities. In 1904 missionaries founded the Albert Academy in Freetown where boys from the Protectorate could be educated along with Creole boys. A school for girls was also established through missionary effort in Moyamba; this was the first attempt to provide education for Protectorate women. In 1906 a school was founded in Bo for the education of the sons of chiefs. The aim of this school was to provide them with the rudiments of a western education in a setting which was in keeping with their village background. It was hoped that in this way future leaders capable of coping with the administrative responsibilities of a chiefdom under the British could be trained, but at the same time, that they would be kept content to remain part of traditional life (Fyfe 1962a; Alldridge 1910). As Porter puts it, 'The peoples of the interior . . . were to remain tribal, uncreolized, unsophisticated and unspoilt' (1963, p. 68). It was hoped that educating them in the Protectorate away from Freetown would accomplish this aim.

During the years that followed the declaration of the Protectorate British policy towards Sierra Leone radically changed. Medical advances had made living in the tropics less hazardous for Europeans. Reports such as those written by Alldridge (1901, 1910) focused on the economic potential of the Protectorate. Whereas the Colony had been founded for what were largely philanthropic reasons, now the attention of the British was turned to the possibilities of economic exploitation. Suddenly the dominant role of the Creoles in trade and administration became a hindrance to the aims of the British. The colonial administration, rather than continuing to encourage Creole leadership, attracted more British personnel to official posts. In 1892 Creoles had held nearly half of the senior official posts, but by 1917 only ten of the ninety-two senior posts were held by Creoles (Fyfe 1962b, pp. 159-60). Many educated Creoles were forced to leave Sierra Leone to find work in other parts of West Africa (July 1968). It was also during this period that the relationships of near equality between Creoles and Europeans began to deteriorate. Previously, they had lived side by side, but now Hill Station, a cooler settlement in the mountains above the city of Freetown, was built for European residence only. Hill Station was connected with the city by a private railway (Porter 1963, p. 98). Colour increasingly became the basis for discrimination in both social and political circles. Spitzer summarizes the situation in which the Creoles now found themselves:

'Having striven for an identity with Britain and Britons in all phases of their lives, these Sierra Leoneans repeatedly saw themselves relegated to subordinate positions, spurned by the very people whose cultural wards they had become' (1972, p. 195).

The extension of the railway and the realization of the vast trading potential of the Protectorate encouraged greater and greater activity by Europeans and, later, by Syrian traders. This latter group had begin to trickle into the country about 1890 (Leighton 1972). The greater capital resources of these two groups of traders, the Europeans and the Syrians, made it almost impossible for the previously successful Creole traders to compete effectively. Gradually they began to lose their near monopoly of trading and business as well as their recognized role in the administration of the Colony. It should be noted that there was a strong sense of nationalism among the inhabitants of the Colony at the turn of the century. Creoles were fully aware that they were quite able to govern themselves independently, a capability which was even acknowledged by the governor in 1870 and in some quarters in Britain (Porter 1963, pp. 52-53). Their ability to develop a strong economy had also been effectively demonstrated. However, the increase in British participation in administration and in business and trade, and the encouragement of Syrian and Lebanese immigration into the country systematically undermined the Africans' participation, reducing the threat they posed to British supremacy.[3]

During the years following the First World War other educational institutions were founded in the Protectorate: an agricultural experimental station, Njala, in 1911, a training school for primary teachers for the Protectorate at Njala in 1920, and another teacher training college begun in Bunumbu in 1933. The Creoles, having lost their control of administrative positions and the trading economy, tended to encourage their sons to enter the professions, particularly the Church and the law. They continued to dominate the lower civil service ranks and were prominent in teaching and clerical posts. However, in 1926 Milton Margai, a son of a ruling Mende family, qualified as the first doctor from the Protectorate and, later, his brother, Albert, became the first lawyer.[4] With the rise of such educated people from the Protectorate the Creoles could no longer even claim a monopoly of the professions.

The attitude of the Creoles towards the tribal groups of Sierra Leone had always been one of superiority and patronage. They had successfully attempted to build a society organized around western values. They had achieved educational and economic status equal to that of their benefactors. They had enjoyed a long period of social equality with Europeans. Their economic affluence had permitted many of them to move back and forth between Britain and Freetown, and for the most part it was with Britain they identified. The encouragement and development of the Protectorate combined with the official change in attitude towards their former uncontested right to control the affairs of the Colony produced considerable anxiety and served to increase the antagonisms between them and the Protectorate people.[5]

---

3. See Van der Laan (1969) for a discussion of the immigration of these traders.
4. 'Ruling families' are those families in a chiefdom which have the right to nominate a member to compete for the chieftaincy.
5. See Spitzer 1968 and 1972 for an excellent documentation of the progressive demoralization of the Creoles by the British.

The prestige role of the Creoles in the society was to rest on their close identification with the British way of life, their dominance of the professions, and their control of educational institutions. They continued (and continue today) to set the standard of acceptance into the upper echelons of social life (Little 1967, pp. 262-264). As Collier puts it, there was a 'certain ambivalence in the Protectorate attitudes towards the Creoles':

'On the one hand, they saw them as exploiters in trade and business and agents of European civilization in their role as teachers and missionaries. On the other hand, the Protectorate tribes somehow admired the Creoles for their progressive ways and for their ability to copy so closely the Europeans' (1970, p. 56).

On the other hand, the Creoles always assumed that their role *vis-à-vis* the indigenous groups was to communicate to them the values of British education, Christianity, and the western style of life. Creoles had always denounced tribal practices as primitive and uncivilized. Yet, as Collier points out, the Creoles faced certain psychological conflicts in this regard:

'In many areas of their personal lives, the Creoles behaved like tribal Africans. Their customs and morals had strong elements of tribal behavior patterns. Yet they professed a code of official behavior in their quest for "civilization" that produced a certain hypocrisy and ambivalence in their attitudes' (1970, p. 56).

In 1947 the British drew up a new constitution for Sierra Leone which would eliminate the former dual system of governing the Colony and the Protectorate (Fyfe 1962b, p. 173). In view of their numerical superiority (more than two million to sixty thousand Creoles) it would naturally be the people of the Protectorate who would take the predominant role in governing the country under the new constitution. Such legislative action was bitterly opposed by the Creoles and campaigns against it brought out all the latent hostilities and prejudices felt by both groups. Nevertheless, in 1951 the new government was introduced. The Sierra Leone People's Party, dominated by the Mendes, won the elections with Milton Margai as their leader.

Under this new constitution the British were prepared to give considerably more support to the development of agriculture, roads, and education in the 'Provinces', as the former Protectorate was now called. It was also during this period that the diamond areas of the country began to be actively exploited by Sierra Leoneans. The Selection Trust, an international company, had been in control of monopoly rights in diamond mining since the 1930s, but the discovery of the vast fortunes that could be earned led large numbers of people to defy the law. During the 1950s there was an enormous migration of men to the diamond areas (Fyfe 1962b; Van der Laan 1965). As a result of the diamond boom the country enjoyed a considerable increase in prosperity, a prosperity of which the people of the former Protectorate actually had a share and which provided the resources for educational and political development which finally led to a concerted movement towards independence from British rule.

Independence

In 1961 Sierra Leone was granted independence. The first prime minister was Milton Margai and he was succeeded in 1964 by Albert Margai. After independence when the Mendes were in control of the government they were accused of blatantly advancing their fellow-tribesmen whenever possible. The Provincials[6] from the Sierra Leone People's Party were often promoted in civil service jobs over Creoles who were usually better qualified. Leading SLPP politicians often openly derided the Creoles and their education with such phrases as, 'So you understand books? Well, even so, you can be pushed out' (*'A lek yu sabi buk te'*) which were openly derisive of educational achievements. The government elected in 1967, headed by Siaka Stevens, claimed its greatest support from the northern Temnes although the Creoles also gave their support to the All People's Congress, the party which won the election.[7]

Competition for positions and political antagonisms continue to be expressed in terms of tribal affiliation. Although the educational gap between Provincials and Creoles has gradually narrowed since independence, the majority of positions in the civil service, the medical

---

6. 'Provincials' as a term of reference for members of the indigenous tribal groups is in general use in Sierra Leone and is considered preferable to the more disparaging term 'native'.

7. The transfer of power to the APC after the elections in 1967 was interrupted by a military *coup*, a counter-*coup*, a year of military rule, and yet another *coup* in 1968.

services, the judiciary, and at Fourah Bay College continue to be filled by Creoles. The Mendes, for the historical reasons noted earlier, are the Creoles' closest competitors in terms of educational achievement. After the upset of the SLPP government many of the senior posts formerly held by Mendes were left vacant. In the absence of a sufficient number of highly trained Temnes, it is not surprising that the APC should allow these positions to be taken over by Creoles. In 1969, seventeen out of the twenty Permanent Secretary posts were held by Creoles (Administrative Postings at 1st September 1969, Freetown, Government Printing Office, 1969, as quoted by Jordan 1971).

Recent criticisms of the present government have focused on the inordinate influence of Creoles on policy and the preferential treatment they have received in terms of political appointments. A new party, the United Democratic Party, was formed by a faction from the APC. The supporters of this break-away from the APC were, among other things, concerned to shatter Creole control of the country, and there were strong indications of future co-operation with SLPP members in order to bring about a unified political movement capable of effectively combating the Creoles' influence. It is not uncommon to hear politicians suggesting that ultimately the Provincials must band together against the Creoles. 'We have more in common with our tribal brothers than with these *opotho*'.[8] The strength of these sentiments is illustrated in the following excerpts from an article in the Sierra Leone *Daily Express*:

> '... The political chaos that has prevailed in Sierra Leone from Albert Margai to the present exists mainly because of the machinations of the top Creole hierarchy. When Sir Milton died his succession by Albert Margai was one of the most nebulous in the history of legal science ... The aftermath of this deal was the political reward that the Creole clique received.
>
> However, later on when Albert Margai decided to get tough with general Creole elements, they calculatedly planned his downfall by supporting his political opponents.

---

8. *Opotho* is a Temne word meaning 'white man' or any person who affects the ways of white men without really knowing how to do it. It is an abusive term. Creoles are especially accused of pretending they are 'black white men'. Provincials also often refer to the enslaved past of the Creoles. Slaves in traditional society had very low status. Of course, Creoles also often refer to the Provincials as 'natives' or 'bush', and refer to their way of life as primitive.

... In their effort to thrive the Creoles have manipulated the two largest ethnic groups in Sierra Leone, the Mende and Temne, to achieve their end. They have acted as catalyst in the political process in Sierra Leone, but they never get consumed in the end. The beneficiaries of the most lucrative jobs extending from the time of Sir Milton Margai to the present have always been Creoles. About ten years ago the argument was that they were the most qualified to man these job[s]. Today I will question this contention very critically.

Creoledom is having a very strong hold on Sierra Leone at the moment. Several of our viable institutions are controlled by them at a point inimical to the provincial people ... Creoledom as a system is a vicious and self-perpetuating system – especially when it comes to "back door" politics.

The effort on the part of the Creoles to dominate the provincial peoples through political chicanery should be understood by all provincial people. The question is not between Mende and Temne, or North versus South, or East, but it is between the provincial people versus the Creoles. As far as the Creoles are concerned we are uncivilized and illiterate people. The National Council of Sierra Leone under the leadership of the late Dr. Bankole Bright had once referred to us as foreigners. Thus, the NCSL platform stated, "We object to the foreigners (Countrymen) prepondering in our legislative council."

Provincial unity is the most essential issue for a united Sierra Leone. Failure on our part to unite, will make us into perpetual servants of Creoles. It is the Creoles who determine our economic and social progress. By virtue of the position they hold in the country they determine who gets what job or what scholarship. It is obvious through experience that they consider their kith and kin first.

Since A.P.C. took over Creoledom has become blatantly entrenched. Creole parasitism has to be eliminated once and for all. We are not blind to the facts previously presented. We want to make it known that Sierra Leone is not Creole property, and an attempt to transform it into another Liberia will be violently resisted.' (July 23, 1969, as quoted by Jordan 1971).

Provincials of the various tribes have their common antagonisms towards the Creoles, but they also share certain cultural affinities with each other. The *Poro*, a male closed society, crosses tribal boundaries, and it still has political significance in the country. But, despite the possibility of political co-operation between Mende and Temne at some future time, ancient, traditional antagonisms continue to maintain the old cleavage between the north and the south. During the rise of the All People's Congress before the 1967 elections, a few Mende did cross over the political division and join the APC, but they did so at great cost to their relationships within their families.[9] There is a Krio saying which expresses just how permanent these traditional enmities are believed to be: 'A rat may be a very devout Muslim, but he is never going to kneel to pray on the skin of a cat' ('*Arata na big mɔre man bɔt i nɔ go pre na pus kanda*').

Educational opportunities continue to follow the pattern established early in Sierra Leone's history, a pattern which favoured first the inhabitants of the Western Area – then the south, with the north falling far behind. In 1966 88 per cent of all children under twelve years of age in the Western Area were attending school, compared with little more than a third of this age group in the Eastern and Southern Provinces. However, in the Northern Province in the same year only 10 per cent of primary aged children were enrolled in schools. The same pattern holds with regard to secondary school. In 1966 about one-fifth of the children between twelve and nineteen in the Western Area were enrolled in secondary school compared with 3 per cent enrolment in the Southern Area, 1 per cent in the Eastern Province, and less than 1 per cent in the Northern Province (Young 1966). Opportunities for higher education continue to favour those from the Western Province: out of eighty-six scholarships awarded in 1969 by the Sierra Leone government or by international bodies for study abroad, fifty-five went to Creoles (Sierra Leone Gazette, 23 January 1969, Freetown, Government Printing Office, 1969, as quoted by Jordan 1971). This despite the fact that the Creoles represent less than 2 per cent of the total population of Sierra Leone.

In spite of the Creoles' minority position in the society, they set the pattern for the social development of the rest of the population. The old established Creole families who had early identified themselves with western culture became the reference group for the behaviour and

9. The latest effort to minimize the problems of these political factions has been for the government to explicitly encourage the 'evolution' of the one-party state in May, 1973.

attitudes of the educated members of the indigenous population. Because of the activity of missionaries in the early days of the Colony, the acceptance of Christian monogamous marriage became the primary measure of being civilized. Creole marriage and family behaviour continues to be the ideal model for educated Provincials.

The attitude of the Provincial towards the Creoles was very much like his attitude towards the white men. While he resented their dominance, he also envied their achievements and measured his advance by the standards which they set. Creoles were patronizing in their relationships with Provincials. The ward system as an institution of the colonial period best exemplifies the relationship between the two groups. The Creoles allowed Provincial children to grow up in their households so that they might acquire some of their civilized ways. Provincial parents were enthusiastic for their children to have such an opportunity despite the risk that these children might later turn their backs on their own families. Although Provincials resent the attitude of the Creoles, their behaviour suggests that they have accepted their inferior status *vis-à-vis* Creoles. Today, although political control is held by the Provincials, Creoles continue to set the standard for prestige and status. They act as advisers and fill most of the important government posts.

Creoles, in an effort to secure their tenuous position, have managed to take advantage of the traditional hostilities between the two main tribal groups, the Mende and the Temne, by giving their support first to one and then to the other. The dependence of the Provincials on the highly educated Creoles and the tendency of the government, which is dominated by the Temne, to favour Creole appointments exacerbates the hostility between all three groups. The result is a situation of extreme tension amongst all these people in the professional group, who are competing with one another for political power.

3

The composition and social background
of the professional group

Tribal composition and education

In view of the educational advantages enjoyed by the early settlers, it is not surprising to discover that 64 per cent of the professionals are Creoles.[1] Mende and Temne comprise 21 per cent, with the remaining 15 per cent made up of several other tribal or ethnic groups in the country. Analysis of the tribal composition of the university students in Sierra Leone reveals that only 40 per cent of all the students are Creole. This might suggest some increase in the representation of Provincials in the professional group in the future. However, when the two university college enrolments are examined separately and some other factors are considered, quite a different picture of the future emerges.

At Fourah Bay College 57 per cent of all the students are Creole compared with ony 17 per cent of the Njala students. This is significant because the students from Fourah Bay College have a far greater chance of entering the professional group than have students from Njala. Njala was originally an agricultural college, although it is now possible to read for degrees in a few other disciplines. The standards for acceptance there have been somewhat lower than at Fourah Bay College, but even so Njala has had difficulty in keeping a minimum enrolment. Studying at Njala is generally viewed as a last resort. Although most of them read some branch of agricultural science, very few Njala students actually wish to enter a career associated with agriculture. Most of them hope to have the opportunity to go overseas

1. As suggested in Chapter Two, it should always be borne in mind that the group of persons who identify themselves as Creoles includes persons with tribal connections.

to enter some other field of study after obtaining their qualifications from Njala. Those who had little hope of changing their careers through further study abroad were very concerned about the very few jobs open for graduates in agriculture in Sierra Leone. In view of these problems it is interesting to note that more Njala students aspired to occupations of higher prestige such as medicine, law, and university teaching, than did Fourah Bay students.

Given the choice, most Sierra Leoneans would choose to study overseas after leaving secondary school. Only a quarter of the women among the professionals and a fifth of the men had obtained their qualifications through study in Sierra Leone only. All the rest had studied abroad and more than half the sample had done all their advanced studies overseas. Creoles place a very high value on sending their children overseas for their university training; some even send young children to boarding schools in Britain.[2] It was not possible to ascertain how many persons were studying abroad at the time of this study, but given the manner in which scholarships for overseas study are awarded and the ambitions and greater economic resources of established Creole families, we can assume that the majority of them were Creole. Therefore, even if the high aspirations of the Njala students are realized, it will be a very long time before the number of Provincial professionals reflects even approximately the representation of Provincials in the population.

Age and birthplace

The average age of the men in the professional group is 38 years, and of women 34 years. Forty-six per cent of the men were born in Freetown, 6 per cent were born in the rural parts of the Western Area and another 8 per cent were born outside Sierra Leone. Among those born in the provinces, about half were born in villages having a population of less than 2,000. The birthplace of the women, both those who were professionals themselves and those who were wives of professional men follow a similar pattern, 40 per cent born in Freetown, 8 per cent born

2. Petersen (1969) points out the importance of an overseas education in ensuring a position of high social status and observes that for the Creole 'An overseas education became second only to the purchasing of land in the city as a form of sure investment' (p. 284).

in the rural part of the Western Area and 7 per cent born out of the country. Another 13 per cent of the women were non-Sierra Leonean spouses and were born out of the country. Only about a third of the Provincial-born women came from villages of less than 2,000 persons; the rest were born in larger Provincial towns.

The birthplaces of the students show some differences from this pattern. While 44 per cent were born in the Western Area, more than a third were born in little villages in the Provinces having less than 2,000 population. Again, there are differences between the students of the two university colleges. More of those born in small villages were attending Njala, while 59 per cent of the students of Fourah Bay College were born in the Western Area.

Marital status

The marital status of the professionals in the sample is shown in Table 1. It should be noted that among the professional women eleven out of the eighteen had never been married, while the rest were married to professional men.[3]

Table 1. *Sex and marital status of professionals*

	Number	%
Married male	120	75
Never married male	20	13
Divorced male	1	1
Widowed male	1	1
Married female	7	4
Never married female	11	7
Divorced female	0	
Widowed female	0	
Totals	160	100[a]

a. Not all totals shown in tables throughout the book equal 100% due to rounding.

3. The reader should not be confused by the fact that the totals in Table 1 and Table 30 are the same while there are differences within them. As is explained in detail in Appendix A, I sampled the entire list of the professional group. The marital status of this sample is shown here in Table 1. I intended to interview half of the professionals in the sample and the spouses of the

The choices of marriage partners by professional men clearly reflect status relations between Provincials, Creoles and Europeans. Both Provincials and Creoles tend to marry within their own group. Among the Creole married men, 69 per cent were married to women who also were Creole. Among the Provincial married men, 34 per cent had married a woman from their own tribal background and another 40 per cent had married Provincial women, but from another tribe than their own.

If a man marries outside his own group it is regarded as more prestigious to marry a non-Sierra Leonean or, in the case of the Provincial, to marry a Creole woman. Almost a quarter of the Creole men and 6 per cent of the Provincial men had married women of European or other non-Sierra Leonean origin. One-fifth of the Provincial men had married Creole women. A union between a Creole girl and a Provincial may not necessarily constitute a loss of prestige for the girl. Usually these are girls from lower status Creole families who would prefer their daughters to marry a professionally educated Provincial rather than someone of their own socio-economic background. Only a few Creole men, 8 per cent, had married women of Provincial background, generally regarded as the least desirable marriage choice for a Creole professional.

The partners to extant unions had been married, at the time of the research, an average of 9.7 years. Most of them had been married under statutory law. Statutory law in Sierra Leone is based upon the British legal system. Six per cent had married under the Mohammedan Marriage Act. Although most of the Provincial couples had gone through some of the rites connected with marriage by customary law prior to their statutory marriage, only two of the couples were married by customary law alone. Two couples admitted to not having been married, although they planned to have a church ceremony at some future date when they felt they could afford the expense. Since these couples had lived together for some time, had children and were regarded by their acquaintances as married, they were included in the group of extant unions. In all, 125 unions were regarded as 'extant' for the purposes of the research.

---

professionals in the other half of the sample. The marital status of those actually interviewed and from whom the data were drawn which describe the professional group is shown in Table 30.

The average age at marriage shows some difference between Creoles and Provincials, the Creoles marrying at an older age.[4] On the average, Creole men married at 30.4 years compared with 28.7 as the average for Provincial men. Creole women married at an average age of 26.5 while the average age at marriage for Provincial women was 23.2.[5] The university students were asked to state what they considered an ideal age for marriage. The results of their responses indicated the ideal age for men to be 26.1 and for women, 24.9. There were no differences between the responses of the Creole and Provincial students.

Although about a quarter of the married couples were not living together, only 6 per cent admitted to being estranged. The others were not living together because one of the spouses was pursuing some educational course or because the husband's work had caused him to be transferred. Two per cent of the couples were apart because the husbands were in prison, having been arrested on political charges in 1968.

Religious affiliation

Since the founding of the Colony, active church membership, the Anglican faith being preferred, has always been associated with the Creole's prestigious position in the society. Only 2 per cent of the Creole professionals claimed to be agnostics, atheists or 'free thinkers', and even these people retained membership of a church. All were church members and over half said they attended services regularly. Sixty per cent were Anglican, 29 per cent were members of other protestant denominations and 8 per cent were Catholic. Among the Provincials, 70 per cent were members of churches, although fewer of them professed to attending services. Most missionary activity in the Provinces has been conducted by various independent protestant denominations. This accounts for the fact that 44 per cent of the Provincials who were Christian were members of such churches, only 15 per cent were Anglican and 11 per cent were Catholic. While none of the

4. Although these figures apply to the present union, only two persons among the married couples had been married before. However, marital history as regards customary marriages and informal unions is complicated, a topic which will be discussed later.

5. Between 1961 and 1968 2472 marriages were contracted under statutory law. The average age of men at the time of marriage for all these unions was 33.5 and of women, 26.3.

Creole professionals were of the Muslim faith, 28 per cent of the Provincials were Muslim, although only about half of these claimed still to practise the religion. Three-quarters of the married couples shared the same religious affiliation, but in only three cases were both the partners Muslims.

Missionary activity had been responsible for the founding of many of the boarding schools in the Provinces and the teachers placed a great deal of emphasis on Christian indoctrination. Thus, while only a third of the university Provincial students claimed to be Muslims themselves, two-thirds of them had parents who were followers of Islam. Many students explained their own conversion to Christianity by stating that it was impossible to progress in school if one insisted on retaining the Muslim faith. As a result of the pressure that is placed on students to convert, many devout Muslims are hesitant to send their children to school.[6] Despite the fact that the majority of the population today describe themselves as Muslim, the religion continues to be more closely identified with traditional life and has considerably less prestige than Christianity.

Education

It would be difficult to think of a more successful innovation in Africa than the acceptance of western education. Earlier it was noted that the colonial period gave rise to a special set of social conditions which had their greatest impact on the elite. Throughout their lives the professional group have had very different experiences from the average citizen of Sierra Leone. Most of these different experiences resulted from the high value placed upon educational achievements and the willingness to make almost any sacrifice in their interest. The majority of the fathers of the professionals were born around the turn of the century at the peak of what Porter (1963) has referred to as the 'period of Creole ascendancy'. It was during this period that the Provincials began to make a serious bid for a share in the trading economy and the British began making gestures towards developing

6. This resistance to western education for religious reasons is a serious and continuing problem for the Ministry of Education. It has attempted to co-operate with Islamic schools by offering support if they revised the curriculum to meet minimum standards. These efforts have met with only very limited success.

the Protectorate. Many of the grandparents of the Creoles in the professional group already had some primary education, and they were highly motivated to see that their children received more education than they themselves had had (Porter 1963, p. 113). All the fathers of the Creole professional men and 99 per cent of their mothers had at least attended primary school and some had gone much further.

However, the relationship between education and economic advance was a lesson that was not lost upon the peoples of the Protectorate compared with the Colony. Despite the fewer opportunities for education in the Protectorate and the lack of financial resources, a number of the grandparents of the Provincial professionals had managed to give their sons and even a few of their daughters some education. Tables 2 and 3 indicate the levels of education attained by the mothers and fathers of the professionals and the university students. As they show, all the fathers of the Creole professionals and students had some western education. However, many more of the Provincial university students than professionals had fathers with no formal schooling. It appears that during the years the university students have been growing up, the value of education for their children has been accepted by an ever-widening group of Provincials who themselves have had no western education.

Table 2. *Level of western education of fathers of professional group and university students by tribal affiliation (Percentages)*

| | Professionals | | Students[a] | |
	Creole	Provincial	Creole	Provincial
Never attended school	0	28	0	49
Literate in Arabic	0	13	0	7
Attended primary school	10	25	8	14
Attended secondary school	67	16	67	17
Education beyond secondary	18	15	21	6
Other ('Don't know' or no response)	5	3	4	7
Totals %	100	100	100	100
Totals No.	96	61	90	136

a. Three university students did not respond to the question asking their tribal affiliation so these three have been excluded from all tables which analyse that factor.

Table 3. *Level of western education of mothers of professional group and university students by tribal affiliation (Percentages)*

		Professionals		Students	
		Creole	Provincial	Creole	Provincial
Never attended school		1	69	2	68
Literate in Arabic		0	1	0	2
Attended primary school		20	18	7	14
Attended secondary school		69	10	82	10
Education beyond secondary		7	1	5	0
Other ('Don't know' or no response)		2	1	4	6
Totals	%	100	100	100	100
	No.	96	61	90	136

More than twice the number of mothers of the women than of men in both groups had attended school and a significantly higher number of these mothers of women had got as far as secondary school. It appears that girls are more likely to be encouraged to go further in their education if their mothers have also had some secondary education.

Having educated parents doubtless increased the chances that individuals would get to school, but often persons other than parents had paid the costs of education of the professionals and the university students. Schools in Sierra Leone have never been free: fees range from £5 to £24 per year, and the per capita income is very low (about £50). Usually government assistance is only available to students after they have completed secondary school. The father in the traditional household is under strong pressure from each of his wives to give equal treatment to her children. He might be convinced of the importance of educating his children but find it difficult to provide money for the education of all of them. Some men resolve this problem by agreeing to pay school fees for all their children at primary level; any further education would have to be financed by other means. The Creole father has a first obligation to educate the children from his 'married' household. Whether or not he educates his illegitimate children depends on his own financial resources, his sense of responsibility, and, often, the attitude of his own wife towards them.

The stories of how individuals managed to get as far as university level are filled with struggle, uncertainty and sacrifice. In a great many cases it was the determined effort of the mother that was most significant. Sometimes a child was sent to live with a relative who had the means and inclination to educate him. Often an interested missionary or a British colonial officer paid school fees for a child. Today it is quite common for European employers to pay school fees for their servants' children. Many students have no security from term to term and are often reduced to soliciting their school fees even from strangers. For example, I was often presented with letters like the following by desperate young people.

'Unfortunately my result was not good again in the last G.C.E. Examination. For this reason I had decided to take the examination again.

My most difficult problem now is getting my examination fees. Unfortunately for me my brother had misplaced his bank book, and is only after three months before he can be given a new one. Secondly he is annoyed with me because of my last performance in the examination.

For the above reasons I am asking you kindly to render me assistance. Sorry for an inconveniency. Closing date for all entries is the 31st of this month. Thanks.'

Often the individual was so determined to continue his education that he worked for a number of years after leaving primary school in order to earn the money for his own fees. However, the possibilities of securing paid employment are extremely limited. A quarter of the Creole university students and almost half the Provincials worked for a year or more after completing secondary school before being able to begin their university studies.

Often the individual took the initiative by approaching large numbers of relatives for financial support. Among the university students who said relatives financed their education, only a quarter named just one relative, usually their father.[7] All the rest mentioned between two

---

7. It should be noted that there is a strong tendency to give fathers the credit for financing educational costs. Everyone would prefer to have a father who took this responsibility, but in many cases the fathers who were reported as having paid school fees had been dead since the respondent's early childhood. However, having a classificatory kinship system, Provincials also apply the English term, father, to their father's brothers or other male relatives on the father's side of the family.

and five relatives who had contributed heavily towards their educational costs, and 8 per cent said there had been so many relatives assisting them over the years they could not count them. One person said that literally every adult person in his village had helped him. Among the professionals 39 per cent gave their fathers the chief credit for support, 27 per cent said it was their mothers who had paid for their education, and 11 per cent said it was their sisters or brothers. Thirteen per cent named relatives on their mother's side, compared with 6 per cent naming their father's relatives. Why it is that a mother and her relatives might be especially interested in the education of her children in this patrilineal society will be considered later in the discussion of the relationship between a mother and her children.

In the case of the Provincial university students it would have been more important to discover if there was a member of their family who had achieved professional status than to have examined the educational level of the fathers as was done. Most professionals are involved in the support of children of ther extended family and it is often mainly through their efforts and encouragement that Provincial students have managed to get to university. Financial support received from relatives reinforces traditional obligations to the extended family. Although few stated they felt they must repay the money invested in their education, most of them felt the obligation to assume similar responsibilities towards others in their family, and many students were supporting relatives out of their grants. Although almost all the professionals indicated they approved in principle the practice of relatives assisting each other financially, women, especially Creole women, were less enthusiastic about the practice than the men.

The location of schools and other difficulties often made it necessary for children to leave home at very early ages in the interest of their education. More than one-third of the Provincial professionals and a fifth of the Creoles were in the care of someone other than their mother before they were five years old. One quarter of the Provincial students had also left their mother's care by the time they were five, compared with only 11 per cent of the Creole students. More than half this latter group were still living in the same household as their mother by the time they were twenty years old. Among the Provincial university students over 90 per cent were living with some other person away from their parents (about half of these were living with relatives) or in boarding school by the time they were fifteen years of age. Only 29 per cent of the Creole students compared with 74 per cent of the Provincials had lived in boarding schools and, among the professionals, 18 per cent of the Creoles compared with 66 per cent of the Provincials had been boarding students. Living in the Western Area gave easier access to schools so that Creoles did not experience such radical changes in residence as did Provincials.

The ward system has already been mentioned. There has never been a systematic study of this institution to warrant any definitive statement about the numbers of children involved. However, twelve per cent of the professionals and 16 per cent of the university students had been wards in homes of persons unrelated to them during childhood. Often Creoles trading in the Protectorate would agree to take children of Provincial families to their homes in Freetown as wards. (In some cases these children were offspring of unions between Creoles and Provincial women.) Although the Creole family was expected to pay school fees, often the heavy household responsibilities of the ward seriously interfered with study and regular class attendance. Usually the ward was regarded as inferior to the other members of the family. As Porter describes it:

> 'They helped with the domestic chores in the house which rendered the Creole children free to undertake more leisurely pursuits . . . tribal people accepted the Creole household as a desirable milieu for the socialization of their children and continued to send them to Creole guardians notwithstanding their minor status in these households. The majority of these wards did not return to the Protectorate but remained in the Colony and passed as Creoles . . .' (1963, p. 64).

Unequal treatment of wards compared with the children of the household was common and produced considerable hostility and competition between them. Such tensions were only increased if the ward got better marks at school. Relationships in adulthood between persons who were wards and their guardians vary considerably. While many were absorbed into the Creole family, in other cases there is no longer any contact and only bitter memories.

Comparisons of the experiences of childhood between the Creoles and the Provincials show that it was the Provincial child whose life was most drastically altered in the interest of his educational advance. Creoles, for the most part, grew up living with their families in the social environment of Freetown in which they had been born. Provincial children were often removed from the care of their mothers at a very early age. In many cases they were moved many times from family to family or from school to school during childhood. Often they were placed among complete strangers in a town where the social environment was alien to the village life in which they had been born. If they lived in a Creole or European home, they were reminded constantly (implicitly if not openly) of their inferior Provincial background. They had to be taught to eat 'properly' with fork and knife, and dress in western fashion. They even had to accustom themselves to sleeping in beds (if they were provided; often Provincial wards slept on mats while the children of the household had beds). They were taught that the ways of the Creoles and the Europeans were superior to those of their traditional upbringing and were reminded of the importance of adapting themselves to the new habits to which they were so privileged to be exposed.

Other stresses were endured for the sake of education. Many described the loneliness and unhappiness of their early years in mission schools away from their families. Missionary teachers often included liberal amounts of physical punishment in their education. Individuals often told of their intense anxiety in the face of examinations since their entire future rested on the results. Their feelings of obligation to the many relatives making sacrifices for them and depending on them to achieve success only increased this anxiety. Many suffered the constant awareness that support could be cut off at any time if the relative who was supporting them lost interest, or had financial losses, or, as so often happened, died. The sense of being part of a 'fellowship of suffering' has developed among persons who were in school together, and it is often described in terms akin to the unity which develops among young boys who are circumcised together in the bush. Provincials were much more likely to be insecure about school costs than were Creoles. Creole families have been committed to the value of education for a very long time and were willing to invest heavily in the education of their children.

Many of the university students already had heavy financial obligations to relatives and dependants; 16 per cent had one or more children and about half of them were married. Provincials especially feel obliged to send regular sums of money home to their mothers, a fundamental obligation of traditional culture. They know that co-wives often humiliate a mother by reminding her that although their own sons may not have gone to England they do, after all, support their mother: (*'Mi yu pikin nɔ go inglan bɔt na im de fid me so'*). Often it is necessary for married men to leave their wives behind when they go abroad to study and they may be separated for many years. Sometimes such separations lead to estrangement.

I visited many Sierra Leonean students studying in Britain. Their living conditions were often far from satisfactory and often inferior to what they were accustomed to at home. Besides the problems of adapting themselves to an alien culture and a cold climate, all of them encounter the trauma of racial prejudice.[8] Those who fail to pass examinations or receive qualifications often feel they cannot go back to Sierra Leone. They try course after course in an effort to achieve some qualification, for, after all, to have come to England and failed is a very deep disgrace.

Today education continues to have an overriding importance to professional couples but most people try to arrange for their children's education without having to send them to another home (although 18 per cent of the professionals had children living in households of relatives or in boarding school). Schools in Freetown are considered much better than anywhere else in the country and many professionals solve their children's educational problem by arranging to be transferred there when they reach school age. Others have houses in Freetown and they leave their wives and children in residence there during up-country appointments.

All but 15 per cent of the professional group had lived abroad (mostly for study purposes) between one and sixteen years, the average number of years abroad being seven and a half. Over half the married couples had lived apart for a year or more during their married life and ten per cent of these had been separated between four and nine years. Most of these separations occurred because one or other of the spouses was studying overseas. And, as was just mentioned, many couples live separately because of the demands of their children's education.

Very few persons obtain their university degrees in the minimum three years. Only three per cent of the professionals had only three years of university training. Half of them studied between four and six years and all the others had over seven years of post-secondary school education.

---

8. This problem was often mentioned by medical students, who frequently have patients who refuse to allow them to attend them.

Among the wives of the professionals, 5 per cent had only primary level education. Twenty four per cent had attended secondary school, most of them having completed From Five. About two-thirds had one or more years of higher education, which included nurse's training, secretarial courses, teacher training courses, catering courses, etc. One quarter of all the wives had obtained a university degree.

Occupation and social status

The professional men included graduate students, engineers, lawyers and judges, doctors, secondary school teachers and principals, bankers, university lecturers and administrators, and civil servants. Professional women included doctors, an accountant, a headmistress, a lawyer, and secondary school teachers. Because some occupational groups are represented by so few persons it is not possible to provide the reader with a table showing the actual distribution of occupations

Table 4. *Occupations of wives of professional men*

	Number
Housewife	42
Secondary school teacher	18
Secretary, typist, stenographer, clerk	14
Primary school teacher	13
Nurse	11
Lecturer in university, university administrative staff	5
Civil service (auditor, accountant, social welfare, assistant architect)	5
Principal (or vice-principal) of secondary school or teacher-training college	6
Self-employed (seamstress, trader, business)	5
Doctor	2
Graduate student	2
Lawyer	1
Saleswoman	1
Total	125

in the sample and still preserve the individual's anonymity. Table 4 shows the occupations of the wives of the professionals in the sample. Two-thirds of the wives of the professionals had worked an average of three years before they were married and three-quarters of them had continued to work an average of almost four years after marriage.

Table 5 shows the occupational status of the married couples in the sample and whether or not the wife was working at the time of the interview.

Table 5. *Occupational status and employment of married couples*

	(Percentages)
Both partners are professional and working	22
Both partners are professional and wife is not working	2
Husband professional, wife has career training and is working	35
Husband professional, wife has career training and is not working	18
Husband professional, wife has no career training and is working	6
Husband professional, wife has no career training and is not working	15
Wife professional, husband has career training and is working	1
Totals %	100
No.	125

As shown here, 35 per cent of all the wives were not working at the time of the research. However, 81 per cent of the Creole wives and 52 per cent of the provincial wives were earning money in some manner although not all these reported they were 'employed'. These 'unemployed' wives earned money in a variety of ways. One professional wife raised pigs and vegetables on a farm outside Freetown. One wife ran a very small catering business although she would not admit to having a job. Another wife was a seamstress; others ran small petty trading businesses. The pattern of financial arrangements between husband and wife, which will be discussed in Chapter 8, makes it almost imperative for women to earn some income of their own. Professional men are, however, generally ambivalent about the question of their wives working and it is a topic of considerable disagreement between married couples. It is generally believed that it is not a good thing for a woman to have a professional-level career because it is thought to lead invariably to an unstable marriage. However, at the same time, if a woman *has* a university education it is believed that she has a responsibility to use this training in a career. In the sample of professional women over half had never been married and three out of the seven who were married admitted being estranged from their husbands.

Discussing the social background of professional Sierra Leoneans in terms of the father's occupation has little meaning in this context. The socio-economic classifications usually employed in sociological studies are hardly an applicable measure of status in this context (Gamble, 1966). Since the turn of the century opportunities for occupational advance for even educated Sierra Leoneans have been very limited. Having the means to earn sufficient money to educate one's children, particularly to educate them abroad, certainly always lent prestige. Almost half of the fathers of the Creole professionals were employed in clerical jobs during most of their lives. Another third were in civil service, managerial or professional positions. Only 4 per cent of the Creoles in the professional group indicated their fathers were farmers. In contrast, one-fifth of the fathers of Provincial professionals earned their living through farming. Half of the professionals' fathers' occupations were coded in the upper two socio-economic groups which include administrative, executive, managerial ranks and teaching. Separate examination of these individuals shows that most of them were paramount chiefs, chiefdom officials, members of ruling houses, or 'factors' (traders who represented large companies in the Provinces). Most of these people also controlled land and received the profits from the farming done on it.

The occupations of the parents of Creole and Provincial university students showed some differences. Almost half the fathers of Provincial students were farmers and about the same number of the fathers of Creole students were employed in clerical or civil service positions. Less than one-fifth of the Provincial students, compared with half the adult Provincial professionals, stated their fathers' occupation as being in the upper socio-economic classifications. On the other hand, 40 per cent of the Provincial students claimed to be from a ruling family, one-quarter of these to be members of a paramouth chief's household.

Social status in the village and in town

The university students were asked to write answers to the questions, 'What do you think it is that determines status and prestige in the city?' and 'What do you think it is that determines status and prestige in the village?'. Three-quarters of the responses distinguished between systems of prestige and status in the two settings. Although the form of questioning tended to produce this distinction, it is significant that more Provincial students than Creoles (82 per cent compared with 65 per cent) indicated there were definite differences between the systems of prestige and status in village and city. Table 6 shows the items mentioned by students and the numbers of times they were given as a response. Although the responses to these open-ended questions reveal an awareness of two separate systems of evaluating social position in the village and the city, it is interesting to note the areas of convergence. Personal qualities, including such attributes as honesty, personal ambition, achievement, and, in this setting, that most important quality, sociability, are regarded as important criteria of high rank in both village and city. Likewise, wealth and owning houses have considerable importance in both. Political positions and political influence are also regarded as important prestige factors in both the village and the city. The political importance of the *Poro* society was mentioned earlier and it would have been appropriate to combine the numbers of answers mentioning leadership in a secret society with political leadership in its more usual sense. Being part of the chief's household or from a ruling family is, of course, also related to political position. The wide acceptance of the prestige associated with western education is also shown in the responses of the students although, according to them, it continues to have less importance in the village.

The largest disparities between the two systems, as the students saw them, arise from the persistence of traditional values on the one hand and, on the other, the impact of western urban values. Although age was frequently mentioned as being important in the village, it is interesting that only one noted that it had importance in the city. Although aged people are treated with considerable respect in the urban setting they have certainly lost the position of almost absolute authority which they hold in family and village affairs. Many people told me that they simply avoid discussing certain questions with their elders since they might give unacceptable advice. Having a large

Table 6. *'What do you think it is that determines status and prestige in the city and the village?'* [a]

	Village	City
The number of wives	46	0
The number of children	35	0
The number of other dependants	9	0
Leader of a secret society	15	0
Tribe	11	0
Number of cattle owned	7	0
Having a house with a zinc roof	3	0
Age	43	1
Amount of land owned	9	5
Areas of convergence { Famyly background (coming from a ruling family in the case of the village)	58	17
Personal qualities (good character, honesty, personal achievement, sociability)	49	35
Wealth (material possessions, owning a house)	95	137
Education	50	130
Political leadership (having political power)	29	52
Occupation	6	63
Owning a car	2	15
Standard of housing	0	21
Membership in social organizations, participation in social activities	0	11
Social class	0	8
Religious affiliation	0	2
Having only one wife	0	2
Total	467	499

a. Since the question was 'open-ended', students could mention as many items as they wished. The numbers in the table show how many times a response was given. It will be recalled that there were 229 persons in this sample.

number of dependants, including wives, children, and other relatives, still figures large as a source of high social position in the village. Professionals who come from such a background find it impossible to ignore completely the traditional way of measuring status and prestige but, at the same time, they are constrained to rate achievement in terms of urban values.

The university students were asked to choose from a list of items those attributes which described their father or their father's family. The choice of these items for the questionnaire came out of many discussions with informants and most of them relate to the measures of status and prestige in the village. Although subjective assessments of social background in such research are also problematic, the students' responses (shown in Table 7) underline the differences in the social background of Creoles and Provincials and provide further evidence of the dual system of prestige and status of which Provincials, at least, are very clearly aware.

Table 7. *Attributes which students indicated as describing their father or their father's family (Percentages)*

	Creoles	Provincials
Poor	2	20[a]
Just average wealth	71	62
Wealthy	12	10
Very wealthy	0	1
Part of a chief's household	1	24
Member of a ruling family	2	40
Influential relatives	23	40
Highly respected	48	74
Leader of a secret society	3	22
A politician	3	10
Owns land	62	69
Large number of dependants	18	60
Owns houses	50	54
A civil servant	33	10

a. Percentages are based on the number of students who ticked the item in the list provided in the questionnaire. There were 90 Creoles and 136 Provincials in the sample. (It will be recalled from the footnote on page 41 that three students did not state what their tribe was, so these three have been excluded from the analysis of this factor.) Although questions about the relative wealth of one's family might be regarded as excessively personal, only 13 Creoles and 10 Provincials did not tick one of the choices relating to their family's financial position.

Monogamy and social status

It is interesting, in view of the emphasis on monogamous marriage among the educated in Sierra Leone, that having one wife was hardly mentioned as important to social prestige in the city, since it was frequently indicated as being of supreme importance in discussions with the informants. Table 8 shows the type of marriage of the parents of both samples by tribal affiliation.

Table 8. *Type of marriage of parents of professionals and students by tribal affiliation (Percentages)*

		Professional		Student	
		Creoles	Provin-cials	Creoles	Provin-cials
Customary rites		2	56	3	60
Muslim law		0	13	0	25
Ordinance marriage[a]		92	21	92	14
Not married by law[b]		4	1	0	0
Other ('Don't know', no response		1	8	4	1
Totals	%	100	100	100	100
	No.	96	61	90	136

a. See Chapter Five for a discussion of the types of ordinance marriage under statutory law.
b. The question about the type of marriage of parents was badly constructed; it left no opportunity for respondents to indicate if their parents were *not* married under any of the three recognized legal systems in Sierra Leone. In my personal interviews with the professionals I finally learned to ask the question in such a way as to allow them to state their parents were not married.

Most of the Creole respondents claimed to come from homes where the parents were married under statutory law, implying that these marriages represented monogamous unions. As shown earlier, most Creole families professed Christianity. Being Christian, educated, and married under statutory law are strongly associated with prestige in Creole society. In the light of this association, it is notable that 43 per cent of the Provincial women compared with only 11 per cent of the Provincial men in the professional sample came from homes where the parents were reported to have been married under statutory law. The evidence suggests that more women than men who achieve a university education (including those who marry professionally qualified men) come from families who have themselves accepted the social importance of Christianity, education, and statutory marriage.

The students were asked if their fathers had ever had more than one wife at a time. Only one Creole student responded 'yes' to this question. On the other hand, 68 per cent of the Provincial students said their fathers were polygamously married. While Creoles would not admit to being polygamous, many men establish liaisons of varying stability which result in offspring. In order to explore the extent of this practice, respondents in both samples were also asked about the numbers of half-brothers and sisters they had on both their mother's and father's side of the family. One-third of the Creole students stated their fathers had no children with any woman other than their mother, but the other two-thirds indicated how many children their fathers had had outside this union. Since divorce is very infrequent we can assume that most of these were born outside marriage. This topic is extremely sensitive, so it is not surprising that this question had the highest non-response rate (12 per cent of the Creoles did not answer the question). The students were also asked about the numbers of half-brothers and sisters they had who were born to their mothers. One-third of the Creoles and 47 per cent of the Provincial students indicated their mother had had other children by men other than their father. Still there clearly is less of a tendency for women to have children outside marriage. Moreover, among those who have borne children for men other than their husbands, it is impossible to speculate how many of such children were born before the marriage, as a result of extra-marital unions, or to know how many were born to unions formed after the dissolution of the marriage by separation, divorce or death.

Because of the sensitivity of this topic it was decided not to ask the professionals a direct question about whether or not their fathers had been married to more than one wife at a time. I did ask them how many half-brothers and sisters they had on both their mothers' and fathers' side. Table 9 shows their responses to this question about fathers. Almost half of the Creole men and 37 per cent of the Creole women in the professional sample admitted their fathers had children with women other than their mother. Again, since divorce is very rare, we can assume most of these children were born outside wedlock. Although Creoles value Christian monogamous marriage, having children with women other than the wife is common.

When the professional sample was asked about how many children their mothers had with men other than their father, only 20 per cent said they had any. There were no significant differences between the responses of Creoles and Provincials. When the responses of the men and women were compared, 23 per cent of the men compared with only 14 per cent of the women stated their mothers had children with men other than their father. Usually in these cases the respondent took care to explain that these children had resulted from unions legalized before or after the marriage of their parents.

Table 9. *'How many half-brothers and sisters do you have on your father's side?' (Professional sample) (Percentages)*

		Men		Women	
		Creoles	Provin-cials	Creoles	Provin-cials
None		52	5	63	21
One		15	8	17	0
Two		9	11	6	8
Three to Five		13	19	10	21
Six or more		11	57	4	46
No response		0	0	0	4
Totals	%	100	100	100	100
	No.	48	37	48	24

The households of the married professionals

Professionals say that it is most desirable for a household to be limited to a man, his wife and their own children. Most of them believe this will be the normative household arrangement in the future. Many indicated that for now it was better to live in a house which was just too small to accommodate many relatives. At the same time, it is generally acknowledged that such preferences have to be assessed in the light of their obligations to members of the extended family which professionals regards as unavoidable under present-day economic conditions in Sierra Leone.

Relatives coming to town expect hospitality from their professional relatives. Professionals are often asked to support and educate some of their relatives' children and such requests are difficult to refuse. Three-quarters of the professional households have kinsmen living in them; 58 per cent were of the husband's family and the others were related to the wife. It is also common for these households to include a number of persons who live with them to assist with domestic work whether related or not. Almost all the persons living with the professionals were described as 'permanent' members of the household group and in 90 per cent of the cases the hosts were either fully or partly financially responsible for these extra persons. It is also common for professional families to have more than one paid servant. Seven per cent of them had paid servants living with them and another 84 per cent employed one or more persons for domestic services, including housework, driving, gardening, etc., who did not live in the house. Table 10 shows the average number of persons per household among the professional group compared with the average household size in the urban areas of all four Provinces. The professionals have, as this table indicates, succeeded in keeping their household size smaller than is average in the Provincial towns, but they are larger than is average for Freetown or the Western Area.

Table 10. *Average number of persons per household* [a]

Profes- sional Group	Freetown	Western Area	Northern Province	Southern Province	Eastern Province
5.5	4.3	4.4	6.6	6.4	6.0

a. These data were taken from this research and from the series of household surveys conducted by the Central Statistics Office in the urban areas of the country between 1966 and 1969.

Although Sierra Leoneans place a strong value on taking care of the aged, only a few professionals' families actually had any older people living with them and only 14 had either of the spouses' parents in the household. In one of these cases it was the aged father who owned the house in which the professional family resided. Most informants held the view that it is preferable to help their parents find other housing and arrange for another relative to live with them, giving financial support when needed, rather than bring them into their own household. Only if the parent is unable to care for himself and alternative solutions are not available is it thought necessary to move the parent in with the professional's family. At the same time, most of the professionals whose parents were alive were giving them money and visiting them regularly. The age structure of the professional households compared with that of the Western Area as shown in Table 11 reflects their bias in favour of supporting and educating young children in preference to offering homes to old relatives.

Table 11. *Age distribution of persons residing in professionals' house-*
         holds compared with all other households in the Western
         Area

	Professional households	*Western Area*[a]
	%	%
0 - 4	15.4	15.2
5 - 9	18.1	12.8
10 - 14	14.3	10.0
15 - 19	10.9	9.1
20 - 24	5.3	8.7
25 - 34	13.5	17.2
35 - 44	14.7	12.6
45 - 54	4.1	7.8
55 - 64	2.0	3.6
65+	1.3	3.0

a. These data came from the *Household Survey of the Western Province, November 1966-January 1968,* Central Statistics Office, Freetown.

The professionals had grown up and been educated during a period unique in Sierra Leone history. If they were reared in a Creole family, they were part of a society which viewed itself as having long ago acquired all the attributes of western culture including its religion and family system. Since the founding of the Colony, the Creoles had assumed an attitude of superiority and patronage towards the indigenous population. Their monopoly of the trading economy and of all other positions which required western education was virtually unchallenged. However, the radical change in the policy of the British towards the Protectorate at the turn of the century suddenly allowed the Provincials to compete for a position of equality with the Creoles. The intrusion of racial discrimination into the social relations between educated Creoles and the British, which occurred about the same time, doubtless intensified the Creoles' insecurities and made the Provincials' rising aspirations an unbearable affront.

Education was the key to success and the lives of these people were organized in line with this priority. Of course, in this the Creoles had a head start. Schools were provided mainly through missionary efforts, and the teaching staff as well as most government administrators were European. These people, who were presumed to represent Christianity and the British way of life, provided the model for educated Sierra Leoneans to emulate.

The process of getting an education did not represent the radical break from family background for the Creole that it did for the Provincial. As we have seen, a dual system of status and prestige has developed and the Provincial professional seeks to achieve status in terms of both traditional and urban values.

The comparison between the professionals and the university students who are about to enter this group suggests that present-day professionals represent a social background and a set of experiences which will not be shared by any succeeding generations of educated individuals in Sierra Leone. More of the university students are Provincial and come from families representing a wider range of social backgrounds than those of the Provincial professionals. The university students have grown up in the period following political independence from Britain. While antagonisms between Provincials and Creoles continue to influence social relations, the predominance of Provincials in the political life of the country has necessarily altered the character of those antagonisms.

These university students have attended schools in which the majority of their teachers have been Africans rather than Europeans. The opportunities for higher education have been extended in a number of different fields of study so that fewer of the professionals in the future will have the long years of experience of living abroad while gaining their qualifications. As far as marriage and family life are concerned, while the western system is regarded as ideal, it is the Creoles rather than the Europeans who are providing the model. We shall now turn to an examination of the ideas and attitudes which people have regarding traditional African family behaviour and how they conceptualize western patterns.

4

Stereotypes of traditional and western marriage and family life

In view of the fact that a significant number of professionals and university students come from small villages in the country, the importance of understanding traditional family organization is apparent.[1] However, to construct a general picture of traditional family life in Sierra Leone would lead us away from the main consideration of this chapter and would be a rather complicated undertaking. For example, one complication is that the population of the country comprises a number of different tribal groups, the two largest being the Mende and the Temne.[2] Almost all of these are represented in the professional group. However, despite the number of ethnic groups in Sierra Leone there is a considerable amount of cultural uniformity between them. As McCulloch noted:

> 'Although falling linguistically into two distinct groups, the peoples of Sierra Leone Protectorate have today many cultural features in common. Factors which have led to this uniformity include long association with Mohammedan Fula and Mandinka, who, while possessing no corporate territorial rights, have settled throughout the Protectorate; the dominating influence of the larger tribes, especially the Mende and Temne, on their smaller

1. It will be recalled from Chapter One that the term 'traditional' is being used to refer to a pattern of behaviour or belief which has characterized the society for a considerable length of time and which can be found today in villages in Sierra Leone.
2. In anthropological literature the term 'tribe' may be used to refer to '...a politically or socially coherent and autonomous group occupying or claiming a particular territory.' (*Notes and Queries on Anthropology* 1951, p. 66). In Sierra Leone this definition does not apply and I use the term 'tribe' throughout this book only to refer to the several ethnic groups residing in the country with which people, for one reason or another, identify themselves.

neighbours; and, more recently, contact with Europeans' (1964, p. 1).

The small size of Sierra Leone and the relatively easy means of travel available have also contributed to the sharing of cultural patterns. Tribal groups are not, for the most part, localized. As regards tribal affiliation most towns and villages are heterogeneous (*1963 Population Census of Sierra Leone*). While conflicts over such issues as the rights to chieftaincy, land or other political matters are usually couched in terms of tribal identity, intermarriage is extremely common between people who claim to be of different tribal origins.[3]

An important feature which has encouraged the considerable degree of cultural syncretism is the recognition of the male and female closed associations, the *Poro* and the *Bundu*, common to most of the in-digenous tribes of Sierra Leone. Historically, there were variations in practice between these associations as found in different tribes. While many of these differences can still be discovered through linguistic analysis of ritual formulae, songs and the like, today they seem to be regarded as relatively unimportant (Turay, 1971). Participation in these associations not only expresses cultural uniformity but actively promotes the sharing of culture between tribes. A member from one part of the country who moves to another place has the right to attend the meetings of these societies regardless of his or her tribal affiliation.

The case of the traditional background of the Creoles is, of course, considerably more complicated. Their ancestors originated from many parts of West Africa bringing with them at least vestiges of their particular cultures. During their enslavement they were exposed to foreign cultures and they were subject to intensive cultural, religious and educational influences during the colonial period.[4] At the same time, from the beginnings of the Colony there has been extensive contact between the indigenous people and the Creoles, not only through the early trading activities of the Creoles but also through intermarriage. Furthermore, Islam has had a profound impact on all

3. Although it has often been politically expedient to claim great differences in the customs and laws of the various tribal groups, subsequent research (1971-1973) on family law showed that the principles of family organization were remarkably uniform across the country. The significant differences that were found were mainly of a ceremonial nature.

4. Petersen has stressed the significance of the 'solid base of traditional culture which at least the liberated Africans shared and which influenced the development of the Creole society' (1969, p. 195).

the peoples of Sierra Leone (Turay, 1971). Although Creoles, with the exception of the Muslim Creoles, claim to follow western patterns of family life there is, no doubt as a result of all of these factors, a surprising degree of concordance of many of their traditions with those of the indigenous groups.[5] And, although many Creoles deny that they have the extended family with its attendant obligations and involvements, even very superficial observation would prove this is not the case.[6] Creoles share certain other traditional beliefs and practices with the indigenous population. These include the role of the ancestors, the practice of witchcraft, etc. (Sawyer 1965, 1966, 1967). However, in many ways, the structure of Creole family life differs from that of the Provincial. For example, the Creoles, with the exception of those who are Muslim, have always claimed to practise Christian monogamous marriage. The introduction of British law in the Colony, as will be discussed in the next chapters, imposed certain constraints on family structure.

Anthropologists have often taken a description of traditional organizations as a reference point or basis for the measurement of the amount of social change which has occurred in the societies they were studying. There has been the tendency to assume that European contact was the only significant factor precipitating change and that before this contact these societies were in a state of equilibrium, static, and perfectly adapted to their environment. Although such assumptions are no longer regarded as tenable, research and analysis of the process of social change continues to be hampered by the use of the old terminology. For example, such concepts as tradition and modernity are often dichotomized as though elements of tradition do not persist in modern societies or the potential for modernity and change does not exist in the so-called traditional societies. The Rudolphs, commenting on this problem, note:

> 'The cumulative effect of the misdiagnosis of traditional societies and the misunderstanding of modern societies has been to produce an analytic gap between tradition and modernity. We find the literature speaking of an abyss between them; stressing incompatibilities between their norms, structures, and personalities;

---

5. For example, birth, engagement and funeral ceremonies are, in outline, very similar.
6. The difference is a matter of the degrees of involvement and of the mechanisms whereby the Creole is able to limit his obligations to kinsmen.

and describing the hollowness of men and institutions in mid-passage. Because they are seen as mutually exclusive, to depart from one is disorienting and traumatic, to enter the other alienating and superficial. Nor does the notion of transitional society escape the preoccupation with the dichotomy between tradition and modernity for it assumes rather than challenges it' (1967, p. 6).

Perhaps studies of marriage and family life are especially prone to such analytical problems. Indeed, as discussed earlier, the assumptions behind this research were that marriage patterns in West Africa were becoming more like those in the West, and that the instability of those marriages was a direct result of the lack of 'fit' of the western pattern with the traditional one.

The Rudolphs have commented on another facet of the separation of the concepts of tradition and modernity. This is '... the view held by historically ascendant classes, races, or nations of those that are or were subject to them.' As they put it:

'Dominant classes, races and nations attribute causal potency to those attributes associated with their subjection of others. The mirror image of others as the opposite of oneself becomes an element in the civilizational, national and personal esteem' (1967, p. 9).

From the beginnings of the Colony, acceptance of monogamous marriage and the establishing of a 'Christian home' were the keys to communion in the white man's world.[7] So the professionals in Sierra Leone have long been exposed to the ideology of the monogamous companionate marriage which they consider a standard form of marriage in the West. They regard it as preferable to the traditional African pattern and their adoption of western marriage supports, in a very fundamental way, their position of superiority in the society. Despite the fact that these professional people have educational qualifications and economic standing which already set them apart within the society, the importance of being seen to conform to the western pattern of marriage has an enormous significance for their sense of personal esteem, of being 'civilized' and, finally, of being superior to those who have not conformed to this pattern (Little 1966a). They

7. Full membership of the church was available only to persons who rejected polygamy. In the Protectorate exceptions might be made in the case of the wives of a polygamous household.

refer disparagingly to the traditional marriage system as the 'native' way of life.[8] Some excerpts from student essays will illustrate this:

'The more one thinks of African traditional family and married life the more one is inclined to discredit it' (Essay No. 189).

. . .

'On the whole I prefer western marriage and family life than that of traditional African family and marriage. This is because the traditional African family and marriage seems primitive' (Essay No. 229).

. . .

'I conclude by saying that I only wish everybody would adopt the western marriage and family life since this is now a modern world and Africa needs to be developed' (Essay No. 64).

. . .

'Summing up, I must say that on the whole the Western marriage and family life is more civilized than the African . . . The Westerners brought civilization to Africa and it is likely that they are better off than the Africans' (Essay No. 200).

So we see adapted as far as marriage and family life are concerned that western-educated Sierra Leoneans have *themselves* adopted the concepts of tradition and modernity and set them in opposition. Moreover, despite their different backgrounds, there is considerable agreement among them on the meaning and evaluation of these concepts when applied to marriage and family life. It is their ideas or representations of traditional and western (modern) marriage and family life with which this discussion will be concerned. The content of these representations may give some clues about the relationship between tradition and modernity and the process of social change.

---

8. This association of status and prestige with western-style monogamous marriage is of most importance to women, but men also find it extremely embarrassing to admit when their own marriages do not exactly conform to their image of it. One man decided to discard his wife after many years of marriage. Because of their strong connections with the church, it was assumed they were married under statutory law. I asked on what grounds he was planning to seek the divorce. He replied that he was extremely reluctant to discuss any intimate thing about his relationship with his wife even though his marriage was breaking up, as it would be unfair to her. The 'intimate' information he was so embarrassed to admit was that he and his wife had been married by customary law, not in the church.

Stereotypes of traditional and western marriage and family life

Jahoda (1961) examined a related phenomenon in Ghana. His study was an investigation of the stereotyped ways in which Africans look upon white people and how they feel about them.

Jahoda, considering the question of what were the sources of the stereotypes which Africans held about white people, looked to the history of contact with Europeans and the present-day relationships between white people and Africans for the answer. For Sierra Leoneans there were several sources of information upon which to base their stereotypes of western marriage and family life. They are told about it in school and, through their religious training, they are given a highly idealized view of the Christian model of marriage. They also have the opportunity to observe the lives of married Europeans who reside in the country. Moreover, they see films and read novels and magazines. Probably the most important sources of information about western patterns for many of the professionals were their first-hand experiences during the years they lived abroad in western countries.

Jahoda found that the younger and less experienced his informants were, the more positive they were in their views of the white man. A similar phenomenon was observed in Sierra Leone. The data about social images were drawn from three groups of western-educated persons: students aged seventeen to twenty-one in their last two years of school; university students studying in Sierra Leone; and the professional men and women, most of whom had lived abroad for some time.[9] As we shall see the attitudes of these three groups of persons were progressively more equivocal in their positive evaluation of western patterns. It is also interesting to note that a few of the Creole

---

9. In addition to interviews on this topic, two other methods were used to collect information concerning the stereotypes which people held of modern and traditional marriage and family life. First, secondary school students were asked to write essays on an assigned topic but in the neutral setting of the classroom with no reference to the research. Secondly, a list of attributes of western and traditional patterns was elicited through interviews and from this an attitude scale was devised. This scale was administerd to a sample of the professionals and to a group of university students. See Appendix A for a more complete discussion of the methods used and Question 100, Appendix B, for the list of attributes that were elicited and the form in which they were presented to the subjects.

professionals even denied that any important differences exist between the two patterns of marriage and family life.[10]

Choice of a marriage partner, courtship and marriage ceremonies

Educated Sierra Leoneans favour western patterns of courtship and the choice of a partner which is based upon the love individuals feel towards one another rather than the traditional pattern where the spouse is chosen by relatives.[11]

> 'In the case of the Western marriage the couples have to know each other for a considerable length of time before jumping into marriage. Whilst in the cases of the traditional African marriage, in most cases the couples do not choose themselves[12] on their own free will and in a very short time a marriage is arranged for them by their parents. I prefer the western way because I think it is high time people start making their own choice and that people should only get married when there is real love between them. The traditional African marriage is more of a punishment rather than happiness for which it was meant. This is because in most cases, there is no existing love between the couples and usually this led to misery' (Essay No. 24).

Young people often expressed the belief that the freedom to choose one's own spouse, as it is done in the West, will result in a home life and a family which is

> '... united in love and there is always peace and quiet in the home. There is not much differences ... In the traditional African marriage life, the girl or boy is always forced to accept the person his or her family chooses for them. They have no interest in the home nor in the person chosen. The man has too many wives so

10. They preferred to think that education, social status and monogamous marriage were correlated everywhere in the world and that the differences which they observed in Sierra Leone were simply a function of social class.

11. Throughout this section when I refer to traditional or western patterns I am referring to the *stereotypes* which these people hold of them. Many Provincial students believe that Creoles already practise western ways.

12. 'Themselves' is often used instead of 'each other'. These excerpts are reproduced just as the students have written them, including spelling and grammatical errors. It should be noted that for most of them English is a second language.

he doesn't pay attention to one or takes her out so he just takes them for granted. The wives are always in the back yard, dirty and eating in the pots with their hands ... He the husband is never happy for his wives are enough to make him ill. He must love them for it is his parent's wish' (Essay No. 8).

The professionals and the university students were asked whether they thought that western young people had a freer choice than Africans in the selection of a spouse and whether or not this was a good thing. In response to this question, 89 per cent of the university students compared with 69 per cent of the professionals indicated a positive attitude towards the western pattern where individuals choose their own spouses. The professionals were significantly less enthusiastic about individual choice of a spouse than were the younger informants. This may be because they were already considering the marriages of their own children and were unwilling to entrust them completely with such a decision. Some would remind me that marriages in the West are unstable just because young people have so much freedom in this matter. Others pointed out that in Africa it is impossible to maintain a marriage when the relatives do not approve of one's spouse.

There is a general rejection of the traditional African custom of bridewealth. Professionals often refer to this method of marriage as simply purchasing wives and refer to women married in this way as 'mere chattels'. Some of the students accused parents of agreeing to a particular marriage partner only because of the economic gain they would receive. This practice was thought to destroy the possibility of any love relationship in the marriage.

'In some cases the girl concerned would be forced by her parents to marry a man just because the man would have paid a heavy sum of bride price for her' (Essay No. 55).

. . .

'In this system [the western] no bridewealth is paid by the male to the female parents thus showing us complete affection for each other. Moreover men do not marry forcefully' (Essay No. 115).

. . .

'In traditional Africa men don't find time to understand a woman before proposing to her parents. This happens because parents are very unreliable and inconsistent so far as the variation of dowry [Sierra Leoneans refer to bridewealth as dowry] is con-

cerned. The suitor who pays a higher dowry for the girl eventually marries her. In the long run, however, difficulties begin to
arise, as regards understanding each other. At other times the girl
may begin to disturb the peace of the husband by giving con-
tinuous trouble either because she did not like the man her
parents had chosen for her, or because the man turns out to be
difficult to understand' (Essay No. 35).

Traditional African marriage rites were also described as cursory,
lacking ceremony, leading to an attitude of disrespect for the institution of marriage. The religious ceremonies of Christians or
Muslims were much preferred. Many emphasized the sacred nature of
the religious ceremony in contrast to the traditional marriage which
was often viewed as not much more than an economic transaction.

'African marriage is a great mess to people. When a man wants
a wife he reports the matter to the girl's parents by giving a small
amount of money because he wants to get her. As soon as the
time is near he give the remaining money he was charged for
her before he will take the girl. At that very spot the woman goes
at the husband's house she is married' (Essay No. 26).

Today, most marriages among the educated do take place in the
church or mosque. Weddings are such important social occasions that
people are constrained to make enormous expenditure. The groom is
responsible for most of the expenses of the wedding and often a young
man incurs heavy debts even before he begins married life. One
informant told me that she and her family had spent well over £200
and that she had no idea how much more her husband had spent on
their wedding. Because this is the typical pattern for Creoles and
other educated persons, many students assume that it is peculiarly an
African pattern and imagine that such displays do not occur in the
West. Creoles have celebrated weddings in an ostentatious manner
almost since the Colony began (Fyfe 1962a, p. 200). Some students
assumed that all western marriages take place in the Registrar's office
without the expensive display which is part of the ceremony they are
familiar with.

'African traditional marriage is much more expensive than that
of the Western marriage. In Africa after the wedding there is a
display of cake and wine, which is usually called "Cake and Wine".
Also the party is held after the reception in which there is a
display of liquor and other edifies. They dance till late at night.

Whilst in the Western marriage there is no such thing. Instead, after the marriage the couple go for a honeymoon and enjoy themselves for about a week. In African traditional marriage after the wedding feast the husband is left in debt. But that does not happen in western marriage' (Essay No. 1).

. . .

'This marriage in the west is not always so grand or inviting thousands of guests. All that happens is perhaps a party is organized after the wedding in the church' (Essay No. 55).

Of course, the traditional practice of polygamy was frequently compared with the preferred pattern of monogamous marriage characteristic of the west. Polygamy was thought to lead to unequal treatment of children, jealousy and bad relationships between co-wives and brothers and sisters.

'In the western area [meaning among the Creoles] most likely people marry one wife, and that one will produce her children. There will be no despite between them because all of them are from the same mother. So after death of their father, things won't be difficult for them . . . To the Africans the husband will marry as man when he takes many wives he will luckily provide [have] many children. And when this happen there will be conflict between the women and the children. Whereas he won't love them equally and the children won't love each other hence their mother's [co-wives] won't like themselves. There will be a split in the family which is very bad' (Essay No. 16).

. . .

'African society is a polygamic society. There is an absence of the western christian doctrine of one man, one wife. Consequently, the family becomes very large and the home becomes dull and sick. In contrast the western family home is bright and it is well-planned. Polygamy is not practised in western culture since men fear veneral disease. The husband is so restricted by his wife so as to do nothing without her knowledge' (Essay No. 56).

And another student linked polygamy with venereal disease, which is in fact an extremely serious and widespread problem in the country:

'With my own initiative, the western culture is far better than that of the Africans as it discourages broken families, polygamy, and the prevention of veneral disease' (Essay No. 7).

Marriage relationships

Relationshops between husbands and wives in the West are usually highly idealized as being based upon co-operation, mutual respect, love and trust.

'The husband and wife live together happily especially if they have a little child who complete their happiness. In some cases the husband goes to work and after the hard days work, he comes home. Immediately the wife sees her husband coming, she runs before him, take from him anything he is carrying into the house. She asks him how he feels and how the job. How is he feeling, etc. Quickly the woman prepares the table for supper which both sit together and eat happily. When the man wants to go anywhere he goes with his wife. They do everything in common. When the husband dies the woman and her children possess his property' (Essay No. 118).

. . .

'They live by themselves making their own decisions about things and planning their own family. They are very happy about the arrival of their children. The children are born in a home of love and peace. The woman takes care of her children and her husband helps her when he is around. She has no rival so she knows that she and her children come first with her husband. They educate each one of their children. They have their ups and downs but they settle them out between themselves. The family is always seen together for instance at the zoo, the cinema, games and parties. The man in the west give his wife enough money so she doesn't go with other men for money as the African force their wives to do. The pair makes their own decisions without asking other people for theirs. No one comes and stays to take care of the children and there is no such thing as the extended family. A ward may come in to help but she goes home in the evening. When you enter such homes you feel that there is real love' (Essay No. 8).

Some believe that couples married in the West quarrel less than do African couples. This is thought to be the result of the practice of long courtships in western society.

'In traditional African marriage it takes quite a long time for husband and wife to understand and be acquainted with each

other. For this reason they are faced with a lot of misunder-
standings which may probably result in friction between the two.
This condition does not apply to the purely western marriage.
The husband and wife are so acquainted with each other it is
impossible for them to have any friction. In most cases their souls
and characters are so compatible with each other there is a
tendency for the wife to choose the type of dress [clothes] she
will like her husband to put on. She sometimes does the purchasing of her husband's dress. They also have everything in
common. When having their dinner and supper both husband and
wife dine or have their supper together. This condition is uncommon in a typical African marriage where the husband and
wife do not dine together' (Essay No. 201).

People often commented favourably on the western practice of
families eating together at the same table and sharing the same food.
In traditional society, the best food goes to the father and other men,
who eat separately from the women and children.

Western homes are also believed to be characterized by an absence
of physical violence while African husbands are said usually to beat
their wives.

'Traditional African family life is too burdensome . . . The wives
and their husbands quarrel and in some family the husband come
home and [if he] find the meal is not ready he beats the women
so mercilessly' (Essay No. 158).

One university student discussed the problem of physical violence in
marriage. She described how an uneducated husband may beat his
pregnant wife, sometimes 'dissolving the pregnancy'. 'Because he isn't
educated he doesn't realize that her bad temper may be associated with
her pregnancy. It's only education which can change the African man.'
The university students and the professionals were asked to indicate if
they thought African husbands were more inclined than western husbands to use physical punishment to control their wives. Eighty-three
per cent of both examples indicated this was characteristic behaviour
of African husbands and disapproved of it. There were no significant
differences between the responses of men and women; however, among
the students more Creoles, 91 per cent, compared with 77 per cent of
the Provincials, expressed approval of the absence of physical violence
in western marriage.

There is general agreement that husbands and wives in the West express their feelings of love and affection more freely than do African couples. Many wives discussed how much they enjoyed their time living abroad with their husbands, because there their husbands were not ashamed to hold their hand in public or show affection towards them. In Africa such behaviour is frowned upon. Among the university students 92 per cent positively evaluated this characteristic which they associated with western, not African, marriage. On the other hand, this was one characteristic of western behaviour which came up for strong criticism among the professionals. They found it 'embarrassing' to see couples holding hands and kissing in parks or on buses or 'anywhere' and they condemned such public displays of affection as being insincere. Although the question asked the respondents to indicate whether or not western husbands and wives display more love and affection towards one another than do African couples, the association for most professionals was with the public display of which they disapproved. Significantly fewer professionals than students, (70 per cent compared with 92 per cent) positively evaluated this western characteristic.

Students also commented in their essays on the absence of emphasis on love-making in the traditional African family. Women, in traditional society, are said to be regarded as only useful to satisfy their husband's sexual needs.

'The wives in traditional African lives are treated as tools to satisfy their husband's sexual needs, and since they practice polygamy they [the women] are often dissatisfied. But the western wives have pleasure with their husband, can please them and extend jokes to them. They have most things in common and share with one another, but the traditional African woman is afraid of her husband and treats him as a lord' (Essay No. 219).

One student said, 'Kissing is not a custom of African life' and another commented:

'Farmers do not romance at night. I mean most illiterates. They just perform the affair' (Essay No. 169).

The lack of affection ascribed to African marriage follows quite naturally from the kind of relationships between husbands and wives as the students described them.

'When an African husband is tired of one wife he just abandons her and finds another one. The wife has no right to be around

When friends [men] come to her husband and if she does she is in
is in for a high jump' (Essay No. 19).[13]

It is generally assumed that western husbands share more in the
conduct of household work than do African husbands and 70 per cent
of the university students and 71 per cent of the professionals considered this a positive attribute. This tendency for western husbands
to share the burdens of housework with their wives frequently came up
for comment in the essays.

'If a husband and wife are walking in the street the husband
allows the wife to carry the heavy load when he perhaps carries
a walking stick ... with western marriages, the husband does all
the heavy jobs and leaves the light housework to the wife and if
they are well off he may employ a servant' (Essay No. 45).
. . .
'In traditional marriage life men have no respect for their wives.
They think women are their slaves for example when a wife is
sick the husband would never help in doing the housework. Whilst
in the western marriage the husband would give the wife due
respect and help her in doing the housework' (Essay No. 64).

The question of sexual fidelity came up for comment by the secondary school students. They were inclined to think that western couples
are faithful to one another, while Africans are not.

'Also the man in a Sierra Leone home is taken as a boss and he
controls everything around the house. He very often leaves the
house, stays out late and loves other girls. These are things which
he does not expect his wife to do ... The men are never seriously
blamed by society ... In Britain I have the feeling that husband
and wife are somehow equal in many aspects at home. And very
often a husband goes out together with his wife instead of just
staying out late at night leaving her in the house' (Essay No. 166).
. . .
'In most homes in Africa there is at least one illegitimate child
due to the father having a child outside his home while he is still
having a family in most cases' (Essay No. 167).

However, university students and professionals were not in agree-

---

13. Since it might be assumed that girls would express more negative attitudes
towards the role of the traditional wife, I have deliberately chosen excerpts from
essays written by male students in this section. However, there were no important differences in the contents of the essays by boys and by girls.

ment that sexual infidelity was more characteristic of African society than of the West. Only 48 per cent of the university students and 38 per cent of the professionals thought male sexual infidelity was *more* a characteristic of western society than of African society. Often, however, the greater seriousness attached to sexual infidelity of men in the West was referred to and disapproved. Some criticized the fact that western couples might divorce or even murder over a husband's unfaithfulness. They favoured the more tolerant attitude of African women towards this 'natural' behaviour of men. On the other hand, almost everyone regarded a wife's unfaithfulness as a very serious matter indeed and bound to lead to divorce.

The role of the wife

The role of the wife in traditional African marriage was always described in the essays in very unfavourable terms. While relationships between couples in western marriages were described as being based upon equality, in Africa the wife is inferior.

'She is almost a servant to him [her husband] because he doesn't even regard her as his wife . . . His wives are always in the back, afraid and they have no say. They are treated as slaves and if one displeases him he can send she and her children home and forgets about them' (Essay No. 8).

. . .

'In the western lands both husband and wife have equal rights. The husband cannot do anything concerning family affairs in the absence of his wife, neither the wife do the same. But in Africa the wife has no right whatsoever to her husband. Even after the death of her husband she does not have any right over the property' Essay No. 22).

. . .

'. . . The African arrives home with his friends and calls at his wife who comes stealthily almost stooping, arranges the food quickly and vanishes to the background obviously thinking herself unfit to sit in the midst of her own brand of people' (Essay No. 3).

. . .

'In the traditional African family life the husband is the head and commands and the fun of the house. The wife is only concerned with the domestic affairs and do not discuss things with her husband. He is feared and respected by the wife. The wife is not considered an equal to the husband . . . On the other hand the western family is one of equal balance on both side. There is common understanding between the husband and wife they sit and discuss family problems and suggest ways of combating them' (Essay No. 3).

The university students and the professionals were asked if they thought the tendency to treat wives as equals was an attribute of western marriages and not of African and if they thought this was good practice. Eighty-five per cent of the professionals and 76 per cent of the students indicated positive attitudes towards the greater equality of western wives. However, there were significant differences between the responses of the Creole and Provincial students. Only 70 per cent of the Provincials saw husband-wife equality as a favourable attribute of western society compared with 81 per cent of the Creole students.

The economic independence of western women is regarded as a threat to a successful marriage. As one professional commented when describing what he disliked about western marriage, 'I would hate to hand my pay packet over to my wife – couldn't have a marriage then.' But, at the same time, African women are thought to be more difficult to 'control' than are western women. Thus professionals are ambivalent about education, careers and economic independence for women. When asked whether western men prefer their wives to have a career more than do African men, 76 per cent of the students indicated this was a positive attribute of western society compared with the African pattern. Once again, the Provincial students were considerably less enthusiastic about this aspect of western attitudes: 64 per cent of them compared with 88 per cent of the Creole students favoured it.

Children and family relationships within the home

It was generally asserted that Africans do not plan the size of their families nor do they attempt to limit the number of children produced. Reference was often made to the fact that having large numbers of children was important for the status of the father, but that the result was poverty and homes filled with quarrelling and competition.

'Another difference is that most Africans feel that having many children makes one great. These have many children with barely enough to live on and in the end poverty strikes them. The western man on the other hand does not ask for a large family he cannot support. With a large family the home is often unhappy because jealous among each other ... The Western family is content to live peacefully with only four in the family' (Essay No. 215).

Many students and adults commented on the tendency of traditional fathers to neglect the education of their children when they had so many.

'When the western man gets married he always had prepared to take care of his family that is he had got a home or a house and some income at least to up keep the family ... They also decide on the number of children they should have so that each child in the family would be given the average education he deserves' (Essay No. 55).

Moreover, western relationships between parents and children are idealized by Sierra Leoneans. Western children are thought to be allowed more freedom to discuss their problems with their parents. Because the western husband is not so concerned with maintaining absolute respect and authority, he can afford to allow his children to approach him freely and discuss any topic with him.

'In western countries it is usual for children and parents to exchange their opinions on any subject and the parent to try to teach their children the simple facts of life. In other words western children look up to their parents as people whom they will go to in times of difficulties whilst African children because they have not been encouraged to talk freely with their parents will feel shy to approach their parents and tell them of their troubles' (Essay No. 100).

. . .

'How often an African child needs his father's love and understanding but because there are many wives and there are many children competing for the father's attention and in most cases the children grow up with the feeling that the father hardly cares and he's not someone to tell your troubles to' (Essay No. 24).

. . .

'The European husband believes that comfort and generosity are not the only thing a family needs. He believes that as the head of the house he should be a person from whom advice and sense flows. The African father, generous and although he has the same amount of love for his family believes in a different approach. He does not believe in showing his love for his family openly and prefers to be a figure of sternness and one who is feared and respected by all members of the family... For example the European father will sit at the table and make jokes about his daughter's last boy-friend or tell his son that his shirt is too long... in a nice jovial way. The African father will prefer to [be] above all these kinds of talk and will not even make jokes to this effect as he wants to appear serious minded' (Essay No. 107).

These examples could be multiplied because this topic was one that came up for most comment in the essays by the secondary school students. We can assume that they were at an age when their need for communciation with parents was great. The university students and the professionals were asked whether they thought African children fear their parents more than do western children, and if this was a good thing. Among the professionals 85 per cent indicated a positive attitude towards the more relaxed relationships between western children and their parents and were strongly critical of African patterns. Many of them were trying to implement western ideas about child rearing; 59 per cent agreed it was better for a child not to 'fear' his parents.

Western families are often commended because they look ahead to the future of their children.

'Now let us come to our third point. During the marriage life of the whiteman he saves money and install it in the bank, so that his children will live happily and if he dies. He lives entirely for his children. When it is time to eat, the whiteman eats at the same time as his children. Whereas the African doesn't keep money in the bank and leaves practically nothing for his children after his death' (Essay No. 20).

An observer of family life in Sierra Leone is struck by the amount of contact and interaction between relatives and yet it is generally believed by them that western families, that is, husband, wife, and children, have closer relationships and spend more time together as families. They were described as 'doing everything together'. Ninety-four per cent of the university students and 81 per cent of the professionals agreed that western families spend more of their leisure time together as families than do African families and that this is a good thing.

Relationships between married couples and their relatives

Sierra Leoneans believe that there are great differences in relationships with relatives in Africa and in the West. In Sierra Leone relatives feel free to visit one another and can depend on each other for assistance of all kinds.

'As had been mentioned a family in Africa usually extended to the in-laws and these use this fact as an excuse when they find themselves in difficulties. For example, a man in the provinces may have to come to town on business. Instead of informing a relative that he will be coming to stay for a night or two, he will think it is unnecessary and that as relatives they are bound to put him up for the night. In western countries this is not so usually the case. If the man has enough money he might book a room in a hotel. Even if he intends to stay with some relatives he will do his best to inform them before hand' (Essay No. 100).

. . .

'The wife who is loved by her mother-in-law is in most cases loved by all her relatives and in course of time the home becomes a free-for-all-guest-house where relatives visit as often as they wish and stay as long as they like. This is quite common in the traditional African family, but it is quite uncommon in European family life. Most of the Europeans being literates they can write and tell their relatives the date and duration of their visit and since most people are busy with their personal affairs, this is not a regular occurrence' (Essay No. 34).

Although these students refer to the inconvenience of having relatives dropping in at odd times, I never found anyone who would consider turning a relative away. Many were highly critical of family life in the West, where, as they say, it is necessary to call to make an appointment before you can visit a relative. When the professionals were asked what they disliked about western family life, the neglect of relatives, particularly elderly relatives, came up for the most severe criticism. Many recalled the shock they felt seeing old people still working for their living in Britain. In Africa, failing to support one's elders is a disgraceful thing.

'Western marriage homes appear to be greedy and unhospitable. Unofficial visits by anybody deserves no entertainments even if you meet them at the table. Husbands and wives in Africa leave their basins for visitors at anytime such an occasion calls. That is why in fact they cook abundantly' (Essay No. 23).

. . .

'A pity however that there is little or no link between marriage partners and their parents in law. For African philosophers it looks as if the Englishman prefers taking care and responsibilities of his dog than that of his nephew. There is nothing like supporting parents and parents-in-law for the couples. Frankly speaking relatives had little to do with marriage partners' (Essay No. 113).

. . .

'Unlike Europe and America, when a couple marries in Africa they are still responsible for their parents. If they happen to move away to a new house their parents sometimes go with them. At times their younger brothers and sisters or cousins grandparents, aunts and uncles all live with them, if the house is large enough. The couple is sometimes responsible for the education of their younger brothers and sisters or nephews and nieces, etc. This is very rarely seen in the western white world. Once a couple get married they are completely on their own, entirely by themselves. Sometimes, of course they may call on their people for a visit, or when an accident occurs, but it is very rare to see a married couple living with several other relatives in the same house however large the house might be' (Essay No. 84).

On the other hand, some students saw certain advantages in the western system where the couples are isolated from their relatives.

'Westerners do not live in large groups. No quarrels grows among them' (Essay No. 54).

. . .

'Extended family obligations hurt the national economy and keep standard of living very low' (Essay No. 38).

. . .

'Here now is the striking difference: In the west the couple are left alone unless the parents are so poor that their help is indispensable. There is no "family humbug" in the African sense. Sometimes they are both employed. It makes it all the better' (Essay No. 190).

. . .

'The Europeans on the other hand are quite independent [of obligations to kin]. If only we the African will try to be independent we shall surely have a better Africa' (Essay No. 109).

Relatives sometimes get involved in family problems. In fact, the traditional method of settling marital disagreements was a discussion in a group of relatives rather than between the couple themselves. This practice is largely disapproved of and the western practice where the couple discuss problems alone is preferred. The university students and professionals were asked about this question and 80 per cent of the students and 89 per cent of the professionals positively evaluated what they saw as a western method of settling disagreements.

Summary

Some people mentioned that among Africans there is more brotherly love, and others expressed considerable approval of the co-operation which exists between members of the extended family. Some did criticize the Westerners for what they viewed as an excess of individualism and selfishness causing neglect of relatives, especially of the elderly. However, the over-all picture of almost everyone's attitude towards western family life is a positive one. At the same time, and in seemingly violent contradiction with their positive evaluation of western family life, they see these marriages as highly unstable.

As one university student said:

> 'Westerners take divorce too lightly. In Africa we always keep up hope that things will work out, will improve. Even if an African couple separate we keep hoping things will change'.

Only 1 per cent of the professionals and 2 per cent of the university students indicated they believed western marriages to be more stable than African marriages.

One of the purposes of examining the attitudes of these educated Sierra Leoneans was to explore their views of western and traditional family life in order to discover areas of possible future change. I shall list some of the qualities which they ascribe to each in three different lists: those where the western characteristic was favoured by most of the respondents; those were the traditional characteristic was favoured by most; and those where the contrast of difference was distinguished but the respondents were generally divided or neutral in their evaluation.

List 1: *Western attribute generally favoured*

Traditional	Western
Marriages are unhappy	Marriages are happy
Parents involved in choice of spouse	Individual chooses his own spouse
Polygamy	Monogamy
No marriage ceremony	Marriage ceremonies
Early marriage for women	Later marriage for women
Large families living together	Small families living on their own
No courtship	Long courtship
No emphasis on love-making	Emphasis on love-making
No privacy	Privacy
No assistance from husband in domestic work	Assistance from husband in domestic work
Bridewealth	No bridewealth
No birth control	Birth control
Jealousy among wives	No problem of jealousy
Inequality of the partners	Equality of partners
No freedom or communication in parent/child relations	Freedom and good communication between parents and children
No property owned or inherited by wife	Property owned and inherited by wife
Families do not eat together	Families share their meals
Relatives interfere in quarrels	Relatives don't interfere in quarrels
Children reared by large number of relatives	Children reared only by their parents
Marriage is based on economic motives	Marriage is based on love
No expression of affection	Affection expressed
Families do not share leisure	Families share leisure

List 2: *African attribute favoured*

Traditional	Western
No public display of affection	Public display of affection
Parental authority remains intact	Parental authority undermined
Families care for the elderly	Families neglect the elderly

Divorce unusual	Easy divorce
Tolerance for male infidelity	No tolerance for male infidelity
Women are submissive husbands	Women are domineering and nagging
Co-operation between relatives	Little co-operation between relatives
More brotherly love and unselfishness	Selfishness of the nuclear family

List 3: *African and western pattern compared, opinion or evaluation very divided*

Women are not educated equally with men	Women receive the same education as men
Women are not encouraged to have careers	Women are encouraged to have careers
Emphasis on virginity	No emphasis on virginity

Although educated Sierra Leoneans are not blind to some of the characteristics of western family life which they regard as undesirable, almost all of them appear to desire some major changes in African family life following the western pattern. While favouring their image of the western marriage, they also would like to retain certain qualitative aspects of African family life which they see as absent in the West. Creoles are usually credited with attempting to follow this western pattern. As one student put it:

'In summing up I would say that Africans are now trying to copy the western family life and the western marriage. In Sierra Leone the people who have tried the most to be like the westerners are the Creoles. The Creoles have been doing their best' (Essay No. 216).

It should be noted that over some issues Provincial university students were less enthusiastic about western patterns than were Creoles. Perhaps, with the growing appreciation of the 'African personality' and culture, they are beginning to prefer to assert that progress is not necessarily equated with whole-hearted acceptance of western values.

5

The legal setting of marriage

English law had been the informal basis for administering the Colony since its founding, although the necessary legislation was passed much later, in 1857.[1] Efforts to enforce the laws of England met with problems from the very beginning. As Petersen notes, '. . . the presence of Liberated Africans as well as increasing numbers of people from the Sierra Leone interior meant that English law could be administered only in a modified form' (1969, p. 203). He describes how missionaries and other administrators of the new settlers' villages were forced to resort to traditional systems of law which included such practices as the use of ordeals to establish guilt or innocence. When the Protectorate was established the situation became more complicated. It was the intention of the colonial government that the population of the Colony should be administered under English law while in the Protectorate efforts would be made to retain the structure and content of native law and custom in civil matters (where not 'repugnant to natural justice, equity and good conscience'). This included allowing the native courts to function in the traditional manner under the leadership of the chiefs. Issues which were beyond the competence of native courts were to be covered by legislation specifically introduced for the Protectorate (Smart 1970). The courts of the Colony were of the English type and the laws affecting the Protectorate were also administered through such courts. However, the situation in Sierra Leone did not simply involve two systems of law and two types of court. There are eighteen different tribes living in Sierra Leone each claiming to have its own

1. 'Ordinance No. 96 of 1857 provided that English law as at January 1, 1857, not being inconsistent with a local ordinance or a charter of justice in force in the Colony, shall apply. The present reception date is January 1, 1880 [Courts Act 1965, s. 74]' (Smart 1970).

distinctive laws. Moreover, Islam is practised in Sierra Leone and statutory provision has been made pertaining to Islamic marriage, divorce and devolution of property (Cap. 96 of the *Laws of Sierra Leone*, 1960).

Although legislation provided that English law should be the sole basis for administering the Colony (or what came to be the Western Area), its population included Temne and persons of other tribal origin as well as the early settlers and expatriates. Although the personal law of these people was their own tribal law, no courts were ever provided in the Western Area for the practice of customary law.[2] Further, it was intended that customary procedures should be allowed to continue as the basis for the execution of justice among the tribal people of the Protectorate. However, tribal groups are not, except in the broadest sense, territorially distinct and there is no separate body of customary law for each tribal group.[3] Furthermore, no ethnic group has remained separate; there has been a considerable amount of inter-marriage between them. And, as has already been observed, there has been a considerable amount of intermarriage between Creoles and persons of tribal origin. These latter marriages give rise to certain 'conflicts of law'.[4] Of course, these problems are not unique to Sierra Leone. Afreh (1968) has discussed the similar situation which exists in Ghana, and they are general all over post-colonial Africa. As Fallers has noted:

> 'The pattern of legal pluralism inherited from the period of colonial control, in which a national body of law and hierarchy of courts sits atop a welter of local court systems administering diverse bodies of ethnic "customary" law, is one that many African leaders find unsatisfactory' (1969, p. 7).

2. Tribal headmen did hold courts, settle disputes and impose penalties in the Colony and they have continued to do so even since Independence. However, they have always been acting beyond their jurisdiction.

3. Customary laws have not been recorded but the findings of our subsequent research (mentioned in the preface) on customary law suggest that there are very few differences in the family law practices of the various tribes. The data suggest it would be possible to enact an integrated system of law for the country. Of course, the amount of syncretism has also been encouraged by the administrative system which supervises the practice of customary law.

4. Conflicts of law, according to Allott (1960) occur '... when a Judge is required to choose between two or more systems of law which are not territorial-ly distinct, i.e. which apply, concurrently and without spatial separation within a single jurisdiction' (p. 154).

This chapter will outline the law affecting the marriages of professionals and present some case material to illustrate the kinds of problems which have resulted from the plural legal system which exists in the country. Frequent reference will be made to customary law and to traditional practices and attitudes, as the personal law of many professionals continues to be customary law. Moreover, traditional attitudes continue to affect both behaviour and the laymen's interpretations of the law as well as the decisions handed down by judges. The material from court records has been selected to illustrate problems faced by professional couples. However, the problems resulting from the plural legal system reach beyond the professionals, affecting all Sierra Leoneans. These problems are especially acute in the Western Area where the general attitude towards the traditional family system is unsympathetic, even denigratory. As a result traditional authority within the family has deteriorated, with attending social consequences of far-reaching proportions. While the plural legal situation in Sierra Leone may be 'unsatisfactory', as Fallers has suggested, as yet there have been no concerted efforts to do anything about reforming family law. Understanding just why this should be is the key to the understanding of professional marriage relationships.

Marriage law

As far as marriage is concerned there are three systems of law in Sierra Leone. First there is statutory (general) law comprising English common law and equity and all the enactments in force in Sierra Leone which do not pertain to customary law or Islamic law. Secondly, there is the customary law of the various tribes in the country and, finally, limited statutory provision has been made for marriage under Islamic law. These three legal systems were intended to accommodate three separate and distinct groups of people in the country. Customary law was to apply to those persons termed 'natives'. According to the law, a 'native' '. . . means any person who is a member of a race, tribe or community settled in Sierra Leone (or the territories adjacent thereto), other than a race, tribe or community – (a) which is of European or Asiatic or American origin, (b) whose principal place of settlement is in the Western Area' (Interpretation Act 1971 – No. 8 of 1971).

General law applies to 'non-natives' and 'non-natives' are defined as

any person other than a native (Ibid.).[5] The third group, to be governed by Islamic law, included 'non-natives' or Creoles who practise
the Muslim religion (Sec. 3, Interpretation Act, 1965).[6] These three
systems of law run within a single territorial jurisdiction, i.e. Sierra
Leone. Smart (1969) describes the complications which can arise:

> '. . . a Sherbro permanently resident in Freetown is as subject to
> customary law as a Creole in Freetown is subject to the general
> law. Similarly, a Creole in Shenge will be governed by the
> general law as a Sherbro in the same locality is governed by
> customary law. Finally, a non-native who embraces the Muslim
> faith up to his death intestate will be governed by the law of that
> religion.'

There are further complications. In many cases it is difficult to
determine just which personal law should apply to an individual since
there is the initial problem of identifying his tribe. Tribes are not, as
has already been pointed out, territorially distinct. Many people tend
to identify themselves with the predominant tribe in the area where
they live, regardless of the tribe of their parents. Often individuals
affiliate themselves to the tribe whose language they first learned to
speak. A man may marry a woman from another tribe and live in her
village; although all the tribes in Sierra Leone follow a patrilineal
descent system, the children of this union may grow up considering
themselves members of their mother's tribe for such reasons as the
predominance of that group, the wealth and status of their mother's
relatives, etc. Fortunately, many problems are forestalled because
customary family law is relatively uniform all over Sierra Leone.[7]

It is even more difficult to ascertain who actually has the right to
consider his personal law to be general law, or, in other words, it is

5. After this 'non-natives' will be referred to as Creoles although this group,
as far as the law is concerned, includes expatriates as well.

6. Petersen (1969) notes that 'Neither Liberated African society nor the Creole
society into which it developed, however, was universally Christian. Some
Liberated Africans turned instead to Islam' (p. 238). Around the turn of the
century these people petitioned the colonial government for statutory recognition
of Islamic law (Koroma, 1973).

7. This appears to contradict an earlier statement about the diversity of legal
systems in the country. Most of the differences as regards family law have to do
with the relative seriousness attached to a breach of the law and with certain
ritual practices. However, part of establishing tribal identity involves emphasizing
the uniqueness of one's tribal practices.

difficult to define a 'non-native'. There are probably very few individuals who can trace their ancestry back to the early settlers or Liberated Africans without encountering unions within their families which involved a native. As Smart points out, '. . . according to the definition of a native an issue of an intermarriage between a native and a non-native is himself a native' (1969). It would be impossible to know how many people who call themselves Creoles are offspring of unions between Creoles and natives. Furthermore, many people from the Protectorate have been absorbed into Creole families as wards when they were small children and, as mentioned earlier, have assumed the family name of their benefactors. Until recently the social advantages of being identified with the Creoles were so great that any pretext which would substantiate the claim to be called a Creole was seized upon.[8] It is believed that the general acceptance of the superiority of the Creoles has altered radically since independence. However, I found that the status associated with being Creole continues to have a bearing on the way respondents identify themselves. The university students were asked to indicate the tribe of each of their parents and then their own tribal affiliation. It would be expected that these students would identify themselves with their father's tribe. However, if a student had a Provincial father and a Creole mother, there was a tendency (though not statistically significant) for such a student to call himself Creole. So we see that the definition of a non-native or Creole is a very arbitrary one.

However, there are not only the problems of a plural legal system and difficulties in determining personal law; the vested interests of the missionaries introduced even more complications. The overall policy of the British colonial government had been one of non-interference in the domestic sphere of traditional life. At the same time the missionaries made monogamous marriage a central issue in their efforts to convert. It was in their interest that the law should allow natives who were converted to Christianity to be married under the ordinances and in the church. So the Christian Marriage Ordinance (1907) made

8. As one man explained, it is only during the last few years since he has returned from studying abroad and has married a European wife that he has begun to admit openly that he is a Limba. He grew up as a ward in a Creole household. He accuses this Creole family of having taught him to be ashamed of his Provincial background. He admits that most of his colleagues in the office assume even now that he is Creole.

provision for natives to be married, but with a special condition placed on them. Non-natives could be married either after publishing banns or after obtaining a licence, but the native had to publish banns (Cap. 95, Sec. 3, *Laws of Sierra Leone*).[9] The most obvious stumbling block to conversion and Christian monogamous marriage, that the native was already a party to a polygamous marriage, was neatly circumvented by the fact that the Christian Marriage Act[10] did not recognize a customary union as a marriage:

'For the purpose of this section a marriage made in accordance with native law and custom shall not be deemed to be a marriage' (Sec. 16, Cap. 95).

Natives were specifically prohibited from marrying under the provisions of the Civil Marriage Act:

'Whenever after the commencement of this Ordinance *any person, other than a native*, desires to be married in the Office of a Registrar, one of the parties of the intended marriage shall sign and give to the Registrar of the district in which the marriage is intended to take place, a notice according to the form in Schedule A hereto and shall pay the prescribed fee' (Sec. 4, Cap. 97, my italics).

In 1965 the marriage law was revised and the words, 'other than a native' were deleted from the Civil Marriage Act (The Civil Marriage Amendment No. 2 Act, 1965). This amendment established a difference in the minimum age of marriage for persons whose personal law was that of one of the tribes of Sierra Leone. The minimum age for a native is 18 years of age; for non-natives, the minimum age is 21 years. This difference in minimum age of marriage for natives and non-natives recognizes the tendency, in traditional society, for girls to marry at a young age. The age limitations of the revised Christian Marriage Act corresponded to those in the Civil Marriage Act.[11]

The most radical alteration in the 1965 amendments was to make the Christian Marriage Act recognize marriages contracted under native law and custom by specifically forbidding anyone to contract a

9. All the references to laws are taken from the 1960 edition of the *Laws of Sierra Leone* or from subsequent legislation. From here on only the chapter and section cited or the name of a piece of subsequent legislation will be listed.

10. All Ordinances are now referred to as 'Acts' (Interpretation Act 1971 – No. 8 of 1971).

11. There was another, but unsuccessful, attempt to revise marriage law in 1966 which will be discussed later in this chapter.

marriage under its provisions if they were formerly married by cusomary law: |. . . that neither of the parties is a party to a subsisting marriage, whether by customary law or otherwise' (The Christian Marriage (Amendment) (No. 2) Act, 1965).[12] The amendment to the Civil Marriage Act, while allowing natives to marry in the Registrar's office under its provisions, does not specify that a marriage by customary law is an obstacle to marriage. It is likely that the amendments were intended to be uniform in their content, but there remains the possibility of a different interpretation.[13] In fact it is quite possible that this ambiguity in the law was intentional for the benefit of those who, having earlier contracted a marriage by customary law, want to marry a woman under general law. More than one lawyer expressed the view that it is important, in this setting, for the law to retain a high degree of flexibility to accommodate the variety of conjugal unions which are socially accepted. In the light of such opinions it is interesting to examine the bigamy law. Although the marriage acts were revised in 1965, and the Christian Marriage Act, at least, made to recognize marriage by customary law, the definition of bigamy was not altered. It continues, 'For the purpose of this section a marriage made in accordance with native law and custom shall not be deemed to be a marriage' (Cap. 95, Sec. 17).

Even in its amended form the Christian Marriage Act does not recognize that there are several types of conjugal unions under customary law, nor does it say that a man may not take a wife under customary law *after* marrying under the ordinance. Widow inheritance is one form of customary marriage which is an important case in point. When a man dies his widows are usually given the opportunity to name (or accept the offer from) one of the male members of his

12. The marital status of six men and seven women at the time of marriage under the Christian Marriage Act was recorded as 'married', as shown in Table 12. These may simply be recording errors, or they may indicate the partners were 'converting' their customary marriage to a marriage under general law. It is also quite possible that these thirteen people may already have been married to other persons by customary law. Whatever the explanation, these marriages of 'married' persons were recorded after the amendment was passed which made a previous customary marriage an impediment to a marriage under general law.

13. That the matter is still ambiguous is illustrated by the fact that a prominent Freetown lawyer recently advised his client that his marriage by customary law was no bar to a civil marriage either in Sierra Leone or Great Britain. However, such a case has never been tested in the Sierra Leone courts.

lineage as husband. Several of the professional men from the Provinces had such 'inherited' wives. It may well be argued that according to practice these 'inherited' wives are better described as dependants, since apparently most professional men do not cohabit with them. However, under customary law, any children born to 'inherited' wives, regardless of who is the biological father, belong to the husband, and, of course, there is no reason why these men may not claim sexual rights with these women.

There are also numbers of cases where men married under statutory law have subsequently taken wives under customary law. In one case, a Catholic who was already married in the church was elected a Paramount Chief. In his role as the chief he felt himself compelled to follow the traditions and accept wives from the families in the chiefdom. Despite such cases, there has never been a charge of bigamy tried in the courts of Sierra Leone.[14]

Both the university students and the professionals were asked to express their attitudes towards polygamy and most were not in favour of it. Only 17 per cent of the professionals and 18 per cent of the students agreed with the statement, 'I would prefer a system which allowed a man more than one wife at a time.'[15] However, significantly more of the Provincials than Creoles agreed with the statement. Among the professionals 34 per cent of the Provincial men and 17 per cent of the Provincial women compared with 19 per cent of the Creole men and 4 per cent of the Creole women indicated approval of polygamy. The tacit approval, among some Provincial men at least, of the practice of polygamy is illustrated by the reaction to a recent case involving a politician who married a foreign woman in the Registrar's office while still married by customary law to a Sierra Leonean woman. In discussions of the case several of these Provincial men dismissed the suggestion of bigamy as complete nonsense. After all, how could an African man commit bigamy, since in Africa there is no such thing?

The Mohammedan Marriage Act provides for persons who are non-natives professing the Muslim faith to be married according to the regulations of that religion, and provides for the registrations of such marriages and any subsequent divorces (Cap. 96). As Daniels has

14. Personal communication with Acting Attorney General.
15. These findings are similar to those of Little (1966) in his investigation of attitudes among secondary school students.

noted, 'The main differences between the "English type" marriage and the other two types (Islamic and customary) is that the former insists on monogamy whilst the other two types accept polygamy' (1964, p. 379). Table 12 shows the marital status at marriage of the men and women of all registered marriages in Sierra Leone between 1961 and 1968. Thirty-nine per cent of the registered Islamic marriages were contracted by men who gave their marital status as 'married' at the time of the registration of their marriage. Moreover, 85 per cent of these polygamous Islamic marriages were contracted by men who gave Freetown as their address and another 6 per cent came from the rural part of the Western Area. This shows that living in the city has not significantly influenced the practice of polygamy among the Muslims. None of the Muslims who were interviewed as part of this research had more than one wife, although the possibility they might take another wife in the future was a source of friction between husband and wife.[16]

Almost all the professionals who originated in the Provinces began their marriages by observing the rituals of customary marriage. At the least this involved obtaining the consent of both families and giving a token marriage payment to the bride's family. A church ceremony is an expensive affair and for this reason the marriage under general law is often delayed. Although the law states that customary marriage is an impediment to one under general law, it does not specify whether or not a monogamous customary marriage may be converted to one under the statutes.

There have been some efforts to raise the standing of customary marriages by providing for their registration. Each chiefdom has the right to administer customary marriage and divorce under the Chiefdom Councils Act (Cap. 61). When registration is undertaken in a chiefdom the action is published in the form of a by-law. Although regulations included in these by-laws are uniform, the charges made by the chiefdom councils are not.[17] Only a few chiefdoms have made

16. One professional husband of my acquaintance did formalize a customary marriage with another woman. This was a relationship of long standing and the other woman had produced several children for him. Although he did not marry her in the mosque or even register the marriage, the fact that he honoured tradition by giving a marriage payment to her family was a source of great anguish and embarrassment to his wife.

17. Marriage registration is a source of revenue for the chiefdom and some charge the parties as much as the equivalent of £10 for a marriage certificate.

provision for the registration of marriage and in these chiefdoms there has been a remarkably poor response.[18] Further moves to reform customary marriage resulted from the deliberations of the Customary Law Advisory Panel formed in 1959.[19] The first report of this panel dealt with two problems relating to traditional marriage: widow inheritance and disputes over refundable marriage payments in the case of divorce.[20] The panel noted a 'growing reluctance' of women to marry one of their deceased husbands' relatives. If a woman refused to be 'inherited', his family, under customary law, had the right to sue her family for the marriage payment and all other contributions the husband had made to them throughout the years of the marriage. The report observed that, with the spread of education, it was desirable to 're-assess the intrinsic value of this aspect of customary law'. It continued by noting that in the days when a girl's consent was 'immaterial for her betrothal' this practice of requiring widows to remain in the family of the deceased was justified, but nowadays, when girls had the opportunity of giving their consent, 'such a system seems untenable'. As a result of these deliberations, a directive was sent to all the chiefdoms forbidding mandatory widow inheritance and stating that should the widow decide to leave her husband's family no marriage payment would be refundable (*Directive on Customary Law*, April 27, 1963).[21]

The second problem considered by this panel, disputes over refunds of marriage payments at divorce, also resulted in a recommendation limiting the amount of money which could be demanded by the husband. This recommendation was also made part of the directive (April 27, 1963). Despite these efforts to eliminate some aspects of traditional practices deemed undesirable, and to elevate the status of customary

18. The cost deters many but there is an even more serious problem. Part of the registration form requires the amount of marriage payment to be noted. Repayment of this money occurs at divorce and determining the amount is a long litigious process. To assess the amount when the marriage is being formalized is regarded as taking the first step in divorce proceedings.

19. This panel was formed by the Judicial Adviser but ceased to function after 1963.

20. Report of the Customary Law Advisory Panel, April, 1963.

21. Directives are often issued from the office of the Ministry of Interior which administers the courts dealing with customary law. However, these directives do not carry the force of legislation although they are often accepted by the chiefdom councils as law. Subsequent research which I conducted in customary law indicates that widow inheritance practices have been only slightly influenced by this particular directive.

marriage, there are still disadvantages to being married under this system of law. For example, the Married Woman's Maintenance Act (Cap. 100) does not recognize customary marriages. If such a wife has been deserted by her husband and wishes to sue him for maintenance, she must do so under the Bastardy Act just as she would were her relationship illicit and her children illegitimate' (Bastardy Laws Amendment Act, 1872 (35 and 36 Vict.) Cap. 65]. There is a further disadvantage. As Daniel notes:

> 'In the sphere of criminal law and evidence some of the local laws make a distinction between competence and compellability of witnesses according to whether they are married in the so-called Christian form or under customary law.
>
> In Sierra Leone, Gambia and Nigeria spouses of customary marriages are competent and compellable witnesses against each other whilst those married under the Marriage Ordinances are not' (1964 p. 387, and also see Sec. 77, Cap. 39, *Laws of Sierra Leone*, where 'husband and wife' are defined as 'husband and wife of a Christian marriage') (*op. cit.*).

It is not surprising that the general view among the professionals is that a customary ceremony is not really a marriage; nor that they attach great importance to statutory marriage. One man, for example, a lawyer, gave his marital status as 'single'; he did admit to being 'engaged'. However, his fiancée was expecting a child within a few weeks, they lived in government quarters allocated to married couples and the girl was addressed by their acquaintances as 'Mrs. —'.

He was the son of a paramount chief and they had celebrated the traditional customary marriage in his own chiefdom headquarters, but they planned to be married in church at some later date. This example is not exceptional. Most of the couples from the Provinces, as noted earlier, have married by customary law and have cohabited for some time before being married under general law. As one wife put it, she and her husband had been 'loving' for a long time before they were 'married'. He had given the customary marriage payment to her family, but after the birth of their second child the wife reported that she 'felt badly' not being married. They, being Catholic, asked the priest to arrange a church ceremony. Then, to their dismay, they discovered that, from the point of view of the church (not according to customary law), they were too closely related to have a Christian marriage. The priest, considering their long period of cohabitation and their two children, sought special permission from Rome for their marriage.

Little (1967) states that generally in West Africa 'The men ... favour monogamy partly because for most of the educated class it is the socially approved form of marriage. Indeed, it is virtually incumbent on professional people as well as upon churchmen'. Jellicoe, writing in 1955, found that in Freetown only a church wedding is socially recognized and that marriages under the civil ordinance are still relatively rare. As shown in Table 12, 80 per cent of all marriages under general law registered between 1961 and 1968 were contracted under the Christian Marriage Act. Only 5 per cent were under the Civil Marriage Act and 14 per cent under the Mohammedan Marriage Act. It is impossible to know how many Sierra Leonean couples marry when they are abroad. The tremendous expense of a church wedding in Freetown makes a simple Registrar's ceremony in England attractive. In one case where the couple planned to 'convert' their customary marriage to one under general law, the husband stated that he could better afford to travel to England with his wife and some of their children for the ceremony than to finance a church wedding in Freetown.[22] But wherever the ceremony is conducted, it is regarded as a step of some social significance.

As shown in Table 12, there was a drop in the numbers of marriages registered in 1967 and 1968. The first military *coup* occurred in 1967 and the period following was marked by considerable political tension. People strongly disapproved of a military government and many said they had sworn that as long as there was a soldier on the streets they would hold no parties or other social events. This attitude appeared to have nothing to do with any fear of the military but revealed their very strong aversion to military control and to violence. In April, 1968 another *coup* was staged and shortly afterwards the country returned to civilian rule. After this there was a remarkable change in the atmosphere in Freetown. Whereas before very few people walked in the streets at night, now evenings found the streets filled with people

22. Christenings are also important and expensive social occasions. I attended a christening in England where both the parents were returning to Sierra Leone within a month. They could easily have postponed the event until they were home with their families. However, they found it was less expensive to do it in England. After all, the photographs which documented the event did not reveal the small size of the party which followed the christening.

Table 12. *Marital status of males and females at time of marriage by type of marriage annually (1961–68)*

Year		Christian					Civil					Muslim					Un-known	Total	
		S	W	D	M	Un^a	S	W	D	M	Un	S	W	D	M	Un			
		no. %	no. %	no. %	no. %	no. %	no. %	no. %	no. %	no. %	no. %	no. %	no. %	no. %	no. %	no. %	no. %	no.	%
61	M^b	253 72	13 4	10 3	—	1 *	5 1	1 *	1 *	—	—	42 12	—	—	23 7	—	—	349	100
	F	265 76	5 1	6 2	—	1 *	3 1	1 *	3 1	—	—	51 15	1 *	—	10 3	—	—	349	100
62	M	207 73	12 4	7 2	—	—	17 6	—	2 1	1 *	—	27 10	—	—	9 3	—	2 1	283	100
	F	216 76	8 3	2 1	—	—	17 6	1 *	1 *	—	—	32 11	—	—	4 1	—	2 1	283	100
63	M	246 74	9 3	16 5	—	—	13 4	1 *	3 1	—	—	33 10	1 *	—	4 1	4 1	—	331	100
	F	261 79	5 1	5 1	—	—	15 5	2 1	—	—	—	40 12	1 *	1 *	1 *	1 *	—	331	100
64	M	245 74	7 2	11 3	—	—	15 5	—	2 1	—	—	33 10	1 *	6 2	16 5	—	—	329	100
	F	254 77	4 1	5 1	—	—	17 5	—	—	—	—	40 12	1 *	—	2 1	—	—	329	100
65	M	216 70	14 5	5 2	2 1	—	17 5	1 *	8 3	—	—	34 11	1 *	1 *	13 4	1 *	—	310	100
	F	222 72	6 2	7 2	2 1	—	20 6	1 *	3 1	—	—	42 14	1 *	—	4 1	—	—	310	100
66	M	236 72	10 3	8 2	3 1	—	13 4	1 *	1 *	—	—	40 12	1 *	—	15 5	—	—	329	100
	F	240 73	7 2	6 2	4 1	—	15 5	1 *	—	—	—	50 15	1 *	2 1	1 *	—	—	329	100
67	M	221 72	9 3	6 2	—	—	13 4	1 *	3 1	—	—	36 12	5 2	—	17 6	—	—	306	100
	F	226 74	3 1	7 2	—	—	14 4	1 *	2 1	—	—	44 14	—	—	4 1	—	—	306	100
68	M	180 77	4 2	4 2	1 *	—	23 10	1 *	2 1	—	—	15 6	—	—	4 2	—	1 *	235	100
	F	184 78	3 1	1 *	1 *	—	22 10	1 *	3 1	—	—	17 7	—	—	1 *	—	1 *	235	100
Totals	M	1804 73	78 3	67 3	6 *	1 *	116 5	7 *	22 1	1 —	—	260 11	2 *	1 *	101 4	4 *	3 *	2472	100
	F	1868 76	41 2	39 2	7 *	1 *	123 5	10 *	12 1	1 —	—	316 13	11 *	13 *	27 1	1 *	3 *	2472	100

a. These statistics were gathered from the records of the Registrar General in Freetown and include all marriages registered in the country between 1961 and 1968. S = single, W = widowed, D = divorced, M = married, Un = unknown.

b. M = male, F = female.

c. * < 0.05 %.

talking together in an obviously more relaxed manner. And indeed, many more parties were held after this change in the political situation. Since weddings are primarily social events, it may be that the drop in numbers of registered marriages during these two years does reflect the attitudes so many people expressed. It is unfortunate that it is not possible to compare the statistics for 1969, but on one Sunday in Freetown, following the return to civilian rule, there were twenty weddings!

Divorce law

Divorces under the statutory law in Sierra Leone may be granted on the grounds of adultery, desertion, or cruelty (Cap. 102). Table 13 shows the number of divorce petitions filed annually from 1961 to 1968 and the numbers which have been granted the Decree Nisi and the Decree Absolute. It also shows the number of divorces according to Islamic law which have been recorded. These divorces are granted under the jurisdiction of the Muslim community and recorded with the Registrar General.

Table 13. *Number of divorce petitions filed annually and decrees granted (1961-68)*[a]

Year	Petitions filed	Decree Nisi	Decree Absolute	Islamic Divorce
1961	26	17	17	7
1962	33	21	21	5
1963	33	21	17	2
1964	36	22	17	2
1965	32	20	19	9
1966	41	27	21	15
1967	23	15	13	14
1968	44	17	12	8
Totals	268	160	137	62

a. These data were gathered from the files of the Supreme Court and from the records of the Registrar General.

As shown in this table, only about half of all divorce petitions filed during these years have resulted in a Decree Absolute. This is partly because of delays in court proceedings and partly because many petitions that are filed are later dropped. It is also possible for a couple to be granted a judicial separation (Cap. 102). However, between 1961 and 1968 only two were granted, one in 1962 and one in 1966.

In Sierra Leone a divorce is regarded as a very extreme measure and to be avoided at almost any cost. As mentioned earlier, Sierra Leoneans often criticize Westerners for their casual attitude towards divorce. Being divorced is particularly undesirable for women, since a woman's status in society is very much bound up with her being married, and if she has achieved the high social position of a woman married under one of the Acts, she will not discard her marriage lightly. A wife who complains about the behaviour of her husband will be admonished by her mother or other relatives. 'You must just be patient and bear with the situation' (*Na fɔ biya*). Another Krio saying emphasizes the importance of marriage: 'A bad man for a husband is much better than an empty house' (*Bad man bɛtɛ pas emti os*'). It is far more usual for an estranged couple to separate than to divorce. Among the professionals, separations can be arranged in a number of ways which avoid an open admission of estrangement. A husband may be posted out of town or the couple may arrange for the wife to live abroad for an indefinite period. One professional's wife had lived with her mother in England for the first twenty years of her life because her parents were estranged. Her father sometimes visited them but in the meantime he had taken an 'outside wife',[23] established a household in Freetown and had other children. Among the parents of the university students 27 per cent were living separately. As one woman lawyer described it, 'You know what they do if they are tired of living together? They just live apart and everybody gets on with his own business, his and her own business. Most people don't bother with judicial separation. They just don't live together.' Women who seek judicial separations rather than divorces are criticized as being difficult and vengeful. They are accused of not wanting their husbands to remarry since another marriage could produce legitimate heirs and, as we shall see, women are very reluctant to allow anyone

---

23. 'Outside wife' is the local term for women who enter into more or less permanent relationships with married men.

the opportunity to share the inheritance rights of their own children.

In a survey of Freetown and the Western Area conducted by the Central Statistics Office a total of 10.9 per cent of all households were classified as 'one-parent' households and 8.2 per cent had female heads of household (*Household Survey of the Western Province: Household Characteristics and Housing Conditions*, Central Statistics Office, Freetown, November, 1967). Most of these one-parent households occurred among the Creoles, the group most committed to Christian monogamous marriage. My own research suggests that many of these one-parent households are the result of estrangements.

When a marriage relationship begins to deteriorate relatives will make every effort to reconcile the couple, most regarding divorce as an unacceptable alternative. Even the lawyers are very reluctant to encourage anyone to proceed directly with a divorce petition. They will often involve themselves in lengthy discussions with the couple and with their relatives, attempting to resolve their differences. Even in court when maintenance disputes are heard, the magistrate may also get involved in attempts to reconcile the husband and wife. A sincere interest in preserving marriages is revealed in this magistrate's remarks:

'Some people don't bother with maintenance suits. They go straight to the Supreme Court. Especially if some years have elapsed, they might prefer to get a divorce and get it done with once and for all. But, no, I wouldn't advise them to do that. I always feel that perhaps given time they might be able to make it up. For example, a gentleman brought his wife here and they have been separated since 1939. He came to ask my advice and he wanted me to send for his wife. I sent for his wife, not knowing why. But I didn't realize they had been living apart since 1939.

So, when the man came, he said to me, "I want you to advise this woman to go home". I said, "Well, since when have you been separated?" He said, "Since 1939."

Well, that is a long time. It is nearly thirty years and so I couldn't say anything to the woman. I couldn't advise her to go home, not after thirty years. But if they would have said a year or two years ... That's why when they first come to complain we invite them to come and see us and try to see if we can solve their problems or talk to them. Sometimes it works.'

The following summary of a case from the records of the Supreme Court illustrates a number of themes common to marital disputes and the extremes of marital discord which are tolerated before a couple finally resort to divorce.

'In this case the husband filed for divorce from his wife on the grounds of desertion. He begged for the discretion of the court in his favour "notwithstanding his own adultery".

The couple had married in 1942 and resided together at three different addresses in Freetown for twelve years before they separated. There were no children from the marriage and in 1954, when they separated, the court ordered the husband to pay £5 maintenance per month to the wife.

The couple reconciled briefly, but in 1956 the husband filed a divorce petition. However, the petition was dropped because apparently the couple had again been reconciled.

He initiated divorce proceedings again in 1966 claiming his wife had deserted him with cause for a period of three years preceding his petition. He complained that in 1947 the wife had engaged in business which took her away from the house during the mornings and again in the evenings until as late as ten or eleven p.m. Her absence made it impossible for him to take her to parties or dances and the loss of her company had a "negative effect upon the normal requirements in the matrimonial home of her consortium".

It was during this period that the husband met Mrs. D. with whom he had an affair. He reported having committed adultery for the first time with her in 1953 and that he had continued to do so ever since. As a result of this relationship four children were born.

The wife, according to the court record, became "frantic" over his relationship with Mrs. D. She too wanted to have children and she consulted a midwife for medical advice. At a certain stage she thought she was pregnant but medical examination proved her wrong. She then consulted a religious sect and was told that she could only have a child if she left her husband's house which was said to be infested with evil spirits. The wife finally did leave although her husband visited her at her new location and continued to have sexual relations with her. However, the wife claimed in court that from 1957 to 1961 she and her husband had not had sexual intercourse. The case was heard in 1968.

The judge, summarizing the case, noted that it was ten years after the marriage that Mrs. D. came into the husband's life. He granted the divorce to the husband because, "The Respondent seems to have known all along and was conscious of the fact that the Petitioner had had a relationship with Mrs. D. The Respondent did not seem to care. She seems to have been satisfied with the state of affairs. She said she loved the Petitioner and in spite of everything she was still prepared to have a child for him. It was only after Mrs. D. had children for the Petitioner that the matter came to a head."

The judge justified his granting the divorce to the husband on the grounds that ". . . it is in the interests of decency that he should be able to marry the woman in question",' (Taken from Div. C. 25, 1966. C. No. 2. Supreme Court of Sierra Leone, Divorce Jurisdiction. Cummings *v.* Cummings, November 15, 1968)

Many divorce records reveal a similar pattern. Couples are separated for a long time and often one or both partners have established a conjugal relationship with another person and have had children. The following case illustrates the kinds of rulings judges often make when faced with such complicated situations. In this case both partners were living with other persons, but the husband had filed for a divorce on the grounds of his wife's adultery. She, in turn, had cross-petitioned for divorce on the grounds of her husband's cruelty and desertion. The Judge ruled in favour of the wife:

'I find on the evidence that the acts of cruelty on the part of the petitioner and his desertion of the respondent . . . long preceded the adulterous relationship between the respondent and co-respondent. I find that long before the respondent's adultery commenced, this marriage was irrevocably broken by the petitioner's cruelty and desertion. I am satisfied that the petitioner had irrevocably arrived at the decision that he would never live with his wife again and that in the circumstances his conduct was quite unaffected when he learned of his wife's adulterous association. It is abundantly clear to me that the acts of cruelty and desertion on the part of the petitioner conduced to the wife's adultery' (1960-61 *Sierra Leone Law Reports*, 1966, Vol. 1, p. 71).

Customary law makes no provision for a woman to divorce her husband on the grounds of adultery. The institution of 'woman damage' provides a mechanism for saving a marriage when a woman commits adultery. The offending man is brought to court by the husband and is fined. A woman who repeatedly involves herself in adulterous relationships would finally be returned to her family and the marriage payment would be refundable. Those who marry under general law have no such institution and a wife's adultery is regarded as a very serious matter indeed. Many believe it inevitably leads to divorce. On the other hand, although it may not be considered desirable, it is more or less expected that men will commit adultery. The rather casual acceptance of a man's sexual infidelity is expressed in the Krio phrase, 'what can you expect, it is just man's nature' (*'How fɔ do, nɔ so man tan'*). The university students were asked to respond to the statement, 'Adultery should be grounds for divorce for both men and women' and significantly more Creoles, 86 per cent, than Provincial, 54 per cent, agreed. Perhaps some people are beginning to think that women have as much right to expect sexual fidelity in marriage as have their husbands.

It is, however, still considered very much more difficult for a woman to win a divorce from her husband on the grounds of adultery than for a man to win such a case against his wife. Public sentiment is against them and the people who might be prepared to come forward to testify against a woman who was charged with adultery are said to be unwilling to make such a testimony against a man. Lawyers report that they always advise women against attempting to base a divorce petition on an adultery charge. Out of the twenty-eight divorces granted on these grounds between 1961 and 1968, only five were granted to women against their husbands. Nevertheless, lawyers say most divorce proceedings initiated by women are the result of the husband's repeated adultery.

A review of the cases where divorces were granted on the grounds of cruelty reveal a wide range of interpretations of what constitutes cruelty. In one case a husband (a theological student) was granted a divorce from his wife on the grounds of cruelty because the wife was accused of having placed certain magical items in his bedroom.

> '... the petitioner reported that on one day he found in his bedroom hanging from the head of his bed a piece of cloth in which was wrapped a piece of red kola nut with a needle thrust through the eye of the kola nut. He also retrieved from his pillow another piece of cloth in which he found some horsehair, finger-nails, needles and a piece of paper on which was written something in

Arabic. Also at the side of his bed he discovered a bottle covered all over with cowries. He became frightened and his health suffered to such an extent that he had to seek medical aid in a hospital. As the treatment given was of no effect, he had to resort to native doctors for several months before he became well again. The judge commented, "Whilst conduct of this nature may not in fact be regarded by an English court as amounting to cruelty, yet our court is bound to take notice of the social background in which the parties live and the superstitious beliefs which, like a cankerworm, can sap the very fabric of even a Christian marriage in an African environment. I, therefore, hold that the respondent by her conduct was guilty of cruelty' (Taken from the case Harris *v.* Harris, (1962) (2) *Sierra Leone Law Reports*, pp. 94-97).

In another case the wife was the petitioner for the divorce, charging her husband with cruelty. The husband was described as having an evil temper. He would return home late at night, drunk, and would awaken his wife and beat her. This happened frequently, even while she was pregnant. These conditions continued for several years and the wife was said to live in a state of constant fear of her husband. On one specific date the husband attacked his wife in the streets of Bo, beat her up and tore her dress, leaving her naked but for a pair of knickers. (The torn dress was produced as evidence in court.) Finally the husband began to threaten to kill her and his conduct towards her made her take this threat seriously so she left him and sought a divorce. (Taken from the case of Williams *v.* Williams. *The African Law Reports. Sierra Leone. 1964-66*, pp. 120-23).

In yet another case cruelty was construed to include psychological cruelty. The petitioner in this case, the wife, was described as 'sensitive and highly strung', requiring a certain amount of social life since she liked going to parties. Unfortunately her husband's work and ambitions took first place in his life and he was described as working late hours and not being fond of going to parties. As a result of their frequent quarrels the wife 'came under increasing nervous strain; her health was affected and she suffered from lack of sleep, depression, dizziness, headaches and generalized aches and pains and, eventually, more serious psychosomatic symptoms of an acute anxiety state'. However, the husband, although he had been advised by doctors that he should humour and indulge her and avoid arguments, had persisted in imposing his will on his wife and their quarrels continued. The wife was granted the divorce on the grounds of cruelty. (Taken from Divorce Case No. 27/66. Supreme Court (Cole, Ag. C.J.): January 4th, 1967. Macaulay *v.* Macaulay).

Property settlement and child custody

Divorces involve property settlements and the question of awarding custody of children. In traditional society if a divorce occurred the children remained with the family of the father unless they were too young to leave the care of their mother. If the wife was allowed to take a young child with her, it was understood that later it would be returned to the father and his family. It appears that the English-type courts are not over-influenced by these traditional attitudes, child custody being determined in the light of considerations for the child's welfare. However, traditional attitudes to this matter are very strong and the threat that a mother might lose her children may still be a deterrent to divorce for some people. This is especially true if the wife is not a Sierra Leonean. One such foreign wife said that if she had a quarrel with her husband he would further provoke her by saying, 'Go ahead, divorce me and leave the country, but, if you do, the children will remain here with me.' One lawyer told of a case where a German wife divorced her husband. Since the husband was a doctor and financially able to care for his children, he was awarded custody. She even attempted unsuccessfully to contest this decision after returning to Germany.

In traditional society the husband controls the material wealth. When a wife leaves her husband she leaves without any property. Even her personal possessions may be stripped from her. Property acquired during marriage belongs to the husband.[24] These traditional attitudes towards rights over property continue to persist among the professionals and are certainly reflected in the settlement of property in divorce cases. In many cases the wife had great difficulty in even getting her clothes away from her husband's house. While women believe that their possessions, clothes, and items they have personally

---

24. There are variations in traditional practices concerning rights to property and this is an area subject to dynamic changes. However, one can generally say that when women do have rights over certain property these properties are managed by the male members of their families.

purchased for the household should be regarded as their own, and be awarded to them in case of divorce, they generally accept that such property as the house, car, furniture and the like belong to the husband. This attitude supports the very general practice of couples where each spouse keeps a separate financial account. I discuss this further in Chapter Eight. The professional sample was asked to respond to the statement, 'If a wife leaves her husband, she also leaves behind her the property (other than personal possessions) which they have accumulated during the marriage' and 92 per cent agreed. Very few people had ever entertained the idea that property should be equally divided in case of divorce or that a wife had any possible claim to part of her husband's possessions. In connection with this notion of the ownership of property, it should be noted that when a couple separate, it is the *wife* who leaves the matrimonial home, not the husband. In several divorce cases a wife has been charged with deserting her husband even though the evidence revealed that at the time of the estrangement she had been forcibly driven from the home.

The marriages of professionals are often subject to extreme pressures as a result of the demands of gaining an education, which often entails long separations, financial stress and the obligations which members of the extended family impose. The following case is illustrative of some of these problems.

> 'The husband asked for a divorce from his wife on the grounds of cruelty and asked the court to award him the custody of their child. They were married in England while both were students. After the husband completed his course he returned to Sierra Leone to work as a lawyer. A child had been born to them while they were in England and later the wife sent this child to her husband while she remained to complete her studies.
>
> In the divorce proceedings the husband claimed that he had tried to persuade his wife to return with him but that she had "wilfully and unreasonably" refused. She denied this allegation and told the court that before they had married her father and her husband had arranged together that she should be permitted to complete her training as a nurse before returning home. In fact, the permission to marry granted by her father had been contingent on this arrangement. The wife alleged that the husband had agreed to all this and had not only promised to visit her in England, but when she had got homesick and wanted to return pre-

maturely, he had encouraged her to stay and finish her course. She produced two letters from him as evidence.

The wife completed her training as a nursing sister, but failed to complete a course in midwifery. Because she was homesick and anxious to see her child from whom she had been parted for three years, she decided to come back.

When she returned she found a sixteen-year-old girl installed in their home. She had been given no prior hint from her husband what to expect. This girl was not a relative but was described to her as the daughter of her husband's "great benefactor" who had sent him to study law in England and who, before his death, had requested the husband to take care of his two daughters.

The wife said that at first she tried to ignore the girl, but she accused her husband of giving the girl special attention. The wife finally insisted that the girl be sent away.

This girl, also giving evidence in court, said that when the husband was away the wife snatched her child away from her and slapped and hit her on the head with a pan. The wife, according to her, was annoyed because the girl's father had given her to the husband for a wife.

At this point the wife moved out of the house to a different address and, since the husband was not at home at the time she moved, she took his things with her as well. When he visited her at the new address he told her he was not coming to live with her and took his things away. She lived at this address for two months and during this time the husband maintained her.

Later they lived together again but both husband and wife agreed they had not had sexual relationships since 1963 although they had shared the same home until 1965. The wife complained that she had made advances to her husband but that he had rejected them and said that if she insisted he would move to a hotel. The wife's mother supported her statement saying that on one occasion the wife had left the room she was sharing with her mother and gone to spend the night in her husband's room. Shortly afterwards she had returned to her mother's room in tears.

A further complication arose. The ward of a neighbour was discovered to be pregnant and she reported having had intercourse with the husband. At first he denied this and became very annoyed when the family of the ward reported the matter to his wife. When the wife asked him about it, he replied that other people did worse things and got over them, but whatever he did there was always some trouble over it. He said that he was not perfect and that if she wanted to leave him she had the chance to do so.

The divorce was granted to the wife on the grounds of cruelty even though the husband had originally petitioned for the divorce charging his wife with cruelty. Cruelty in this case was defined to include the unexpected presence of the sixteen-year-old girl in the household and, as the judge put it, "Apart from the other facts I have mentioned the petitioner did not deny that for a year he took no meals at home. These and other facts would certainly hurt the pride of a wife and cause her mental or physical strain ".' (Taken from the case of Navo *v.* Navo. Divorce Case No. 28/65. Supreme Court [Browne-Mark, J.]: May 4th, 1967.)

In Sierra Leone, as perhaps in most societies, women stand to lose most by a divorce. The status of being a married woman has profound significance, and a divorced woman is both socially and economically vulnerable. An analysis of the registered marriages between 1961 and 1968 shows fewer divorced women remarrying than divorced men. Still, a little over a third of the divorce petitions filed between these same years were filed by women. Most of these women were, however, rather well placed in terms of education and occupation. Unless a woman has educational or occupational qualifications which afford her some status it is unlikely that she would seek a divorce in view of the stigma attached to the divorcee.

Inheritance law

As with marriage, there are three systems of law affecting the inheritance of property in Sierra Leone. The deceased's property is administered according to his 'personal' law which is determined, as noted above, according to his ethnic background, religion or place of birth. I have already drawn attention to the difficulties in many cases of determining whether a person is a 'native' or a 'non-native'. As Smart observes:

'The law that governs the devolution and distribution of the property in question, the deceased's personal law, which is determined not by him but by the inevitable accident of birth and ethnic ties or religion; the genre of inheritable property; the trinity of laws – general, customary, and Mohammedan – and the vast congeries of tribal laws, all engender problems of conflict which are hardly known to countries with a monolithic system of laws as in England' (1969).

Marriage between two natives by customary law does not affect the personal law of the husband, but it does alter the personal law of the wife to that of her husband.

'Being regarded as a chattel of the husband the woman herself together with her property becomes an accretion to the husband's estate. Nonetheless, no change in the husband's position is affected by marriage, and his property at all times remains his own and descends on his death just as if he had never been married' (Smart, unpublished manuscript. No date).

If two natives marry under the Christian Marriage Ordinance it does not affect their personal law as regards inheritance.

'The property of parties to a marriage celebrated under this Ordinance shall, if both parties be natives, be subject in all respects to the laws and customs of the tribe or tribes to which the parties respectively belong' (Cap. 95, Sec. 26).

However, since the position of the wife with regard to inheritance is virtually the same among all the tribes in Sierra Leone, the fact that a Christian marriage does not change her personal law is a matter of no consequence. Although the amendment to the Civil Marriage Act in 1965 allowed natives to marry under its provisions, it did not make any alterations in the rules regarding the inheritance of property. If the intention was, as in the Christian Marriage Act, that marriage should not affect the personal law of either the husband or the wife, then there is still no indication in either Act as to which law should apply in those cases where there is a conflict between two systems of customary law. Admittedly most of the time such problems are avoided because, as Smart points out:

'In Sierra Leone as in other African countries, native laws and customs about the distribution of the property of the deceased native initially varied from tribe to tribe as well as from district to district within the same tribal area ... In recent times, however, with more frequent admixture of tribal groups, a certain degree of syncretism is prevailing.' (Unpublished manuscript, no date).

In contrast to a marriage under the Christian or Civil Acts, marriage under the Mohammedan Marriage Act alters the personal law of a non-native to Islamic law. Although the law does not provide for a change in the legal status or personal law of a native who marries under the Mohammedan Marriage Act, Smart suggests that by common practice, '. . . the personal law remains not native law and custom *simpliciter*, but with a variation, its content drawing largely upon Mohammedan law.' (Unpublished manuscript, no date). The fact that marriage under statutory law does not change the parties' personal law as regards inheritance is exceptional in post-colonial British West Africa. In every ex-British colony, except Sierra Leone, we find that marriage under statutory law alters the personal law of parties to marriage under its provisions. Moreover, in Sierra Leone it is widely believed that marriage under one of the acts does alter the individual's personal law to statutory law. One informant who was resisting his wife's demands for a church wedding gave as his excuse:

'I paid £50 dowry and we are married by customary law. I think that is enough. Besides there is my property when I die. My family is from a ruling house in my chiefdom and I want my property to go to my fathers and my brothers when I die. If I marry her in the church, when I die she will get it all.'

The fact that he was so misinformed is the more surprising in that he was a lawyer! However, perhaps it is understandable that there should be such misconceptions of the law, since when natives marry under one of the acts the relationship is governed by general law in every respect *except* in the administration of the estate when a person dies intestate. But in the case of inheritance, it is the personal law of the individual which dictates its administration.

Thus if a native marries a non-native or Creole under statutory law and though they live together all their lives, when the native dies his estate must still be administered by the customary practices of his tribe. Under customary law the wife is considered part of the husband's inheritable property and would, under the traditional system, be 'inherited' by one of the male members of his family. Although customary law dictates that the husband's family should be responsible for the support and care of the wife and dependants of the deceased, in most tribes she can inherit neither money nor property from her husband.[25] Of course, in the case of a marriage between a native and a Creole woman, the responsibility for even maintenance could be avoided since, under customary law (unless the husband has actually given marriage payments for her)[26] the marriage would not have to be recognized, although in practice it always is.

On the other hand, if the Creole wife of this marriage with a native dies intestate, her estate, under her own personal law which would recognize the marriage, would pass completely over to her husband under the provisions of general law (Cap. 45). Upon his death his estate, to which hers has now been added, would be inherited by his patrilineage and their sons could have no more claim to a share in the estate than would any other male member.

Similar problems may arise when a Creole man marries a native woman under one of the ordinances. If the wife has property and dies before her husband without making a will, her estate should be administered under customary law. According to a strict interpretation of customary law, her husband cannot make any claim to her estate since the marriage would not necessarily be recognized; after all, most likely he would not have given marriage payments. But if this same Creole husband dies intestate first, the wife would receive that proportion of his estate which under the statutory law widows are entitled to (Cap. 45).

The complications and potential hardships which can result from the administration of the estates of deceased partners to mixed marriages are illustrated by the following case which the Administrator General described:

'I have one case now which starts out exactly on the lines we are discussing. It is the case of a man who died at Port Loko. He was a native of Port Loko. He married a Christian woman, a Creole, in the Christian marriage way. They have children and he also has native wives and those wives have children too.

What I am going to do is, it seems to me, that I am going to

---

25. That women's rights over property is an area of dynamic change has already been noted. The general rule is that the family head assumes the deceased's property in trust for his children.

26. There are several stages to customary marriage which vary from tribe to tribe and are carried out over a period of time. Some payment of money or goods, locally termed dowry, is given to members of the girl's family.

divide the estate into two parts. [This is] because he has estates which come under the Native Administration and estates which do not come under the Native Administration. He owns bank accounts and all banks are foreign institutions and so wherever they may be in the whole of Sierra Leone they do not come under the Native Administration. So that money in the bank will be divested from the Native Administration and we will have to treat it under the Christian Marriage Ordinance.

So she [the Christian Creole wife] will get the cash. Then we will have to treat the property which is at Port Loko and elsewhere and administer it according to native law and custom. We will ask the District Officer to supply us with the usual certificates. We will tell the "D.O." that this man has married in a Christian way to a Creole woman and they have children. By our law, by the Christian way, by the ordinary law of the land, she is entitled to one-third and her lawful children are entitled to two thirds. We will also tell the "D.O." that this man also married native women under a native law and custom. They have children also. So issue us your certificate and tell us how you think this estate should be divided. [27]

We will need to know which wife was married first, one of the natives or the Christian wife, so we can know who is the senior wife and who is the junior wife. Because in these polygamous marriages they have senior wives and junior wives. Well, we will want to know which marriage was contracted first to be able to tell ourselves who is regarded as senior wife and who is regarded as junior wife. The senior wife has priority and gets more. So if the Creole wife is senior she will get more.'

The Administrator General happens to be Creole, and, of course, received his legal training in Britain. From his remarks, it seems clear that he is unaware that under customary law women do not directly inherit property, but are themselves 'inherited'. [28] It is clear that he is hoping to find that the Creole wife was the first and hence 'senior'

---

27. The procedure in the cases where property must be settled by native law and custom is for the Administrator General to consult with the District Officer who in turn consults with local chiefs and other experts in the particular tribal law.

28. Although here the recent changes in provision for widows under customary law mentioned above should be kept in mind.

wife, which would support his argument to the District Officer that she should have the money in the bank which her husband left.

In this discussion with the Administrator General I questioned the legality of such an approach to the administration of this estate. After all, I suggested, the money which the husband owned in the bank came from the surplus produce from the land he controlled and farmed in the provinces. I was assured that since the bank was a 'foreign institution' it was, therefore, out of the jurisdiction of the Local Court (formerly native courts). He continued by saying how often in such cases the native has invested in property located in the Western Area which is also not under the administration of the Local Courts. In such cases, he said, the property in the Western Area is simply handed over to the Creole wife and the rest falls back to the patrilineage as administered by the local native authorities under the supervision of the District Officer. At this point he reached for the reference on the law and read to me:

> 'Notwithstanding anything contained in this Ordinance, when any native dies intestate leaving assets in Sierra Leone which are not within the jurisdiction of any Native Court, the distribution of such assets after payment of the debts of the deceased and the costs of administration shall be according to native law and custom' (Cap. 45, Sec. 43).[29]

The Administrator General related another case where a Creole woman had married a Paramount Chief recently deceased. The widow was now living in Freetown with her sons and was running a small business in her house. In this case all the chief's property had been distributed according to customary law but fortunately the woman owned Freetown property which could support her and her children. He assured me that in all cases where one of the spouses of the deceased who died intestate had been a Creole he had been able to work out a 'satisfactory solution'. However, he agreed thus far no case had ever been tested in the Supreme Court. Such contests are probably avoided because customary law is flexible, Provincials have a strong

---

29. It would be highly unfair not to emphasize here that the Administrator General and other civil servants facing such situations have an impossible task. Customary law has not been recorded and 'experts' give contradictory information. False claims are numerous. Many District Officers who also get involved in these matters express the view that they must find a balance of 'humane values' and customary practices in their settlement of such cases.

respect for the overriding authority of the national government and, most important, there is a general ignorance about the content of both legal systems.[30]

The important question is how many persons are affected by the conflicts of law which arise from intermarriage between natives and non-natives or Creoles. As shown in Chapter Two, one-fifth of the Provincial men in the professional sample were married to Creole women and 6 per cent had married women who were non-Sierra Leoneans. Unless these men make wills when they die their estates will be administered under customary law with all the attendant uncertainties about the legal rights of their non-native wives. Only 8 per cent of the Creoles in the professional sample had married Provincial women, but again if the husband died intestate before his wife's death, his property could finally come under the jurisdiction of customary law.

It is impossible to know how many such intermarriages there are between natives and non-natives in the general population. Information about tribal background is not recorded when a marriage is registered but the address of both the parties at the time of the marriage is available. Analysis of the addresses of all persons married under the general law between 1961 and 1968 shows there were 3 per cent more women than men who gave their address as the Western Area. Even if we dared to assume that these 3 per cent were Creole women marrying Provincial men, the 3 per cent would only involve about 75 marriages over these eight years. The registration of births in the Western Area does show the tribe of both parents up to 1966; in 1967 the military government censored all official reference to tribe. Analysis of the births from 1961 to 1966 shows that among mixed unions one and a half times more Creole women gave birth to children having native fathers than native women giving birth to children having Creole fathers.[31] In view of the proportion of Creoles (less than 2 per cent) in the population, this trend is likely to continue, but with the present state of the law of inheritance these women place themselves and their children in a highly vulnerable position.

---

30. Of course, nearly all such problems could be avoided if people made wills, but very few do.
31. Among these Creole women giving birth to children having native fathers, three times as many of the fathers were Mende or Temne compared with fathers from other tribal groups.

Maintenance law

The statutory law of Sierra Leone provides for the maintenance of women who have been deserted by their husbands (Married Woman's Maintenance Ordinance, Cap. 100). The benefits of this law apply to everyone who has been married under one of the Acts, native and non-native alike. As noted before, the law does not, however, apply to those women who have been married by customary law. It has been further noted that, if such a woman finds it necessary to take action against her husband for non-support, she must do so under the Bastardy Act along with unwed mothers (Bastardy Laws Amendment Act, 1872. [35 and 36 Vict. c65] and Bastardy Laws (Increase of Payments) Ordinance, 1961). Table 14 shows the number of such cases tried on the two maintenance acts in Freetown.

Table 14. *The number of maintenance cases tried annually in Freetown (1961-68)*[a]

Year	Married Woman's Maintenance Ordinance	Bastardy Act
1961*	144	130
1962*	64	84
1963*	102	116
1964	148	115
1965	83	131
1966*	104	181
1967	137	236
1968*	139	205
Totals	921	1 198

a. When I gathered these statistics it was found that many of the monthly records books were missing from the Magistrate's Court files. These years for which the records were incomplete are marked with an asterisk. The totals for these years shown in the table are estimated by taking the average number of cases for the months available and multiplying by twelve. However, even if the years where records were complete are compared, a substantial increase of cases being tried under the Bastardy Act is shown.

According to these records, the number of married women suing for maintenance has not increased and most certainly the number of such cases in court does not reveal the scope of the problem among married couples. The failure of husbands to maintain their wives and children is the most common problem brought to the family caseworkers at the Ministry of Social Welfare. Although they may advise and even assist women to initiate maintenance proceedings, the present law does not make it particularly advantageous. The maximum amount the law allows a wife to be awarded is £4 weekly. However, the amendment to the Bastardy Act in 1961 has increased the benefits for children born out of wedlock from five shillings to thirty shillings per week (maximum amounts awardable). As one lawyer pointed out:

'If this should happen to me, [as a married woman] I wouldn't go to a Magistrate's Court to sue my husband. Because even if I have six children or ten children, I know that if I drag my husband to court I won't get more than £16 [monthly]. But, on the other hand, a woman with six illegitimate children say by six different men can get the maximum awarded to her – £36 [monthly]. Not for herself, of course, but for her children. Well, financially, for your children you get more if they are illegimate as the law stands today.'

As shown in Table 14, there has been a significant increase in the number of cases of women suing for maintenance under the Bastardy Act since 1961.[32] This does not necessarily indicate an increase in the number of illegitimate births. More likely it is a reflection of the wider knowledge of the greater benefits now available for the mothers of illegitimate children. The increase could indicate that more women married by customary law living in Freetown, cut off from the assistance of their relatives, having no recourse but the courts, are suing their husbands for support. However, as we shall see in the next chapter, there has been a great deal of publicity about the problem of illegitimacy in Sierra Leone society. The social stigma attached to being an unwed mother has lessened and women stand to make considerable financial gain from taking their case to court.[33]

32. The court records only reveal a fraction of the cases which are dealt with by the family caseworkers. Realizing that most men are unable to pay the amounts which would be awarded by the courts, the caseworkers accommodate the men by receiving minimal amounts of maintenance money and handing it over to the women for their children.

33. Subsequent research in family law has revealed that unwed mothers are very sophisticated about their legal rights. They are aware that they stand to gain more if their children are fathered by different men since the court is more likely to award the maximum amount for a child if a man is only being sued for supporting one.

In 1966 there was an unsuccessful attempt to amend the maintenance laws (The Maintenance of Dependants Act, 1966). This proposed
legislation would have repealed the Married Woman's Maintenance
Act and it would have provided for the maintenance of dependants,
legitimate or illegitimate, and for the regular reassessment of the
amounts awardable as the economic conditions in the country changed.
At the time it was drafted, this proposed legislation set the maximum
figure awardable at leones 35 for a child and leones 50 for an adult
dependant.[34] The law would have given the magistrate jurisdiction to
fix the monthly sum according to the earning capacity of the person
liable for the maintenance and education of the dependants in question. The bill also included a very progressive statement about the
legal obligations of *both* parties to the conjugal union to maintain
the other, although this obligation 'shall only apply to the wife in so
far as her husband is incapable of maintaining himself' (Ibid.).[35] The
bill also stated that 'Every father shall be under legal obligation to
maintain and educate his legitimate and illegitimate children until they
reach the age of eighteen years' (Ibid).

Since the increase in benefits to children under the Bastardy Act
amendment in 1961, there has also been an increase in the number of
paternity disputes. The following case is illustrative of the kinds of
disputes which now commonly arise.[36]

> 'The woman sued the respondent for support. She testified that
> she had met him some time in 1956. They had six children, five
> living and one deceased. Four of the children are living in the
> respondent's mother's home and the fifth was living with her. She
> noted that the respondent had given her Le. 10 shortly after the
> birth of the last child but had since failed to maintain her.
> The man admitted that he and the complainant had "started to

34. The official currency of Sierra Leone is a leone. It is equal to fifty new
pence sterling. A leone is divided into one hundred cents, ten cents equalling
five new pence.
35. This bill would have defined a marriage as any '...which is recognized
by the law of the place where it is contracted as the voluntary union for life of
one man and one woman to the exclusion of all others' and embraced Islamic
marriage. It appears that this law, had it passed, could have been construed to
include customary marriages where there was only one wife.
36. This case and many others were collected by reading through handwritten
accounts of court proceedings. Unfortunately, the method of record-keeping is
such that it was not possible to find the disposition of cases or to document them
properly.

love" in 1959 and they had "started to get children" in 1960. By 1964 they had about five children, four living and one dead. He told the court that all of the four children were in his custody and were residing with his parents. He was providing financial support and paid their school fees as well. He testified that the relationship with the petitioner had ended in 1965. Since that time he had not contributed to her upkeep and was not the father of the child born to her in 1966.'

Paternity disputes are not limited to cases involving unmarried women. As one magistrate told me:

'. . . you even find people who are married . . . . You sometimes find husbands and wives coming and the husband telling us he is not the father of the child born to his wife. You have married men disputing paternity even when they are living in the same house with their wives. They come to the court and tell you, "Although we have been living together, the child is not mine. I have not had anything to do with the woman for so many months". Sometimes it is very unpleasant to start asking all sorts of questions especially when it is disputed because it is on the records.'

And often these already complicated cases get even further entangled, as this magistrate described:

'. . . you find a woman coming to court for maintenance. If the case takes a long time, say about two or three months, or if she in fact has been awarded maintenance – you find that when she comes to swear to the information that the husband has not been paying and to have him arrested – you find that she is pregnant. So the next thing you see is the husband coming to have the order varied because of his wife's adultery. This is provided for in Cap. 100 (Married Woman's Maintenance Ordinance).'

The family caseworkers in the Ministry of Social Welfare found the increase in maintenance disputes 'alarming'. One described the situation as she saw it:

'. . . it depends on the individual, but some of them [husbands] just don't want to maintain their homes. If they have their salaries at the end of the month . . . you find they have girl-friends outside and they don't mind spending on the girl-friends instead of their wives . . . some have genuine cases in which they say they have to maintain their mothers, their fathers or relatives. It is here we always tell them that your wife and family come first.

All other obligations are secondary to your family.

But with some, they just don't want to maintain their family at all. Especially if the wife is earning something. Some prefer to go out on the beach with their friends . . . They just expect the wife to maintain herself. [Among] middleclass women you have a lot of business-women. Some women earn more than their husbands especially if they are employed in the government. Some of these women are selfish. They feel that if I earn the money, it is mine just for myself alone. I am not going to spend it on the home. These women are supported by the law; of course, the law says it is the duty of a man to maintain his home.'

The remarks of this caseworker point up one very dramatic difference between traditional values and those based on western ideas as represented in the maintenance law. In traditional society a woman's full energies were expected to be employed in contributing to the upkeep of the home through farming, trading, etc. The idea that a woman should be free from direct involvement in the day-to-day maintenance of the family would be incomprehensible in the village setting. Yet women, married under the Acts ordinance, by law are freed from such responsibilities and can, if they choose, keep all their earnings for themselves, refusing to contribute to the expense of the home.[37]

Adoption

Sierra Leone does not make any provision for the legal adoption of children under any of its three systems of law. This is a problem of some concern among social workers, lawyers and many couples who are raising children they would like to adopt.[38] There has been con-

---

37. That the husband should be fully responsible for maintaining the household is also a departure from traditional values. This topic will be considered more fully in the discussion of household finances in Chapter Eight.

38. There is a children's home in Freetown for orphans and permanent homes have been found for several of these children. At the suggestion of their lawyer, one professional couple who had 'adopted' two children, made a 'Statutory Declaration' of their intent to assume permanent responsibility for the children without the assistance or involvement of their parents. This document would, however, have no legal standing in a dispute with the children's biological parents.

siderable interest in drafting an adoption law, but the problems are difficult. In customary law there is no adoption in the sense that we know it in the West.[39]

Nevertheless, it is very common for children to grow up in the care of someone other than their own parents. As noted earlier, this was the childhood experience of many of the professional and university students. As shown, in the interest of their education, often children are sent to another home to be reared. The ward system, also described before, has contributed to the numbers of children growing up in homes away from their parents. In traditional society it is believed that for many reasons it is desirable for someone else to raise one's children. Many are convinced that it is important for the early discipline of a child to be given by a detached relative rather than his own parents, who might spoil him. Sometimes a child is known to be his father's favourite or the offspring of his favourite wife and is therefore in danger of being harmed by jealous co-wives. The practice of sending children to be reared by relatives persists. As we saw, many professional families have taken other children into their homes. In the following case, a professional family gave their daughter to a relative.

'Mr. and Mrs. J. were a professional couple included in the pilot group. Both were Mende and had grown up in small villages in the Provinces. The wife only had a primary education, but was the first of her family to have received any western education at all. The husband came from an educated family; his father was a secondary school teacher. This couple had six boys and one girl. Although Mr. J. was always very respectful in his attitude towards traditional values, he very clearly counted himself among those who had accepted western ideas about family life. This was illustrated in a number of ways. He spent more time at home with his wife and family than did any of the other men in the pilot group of couples. He was active in church life and often took his wife with him to committee meetings during the week. He had spent some time abroad and had made a special effort to arrange for his wife to join him there so that she would have the opportunity to get familiar with "western" ways.

39. Children may be 'given' to a relative and under such circumstances as the childlessness of the relative or the death of the parents and nearer kin, the child may be considered to belong to its adopted parents. In the case of a girl, this is indicated by the marriage payments being given to them rather than her own parents.

He often discussed his family life in such a way as to reveal his familiarity with concepts of modern psychology. He often stressed the importance of the parent-child relationship in the family and he spent a good bit of time supervising his own children's home work.

I had been visiting this family for about four months when one day Mrs. J. casually informed me that they were giving their only daughter to her sister who lived in Bo, who had no children of her own. The little girl was only four and a half years old at the time. I asked several questions about how she thought the child would react to the idea and whether or not they were concerned about her adjustment to the new home and, finally, why they were doing this and would they not be lonely without her.

Mrs. J's responses to these questions indicated she regarded them as totally irrelevant and even uninteresting. Of course, the child was happy about going. She liked her aunt. Why should she have difficulty adjusting? After all "... my sister is the same as me".[40] The reasons they were giving the little girl away were explained. First, the sister had no children and Mrs. J. and her other sisters had for some time been attempting to find a solution to this problem. Secondly, Mr. J. was spoiling the little girl. Mrs. J. would not react to the suggestion that she might miss the little girl; she only replied "I have so many children already".

Later, the father told me how the decision had been reached. His wife's female relatives had been complaining to his wife about his indulgence with the little girl. They frequently visited the household and kept urging Mrs. J. to do something about it. An obvious solution to this problem and to the problem of their childless sister was to give the child to her.

Mr. J. said that although he admitted he spoiled the child, he did not think it harmed her since she was the only girl in the family. He also pointed out that extra attention is beneficial to children

40. Anthropologists sometimes make reference to the notion of 'equivalency of siblings'. In many societies certain categories of relatives are referred to by the same kinship term. Among the Mende, for example, a mother and her sisters are all called by the same classificatory term. It is sometimes argued that behaviour towards persons who are classified by the same kinship term is the same. Apparently, Mrs. J. felt this to be in some way true for her little girl who was now going to be cared for by someone whom she would address by the same kinship term as she used when addressing her mother in Mende.

and noted how bright she was as a result. "But", he sighed, "what could I do against all those women?" He had been forced, he said, to submit to their decision about what was best all round.

During the first months after the child had been moved to Bo, the parents frequently visited her. They also continued to support her and to pay her school fees. After a year had passed these visits dropped off almost completely. The father accompanied me and a party of other persons on a trip which took us through Bo. Although we stopped en route to see his parents, he did not suggest that we should stop to see the child. Clearly, the child now did "belong" to the aunt. The father admitted to me much later that during the first few months after her transfer to Bo he "dreaded coming home after work" but, as he put it, "What could I do?" '

Another wife described her own experience. She had taken one of her sister's daughters with her to her new home when she married. The girl was four years old at the time and had lived with Mr. and Mrs. L. until she was fifteen years old. Mr. and Mrs. L. had been responsible for the girl's education and support all through those years with no assistance from her own parents.

'Well, I took her as my own right from the start. When I hadn't any children when I got married, she stayed with me. She didn't know her mother because she was so young when she came to me.'

I asked how it came about that Mrs. L's sister had given up her child:

'Well, she was just too fond of me and wouldn't go to her own mother. Because I was staying in the house when she was a baby, so when she grew up she came to know me more than the mother, her own mother. She was used to seeing me more than her own mother. So she thought I was her mother, so she wouldn't go to her mother on no account. She hung on to me until I was married and then she asked to come with me.'

Despite the fact that individuals have not grown up in close contact with their parents, traditional attitudes and obligations towards these categories of relatives persist. It is almost as though the appropriate behaviour and response is associated with the category of relative rather than with the person who fills that relationship.

Many people argue that Sierra Leone needs an adoption law but there are others who hold that the present pattern is preferable. They suggest that an adoption law would produce other problems. As it is, relationships can be established, dropped and again resumed, based upon the individual's need for them and upon the traditional ideas about appropriate behaviour towards certain categories of kinship. Whether or not one is in close contact with certain relatives such as one's mother or sister or brother, the fact of the relationship itself evokes certain responses. Some fear that to impose an artificial relationship through an adoption law would interrupt the continuity of these relationships which persist despite long separations and geographical distance, depriving a child of the benefits of a wide number of potentially affective links and resources in times of need.

One of the profound challenges facing newly-independent African countries is the task of enacting a culturally sensitive body of law. When reading through the accounts of court cases one is often surprised that, despite the fact that the judiciary had been totally Africanized, legal decisions often appear to fail to reflect the social conditions, values and practices. On the other hand, in certain matters Sierra Leonean judges appear to be very sensitive to such matters, for example, as was shown, the broad interpretation of cruelty as grounds for divorce, which ranged from psychological cruelty to the use of fetish.

Sierra Leoneans and other West Africans have accepted the form of English-type ordinance marriage. With the exception of inheritance laws, their marriages come under the structure and jurisdiction of a legal system which often imposes values which, at worst, are completely foreign and unsuited to current social practice. At best, they may only be vaguely understood and perceived by most people as somehow being superior. For example, women are convinced that a statutory marriage emancipates them from the 'evils' of their role in traditional society. They are relieved of the primary burden of providing for the household and they no longer have to tolerate the presence of co-wives and their children whose existence threatens their security in such a profound way. Although a statutory marriage imposes certain responsibilities on men for the maintenance of a household which are uncomfortable, even disagreeable to some, it might be concluded that men continue to have the best of both worlds. They have the possibility of enjoying the status associated with a monogamous statutory marriage and at the same time, they are free to establish households with women outside the marriage, continuing to have large numbers of children with them, and thus enhancing their social position in traditional terms at the same time. However, recent legal changes which have imposed rigid financial responsibilities for these extra households have made this practice less attractive. Moreover, certain recent attempts to change the status of these illegitimate children have had dramatic effects upon the men's attitudes and upon relationships between themselves and their wives. This matter is considered in the next chapter.

Those who discuss the trend of West Africans towards the practice of contracting marriages under the Acts of statutory law usually equate this trend with the acceptance of monogamy with its associated values. Mercier (1954) as quoted by Little (1967) differentiates between a 'monogamy of fact' and a 'monogamy of choice' and points to the differences between those people who have only one wife because of their financial limitations and those who choose, regardless of their financial position, to have only one wife. Omari's research (1960) among Ghanaian students revealed that students there regard polygamy as a backward practice and that, as Little (1967) puts it, '. . . a plurality of wives is no longer a way to increase influence and status . . .'. As already stated, my own research bears out these other findings that educated West Africans do reject the idea of a legalized polygamous marriage system and regard with disfavour marriages contracted under customary law. The stress which missionaries placed on the *form* of marriage was enormously effective. It was apparent to educated Africans that to achieve favour with the white man, it was imperative to conform to this institution of statutory, monogamous marriage. Today the ceremony of marriage with all its elaborate trappings has become an almost indispensable symbol of status in town life. The interesting related question to which this study is addressed is to what extent marriage relations or actual behaviour have conformed to the idealized companionate model upon which the law is based.

6

The status of children born out of wedlock

It would be difficult to think of a social problem with wider ramifications in modern Sierra Leone than that of children born out of wedlock. Certainly, as will be shown, the present legal status of children quarrels with Fallers' ideas about law, which he says is concerned with

> '. . . the major institutionalized values of societies, the values to which people are sufficiently committed to be willing to impose them upon themselves in an authoritative manner. Such values are "cultural" in the sense that they form elements in the interrelated systems of ideas shared by a people; and they are "social" in the sense that commitment to them underlies the mutuality of expectation upon which ordered social life rests' (1969, p. 2).

For one thing, such a consensus theory of law fails to account for the situation resulting from imperialism. The legal system prescribed by the colonial government could hardly be described as representing the consensus norms of the society as a whole. In the area of family law the imposed legal system outlined the structure for the transformation of the institution of marriage and this model became a new basis for the measurement of status. The colonial period survived long enough to convince a segment of the population of the superiority of the foreigners' ways. This group became committed to and identified with the new system of marriage and their prestigious position in the society came to be equated with it. As we shall see, these values could be manipulated in the interest of the elite who inherited the positions of power from their colonial predecessors. Legal institutions are, as Fallers says, authoritative, but their authority is not necessarily based on representing the values of the society as a whole. Rather the content of the law often reveals the strength of groups within the society whose interests continue to be served by the conventions they impose.

Thus when any attempt is made to change the law in the interests of the majority to be more in line with common practice, we find such proposals immediately ramify into the political sphere. 'Reform' of the law will only occur when the laws no longer serve the interests of those in power and have become uncomfortably obsolete. Unification of the diverse legal systems in post-colonial countries is not likely to occur until such time as political power has been more widely distributed.

This chapter will discuss the problem of the status of children born out of wedlock in Sierra Leone. A case study of an ill-fated attempt to equalize their legal position will be presented. This case has wider theoretical implications than the consideration of the relationship between law, norms and values, and political power. The attempt to pass legislation equalizing the legal status of legitimate and illegitimate children is an example of an effort to bring about harmony between the societal norms regarding illegitimate children (as they were perceived by lawyers) and the law. Quite by accident the publicity surrounding the event convinced the general public that the law *had been passed*. The effect on the behaviour of individuals of the belief that the law had been passed provides a unique opportunity to examine the relationship between beliefs and social change. As Moore suggests:

> 'Attempts to remold society through legislation presume ideas of what society is, how it works, how it can be changed, and what it should be. Although judicial innovation and legislation by no means always have the intended effects, the models on which they are based imply a way of looking at social life and a "folk" sociology of change implicit in legislation, that may be a way of finding out more about the relationship of ideas to social action' (1970, p. 287).

Moreover, the controversy surrounding children born out of wedlock is central to our understanding of the organization of marriage and family relationships among professional couples in Sierra Leone.

The scope of the problem:
how many children are born out of wedlock?

In Sierra Leone a person is deemed to be born out of wedlock, or illegitimate, if his parents were not married by one of the recognized forms of marriage which include, as noted in Chapter Five, statutory marriages under general law, Islamic marriages, and marriages by native law and custom. Provision is made for the compulsory registration of all statutory marriages (Cap. 95, 96 and 97, *Laws of Sierra Leone*) and, more recently, for the registration of customary marriages (Cap. 61). However, as was noted in Chapter Five, only a minority of such customary marriages are being registered. While provision has also been made for the registration of births all over Sierra Leone (Cap. 92 and 93), the number of births actually registered in the Provinces is insignificant. Since in the Western Area it is necessary to present a birth certificate when a child is enrolled in primary school, most persons there register their children's births. Further, in the Western Area births are usually attended by a midwife who takes the responsibility of registration. Our discussion of illegitimacy will therefore be restricted to births registered in the Western Area. However, this is not inappropriate since we are primarily concerned with the effects of illegitimacy on statutory marriages. Eighty per cent of the women and 71 per cent of the men marrying under statutory law between 1961 and 1968 lived in the Western Area.

The manner in which the birth of a child is registered makes it possible to see if he is legitimate or not. Births are registered under four possible headings: those legitimate children born to couples married under one of the Acts of general law; those legitimate children born to couples married by native law and custom; those illegitimate births where the father has signed the register or permitted his name to be recorded; and, finally, illegitimate births where only the mother's name is recorded. Although according to the law, those children whose births are registered in the third category, where both parents' names are given, are illegitimate, the situation is actually more complicated. Primarily, this column is intended for the registration of those births where the putative father has acknowledged paternity and has agreed to the entry of his name in the registration of the birth. In many cases such putative fathers come to the office of the Registrar of Births to sign the certificate themselves. However, it is possible that another kind of conjugal union is represented by the births registered in this column. Marriage by customary law is, as noted before, regularized by the presentation of a marriage payment to the family of the girl. In many cases this payment may be made in instalments over an extended period of time. Until this payment is complete, the union is not a marriage and, according to customary law, technically these children belong to the girl's family and are registered as illegitimate. It is impossible to know how many of these unions are later regularized by the completion of the marriage payment.[1] Of course, in terms of the law regarding legitimacy, these children can never be legitimized even if their parents' marriages are regularized, since, as we shall see, subsequent marriage of parents of illegitimate children does not legitimize a child.

Table 15 shows the number of all illegitimate births registered in the Western Area between 1961 and 1968.

Table 15. *Number of Children born out of wedlock in Western Area (1961-68)*

Year	Total Number of Registered Births in Western Area	Father's name given or signature present		Only Mother's name given	
		Number	% of all births	Number	% of all births
1961	5 554	1 036	18.7	1 406	25.3
1962	6 072	928	15.3	977	16.1
1963	6 660	980	14.7	1 010	15.2
1964	6 008	1 040	17.3	859	14.3
1965	6 819	1 145	16.8	1 022	15.0
1966	7 116	1 125	15.8	1 007	14.2
1967	6 449	872	13.5	1 064	16.5
1968	6 657	744	11.2	974	14.6
Totals	51 335[a]	7 870	15.3	8 319	16.2

a. The total population of the Western Area is 195 023 and represents 8.9 % of the population of the country (*1963 Population Census of Sierra Leone*, Vol. 1).

1. As mentioned, the registration of many births in this group includes the signature of the father of the child. In many cases these fathers are well-known professional persons who are already married. Their signature is their way of signifying their responsibility for the birth of the child. In such cases there is no question about the fact that the child is illegitimate.

Except for 1961, when 44 per cent of all registered births were illegitimate, the number of children born out of wedlock has remained around 30 per cent of all births in the Western Area.[2]

In Chapter Five the recent changes in the law regarding the maintenance responsibilities of fathers of illegitimate children were described. It may be that the slight drop in 1968 in numbers of children born out of wedlock where the father acknowledged paternity already reflects this change in the law which has drastically increased the father's financial obligations to his illegitimate children. Certainly, as we saw there, many more women are claiming this support under the Bastardy Act and lawyers note that the courts are more severe in imposing these obligations on putative fathers. However, as pointed out, women married by customary law seeking maintenance from their husbands come under this legislation and the increase in such cases could reflect larger numbers of such wives coming to court. However, all the evidence supports the general conclusion that most women who sue for support for their children under the Bastardy Act are unwed mothers. For example, the report of the Ministry of Social Welfare shows that unwed mothers represent by far the greatest number of cases coming to them about this problem. The Ministry's composite report for 1960-65 reads:

'Matrimonial: This included native customary marriages, 104 dealt with between 1960 and 1965. Most complaints were successfully dealt with, although some were incomplete because of lack of co-operation from one side. The women reported chiefly for conciliation, maintenance or applied for the custody of their children.

Affiliation or Illegitimacy: 438 cases were reported and dealt with. Most of these unmarried women complained of non-maintenance from the putative fathers of their children. Few of them requested social security when in danger of molestation or maltreatment. Much difficulty was encountered in securing maintenance when affiliation order was not in force' (Composite

2. Very few data are available to make meaningful comparisons with legitimacy rates in other countries. An attempt by the United Nations (Saario 1967, pp. 7-9) to produce comparative statistics on the problem of illegitimacy produced unsatisfactory results. This is hardly surprising in that there are differing bases for determining legitimacy and for compiling statistics, and the registration of births is incomplete in so many countries.

Report for period 1960-65. Typewritten report for circulation within the Ministry of Social Welfare).

An affiliation order is the legal assignment of paternity. The comment on the difficulties in securing maintenance where an affiliation order is not in force refers to the increasing tendency for men to dispute paternity. Because of the prestige associated with large numbers of children, formely it was unthinkable for a father to avoid acknowledging a child as his own. However, as noted before, this kind of dispute is becoming more and more common. On the other hand, it is probable that many disputes over paternity result from attempts by women to impose the responsibility for their child's support on the man most able to afford it, when paternity is unknown. Awareness of the advantages of having a child by a financially able man is reflected in the Krio saying, 'It's only a rich man who gets children' ('*Na gentry man de bɔn pikin*'). A lawyer told me about just such a case:

'More men are denying [paternity] now. I even handled a case in Bo before I came. A friend came to me saying, "Well, I have been in love with this girl. I believe I am responsible for the first issue but this second one I am not responsible for. I have now married my wife and she is in Freetown. The first child whom I perfectly believe I was responsible for is with my brother attending school. I am responsible for him and so forth. But this one I suspect that this woman was pregnant before she ever came to me – although I interfered with her. She is trying to play upon my simplicity and so forth because I love her."

There is no proof. The only thing to help is that he happens to have caught letters this woman wrote to her [other] boyfriend ... My friend has got all these letters which he is presenting to the Magistrate. So the woman is in a very difficult position before the Magistrate.'

Although the tendency to deny paternity to escape financial responsibility for an illegitimate child may have intensified as a result of the change in the law and the wider knowledge of the right of unwed mothers to claim support, the illegitimate child has come to pose a much greater threat than simply a drain on a man's monthly income. It is not possible to ascertain how many illegitimate children are fathered by married men. To have directly asked the persons in the professional group, if they had such children would have produced considerable resistance. I did ask them if either they or their spouses were financially responsible for any children born to them outside the marriage and 24 per cent indicated they were. In view of the extreme sensitivity of the topic, we can be quite certain that these results do not exaggerate the numbers of persons who have children outside marriage. It does not, however, tell us how many children are involved. For example, one wife admitted her husband had one child *before* their marriage, (wives view this as quite a different problem from the child born out of wedlock after marriage), but I learned from another relative that this same husband had nine children born outside *since* the marriage. Two christenings of his illegitimate children took place while I was in Sierra Leone. Another husband had seven outside his marriage: such examples are not unusual.

While it is not possible to know how many children born out of wedlock are fathered by married men, it is generally assumed in Sierra Leone that *most* of them are. At any rate, the present social and legal status of these children in Sierra Leone directly hinges on the threat they pose to monogamous statutory marriages.

The social position of the child born out of wedlock

The Creole population in Sierra Leone very early accepted the idea of Christian monogamous marriage. It is safe to say that missionaries made acceptance of monogamous marriage the most important symbol of conversion. Rejection of traditional (i.e. primitive) ways, the chief emphasis being on rejecting polygamy, became significantly bound up with status and position in urban life. It cannot be over-emphasized how the fashioning of one's family life along the lines of the western model of marriage came to have a profound importance in supporting the Creole's, and later the educated Provincial's, image of himself as educated and civilized.

Nevertheless, the deep-seated traditional desire for large numbers of children continued, and today still has importance for prestige and status. Men establish liaisons with women outside marriage and have children by them in addition to those produced within their marriages. These women have to be referred to as 'outside wives' and their children as 'outside children' (Baker and Bird 1959; Crabtree 1950; Izzett 1961; Jellicoe 1955; Little 1967a). There is a considerable difference of opinion as to whether or not this practice is more common nowadays than during the early years of the Colony. Many refer to the 'Victorian' quality of life then, and note that formerly the girl who produced an illegitimate child was deeply disgraced in the community as well as within her own family circle. One woman, an 'outside wife', told me how she lost her position as a teacher in a prominent girls' secondary school when she became pregnant. Others believe that advances in women's education which now allow more women to be economically independent, and the increased security afforded unwed mothers through the recent legislative changes, have simply greatly lessened the stigma attached to the role of the 'outside wife'. In fact, today it is not uncommon to hear university girls state that they do not intend ever to marry. Sometimes one even hears married women discussing the position of these 'outside wives' in quite admiring terms, as in the following comments.

'Over the last ten years this practice of being an outside wife has become more and more approved. These girls are secondary educated, my dear! They have several children. I admire them, I really do. Why, the courage they have *and* they are independent! But, of course, they are not safe. Safe? Well, that is they have no one husband to care for them. They are not married. Those fathers [the fathers of their children] could go off and leave them at any time. But they have a kind of courage, these women. You can't trust men anyway [even if you are married] so they can't just sit down. They want to get a family. These children will take care of them, someone to bury them. Everyone wants to have someone to bury them, to do things to her only a woman can do for her.'[3]

Nevertheless, there is considerable evidence that women who bear illegitimate children impair their status in society. The highly abusive Krio phrase, 'It's the girl with the sympathetic bottom who gets the illegitimate child' ('*Sorry hat bomb na in dae born bastar pikin*') suggests that the responsibility for this problem rests on the girl involved and reflects her tendency to be promiscuous. Women who bear illegitimate children seriously jeopardize their chances of ever marrying.

3. These remarks emphasize the importance to women of having children, whether they are married or not, and suggest at least two reasons for their importance. First of all, a woman in particular relies on her children for support in her old age. Secondly, there are certain responsibilities associated with death, such as washing the body, which are preferably assumed by one's daughter.

Although Sierra Leoneans may readily admit that the women who bear illegitimate children suffer from loss of status, they contend that the children themselves are not stigmatized. After all, as I was frequently reminded, children in Africa are always welcome, regardless of the conditions of their birth. It is possible to examine the extent of legal discrimination which illegitimate children suffer, and I shall do so shortly, but it is not so easy to determine the degree of social discrimination they face or the psychological damage they may experience as a result of their position in society. For every example I could find illustrating the social disadvantages attached to being illegitimate, someone could counter with an example proving my example to be quite exceptional. However, the following case does illustrate many aspects of the social condition of these children which were found to be very common:

'I had just completed an interview with Mr. H., a professional who held a high administrative post in one ministry. I was about to leave when he asked, "Will you use names when you write about your research?" After being reassured I would not, he asked me what I did about people who lied to me. Before I could answer he continued, "I want to be very sincere with you. I lied to you in the interview. I don't want you to publish any lies so I had to tell you I lied. Now what are you going to do with my questionnaire? Are you going to throw it away?" The man was extremely uncomfortable and embarrassed at this confession. I asked him if he wanted to talk about it.

"I told you [in the interview] that my father and mother were married in the church. Well, what if I told you now that they were not married at all? Well, they were not. Before I was even born my father went off to America to study for twelve years. While he was away he stopped writing to my mother. A long time later my mother married my stepfather. He rescued her. When I was in secondary school they decided to change my name to his. It saved a lot of embarrassing questions. I am one of those outside children we were talking about. My father is – [and he named a very prominent man in the community]. I am his only child. You know him, don't you? You can tell if you look closely at me. Everyone can see because I look so much like him. He came back to Sierra Leone after twelve years, but my mother had married. He had asked her to wait but it was so long and he hadn't written. She had met Mr. H. and he had *rescued* my mother. My father didn't try to take me back and he didn't support me. He now claims he tried to talk to my stepfather but that my stepfather avoided meeting him. My father also now claims that my stepfather demanded money before he would turn me over, but I don't know if any of these stories are true.

Once I had completed secondary school and was about to leave for England, I tried to visit my father in his home. His wife drove me away. Sometimes I visit my grandmother and my aunt [paternal relatives] but I am not welcome in my father's married home, even now. His wife could never have children. They have adopted two girls, daughters of her sister, so she is more worried about me coming around.

While I was studying in England my father visited me when he happened to be in London. However, he never helped me with my education. I don't think he was ever really interested in me and my progress.

I have been back from U.K. now for several years. I am married, as I told you, and have children. Recently, my father has retired and since then he has begun to come to visit me from time to time. He comes by on Sundays and sits down with us. He seems to want to be there and he likes the children.

But I ask myself why he visits me now? Would he visit me if I weren't in such a high position as I am in now? Would he want to see me if I weren't so high up? It was my mother who educated me with the help of my stepfather. My grandmother could have taken me in but she didn't. Why should he want to see me now? I think about this problem all the time. Why should he want to see me now when all those years he didn't care what happened to us?"

Simply to recount this man's words fails to convey the degree of emotion involved. At many times during the conversation he was nearly weeping. I asked him if his wife was aware of how deeply he felt about this matter. He admitted he had never before in his entire life talked to anyone about his feelings towards his father. "But", as he reminded me, "I just had to be sincere with you since you would have published my lie." '

Not only does the girl who has a child out of wedlock seriously jeopardize her chances of ever getting married, but the status of being illegitimate may also affect a girl's chances of marriage. Family background is one of the chief considerations in the choice of a wife. One informant noted how the status of being illegitimate is considerably more critical for a girl than for a boy. A boy may overcome this handicap through educational and occupational achievements, but, as he said, 'A girl is more subject to the rules, and her chances of marriage are still determined mainly by her family status. These determine her eligibility for marriage.' He believed there was no doubt that a girl tended to identify strongly with the social position of her mother. He illustrated this by going over his genealogy. He showed how those women in his family who had been borne outside marriage tended to perpetuate the system by becoming 'outside wives', raising children for other men.[4]

Whether or not the educational and occupational opportunities of illegitimate children are affected by their status is also difficult to establish. The willingness of fathers to maintain their children and to pay their school fees varies widely. However, the teachers with whom I discussed this problem believe that outside children often have more difficulty in school. Sometimes they find themselves in the same school or even the same class with their half-brothers or sisters, with certain attending stresses. The married woman and her children are accorded the highest status and sometimes schoolgirls and boys try to hide the fact that they are outside children. As one university girl, who was an outside child, put it, 'By hiding you give more respect to the wife. Outside children are second best.'

Relationships between half-brothers and sisters are often strained. One man confided that his father had eight outside children. He only came to know about them when he went to secondary school and discovered several other boys in the school with his name. His mother explained the situation and warned him to have nothing to do with these children. He said that even now, as an adult, he is the only member of his family who, if he meets his father's 'outside wives' or their children on the street, will greet them. All the others strictly avoid all contact with their half-brothers and sisters.

The child born outside marriage is usually deprived of a close relationship with his father. One university student spoke about her

---

4. Subsequent research also showed many of the unwed mothers suing for maintenance in the magistrate's court had mothers who were also unwed.

own experiences. 'When I needed my father to talk about some problem, he was never there. He never came around at those times when I really needed him.' It also makes a difference if the mother of the illegitimate child has other children by more than one man, which is common. As another university student described her experiences to me:

> Her father had ended his relationship with her mother when she was three months old. He went off and married another woman. He never provided for her support. Her mother never married but she had five other children with another man. This man supported his children until he died. This girl complained that these other children didn't respect her because her own father had deserted her. When I asked about her attitude towards her father she responded: 'I just don't know why he went off and left me with that [referring to her mother] woman.'[5]

The relationship between the outside child and the father's wife is most likely to be fraught with tension. Quite understandably, wives hold markedly different attitudes towards the illegitimate children born to their husband before marriage and towards those who arrive afterwards, although their legal status is the same. From the man's viewpoint, the ideal arrangement for the care of his illegitimate children is when the wife allows him to bring these children home to be reared. Such arrangements are described by one informant who himself had outside children. Referring to the practice of rearing illegitimate children in the married home, he noted that:

> 'It happened more regularly in my grandfather's generation than it does now, it is true. In some cases, I am thinking of a particular case here where the wife is what you call really masculine,[6] the husband may be afraid to bring the outside child to the home. In other cases, where there was competition between the wife and the other woman for the husband and the husband chooses the former [meaning the husband continues to see the other woman] the wife may refuse for the child to come home.'

But, apart from these isolated instances, generally speaking once

5. The feeling of loss when deserted by one's father is doubtless increased by the fact that in Sierra Leone children are traditionally thought to belong to the father.
6. By 'masculine' this man means 'domineering'.

the wife knows about the existence of the outside child before or after marriage, the outside child comes in.

You notice that I am stressing the wife. The important person here is really the wife, not the husband. Generally speaking wives are very much accommodating out here. When the wife accepts the child there is hardly any discrimination. Take my own case, Jean [his daughter], it was my wife who made the reception when she got married the other day. I was in England, but she made all the arrangements for the reception. She got the champagne. She did everything exactly as she would do for her own daughter. I was away in England and my wife did everything as though I was there.'

Another husband illustrated how this whole process of bringing the outside child home to be reared might come about by telling of a friend's experience.

'A friend of mine was married to his wife and they had lived together for fourteen years – no issue. Then this fellow, well he said, by accident, he went out and got a child. Soon the outside woman was in the pregnant state and the gossip got to the wife. She got to know about it. And one morning my friend was running up to me. He said, "Bob, I'm in trouble. You know what happened? Round about 3.00 a.m. this morning my wife woke me up and said, 'You, I want to talk to you on a very important matter.' Well, he said, being of guilty in his mind, he thought of nothing else than that one. So his wife said, "I hear you have a woman outside, expecting for you. Don't deny to me if it is true. I don't mean trouble." He said that at first he wanted to deny, knowing our women in general.[7] But the way his wife spoke to him he was impressed. So he confessed and said, "Yes it is true. I have been making up my mind how to approach you on the matter."

The wife went on to ask for the woman's name, address and all that. She told him in the morning she would go and find the woman.

So he came to me when I was out walking. He came up to me and said, "Bob, I'm in trouble." I said, "What is it?" He said that his wife has heard about the girl and she told him that she is going there and he doesn't know what is going to happen.

7. In other words, he knew how Sierra Leonean women usually react to such news.

Well, to cut a long story short, the wife went to the woman,
introduced herself and embraced the woman. She forced her
husband to be supporting the woman. In fact, at the end of
every month the support that was agreed upon was given to the
wife and she took the money to the woman. Until she gave birth
and she took an active part in it. When the child was about seven
months old she used to go there every morning, take the child
from the woman and bring the child to her own home. In the
evening she goes there and takes the child [back to the mother]
and goes home. As soon as the child was weaned, she took the
child into the house and she cared for the child.

You know what happened? By the time the child was eleven
months, the wife was expecting! And that was the beginning of it.
She had four other children and with this one that she took from
outside. If you went to the house you would never pick out the
one which was hers and the one which was not, in fact, hers.'

Such wives are held up as models of the perfect wife. One story
has become almost a legend among the men in Freetown. This story
concerns a certain well-known and accomplished professional woman
who is illegitimate. The story goes that her father's wife, a 'big' woman
in Freetown, heard about the existence of her husband's illegitimate
child who lived with her own mother on the 'worst' street in Freetown.
One day this wife went to get the child. When the people living on the
street saw her coming, they were afraid and waited in their houses to
see what would happen. This 'big' woman is described as striding into
the street and shouting in a loud voice, 'I have heard that my husband
has a child and that the mother is living on this street. I have come to
take the child to its father's home. Bring the child to me'.

According to the story-tellers, the mother fearfully crept out of her
house with the little girl, handing her over to the wife. Men, reciting
this story, dwell on the tender care lavished on the little girl. They
point to her accomplishments now that she is a grown woman and
remark how but for this kind, motherly, and understanding wife,
Sierra Leone would have lost the benefit of her talents.

What about the attitude of a mother who loses her child to the
married home? Why does she agree to such an arrangement? Men
simply brush aside these questions. Such a woman knows only too
well that her child's best interests are served by being with the father.
In the case cited earlier, where the wife took the infant after seven

months, the mother was 'compensated' and permitted to visit her child. Furthermore, as noted before, it is the general view that children belong to their father. One former social worker considered this question:

'First of all it really depends on the kind of woman who has the child and how she is situated. She may be sensible enough to say "Look I have this child, I have not money to take care of it. Mr. X. is the father of the child and he can afford to maintain it. In the interest of the child shall I let him go and give him a chance of a better life? Because if he is here with me and I have only £5 a month regular income, would that be sufficient for rent, and food, and transport and school fees?"

Sometimes men do "pinch" their children away from these mothers and then the children really do suffer.[8] Sometimes the wife may try to persuade the mother by saying, "It's my husband's child. Are you willing to give up the child to us to give him a better chance in life? I don't mind taking the child but the only thing, don't keep worrying the child's life. Don't come and visit, let the child settle down with no questions." '

A professional man discussed the relationships between his 'outside' child, his wife and the child's own mother. I had asked him whether he informed his wife of this child's birth.

'It is difficult, of course, to tell your wife. She asks you if it is true and at first you say no and afterwards you say yes. There is a quarrel and then she accepts it. Then the child comes [to visit the married home] and says, "How do do, mummy" and that type of thing and the wife, she says, "How do do" and she has accepted. It is finished.'

I asked how the relationship is explained to the child:

'No, the child doesn't need an explanation. The child comes up in tender age thinking that she has got two mummies. One with the daddy and the other one at home. That is why the child does not come over. And even when the child comes over she realizes that she has got two mummies. In some cases I know of the child calls the wife, the stepmother, "Mummy" and calls its own mother, "Auntie". We have a tradition here that you realize, of

8. The problem of fathers snatching their children away from these mothers comes up frequently in the case records of the Ministry of Social Welfare.

calling all of our relatives, "Auntie". She [the child] equates the status of her own natural mother to the status of a relative. If she is not properly taken care of [he meant not reared in the married home] it is "Auntie" that she is going to, but it is "Mummy" who is at home'.

Even if the illegitimate child is accepted in the married home and reared by the wife there may be serious problems. Some wives admit it is difficult to treat these children as their own. Often husbands force their wives to take the child and wives give vent to their resentment in their relationships with the child. And 'outside children' may reason that punishments they receive from the wife, represent discrimination against them, 'You treat me this way because you are not my real mummy'.

However, probably only a minority of illegitimate children are actually raised in the married home. As one man put it, 'There are two kinds of wives: the understanding kind who accept the child and the *majority* of women who are adverse to outside children.' Women tend to regard the former type of wife unfavourably and make such comments as, 'She is a fool to do it. *I would never do it.*'

Certain abusive phrases bear out the fact that the child born out of wedlock has an inferior social position. For example, to use the phrase, 'You are born a bastard' (*'dis basta pikin yaso'*) or to say 'You were born without a coat at the back of the door' (*'Yu bɔn yu nɔ mit kot behɛn do'*), meaning there is no father in your house, is seriously abusive.

The church also discriminates against illegitimate children. Christenings for children born out of wedlock cost twice as much (five shillings) as christenings for legitimate children. And, in most churches, such christenings may not take place on Sunday, only on weekdays. The rule of reserving Sundays for christening only legitimate children is sometimes relaxed if the father of the illegitimate child is a prominent man.

Attitudes towards husbands' extra-marital affairs

In interviews with the professional group and the university students both men and women ranked arguments over men's extra-marital affairs as the greatest source of marital conflict. These extra-marital relationships are perhaps *the* most significant factor influencing the organization of the family. Despite the widely ramifying and disruptive effects on their marriage, men continue to establish liaisons and have children outside marriage and women appear to accept them as inevitable. As one man put it:

'... I think that the whole thing is that inherently in the Sierra Leonean man, inherently he is a polygamist. I think inherently I am. Speaking for myself and I have thought about it, I think inherently I have got a polygamic germ in me. It isn't that this woman [referring to his girl-friend] is better or more sociable than my wife, but men just go about because they are polygamous-minded.

Men may not want to face it, particularly those who are Christians would not want to face that they are polygamous at heart by nature.'

I asked this man if he thought Europeans were different from Africans in this respect.

'I think the European man is really not polygamous. He is not. I have come across a good number of them. Perhaps I have just come across the wrong type but I don't think you get people [in Europe] who are polygamous.

We do read about the film stars and the number of women they get married to. We read about those [and] about people who run away with little girls eighteen or nineteen, but those are the exceptions. I do feel that is why they catch the public eye.

Out here, if for instance, I had three or four sweethearts, it would not be in the papers. Even if I was going about seeing them in official hours, etc. But in England if the Minister of [he named his own post] had two or three sweethearts and was going to see them in official hours, you are going to find it in the personal column of some paper.

People [here] generally accept these things. I mean I don't say I do that, but it is the attitude in the community. I don't say polygamy is a good thing. The only thing is I think that it exists and there is no point saying something which exists and is basically not wrong – I don't say it is good, but there is a vast difference between goodness and wrongness – I don't see why it should not be recognized and legalized.'

Men's extra-marital sexual relationships cannot be understood without appreciating the status associated with large numbers of children. Despite the trouble which may be occurring within the marriage as a result of the birth of an outside child, a man will be receiving congratulations from his friends and even from his relatives who usually welcome the new addition to the family. Further, it should also be noted that unmarried women achieve considerable prestige through unions with educated men. Unmarried girls, particularly those who cannot hope to get married to high-ranking men in the community, are often quite willing to become their mistresses or outside wives, rather than to marry men of their own social position. As one former social worker pointed out:

'Well, if they don't want to get married to the kind of man who would like to get married to them – you see it may be a man of the same or lower status to themselves – they think it is better to be the mistress of Honourable so-and-so, than to be the wife of a carpenter. They will have their own status in their own social set-up. She would probably be better dressed than her other friends because Honourable so-and-so would be able to give her £10 to £20 more than the other girl who has a carpenter or who has a works foreman. So that would reflect in her appearance and will put up a big "spree". For them it is the status, temporary though it might be.'

The combination of the 'polygamic germ' together with the social ambitions of unmarried girls have resulted in a situation which has drawn considerable unfavourable attention:

'Dear Editor: First of all I must congratulate Kongosa Bench[9] for taking such a keen interest in the situation surrounding the behaviour of our girls and those who eventually become child mothers as a result of their own fault or otherwise.

I was very much moved by the question, "How can we curb it a little?" This is no doubt a burning question lurking in the mind of all serious minded parents, teachers and religious leaders.

... If we are to curb this kind of disease in our girls I feel something ought to be done with those big men, married men at that, who roam our streets in Mercedes Benz and Admirals. These men intice young innocent girls with money and luxuries. They even build castles for them with sugar coated tongues and when the

9. 'Kongosa Bench' is a regular column appearing in the Sierra Leone *Daily Mail*. 'Kongosa' is the Krio word for gossip.

obvious happened, the girls are left holding the baby whilst the men continue their chase for others.

In this way misery has been brought on many houses, as the parents are left to bear the heart-break because of the disgrace which is often said, "their children have put them".

But what happens to these Big Men? They are in Freetown and hold key posts so therefore can do any wrong. Nobody dares say anything against them. The big bosses take advantage of girls who are badly in need of jobs – what a state of affairs.

. . . As things are, our young girls have no protection from the state. But, of course, those who should or are expected to give that protection are the offenders in the first degree' (Letter to *Daily Mail*, 17 July, 1968, entitled "Shocking Report – We need Legislation").

But despite such criticisms, not only men but married women seem to accept the situation as natural and few girls enter marriage expecting their husbands to be faithful. In interviews with the professionals I asked for a response to the statement, 'It is unfair for a wife to expect her husband to have sexual relations only with her'. One would certainly not expect any accurate measure of either attitudes or behaviour from such a question; the discussions following this question were of more interest to the inquiry. But despite the inadequacy of the question, 15 per cent of the women immediately responded that they agreed, they would not expect sexual fidelity. Another five per cent thought they would only tolerate sexual infidelity if they had no children themselves. The responses of the Creole women compared with the Provincial women showed significant differences: only 9 per cent of the Creole women agreed, compared with the agreement of 29 per cent of the Provincial women. Among the university students 23 per cent of the Creole girls and 39 per cent of the Provincial girls agreed with this same statement. This difference between the attitudes of Creole and Provincial women in the professional sample may reflect a greater acceptance of the 'polygamist nature' of men by the Provincial women compared with the Creoles, who have been under the influence of Christian ideas for a longer time. But more likely it reflects a quite different matter, an issue directly related to the fears that Creole women share regarding the legal status of illegitimate children. I turn to this question shortly.

As suggested, women's tolerance of men's sexual infidelity is related, among other things, to the general attitude about the importance of children. No one can envisage a successful marriage without them and, although a few informants suggested fostering children as the only alternative, the usual attitude is that childlessness fully justifies a man having them with another woman. However, one Mende wife expressed the ambivalence most wives feel about the matter:

'If I were unfortunate not to have a child in my marriage, I think I'll adopt a child. It is quicker than having someone your husband is loving and that is always ending in failure. They [the outside wives] will walk into your house and say they are already having the child and you have nothing.

Well, they [villagers] are having their own customs, but we in this town – we usually say that now we are civilized. We don't go much into the customs of the village. Here in this town if you take your husband's girlfriend she will want to equalize herself with you and pretty soon she will think she is the wife and you are the second missus. That is why people in this town do not accept these girlfriends or these children. Always these mistresses look down on the wife.

... Well, it is up to the father to decide if he will accept the child. As for me, if I am unfortunate enough to allow my husband to have a child outside, I will not accept it. [That is, rear it] *I will not*. That would be a difficult position. The child's mother would be interested to know how you are getting on with the child and she would always want to come and see the child. I don't know for other[s] but I wouldn't accept it. If he wants a child [outside] he can do whatever he wants for the mother but don't include me in it. I won't accept it.

[Regarding the financial position of the outside woman and child] They take you to court in this town and you just *have* to pay. You just have to be responsible and that puts the wife in a difficult position. When you have to give something to your own wife and take some more to give it out to the other woman. I don't think it is really nice to have a woman who is bringing forth children and then go and have another one. You just give yourself unnecessary responsibility. For my own part, if I was a man and I got a wife and she has not got a child I just have to tell my wife, "We stayed for quite a long time. Will you allow me to let me have a child out?" If the woman allows, well fair enough because you want a child and you have not got one from her. Don't you think it is really nice?'

The terrific conflict between awareness of the importance of children and the difficulties associated with having them outside marriage is shown in the responses of the men and women in the professional group and among the university students to the statement, 'If a marriage does not produce children a wife should be understanding and allow her husband to have children outside' in Table 16.

Table 16. *'If a marriage does not produce children a wife should be understanding and allow her husband to have children outside' (Percentages)*

		Males		Females	
		Profes-sional	Student	Profes-sional	Student
Agree		54	64	43	56
Other (only with the wife's permission)		9	1	13	2
Disagree		36	31	43	41
No response		1	4	1	0
Totals	%	100	100	100	100
	No.	85	142	72	87

To appreciate fully why illegitimate children pose a growing threat to the marriages of Sierra Leoneans we must now turn to the legal status of these children and the story of a recent attempt to revolutionize their position in the society. In a sense it can all be summed up in the Krio saying, 'Before the body is even cold, the fight for the property begins' (*'Di bɔdi nɔ kol yet, dɛn dɔn bigin fɛt fɔ propoti'*).

The legal status of children born out of wedlock

'In construing this will, regard must be given to the intention of the testator, a Sierra Leonean, whose will follows the pattern of most Sierra Leoneans in wanting to preserve their properties as a family property *for as long as possible.*'[10]

10. George *v.* George and Four Others. Sierra Leone Court of Appeal, 13 March, 1967 (Civil App. No. 20/66). (My italics).

This comment made during the settlement of a disputed will leads us immediately into the key concern which makes the outside child such a threat to the married woman and to her children, namely property and inheritance. In Sierra Leone, under the present law, illegitimate children have no inheritance rights from either of their parents, although today *most people think they do!*

The question of the legal status of illegitimate children became the subject of public debate in 1965. A bill was drafted by members of the judiciary which would have eliminated the notion of illegitimacy and equalized the inheritance rights of all children.

Copies of the proposed bill were sent to the Bar Association, the National Women's Federation, and to leaders of the various church organizations, for discussion and consideration. There were radio broadcasts and articles in the press devoted to an explanation of the aims of the bill to the general public. A remarkable furore arose over this issue.

Sir Albert Margai, the Mende Prime Minister, publicly supported the bill and was accused of being its author. Critics said he had instigated the bill primarily to justify his own chaotic marriage situation. Sir Albert is a Catholic but, in addition to the wife he married in the church, he also has children with women whom he has presumably married by customary law. Moreover, his interest in the bill was construed as part of a general effort to corrupt Christian Freetown society with the traditional 'primitive' practices of the 'natives' of the Provinces. The controversy over the proposed legislation shifted immediately into the political sphere. Sir Albert Margai's popularity with the Creoles had already waned.[11] Opposition was so effective that the bill was dropped before it ever passed draft stage and was never brought to a vote before Parliament. Nevertheless, the widespread publicity given the entire controversy has had important and continuing social consequences.

Although it is quite true that Margai was a keen supporter of the proposed legislation, it is not true that he was the author or even the one to initiate an attempt to pass such a law.[12] Interest among members of the judiciary arose from quite a different source.

11. See Kilson (1966) for a full discussion of the political events leading up to this period.
12. I had the opportunity to discuss this proposed legislation with Sir Albert Margai in his home in London where he now lives in political exile. He dismissed

In 1962 the United Nations Sub-Commission on Prevention of Discrimination and Protection of Minorities was authorized to undertake a global study of discrimination against persons born out of wedlock (Saario 1967, p. 183). This commission circulated an outline for the collection of information about the position of children born out of wedlock among member nations. The collection of these data began in 1963 and extended over the next two years (Saario 1967, p. 184).

When members of the judiciary in Sierra Leone set out to provide the information requested for the United Nations study, they were confronted with an impressive discrepancy between what they *thought* to be the social status of illegitimate children and their present legal position. They had been asked to:

> 'Indicate whether the social status of persons born out of wedlock is inferior to that of persons born in wedlock (on any grounds such as ethical standards, religious ideas, the social concept of the family, etc.). Indicate also whether the fact of being born out of wedlock has any effect on membership in a religious community. Describe any other important aspect of the problem' (Saario 1967, p. 184).

Sierra Leone's response to this question was simply to state, 'Generally, no distinction [exists] in political or religious life between persons born in wedlock and those born out of wedlock.' ('Answers to United Nations Questionnaire. Persons Considered to be Born out of Wedlock': typescript copy from Attorney General's Office). Again, the inquiry asked, were any distinctions made with regard to public rights or access to social services? The response in the report from Sierra Leone was unequivocal: 'There is no discrimination against persons born out of wedlock.' Even if lawyers sincerely held these statements to be true, their subsequent review of the legal status of these children for the study revealed quite a different picture.

As noted above, in Sierra Leone a person is considered to be illegitimate if his parents were not married *at the time of his birth* under one of the marriage Acts or by customary law. There is no way for a child born out of wedlock ever to acquire the status of a legiti-

---

the idea that efforts to pass the law were dropped because of the extreme opposition that arose. He said the more difficult and pressing political events had to take precedence at this time.

mate child, not even by the subsequent marriage of his parents.[13] In such cases where a decree of nullity is granted, any child who would have been the legitimate child of the parties to the marriage, had it not been dissolved, is considered to be their legitimate child. Although annulment of marriage does not make a child illegitimate and there is no specific procedure of disavowal of paternity, a person may be declared illegitimate by an Act of Parliament, or the question may be decided incidentally in deciding a claim to property or other legal rights, or in proceedings for maintenance.

With reference to the question of family relationships, the child born out of wedlock has no legal familial relationship with his mother, although the law makes her liable for his maintenance. He is also not legally related to his father, but if paternity is established the father is liable for maintenance. There is also no legal relationship between the illegitimate child and the relatives of either his father or his mother.

An illegitimate person has no surname by inheritance although he may establish one by reputation. Nationality depends 'principally on descent from a father and a father's father of Negro African Descent who are or were citizens of Sierra Leone' and for this purpose the term "father" includes a natural father.'[14]

A child born out of wedlock acquires the legal domicile of his mother at birth, but he has the possibility of acquiring a domicile of choice when he is of age, just as does any other person.

Although the mother of an illegitimate child has no legal rights to the custody of her child, the court recognizes a blood relationship. The court is governed by equitable rules and so, in equity, regard must be paid to the mother, the putative father and to the mother's relations.

13. This discussion referring to the laws about the status of the child born out of wedlock is drawn from a typescript copy of the report to the United Nations. 'Answers to United Nations Questionnaire. Persons Considered to be Born out of Wedlock' prepared by and obtained from the Attorney General's Office.

14. This definition of nationality included in the report to the United Nations commission stems from a parliamentary decision regarding its membership. The Afro-Lebanese, that is persons having an African mother and Lebanese father, are viewed as a growing political and economic threat within Sierra Leone because it is believed there are many such children now being educated in the Lebanon. It is feared they will return to Sierra Leone as Africans with a 'Lebanese mentality' and take over political control of the country. Nationality, for the purpose of limiting membership of Parliament, was defined in this manner.

The court has the power, however, to appoint someone else to have custody of an illegitimate child.

The mother of an illegitimate child must give him a mother's care and nurture and must not neglect or abandon him. She may not conceal his birth (an offence by statute) and she must maintain him until he is sixteen, or in the case of a girl, until she marries. The putative father may be compelled to contribute to his child's support by legal proceedings.

An illegitimate person has no right to inherit from either of his natural parents although there is no limit to what may be given him by will. However, unless there is clear indication to the contrary, the expression 'children' in a will is construed as referring to legitimate children only.

The position of children with regard to inheritance rights under customary law is very similar to that of children under the statutory law.

'(a) *Legitimate Children:* Children born in wedlock belong under all circumstances to their father and are heirs to his personal property which includes houses and plantations.

(b) *Step-children:* are children of a woman's first husband. They are usually left with their father's family. Such children can under no circumstances inherit any property from their stepfather. They can only inherit property from his own father and father's family. [sic]

(c) *Adopted sons:* A man can adopt a child as his son. The adopted son has no rights to the family land of his adopted father. He can only claim rights to the family land of his (biological) father.' (Massally, A. J., Police Magistrate, Kenema, Sierra Leone. 'Questionnaire on Points of Customary Law', December, 1964).[15]

15. This pamphlet was prepared and distributed among some Paramount Chiefs in the provinces. It was an effort on the part of its author to discover how 'customary laws as affected by social and economic changes are being administered by the Local Courts'. Massally states: 'The need for such a guide has, in my view, become apparent in view of the fact that appeals from Local Courts now lie to Courts whose judges have been trained in a different Jurisprudence. Secondly, Lawyers are now for the first time allowed to plead before these appellate Courts on appeals from the Local Courts on matters affecting customary laws' (p. 2). The pamphlet is described and was circulated as a questionnaire, although, in fact, it makes statements about the content of customary law as in the above case.

The attempt to eliminate illegitimacy

So we see that in a society where it is contended that the illegitimate child faces 'no social discrimination', he certainly does suffer considerable legal discrimination. Although he may assume Sierra Leone nationality, he has no legal relationship to either his own parents or their relatives, he has no surname, no inheritance rights, and he can never be legitimized. It is little wonder that members of the judiciary sought to remedy the situation with new legislation. They drafted a bill which would have eradicated legal discrimination against children born out of wedlock. The government newspaper published an article headlined:

'BID TO END ILLEGITIMACY IN SA. LEONE. All Children of Sierra Leone citizens formerly regarded as illegitimate will become legitimate when a New Bill to this effect is passed into law' (*Daily Mail*, 3 September 1965).

It should be noted, however, that the provisions of the proposed legislation were *not* intended to be retroactive. That is, the present number of persons in the population born out of wedlock would not be legitimized under its provisions. The aims were stated as follows:

'The object of this Bill is firstly to declare all children citizens of Sierra Leone born after its passing, to be legitimate; and secondly, to provide that the children of parents who subsequently marry under the Civil or Christian Marriage Acts or outside Sierra Leone shall, if the father is resident in Sierra Leone at the time of the marriage, be legitimated as children of the marriage. The Bill also provides a person legitimate under the laws of another country by the subsequent marriage of his parents shall be treated as legitimate in Sierra Leone if his father was domiciled in that country at the date of the marriage. The remaining sections deal with the effects of legitimation with regard to the succession to property and also with the right of [il]legitimate children who have not been legitimated to succeed to the property of their mother and the corresponding right of the mother of such illegitimate child to succeed to its property. Finally, the Bill provides for children of all citizens of Sierra Leone who are born after the date it becomes law, to be regarded as legitimate. There is a provision however to the effect that nothing in the Bill when enacted, shall affect the operation before the commencement of the Act, or affect any rights under intestacy of a person dying before the commentcement of the Act' (From a typescript copy of the Bill supplied by the Attorney General's office).

The supporters of the Bill argued that the notion of illegitimacy itself was an evil by-product of Western influences. For example one Sierra Leonean wrote an article which appeared in *Flamingo* magazine:

'Good news for the kids – and possibly for their mothers too! Sierra Leone is going to wipe off one more stigma from its social life, which has been one of the ugly relics of the colonial past! – the stigma of the "illegitimate child".

The impact of Western civilization on this part of the continent brought with it certain advantages and disadvantages. For closely tied up with its religious influences was the doctrine of "one man, one wife", which was meant to provide some security for the women.

Western civilization in Sierra Leone particularly, did not recognise any child born out of wedlock. The right of parenthood became a question of challenge and so started a new generation of unwanted children labelled by law, illegitimate.

While this problem may not have been so acute in Ghana and Nigeria, because of the strong desire of their peoples to preserve their own basic traditions [,] for the settlers of Sierra Leone's former colony area who had not only imbibed a lot of Western culture but had also become completely detribalised, there was hardly a place for the illegitimate child. At least, the law did not recognise them. And this influence has spread in Sierra Leone' (Bangurah, 1965).

The argument that the whole notion of illegitimacy resulted from western influence and was not part of traditional African society is not actually true. There is sufficient evidence which indicates that illegitimacy is not a foreign concept in traditional culture.[16] However, the emphasis in traditional society seems to be on 'illegal' sexual relations, since generally all women who are past puberty are married. Further,

16. For example, among the Mende '*bi pueloi*' is an abusive term meaning 'you are a bastard'. *Poae loae* is the Mende term for a son of an illegal sexual relationship. *Wan ka pure* also refers to any child born of illegal sexual relations. The practice of burying the umbilical cord of a new-born child in the father's village is carried out by all the indigenous tribes of Sierra Leone and it is the father who buries it. When the father is not given the cord it is one indication that the child is not his legitimate child.

it seems that legitimacy in traditional society is of most importance with regard to succession and inheritance, particularly in contests over chieftainship. Otherwise, there seems to be relatively little evidence of social discrimination against the child conceived under these conditions. But Provincial informants say that if a person is accused of having been born as the result of an 'illegal' sexual relationship he would just have to leave his village.

Concern over inheritance and succession has considerable effect on relationships within the traditional household and it continues to do so in the household of the couple married under one of the statutes. The status of the legally married wife is analogous to the position of the head wife in the polygamous household.[17] Ideally, compared with her husband's other wives, the head wife enjoys the position of highest prestige and authority. Ideally, her son should inherit the position and property of his father. But more often the father does not get round to considering the question of succession until he is old and then he is often likely to name the son of his favourite wife. She may be the most beautiful, youngest and most recent addition to his household. Women depend almost entirely on their sons for support and security in their old age. Thus, since the choice of who will succeed the father remains an open question until the father's death, competition and rivalry among wives for favour for their sons continues over a very long period. However, in the case of the woman married under the statutes the question of inheritance was thought to have been resolved, once and for all. Only the children of this union could inherit from the father, unless he happened to make a will which very clearly excluded them or included other heirs such as his illegitimate children. But, as we saw in Chapter Five, this is not true except for those persons whose personal law is statutory law.

Through a statutory marriage a woman secures a position in society of considerable prestige. She cannot countenance the suggestion that any other woman should have the right to infringe on her position. Most of all, she jealously guards the privileges and position of her children. It is intolerable to her to think that the contributions she makes to the building-up of family property will be dissipated to the illegitimate children of her husband. As women often asked, why should these women (the mothers of outside children) who have done

17. Baker and Bird (1959) make the same comparison.

nothing for the husband over the years except drain away his monthly earnings, suddenly gain from the inheritance that would come to their children? It is little wonder that wives were adamant in their opposition to the Bill.

While women do recognize the obvious injustice to illegitimate children resulting from their present inferior legal status, rather than make legal changes which threaten their own present status and their children's future, the members of the Women's Federation recommended that the problem should be attacked at its source:

'Women's meeting adopts resolution. WOMEN DEPLORE BIRTH OF UNLAWFUL CHILDREN. Sierra Leone's National Federation of Women's Organisations have passed a resolution calling for a reduction in the number of unlawful children born in this country' (*Daily Mail*, 31 August, 1965).

Not surprisingly, the church organizations of Sierra Leone also bitterly opposed the proposed legislation, on the grounds that it would destroy the sanctity of the Christian home. The Bar Association, who also opposed the bill, did so on the grounds that it was a very inadequate way of attacking the problem of revising family law. Acknowledging the need for such reform, they argued it would require much more thought and consideration than the authors of this measure had given it.

In my interviews I asked people to respond to the statement, 'A man's inheritance should be divided equally between all his children, whether born within the marriage or outside.' Table 17 shows the results:

Table 17. *'A man's inheritance should be divided equally between all his children born within the marriage or outside' (Percentages)*

		Males		Females	
		Profes-sional	Student	Profes-sional	Student
Agree		75	57	50	49
Disagree		23	40	48	49
Other		1	2	2	1
Totals	%	100	100	100	100
	No.	85	142	72	87

The professional men clearly favoured equalizing the inheritance rights of all their children. Even though women were divided in their view, the overall response to this question suggests that perhaps a sufficient margin of professionals might have voted in favour of the bill had it come to a vote.

Even more interesting than the response to the question is the fact that the respondents *thought* they were being asked to express an opinion on a law already in effect! Almost without exception the informants answered the question and then patiently explained to me that this was now the way the law stood in Sierra Leone. I was informed how legislation was passed a few years ago which provided just such inheritance rights to all outside children. Only lawyers (not even their wives) and a very few other professional people in the sample realized that this attempt to reform the law had been dropped. The publicity surrounding the issue apparently had had considerable impact on them but they had not followed its development. The Administrator General reported his experiences with clients who came to him about the distribution of an estate. He told me that time and again widows had come to his office about the settlement of their husband's estate assuming that it would be divided among *all* his children. 'You can imagine their relief, he said, 'when they discover the law was not passed!'

As a result of the belief that the law had been passed, quarrels between couples over husbands' extra-marital relationships have increased. Perhaps this belief, together with the stiffening of the maintenance laws for children born out of wedlock, has encouraged men to avoid pregnancies in these outside relationships, as I found that married men were far more likely to be using contraceptives (or encouraging their use) with women outside marriage than with their wives.[18] Perhaps the belief that this law had been passed, which increased conflicts within households over outside children, had already begun to decrease the number of children, fathered by married men, born into this stigmatized social category.

The authors of the bill that would have eliminated the legal discrimination against children born out of wedlock must have known they would encounter fierce opposition from some groups. Never-

18. These matters will be considered in more detail in Chapters Nine and Ten.

theless, they must have also been convinced that such legislation would bring the law into line with general social practice and would be supported by the majority.

In view of the numbers of children born out of wedlock and the extent to which it appears that they are socially accepted, obviously the present law relating to illegitimate children in Sierra Leone does not represent the values and practice of the society as a whole. Rather the law as it stands protects the interests of a tiny segment of the populaiton (the Creoles and educated, Christian Provincials) who have identified their superior position in the society with the practice of Christian monogamous marriage. Restricting the inheritance rights to the legitimate offspring of such unions avoids dispersing economic resources to a wider group, permitting a couple to build up and control wealth and property. This small group of persons wields tremendous power and influence in the country. Such findings severely challenge the view of the relationship between law and 'consensus norms' as Fallers (1969) discussed it.[19] Instead these findings reveal a very close connection between the law and political power. Barnes (1969) also found this relationship in his examination of Ngoni Native Courts.

'Each subculture provides its own set of legal norms, and within a plural society the norms of one segment may conflict with those of another. The important characteristic of plural societies is, however, not the mere diversity of legal norms and other aspects of culture. Characteristically, one segment imposes, or endeavours to impose, its norms on other segments that do not accept them but are coerced into partial conformity' (p. 102).

Perhaps the belief that legal systems are completely insulated from political factors, or our 'Utopian model' as Barnes (1969) puts it, has obscured investigation into the manner in which political power is maintained and manipulated through legal institutions.

In Sierra Leone we have seen how the dispute over the legal status of children born out of wedlock exposed a number of conflicts of interest between opposed segments of the population. It revealed the political struggle between the Creoles and the Provincials; the con-

---

19. It should be observed, however, that there were serious conflicts of norms *within* the group opposing the bill. On the one hand, all children were welcomed. On the other hand, building up the family assets and limiting the number among whom they may be distributed was a matter of even greater concern.

flicting systems of status and prestige as represented by the traditional society and that of those who try to follow western patterns; the conflicts between men and women as women seek economic security for themselves and their children, and husbands seek prestige and status through having many children; and the opposition between married women (or 'principal wives') and unmarried mothers in their separate struggles for economic security and status. It is noteworthy that both those who promoted the bill and those who fought against it, in order to buttress their arguments appealed to values imposed during colonial rule. On the one hand, supporters blamed western values for introducing the idea of illegitimacy, creating a group of persons who are discriminated against. On the other hand, those who rejected the bill defended their position by appealing to Christian ideals regarding the sanctity of monogamous marriage.

Moore (1970), cited earlier, noted that laws are passed because legislators presume they will affect behaviour. As she points out, laws do not always have the intended effects, but the observation of behaviour after a change in legislation may help us to know more about the relationship of beliefs to social action. Although the attempt to change the legal status of children born out of wedlock failed, the people who would have been most affected by its passage *believed* that the law had been passed. The result is a kind of experimental situation which is fairly unusual in social research. Those who fought the bill presumed its passage would have a detrimental effect upon Christian monogamous marriages, encouraging promiscuity among married men and an increase in outside children. It appears, however, that they were quite incorrect in their assumptions.

We have seen how the publicity surrounding this attempt to eliminate the concept of illegitimacy and equalize the inheritance rights of all children led to the belief that the law had been passed. This belief, together with the stiffening of maintenance laws, resulted in an increase in paternity disputes. Paternity disputes were unheard of in traditional society, since every one welcomed more children in the family. The threat to the inheritance rights of legitimate children increased tension between married couples over the practice of married men establishing extra-marital liaisons. Men have become less eager to father illegitimate children and have even begun to use or encourage the use of contraceptives in their relationships outside marriage although, as will be seen, they are less willing to encourage their wives to use them. Finally, the belief that the law has been passed has effectively eroded the former sense of security married women had in what was unquestionably their superior role *vis-à-vis* other women in the society and particularly in relation to the 'other women' in their husbands' lives. This insecurity has had a far-reaching effect upon marriage relationships and is central to the understanding of many aspects of the organization of family life. Before turning to the examination of relationships between husbands and wives we will first look at courtship behaviour among young educated Sierra Leoneans. As will be shown, the expectations about marriage which are built up during courtship are in rather dramatic contrast to the situation women find themselves in once they have married.

7

Choosing a marriage partner

'If mared na lɛk pam wain, yu go tes an fɔs!'[1]

The time required to complete a western education has afforded the occasion for a dramatic change in relationships between young men and women. Traditional culture provided no guidelines for the behaviour of young women who were unmarried. Intensive training in domestic skills in preparation for marriage was given in the *Bundu* society and girls were initiated into the organization shortly after puberty.[2] The period of seclusion in the 'society bush' could last up to a year or more.[3] Shortly after graduating from the society, girls, presumably still virgins, were handed over to their husbands who had previously made arrangements with their families.[4] Today all this has changed. Even the *Bundu* society has accommodated itself to school calendars, initiating girls during the holidays. The period of seclusion has been drastically shortened, in some cases to a matter of days, and the educative function of the society has almost disappeared. Instead of marrying after leaving the society, schoolgirls return to their

1. 'If marriage was like palm wine, you would taste it first'.
2. The *Bundu* society (or *Sande*, as it is called in Mendeland) is a closed association for women which exists in most parts of Sierra Leone. Muslim Creole families initiate their daughters into the *Bundu* society although other Creoles do not. For a description of the organization see Little 1967, pp. 117-130.
3. A special enclosure is built for the girls during their training. Part of the time they are completely isolated from all contact with the villagers. Later, they may work in the fields and move about the village but they are clearly identified by the clothes they wear and by the practice of rubbing their skin with white clay so that men know they must not approach them.
4. This is not to suggest that the girls have absolutely no voice in the choice of their husband. There is an occasion while they are still secluded in the bush when they have the opportunity to confirm their willingness to accept a prospective husband. However, one can be very sure that strong pressure would be brought to bear on the girl who hesitated to agree to a partner her family strongly favoured.

classes. Since schools are located in the larger towns, most young people spend their schooldays away from the direct supervision and authority of their family.

Creole families who are Christian have always had the several years of their daughters' adolescence to contend with. However, if they lived in Freetown it was not necessary for them to leave home to attend school. The rules for the correct behaviour of unmarried young Creole women have always been very strict. The heavy obligation for rearing a daughter with an unblemished reputation falls on the mother and other female relatives, a duty which is taken very seriously.[5]

However the problem of supervising the behaviour of unmarried young women is approached, the phenomenon of adolescence has provided a fertile ground for the enthusiastic reception of western ideas of courtship. Today young people expect to have the right to choose their own marriage partner and on the basis of western ideas of romantic love. This is not to suggest that traditional ideas about the roles of husband and wife, the importance of family opinion and the criteria for selecting a spouse have no more influence. As will be shown, young people must somehow resolve the conflicts between traditional ideas about these matters and contemporary values. Many of these conflicts arise because of the new ideas about relationships between unmarried men and women which they form during the years they are pursuing an education.

Today almost every girl who has some secondary education would prefer to marry a man with professional qualifications but unfortunately there are very few such men compared with the number of aspiring young women.[6] To succeed in marrying a high status husband requires that a girl should conform to a very exacting pattern of behaviour, but the rules for this are ambiguous and sometimes contradictory. As one university girl remarked when discussing the question of premarital sex, 'In order to get a good husband you have to be good, but you also have to be careful not to be *too good.*'

5. From the onset of a girl's menstruation some older female relative in the family, often her grandmother, takes the responsibility for checking on the regularity of her period.

6. As noted earlier, a girl may decide it is preferable to establish a relationship with a married man in a high position and even to bear his children than to marry someone of her own or a lower social position.

Criteria for selecting a spouse

University students, both the men and the women, indicated that the most important factor in choosing a marriage partner is being in love. They also place a strong emphasis on physical attractiveness. Naturally ideas on this topic vary widely, but both men and women are very conscious of western ideas of beauty. This concern is borne out in a newspaper article which questions that there could be any international standards:

'... Various opinions have already been voiced, especially in Africa. There have been quiet disagreements as to how a woman's beauty should be judged. Simply because the way an African looks at a woman's beauty very much differs from the way a European or Oriental looks at it.

... A European has his own tastes of a woman's beauty as has [the] man from the Orient. It would be sheer pretence for the different people to agree on a particular white, black, yellow, or red girl and judge her as the most beautiful' (Sierra Leone *Daily Mail*, January 6, 1968).

However, few men agreed with the ideas represented in this article. Most girls on the campus were slim and conformed with western standards of the ideal feminine figure and most men stated that this was their preference.

There is a remarkable emphasis upon fashionable dress among Sierra Leonean women. Almost all secondary school and university girl students wear western styles and many also affect western hair styles or wear wigs. Their interest in fashion keeps the sewing machines of Freetown buzzing. Articles in the local press are often devoted to discussions of fashion. Although the introduction of the mini-skirt faced a rather stormy protest in some quarters, articles on the woman's page in the local newspaper favoured this style. Many articles also stress the importance of a woman's beauty and how to dress to attract men.[7]

---

7. Beauty is emphasized by traditional society as well. When girls graduate from the *Bundu* they are presented before the entire village dressed in their best. The songs and speeches on this occasion stress their attractiveness as, for example, the song sung by the women: 'If I had a daughter as beautiful as this one, I would be madly happy'. See also Little 1967, p. 118, for his observations on the western style dress of village girls graduating from the *Bundu*.

'It is a woman's beauty that determines most of her future successes. It is the one thing that brings almost everything under spell as though touched by a magic wand. A woman's beauty attracts a string of men to bow to her charms and ask her hand in marriage. In many cases, beauty makes women rich. Look at the film stars and winners of beauty contests' (Sierra Leone *Daily Mail*, January 6, 1968).

The title of another article in the Sierra Leone *Daily Mail* posed the question 'How do Men like to see women dress?':

'... I have discovered that the vast majority of women haven't the slightest idea of men's preferences ...

Men love long hair. But that is hardly news to us. I am willing to concede that a girl must move with fashion and so make one small point. The texture of a girl's hair is more important than the length. Women like their hair to look well. Men are concerned with what it feels like. They hate sticky lacquer. Oddly enough, they don't mind wigs and false hair pieces. But, they warn, false hair must match the natural hair and it must be anchored firmly to the head. It is embarrassing they say, to have girl's hair come away in your hand.

... Men don't like evening skirts. A woman always look strange and formal in a long skirts. In fact, long skirts make a man feel shy. Besides, he is always terrified he will treat [tread] on it and rip it to pieces.

... Men disgust (sic) women in evening trousers. A woman may wear trousers in the daytime for convenience but she should try to look as feminine as possible in the evening.

A few men go for bell-bottomed trousers, most of them prefer the more shapely trews. But all men agree that women with large bouts should never wear trousers at all.

... They say we look sexy [in] lacy stockings. Never on fat legs, they say.

... Men love perfume. The like to associate particular scents with particular women. But don't overdo it, they warn. A tantalising whiff is much more effective than an overpowering dose' (March 9, 1968).

Although most people agree on the importance of romantic love as the basis for marriage and on the desirability of choosing a spouse who is physically attractive and who dresses fashionably, university students have specific ideas about the other characteristics necessary in a prospective spouse. Those criteria represent a combination of traditional and contemporary values. Family background is a chief consideration. It is important to know if there is any insanity or some other weakness thought to be inheritable in either family, and checks are made as far back as genealogical knowledge allows. Sometimes an old relative will remember some quarrel which occurred between members of the two families several generations earlier and this ancient dispute will be used as an argument against a marriage which would unite them. As one student said, 'If a family discovers anything adverse about another family which occurred as long ago as fifty years, they will say no to a marriage between them.' Being of the same religious faith, which students ranked as being an important consideration, is a requirement strongly associated with a good family background. This is especially true among Creoles.

It is very difficult for a girl to rise very far above the social reputation of her family except through very circumspect behaviour. On the other hand, a man may be judged more on his individual achievements than on his family background. Women regard a man's standard of education as very important and they prefer their husbands to have more education than themselves. Of course, education and occupational opportunity are closely associated with financial standing. Over half the girls ranked wealth as a very important criterion in the choice of a spouse, while only 16 per cent of the boys in the university sample indicated this was important.

A young man will also be interested to know the standards of discipline under which his prospective bride was reared. It is considered the family's (but especially the mother's) duty to train a daughter carefully for marriage. In Krio it is said, 'A child who does not learn his lesson from his mother will be trained in the street' (*'Pikin we nɔ de yɛri in mama in wɔd na trit go tren am'*). There are very strict ideas about what is the correct behaviour for a respectable girl. One woman summed it up, 'She should be respectful, kind to her sisters, good to her parents and careful in her relationships with men'. There are firm ideas about the general deportment of women, especially when they are in the presence of men. They should be quiet and never argumentative when they do speak. One student said he had immediately dropped a girl-friend after she had dared to discuss politics with his relatives.

It is not acceptable for a girl to have more than one boy-friend at a time. If she is seen going out with a different man on different nights, it is assumed she is a prostitute. As one woman commented, 'That is the *only* thing our society really believes in. And men are always watching.' Standards for the proper behaviour of a young woman emphasize all the Victorian qualities of womanhood. People are very conscious of these standards for judging character and, when a girl's name is mentioned, comments are often made about her reputation in the community. Everyone is very interested in the behaviour of un-married young women.

A man prefers the woman he marries to have less education than he has. One man conceded that the wife of a professional man should have *some* education:

'The wife with no education will always be a bit insecure. At least she must have a primary education. Like my wife – she has her primary and [also] teacher's training and one year at Fourah Bay College. Well, she has a job now and she is almost a professional person. She can feel secure.'

Although men want to marry a girl with some education, the man who marries one with more education than he has had may well be the one to feel insecure, as this student explained:

'Well, as far as I am concerned I would not be for marrying a village girl. If I had a girl-friend here [at university] we would understand each other better. As for a village girl, I would just run after her and get married, but I would not understand her as much as I would a student here. In that case I would prefer, well, I must have my own education above her own. There must be that gap. Why? Well, I am basing this on our own African ladies. Because it is my own frank opinion – say we are on the same footing and the man is earning £60 per month and the woman is earning £60 per month. It would only need a financial crisis to come up in the family and it will soon be said that "I earn £60 per month". But say you are earning about £60 per month and the woman between £20 and £30, then that man really definitely knows that she is earning money but not up to the same amount, so that gap is really there . . . I think that the husband having the higher education is better, that is the way I feel about it.'

The expression of reluctance to marry a girl with a university education is a stronger tendency among Provincials than among

Creoles, who have had a longer tradition of educated women.[8] It was noted earlier that men fear that marriage will be unstable when a wife has too much education. Most men expressed strong feelings about this potential threat to marriage. They say that educated African women do not know the limits of a wife's authority in the home. Men often complained that while educational or economic equality might work in the West or even in Sierra Leone if the wife was of European background, their own African women do not know how to handle it. According to these men, African women are so accustomed to being subservient to their husbands that when they achieve equal qualifications or income, they lose all sense of proportion.[9]

We have seen that only a quarter of the professional men were married to women with university degrees. One of the first university-educated women in Sierra Leone, an accountant, is single. She told me that the men in her class at Fourah Bay College often told the girls they would never marry a woman who had a university degree. She reviewed the list of those women who graduated with her and noted how almost all of them were still single. Today university girls recognize that men fear to marry highly educated women. As a result, very few of them aspire to occupations requiring more than a first degree and some claim that, after graduating, they want to be hairdressers or secretaries. Perhaps it is their awareness of the few opportunities to marry men of their own or a higher educational level which influences not only their career aspirations but also their social life while still at university. Many of them are accused of having men who are already married as boy-friends, and usually these boy-friends are high-ranking civil servants. Certainly the wives of the professionals regard university girls as their worst competitors. The following article from a college newspaper outlines the problem as seen by the young men on campus:

8. The university students were asked to respond to the statement, 'It is preferable for a wife to have no more than a secondary school education'. Most of the men agreeing were Provincials (19 per cent Provincials as compared with 8 per cent of the Creoles).

9. It should be noted that my data do not support the findings of Little (1966a) who found secondary school students favour *equal* education for marriage partners. His data were gathered from secondary students who may not have been considering the question of wives having a university education. Further, his questions were slanted to investigate attitudes about companionate marriages and his sample was very small, including more women than men.

'*LATI HYDE ON THE MOVE:*[10] It is true that Fourah Bay College offers boundless and limitless opportunities to everyone to become anything – from a prostitute and madam Dracula to a virtuous and honourable person. Do we need a campus code of ethics? Of course, we have it. In a nutshell it is: "Winner takes all, God dam the loser" and "all" means all the boys around the campus who come their way. God bless the madam Draculas!

Our girls care less about international ethics, good morals, and even good home training. To quote . . . she said, "the boys up here are immatured". To show her fellows that the boys are really immatured she has decided to fall in love with a married man. The man even comes up here with his official uniform to visit this . . . [girl]. Well I am glad you have found a matured man. I wish you luck.

When the boy friend of Miss D. D. got married sometime ago, I thought that was the end. But to my surprise, a car was sent for her to attend the ceremony. It is believed that the boyfriend will divorce his wife very soon to go steady with her. Can't our girls be reasonable. Is it because of the legal head behind this affair? The boy pays visits frequently and both of them usually go for a drive. Have a conscience madam.

Would you like your lawful wedded husband to treat you like your boyfriend is treating his wife? What are your prospects with the boy? Think and decide.

Our girls really like married men. [It] is believed that a former first lady of Lati Hyde is also in love with a married man. Whether the boyfriend is unaware or not is difficult to tell. But, one thing is certain, the girl knows how to play her cards.

Another blistful disclosure came few weeks ago, when it was rumoured that two of our girls slept in the house of a married man. Whatever they may think about the idea, I say it is very bad. Think about your future in our society and not only the present!' (*The Clarion Weekly* mimeographed, no date).

Traditionally the virginity of a bride was a matter of utmost importance. Initiation into the *Bundu* society was regarded as the time of preparation for marriage and when girls joined they were examined to ascertain that they were virgins.[11] The time of seclusion in the

10. Lati Hyde is the women's hostel at Fourah Bay College.
11. A girl who was found to have lost her virginity was a source of deep

society was also thought to protect them from engaging in premarital sexual relations:

> 'Generally, before girls reached puberty or a little after that stage, they were initiated as members of the Bundo [*Bundu*] society. They stayed with the organisers of the society for at least a year, mothers preferred to leave them [their] daughters there until eligible bachelors asked for their hand in marriage. This they believed would keep them out of mischief for the time being and avoid the shame that they would have brought upon themselves and their parents. In this kind of "boarding home", under the strict eyes and guidance of the supervisors and the law that restricted boys around the area of this sacred society, they were considered pretty safe' (Deen 1968).

Although today the educative functions of the *Bundu* society have almost disappeared, the period of seclusion has been radically shortened and the notion that the *Bundu* society is a preparatory school for marriage has largely been lost, the idea that initiation into the society marks an important step into adulthood persists. One reason for the continued importance of the *Bundu* may be related to men's attitude towards women's sexuality. The popular explanation for the cliterodectomy (part of initiation into the society) is that it reduces women's sexual appetite, preparing them to be steady and reliable spouses. It is still considered very important that a girl be a virgin upon her initiation into the society. As one girl explained:

> 'We have a secret society and they check on us. I haven't joined it yet. I am afraid if I go to that and I am not a virgin then something will go wrong. It would be embarrassing because your parents would be very hurt. They should be proud, not ashamed.'

With such an emphasis upon virginity before initiation it is perhaps not surprising that girls assume that the freedom to enjoy sexual relations is part of their new adult role once they have graduated. Normally girls join *Bundu* when they are about fifteen or sixteen years old. But even village girls urge their parents to allow them to join *Bundu* earlier because they anticipate that the constraints on their sexual behaviour will largely be eliminated. Recognizing the tempta-

---

disgrace to her family. Society leaders could charge more for her initiation. A prospective husband could even refuse to go on with the proceedings.

tions that will be open to their daughters, some parents try to delay their joining the society until they are much older and some girls are initiated even after they have come to university. But once a girl has graduated from the society apparently most parents assume they can no longer control her. As one girl explained, her mother was not surprised to learn she was no longer a virgin, 'Because being educated she knows that at the age of twenty-three and in college she must expect that.' And another girl said:

> '. . . my parents still regard me as being a virgin. When I was in school, they would examine me anytime I went for holidays. They hired some old people to examine me. I told my mother and father I was not pleased with this because I was thinking at this time of making love and I knew they would examine me on holiday. Since I have been to college they have not done this.'

Another girl assumed that she had been encouraged to join the society as a way for her step-mother to check on her virginity before she went to university:

> 'My dad, because of his profession, he is not so interested in secret society. Before my mother was married to him, she was a member of a secret society, and even his sisters. I came to college when I just left school [and] my aunt's foster-daughter made me to be put into a society so as they could check my virginity.'

I asked this girl how she felt about it:

> 'Well, I didn't feel embarrassed because I *knew I was*. And if you want, you can bring your mother in and so be honoured.'

In the villages, the number of individual *Bundu* societies is increasing, largely as a result of the competition between older women who wish to form their own society in what is a highly lucrative avocation.[12] However, in view of the fact that only half of the Provincial men in the professional sample are members of the *Poro* and less than that (43 per cent) of the Provincial women are members of the *Bundu,* it appears that the importance of membership of secret societies among the professionals has lessened. Moreover, women appear to be less enthusiastic about their daughters joining *Bundu* than their husbands are. Only one-fifth of the Provincial women indicated they wanted their daughters to join *Bundu*. Among the Provincial men 42 per cent

12. Some small villages will have as many as three women heading their own societies. They compete with each other to get the girls to join their own group. Parents and suitors are required to pay these *Bundu* heads fees for their services.

preferred their children to join a secret society. A few of the Provincial men did express strong objections to their daughters joining *Bundu*, but only two of them thought they had even the slightest hope of keeping them out of the society because of pressure from the other more traditionally-minded women in their family circles.

The responses of the Provincial university students showed more enthusiasm for secret societies. Three-quarters of the Provincial men and 64 per cent of the Provincial women stated they would prefer to have their children initiated into a society. (Generally these Provincial students showed more interest than did the professionals in the preservation of many traditional customs.) The students were not asked whether or not they themselves were members; the topic is too sensitive to include a direct question about it in the questionnaire. However, from observations and personal interviews with a number of them, I concluded that most of the Provincial girls had already joined or would do so shortly. But even if initiation continues to be an important step to adulthood, the *Bundu* society can no longer guarantee a husband that his bride will be a virgin when they marry.

On the surface it appears that premarital sexual relations are quite generally accepted among young people. Students were asked if they thought it was important for a girl to be a virgin when she married. Forty-four per cent of the men compared with 14 per cent of the women in the university sample agreed that it was important. But although a man might prefer to marry a virgin, not many thought it was very likely they would. As one young man explained:

'I don't think that it is that important because you don't have virgins that much around. It is very difficult now to find a virgin by the time you get married. The girl you might marry has been in school up to when she is about twenty-two or twenty-four if she has to go to university. You don't normally expect virgins about then. No, it is not important.'

Although it may be thought difficult to find a bride who is a virgin, many girls still feel premarital chastity is worthwhile. As one girl put it, 'I wouldn't say it is very important to be a virgin but if I was married and not a virgin, it would hurt my pride.' And another said:

'I feel that my mother and father feel that it [premarital sex] is wrong. One of my aunts got married two years ago and she was twenty-seven and she was a virgin. I don't know whether I will keep as long as that anyway.'

But girls who maintain such personal standards often find themselves embarrassed to admit it to other girls who presumably are not so strict.[13]

> 'I don't think I should keep on saying it [that she was a virgin] because perhaps they won't believe what you are saying and then they feel you are trying to look down on them. So you just keep quiet. They laugh about it without knowing if you are or not. They keep on saying that you feel like you are out of society. They tease you and laugh at your boyfriends. They feel you are out of the way because you are trying to keep it that way.'

Whatever the attitude of other girls towards those girls who do avoid premarital sexual relations, some boys seem to appreciate them. Although a young man may be having sexual relations with other girls he may avoid having them with the girl he intends to marry. One such young man told me about his girl-friend:

> 'She is a virgin, I am convinced about that. I want her to remain a virgin until the time of our marriage. That is provisional, a kind of bond between us. If she breaks it, I will choose another girl.'

And another, referring to his fiancée, 'Yes, she says she is a virgin. I wouldn't like her any other way.'

Girls claim that they usually experience their first premarital sex with boys they think they will marry. Many reported having 'given in' to their boy-friend just before he went overseas to study since they would marry upon his return. Of course, 'clashes' sometimes occur and a girl may find herself having to explain how it came about that she lost her virginity to a new boy-friend. Quite understandably such explanations may be very difficult and the anxieties girls feel are expressed by one girl who even tried to convince herself the first experience hadn't robbed her of her virginity:

> 'The first one, I had it in August of 1967 two times before he went overseas. From then I did not have it till February 12, this past month, I had one with this [new] boyfriend. It was very

13. I invited a group of students to my flat after one pre-test of the student questionnaire to discuss some of the topics covered in it. When the question of virginity came up the girls quite freely talked about it before the boys. They laughingly pointed out the one of them who was still a virgin. The girl was not particularly attractive and the implication of their remarks was that she was a virgin only because she had had no opportunities to be otherwise. Understandably this girl was exceedingly uncomfortable and at one point almost contradicted them by saying maybe she too had her own secrets.

difficult, I felt pain. So I was wondering if I really had the first intercourse with the first one. We were discussing it. I think it was the first one I had in February.'

Boys, too, feel considerable ambivalence over the question of the relative importance of a girl's virginity. As one boy asked:

'Supposing you come across this girl and you are somebody who is not really particular about if this girl is a virgin or not. You are basing everything on true love. It is just true love that matters, but whilst you love this girl, she keeps on telling you she is a virgin. You have no way of proving that she is a virgin or not so you just have to accept. Then after marriage you discover that she is not a virgin. How would you feel?'

Another student described his relationship with his girl-friend who, at least at the beginning of their relationship, had been a virgin:

'My girlfriend, I have been informed two weeks ago that she is in love with a man I do not know. I went down last week and I checked out and I found that this is true. I have not really faced her. I don't really want to face her. I know she would be annoyed. I have no solution to that. He is an older man than me. He is working, he has a big car and all that. He stays in the same village as her.'

I suggested that perhaps the relationship wasn't a serious one and that maybe, after all, she was not having sexual relations with him. He asked, 'Well, supposing I found the information is true, what shall I do then?' I asked what he could do and he replied, 'Well, I will just give her up and look after somebody else.'

While many university girls are not casual about engaging in premarital sexual relationships and some boys practise self-control in their relationships with those girls they may marry, most men engage in regular premarital sex. They seem to divide girls into those who are seriously pursuing an education and whom they might possibly marry, and those girls who, for one reason or another, they would not consider marriageable. Most university men had their first sexual experiences at about seventeen years of age. The following responses to questions about this are typical:

'Seventeen years. It was a married woman. I was curious to know what it was like and then she indicated to me that she wanted to have a go so I did. I don't remember much about it now.'

. . .

'Eighteen or nineteen years. She was someone older. It wasn't her first experience. It was arranged by someone, another intermediary, someone else who arranged it. I didn't pay any money, not on that particular occasion, but she was expecting money later.'

. . .

'The time that I was intelligent enough to remember, about fifteen to nineteen years. It wasn't a girl friend, it was another girl. Actually, I was going on a census and I just had the urge that minute so I just paid money. . . . Well, I think she was married, I can't say definitely. Actually I asked her but she seemed reluctant but we offered her money, about forty cents. This was just my first experience. There was nothing to really gain from it so it was just a joke. I asked for my money and so she said, "Okay", and I said, "No, I am just kidding".'

. . .

'Seventeen years old. She was younger than me. It wasn't the first time for her. She was my girlfriend. You see, my boy friend was looking out for her, using her. He went abroad. I knew she had engaged in sex relations.'

. . .

'Fourteen or fifteen years old. She was older than me. She is someone who taught me how. One night my parents were out and so both of us came to the house. She called me in and asked me to do it.'

The question of premarital sexual behaviour is connected with the question of social attitudes towards any pregnancies which may result and the use of contraceptives.[14]

Although friendships on the university campuses tended to be divided on Creole/Provincial lines, only about a third of the students thought it was important to consider tribal background in choosing a spouse. Parents of Provincial students might prefer that they should marry someone of their own tribe, but few students thought it was a matter of serious importance to them so long as they married a *Provincial*. Often Creole parents *do* strongly object to their children marrying someone of Provincial origin. We have seen that most

14. The problem of children born out of wedlock was discussed in the last chapter and I take up the topic of the use of contraceptives in Chapter Ten.

Provincial professionals had married outside their own tribe and also that more Creole women had married Provincial professional men than Creole men had married Provincial women. As suggested there, with the shortage of professional qualified men, Creole women, given the choice, may find it preferable to marry a Provincial professional man rather than not to marry a professional at all.

Almost every discussion of marriage in West Africa notes the increase in the element of personal choice of a spouse and the reduced role of the extended family in marriage arrangements. (For example, see Omari 1963; Little 1966a, 1967; Mair 1969.) Certainly most young educated Sierra Leoneans consider the choice of a marital partner very much an individual matter. However, very few marriages *anywhere* in Sierra Leone are arranged without at least the tacit consent of the partners, although occasionally wives are still offered to paramount chiefs when they are quite young.[15] And, even in the most traditional setting, as pointed out before, the girl's consent had to be given before a marriage was consummated. Among the professionals I often heard of cases where family members made suggestions about the suitability of a certain girl, and the young man sought her out and courted her. There have been other cases where parents have sent or offered to send suitable brides to their sons studying overseas. And a few of the professional couples I interviewed had only met very briefly and had done their courting entirely by mail. But on the whole, these are very exceptional cases. Most marriages result from a period of courtship after the partners have met at a friend's home, at school or university, at a fête or some other social gathering beyond the reach of direct parental control. However, marriage in Sierra Leone is still part of a cultural context where the status and authority of elders is very strongly recognized. Family approval of the choice of a spouse is still important. Parents may pointedly remind a young person in Krio, 'Okra is never taller than the farmer' ('ɔkrɔ nɔ ba lɔŋ pas in masta'). In other words, a child never escapes from his parents' authority.

Sometimes this approval is requested simply as a token of respect

15. One chief explained how he handled this situation. He educated all these girls as far as giving them some secondary school education. After they had joined the *Bundu* society, they were given the opportunity to decide whether to remain in his compound as his wives or to marry someone else of their own choice.

for the authority of the family. Many couples meet and marry during the course of their studies overseas but they usually write letters to their parents asking them to approve. Although it does happen, very few couples completely ignore this responsibility or deliberately marry without at least a semblance of family approval. Sometimes families recognize their inability to control these decisions and relatives may be so impressed by the educational or economic achievements of a young man or woman that they feel inadequate to interfere in their lives to this extent. Approval may be coerced or only tacit, but no one feels very comfortable marrying without it or against the expressed disapproval of his or her family. The continuing social and economic structure of the extended family makes this a very important matter. One young man even mentioned how he would fear that his mother would curse him should he marry against her wishes.[16] The students in the university sample were asked three related questions about this topic and their responses show how uncertain they were when asked to compare the importance of love with the question of family approval.[17] These responses are shown in Table 18.

Table 18. *The importance of love and parental approval in the choice of a spouse*

	Total university sample	Agree Creole Students	Provincial Students
Love more important than approval	61 %	70 %	54 %
Approval as important as love	45 %	38 %	52 %
Strong disapproval more important than love	33 %	30 %	36 %
Total No.	229	90	136

16. The belief in the mother's curse and the role of the husband's mother in marriage will be discussed later.

17. The questions appeared at different points in the interview schedule. They were as follows: 1. If I love a person, I shall not be concerned with whether or not my family approves my choice of a marital partner. 2. When choosing a mate the approval of one's family is as important as the love a couple might feel towards each other. 3. If my parents strongly disapproved of the person I chose to marry, I would not marry that person.

It is clear that most students value the right to make their own choice of a spouse on the basis of love rather than on the approval of their parents. At the same time, almost half of them rated family approval as being as important as love in the choice of a spouse. The results show how much more concerned are the Provincial students than the Creoles with the opinions of their families in such matters. However, the responses to the last question as shown in Table 18 suggest that if the matter came to a real crisis both Provincials and Creoles believe they would be inclined to act on their own individual prerogative in their selection of a marital partner. There were no significant differences between the responses of men and women to any of these questions.

One very prominent Creole professional man told me about his own courtship and marriage which took place in the early 1930s. Before going overseas to study he had been engaged to marry a girl who had been for a very long time his family's choice for him. The arrangement had been highly satisfactory to both families, but just before leaving Sierra Leone he played a game of tennis with a young girl and had 'fallen completely in love with her'. He wrote to her during the years he was studying in England and made up his mind he was going to marry her, not his fiancée. When he finally arrived back in Freetown his family, his fiancée and her relatives met him at the pier. Without informing any of them, he arranged a private ceremony in a small church in Freetown, secretly marrying his tennis partner! In those days, he said, such action caused an enormous stir of disapproval in Freetown and he praised his wife for the way she was able to cope with the long period of hostility from his family. But, he said, there was never a happier day in his life than the day his mother finally gave the marriage her blessing.

There is a very strong value placed on family members being able to get along with one another. Relatives expect to be able to move in and out of one another's households, to receive and give hospitality, and to depend on each other in any emergency, financial or otherwise. Moreover, the couple may have to request family intervention should a quarrel or some other problem develop in their own relationship. It is considered very risky to attempt to make a marriage work without the good wishes of one's family. I was told over and over again that should a quarrel occur between a couple whose families had not approved of the marriage, or should the couple separate, no relatives would come round to assist. There would be no one for either of the partners to turn to and everyone would say, 'We told you so'. The traditional attitude of respect for the good judgement of older people also continues to be a strong motive for allowing families to express their opinions in the choice of a spouse. The attitude in Sierra Leone is much as the Grahams found it in their study of Thai family life:

> 'The young couple who marry without consent can hardly expect the securities of living with the older folks, financial aid in establishing their own home or aid, advice and comfort in meeting life's emergencies. They are on their own in the strange, and often threatening, world of married life' (Graham, Henry M. and Graham, J. K. 1958).

Other and more obscure factors may influence the choice of a spouse. As one young man put it:

> 'When I first meet a girl and during the first few weeks we see each other I watch very carefully to see how things go with me. If I have good luck or things are fine, I think, "Well, she is bringing me good luck." But if I start having troubles after meeting this girl I will say to myself, "This girl is bringing me bad luck, this isn't a good choice." Then I will stop seeing her quickly.'

Relations between the unmarried: courtship

Creole women have always enjoyed a considerable amount of economic and social independence, as education for women is almost as old as the Colony of Freetown.

> 'The independence Creole women enjoyed contrasted strikingly with Europe or neighbouring Africa. From an early age they roamed the streets as petty traders. With or without husbands they would venture up-country selling soap or trinkets; some had their own factories on the rivers, with a clerk to take charge in their absence. Some went to trade in the Gambia. Marriage ties remained loose or were disregarded. Mandinka women were said to sigh for Freetown where wives were "free" to leave their husbands. Men enjoyed the same freedom. Traders would bring from up-country children by their "country wives" to work as servants for their legal wives at home. One rich trader, a pillar of his church, died leaving eleven illegitimate children' (Fyfe 1962a, pp. 379-80).

Today Sierra Leonean women are employed in almost every sphere of life. Nevertheless it is generally assumed that the only reason for friendships between men and women is to facilitate sexual relations. The private lives of women who are active in public life but not married are looked upon with suspicion. If a woman is seen in the company of a man, it is assumed that a sexual relationship exists between them. Such attitudes have the effect of dividing women into three groups: those who are married, those who are young and un-married whose movements are restricted and under the strict sur-veillance of their relatives, and those who are single, employed, and who are more or less emancipated from family control. It is generally assumed that this latter group of women freely engage in sexual relations with the men they meet in the course of their daily working life. As a result it is extremely difficult for single working women to keep a respectable reputation and thus remain marriageable. Many of the young professional women live at home with their parents. They live very restricted lives, usually only moving about the town in the company of relatives. An item in one local news-sheet alludes to the general problem of the single employed girl:

'*Bang! Bang! What a Scandal?* If what has been decided upon by some sychophants in a particular department in connection with our Editorial for last Monday, May 5, is to be implemented, we hasten to ask: What a shame? What a disgrace – in the final analysis what a scandal for those scape-goats?

In our editorial on Monday, we started by asking "WHICH DEPARTMENT IS IT?" What we said about the department was nothing but a challenge to the Head of the department who thought he can use a government office as a brothel by being more interested in his so-called secretaries than the job for which he is being paid out of public funds. Amongst many other things, we said we will continue to embarrass him as long as he continues to head that department without changing his attitude towards his junior workers.

. . . So far, we await any action any idiot of any department will take against us in connection with that particular editorial. It would be reasonable if all heads of all departments in Sierra Leone should institute legal actions against us, other than one man gets up to say that the "RED CAP" fits him. The first head of department to take action against us will serve as a scapegoat and we will disgrace him to the end, regardless of what we are to sacrifice to fulfil our task against us' (*The Truth*, Freetown, May 9, 1969).

As shown in Chapter Six, there is widespread concern over the temptations open to young girls, and their increasingly lax morals. An article in the local press questions the propriety of girls having more than one boy-friend. This is only one of many press comments on what is described as a decaying society where morals, especially among young women, have become very loose.

'CAN A GIRL LOVE TWO BOYFRIENDS? We are worried. We show anxiety over the attitude of our young people – especially the attitude of our young women. And here, apart from anything, I must confess I find it hard to explain the differences between women and some of our present day girls.

. . . I have ventured to find out the reason why girls love more than one boyfriend. Don't ask me who say they do.

To answer this question I do not really know whether a girl who is said to be in love with more than one boyfriend understands the word love or in other words whether she really knows what she is doing or what she is after . . .

Fifty per cent of the girls I chatted with agreed that a girl . . . can love more than one boyfriend at one time but they put the pointer on the men and boys who they charge with acts which they said could give cause to a girl having another boyfriend.

They say the boys are unreliable and their pleasure is to move around with as many girls as possible without any intention of helping the girl friends mold a prosperous career. They said the boys are all liars and they tell fantastic stories which at first sight are believable.

After the heavenly sweet talks from the boys and all turned out to be false you are left at sea; wondering with disappointment that may ruin your entire career.

Therefore they agree that because of this, they justify girls who took such a line in love.

Twenty-five per cent say the reason, though they consider it immoral, that girls today don't actually love, all they are concerned with is money. They need expensive dresses which one and only boyfriend could not afford. They say these sets of girls do not actually love, but are only looking out for material benefits.

And they care less. All they need is money to buy dresses.

Of course such girls they say think little of their career and do not have anything to look up to. Perhaps most of them end up as prostitutes . . .

In some quarters, it is believed that the public plays another part in shaping a girl's career. If the girl is brought up in a community [where] everybody has more than one boyfriend through curiosity she may be influenced to follow on an exercise her rights in having even three or more boyfriends. These are some of the ideas I honestly got from my survey.

Here we welcome different ideas on the problem "Why do girls love more than [one] boyfriends?" Your ideas are welcome and we will publish all contributions' (Sierra Leone *Daily Mail*, May 25, 1968).

The main reason parents give for insisting on their daughter having only one boy-friend at a time is that, if she becomes pregnant, they will know who is the father.

'Career' as it is repeatedly mentioned in this article refers to *marriage* which is thought to be the only suitable aim for the serious young woman. The importance of achieving the status of being married is reflected in the Krio saying, 'It's just the ring that I want' (*'Na di riŋ nɔmɔ a want'*).[18] This phrase is thought to express the primary interest of every normal young woman. If couples have a disagreement during courtship a girl's family may warn her to be careful, 'Wait until you get the ring' (*'Weyt te yu get de riŋ'*). Such a girl would be admonished to avoid any criticism of her fiancée until she got him to the altar. Men complain that women are so intent on getting a husband they pretend to be docile and obedient, but as one man said, 'The moment they've got the ring, everything changes, they become dictators!' Another man, active in politics, referring to his girl-friend as his 'paramour', described her as behaving so sweetly now, but he said he was observing her very carefully and would continue to do so for a very long time because perhaps she was simply ambitious to become the wife of a politician.

So we see that young people, particularly young women, in Sierra Leone are faced with some serious problems. Every young girl would

18. Men may use this phrase sarcastically to describe a woman's attitude towards them.

like to marry and to marry someone of high status in the society. There are not enough such men to go round. The basis for selecting a spouse, while involving modern notions about romantic love, physical attractiveness, and the right of the individual to choose his own mate, also includes traditional criteria for assessing the suitable wife. These traditional values are almost impossible to maintain in the social atmosphere in which young women find themselves once they have entered secondary school. While these problems are common to adolescence in many societies, unmarried adolescence is a relatively new phenomenon in Sierra Leone.

One young newly married professional couple discussed courtship and some of their own experiences. Their case illustrates several aspects of modern courtship. They met when she was a student at Fourah Bay College where he was employed as a lecturer. He was a Provincial and since she was a Creole they both had difficulty in obtaining their families' approval of their plans to marry. While the husband did most of the talking in this discussion, the wife was also very interested in the topic and contributed more to the conversation than is usual for wives when their husbands are present. The husband began:

> 'When a boy and girl first decide they like to go out together the boy meets the girl *outside* the house. He doesn't go into the house. Before he can even come to the house he has to write and ask the father's permission. That is my experience. You know these mammies, they are difficult to deal with.'

He quoted a Krio saying which is said to describe the character of older Creole women to whom he referred: 'These mammies, they are sticky handed' ('*Den mami ya gena han*'), and he and his wife laughed. He continued:

> 'They don't let their daughters be *officially* engaged in love affairs so they [the boys] have to meet these girls in the street, at dances or at college. They start being friendly and this goes on and on and on until you both decide to get married. Some families never allow you in the house. You just have to write to the girl. I was never permitted to visit Gladys [his wife]. I had to go and stand outside and watch to make sure that her aunt was not looking at me very ferociously. This was before we were engaged.'

I asked when he was first allowed into Gladys' family's house and he replied: 'Not until last year, in August.' They both said that during their entire courtship Gladys' family had pretended not to know of it. The husband went on to discuss this masquerade:

'But they *were* knowing, you know. They all *knew* about it but they just wouldn't let me in the house. So when you want to see her [the girl-friend] you just have to be patient and bear to come outside and stand and wait. Some of them [the boys] will stand there whistling and calling for the girl.'

I asked what is happening inside the house when all this activity is going on in the street.

'Oh, since the girl is not allowed to go out, she is inside thinking of excuses. She may say, "Oh, Auntie, I have to get an exercise book from my neighbour, can I run for it quickly?" Auntie will say that she can *run* for the book. After that the man, this man who has been whistling or calling for the girl for two hours, sees the girl. She runs down and says, "I just told a lie, I am going get my exercise book, Good night." This is how they meet, or they meet in cinemas. Later on when you get engaged or be serious you write a letter to the parents and they ask the girl. Then they have to find out about the boy's family background. In Creole society they start digging into your background – where you come from, whether you believe in God and so on. I had to lie that I was a Christian. I had to be dragged to the church against my will to get married. I do not believe in all these ceremonies, but because I wanted to get married, I had to go along with them.'

I asked if Gladys, his wife, had known he didn't believe in all this.

'She knew, but she knew that if her aunt and uncle knew that would be against me getting permission. But, of course, I was already educated. I had a *big degree*, you know. The degree to them was the *most* important. I was already *up there* in the society. And my father was a chief and all of that sort of thing.'

His tone was very sarcastic and he emphasized how a Creole family would never accept a Provincial *unless h*e had such qualifications.

I found it difficult to believe that this husband had actually been prohibited from entering Gladys' home but both assured me that it was true; not until the engagement party did he walk into her home. The husband described what would have happened to him if before that he had just knocked on the door asking to be allowed in:

'They would throw dirty water on you, literally. They are very strict about their girls. They have very strict control of their children. It is wrong to think that children can be left to do what they want to do.'

Of course, I had noted many inconsistencies with this idealized view of such strict upbringing of girls and I questioned this couple about the many girls who get pregnant before marriage. The wife responded that this could *never* happen to a girl from a home such as hers, but the husband argued that it was happening all the time. He continued to describe their own courtship.

'We went through the whole engagement ceremony. Yes, we went through with the whole comical ceremony. Before that I wrote a letter to her parents in my very best English. I talked about how good I was in this letter. They never spoke to me, but they had been seeing me. I never spoke to them, either. I would pretend to be walking past and then, when they went into the house, I would stand and talk to her. So when I wrote to them, they knew me. I said that Gladys had been my girlfriend for over four years and I wanted to get engaged to her with a view to getting married to her immediately afterwards. I said I was a Temne and my parents were in Makeni. I did not tell them that I have over thirty brothers and sisters. I said I had five brothers! I told them about my family. I told them I have a B.A. and am going to take a Doctor's degree and am now about to go to London to do this graduate course.'

The wife then described how her aunts had sent the letter to her father who was living abroad and had also written to her husband to let him know they had received his letter and that the matter was being considered. After permission was granted the engagement party was held and after this, finally, he was allowed to come freely to the household. I asked the wife, 'What about the fact that you had this boy-friend for more than four years; was he never discussed among your parents or grandparents?' She replied:

'No, only amongst my sisters. It was never discussed otherwise in the family. In some families it is the practice that if a boy wants to start seeing a girl as a girlfriend, he must write to the father asking for approval. Then they are allowed to see each other. Before you go to see a girl you have to write to the father to ask his permission so he can give his consent or tell you that you cannot see her.'

She emphasized the strictness of her training:

'When I was a teenager, I was very carefully watched. I was not allowed to go anywhere. I had to just stay around the house. It was worse than boarding school. So long as there was any activity connected with school, you were allowed to go, but that was *all*.'

Throughout courtship the attitude of the girl's family towards her suitor, the letters for permission that he must write, the long waits outside her house to see her, all suggest that he is being tested to see if he is worthy of the girl. All this attention to the girl must also increase her sense of importance. Moreover, the boy who is courting gives his girl-friend extremely solicitous attention. Girls often receive gifts of money, handkerchiefs, dresses, jewellery, head-ties, and the like. Boys always give their girl-friends gifts on their birthdays and feast-days, if they are Muslims, and in any case at Christmas and Easter. Those boys who are able to afford it may take their girl-friends to eat in a restaurant or to spend an evening in a club. Girls also expect their boy-friends to remember their various relatives on such special occasions as a birthday. They may also ask him to donate some money for the cost of a new dress for a cousin. A crucial part of the image of a good husband is that he is generous towards his wife's family, and during courtship is a good time to establish his reputation for this! A young suitor is under great pressure to please her and her family in every possible way.

A part of courtship includes the writing of highly stylized letters filled with romantic imagery. The following collection of these letters provides considerable insight into the lives and attitudes of young courting couples. The following letter, written by a young man to a girl he was interested in courting, is an example:

> Fishes Love Water
> Boys Love Girls
> I LOVE YOU

Look before you observe
Observe before you venture
Venture before you engage
Engage before you marry
To the rose of my heart Reme,

After surveying the sweet contours of your face, I now make bold to put it down in writing that I love you with all my heart, and if you respond positively you shall have not have any cause to regret.

I am a Form V pupil at the Sierra Leone Grammar School, getting ready to take my G.C.E. O level and also form captain of thirty five pupils. This is just to show you that I am a responsible young boy who will take all possible care of you in the future.

If my request is granted, I would like to have your particulars and a photograph of you, the letter is to sweeten my heart before and after bed.[19]

Yours to be,
Victor

Sometimes girls initiate a correspondence with a boy they have met. Here is one such letter.

Let love represent
the date

In the garden of love where
two friends meet doing
nothing but x kissing x

    xx

          xx

Hello Sweet,

It gives me the greatest pleasure to write you this letter just to tell you that I love you with all my heart. I had wanted to tell you but I was too shy.

Till then its your darlilng
Doris

This next letter was received by a young man after he wrote to the girl expressing his love:

Dear Richard,

Thank you very much for your lovely letter written to me proceeding. I must say how sorry I am for not giving an early reply this I did Intentionally and was waiting for the result.

I did promise to give you my particulars which are as follows. I am sylvia Thompson born on the 21st day of July 1946 and of

---

19. By 'request' the writer explained to me that he was asking the girl for permission to fall in love with her and have his love returned. His request for 'particulars' includes information regarding her birth-date, age, hobbies, address, school, her place in school, the number of brothers and sisters she has, and whether or not her parents are alive. For obvious reasons all the names in the letters reproduced in this chapter have been changed. Otherwise, they have been exactly copied, complete with grammatical and spelling errors.

the above address. I then later attended the Wilberforce Rural School and afterwards the Y.W.C.A. Vocational school in which I was a foundation member and on the 23rd of July 1965 finished a four year cause and on August 12 appointed to work at Paterson Zachonis Stores Stationery shop as sales clerk.

My dad is a retired civil Servant of the Ministry of Works. He was an Inspector of Works. My Mum is a housewife. I have two brothers, James and Stephen (both married), Stephen is at present studying Telecommunications and James is working at the Liberian Embassy in Freetown. Then comes Victoria whom I am shure you know all about and my two Little sisters Felicia and Leila both attending the village school. Felicia class seven and Leila class five.

Before closing I wish to promise that I will be a true and faithful friend of yours.

That's all for now

It's
Affectionate
Sylvia

Here is another example of a girl's response to a boy's letter:

My dear Thomas,

I am very please to receive a missive from you telling me all about yourself. I thank you very much for all the nice things you have said I only hope you will put them into practice. As for me you have nothing to doubt I can assure you. As you have told me all about yourself I think it will be fitting to tell you all about myself.

My names are: Mary Doris Clarke

Date of Birth 29th March 1945. Schools. St. Joseph Convent Primary, and Freetown Secondary School for Girls. I left school in July 1963, after gaining my higher Grade Domestic Science Certificate. As you know I teach at Holy Trinity Boys' School Freetown. Hobbies – Dancing and Netball. I am a West African Methodist by faith and I attend Judea West African Methodist Church Wilberforce. I was baptised and confirmed in the Catholic Church as my father is a Catholic but there arose a dispute which led me to join the faith which I now hold.

My father is Mr. Albert Clarke who is presently in England reading law, he has been there for the past seven years.

My mother is Mrs. Fanny Johnson-Cole of North Kensington Maternity Hospital. She is a qualified Midwife, she has been in England for the past six years.

As you know I life with my grandmother and uncle. I have two half sisters Susana Clarke who is my elder sister and Daphne Johnson-Cole, my younger sister who attends F.S.S.G.

I have not got any recent photograph of myself, but I will let you have one soon.

Yours Affectionately,
Mary

N.B. Please excuse bad handwriting.

Young couples sometimes meet in the home of a mutual friend. In the following case, the young man asked his friends to interrogate the girl carefully about her past relationships with boys and inform him. However, the girl writes herself, giving him the information he had planned to obtain surreptitiously:

Secondary School Taima,
Via Mano
29th Jan. 1968

Hello Desmond,

Thank ever so much for your letter which reach me last week. I was at lost wondering who the Individual is before I came to know you are the person I cam across the other day I visited the Johnson's as you stated. You letter was amusing especially in a particular photograph which I shall reply in later paragraph.

The last time you visited us together with Mr. and Mrs. Johnson, Mr. Johnson heated [hinted] on the point about your affairs but we didn't finish our conversation as I was engaged with some domestic work where as he was in haste I support. The second time was at the time of my confirmation party, during the time he was about to leave he explained everything to me but I was indefinite in my answer as I wish a direct contact [from you] which you have done.

Your Interest in me based on love seems doubtful [in view] of you[r] request. You might answer this statement in a different way. Well it's clear that you won't expect a girl of my age and standard to be without a boyfriend, to be Frank it's impossible, as I won't expect you to be without a girlfriend. I don't think you will ever have a single girl. As you have made your answer impossible by making the point clearly at that if at all I have a boyfriend I should turn your request down it['s] okay. But I don't think I should hide from my shadow. I've got a boyfriend but not a lover (take note of the two words!) That your answer if its Okay or not solve your problem and reply to inform me about the result.

I needless say much as I've left you in suspend. How are you getting on with studies and with life? I hope fine and things are not tough. My address in full is Taima Secondary School.

Fondest love and best wishes, my regard to you, Mr. and Mrs. Johnson and friends,

Sincerely yours,
Glenna

Letters are not usually sent directly through the post; there is too great a danger they might fall into the hands of interested parents or other relatives. Instead, they are delivered by friends. This next letter points out the difficulties some young couples have in getting time to spend alone even on those rare occasions when they do meet.

Taima Secondary School
21st Feb. 1968

Dear Davidson,

Happy to report about my safe arrival at school. I had a nice and Interesting journey to school though I left loved once behind. I'm sure you were not please or happy as we didn't have a conversation or discussion before my departure I was at first move when you were with me but I became embarras when my parents had to join the company. I also notice you had been uneasy. I hope you didn't mind it much as you intended plenty of time for private discussion. I'm sad. You didn't say goodbye to me. Thanks ever so much for the little lunch you gave me, it was greatly appreciated as I was not expecting it. I shall take the greatest care over the pictures you gave, they shall be a souvenir in my Album, I wish to get yours to serve as a sourvenir to me within the campus till I see the true image it portrays will it be okay?

Your questions asked by you the last time were to hard on me. As first acquaintance I was very shy to answer, I hope as time goes we shall be more familiar with each other. I think you last reply requested my particulars thought it might have been said verbally Its better I make a written one for you.

Name:
Date of Birth 26th November 1949
Tribe: Fullah
Form: IV (Science)
Subjects: Maths, English Lang. Literature, History, Biology,
           H[Human] Science and General Science
Parents: (Family) You are familiar with them needless to pro-
           ceed about it.
Customs: Jealous, Playful.
Hobbies: Kissing, reading, singing, dancing, swimming and writing.
I've give you my photograph I need not say anything about it
again. I had wanted to list down the words written on your last
reply unfortunate my friends have missplace it in my absence
when searching for books. Was my argument about the signing of
scythe satisfactory to you? If not, let me know.

How are you getting on with studies up there? I hope pretty
nice. I've just tried to be settled to start serious studies. Fondest
love, and best undertaking for you. Convey hearty greetings to
your close friends. Mine join into say good-bye and good wishes
of the day.

Yours to be,
Margaret

The girl who wrote the following letter found it easier to explain
her reasons for rejecting her boyfriend's advanced by post than in
person. In this letter the theme of proper behaviour for a young girl
again emerges:

At home
Today's Date

Hi dear!

It's indeed an unfortunate event for me, for not sending the
missive by Sylvia yesterday. Anyway it was not my fault because
the letter was written the same Saturday when you said Good-bye
to me, and I placed it inside my bag but when I looked for it to
be handed over to Sylvia I can't find it, anyway, I hope that you
were not annoyed if you were I'm very sorry. I think I must start
with the main body of my letter which you have been waiting for.
At first when you told me about something concerning love I was
troubled as I was not expecting you to say such thing to me, but
I thing [think] what it must be said as time waits for no man.

You would have been thinking why I neglected your request or gave you a negative answer to your request, but it should be done as I had planned not to love more than one boy as this leads me to a great crime last year. I hope you were not all disappointed, but, not to be so disappointed. As you had said that you want to have some connection with me. I suggest that both of us will be sister and brother, because there is no other way by being a somebody to me, if you want to be a brother of mine its left with you. If no you are not. It's left with you also. Anyway, that's all for now. I am pressed with different assignment to be done tonight and time is against me.

Till then it's cherio for now till your reply is handed to me.

That's me

Frances

N.B. Sorry, I just can't send my diary as it had been siezed by one of the readers in the B. Dept. when she gave it to me I will send it. Thanks. Excuse scratches as I'm in a very high speed to finish it and my assignments before 8.45 p.m. when the bell will be rung for end of studies.

Engagement

The Creoles have long practised the engagement ceremony called 'The Gage'.[20] This ceremony is a very enjoyable social event and although today many Creole families do not observe the custom, it has been taken up by educated Provincials. It incorporates Christian as well as traditional elements.[21] At this ceremony several members of the groom's family make a formal application to the girl's family for

20. Formely there were two ceremonies, the first was called the 'Put Stop' or the 'Marking'. At this ceremony a date for the wedding was set and it served as a formal anouncement that the girl was now unavailable to any other suitor. 'The Gage' was a shortened version of the first and occurred just a few days before the wedding. Today only one ceremony is observed and it may be called by any one of the three names, but usually it is referred to as 'The Gage'.

21. Alldridge, writing in 1910, describes the betrothal ceremony of the Mende and one is struck by the close parallels between his description of it and the present-day Creole 'Gage'. For example, Alldridge quotes the words of part of the ceremony where a gift is presented to the girl's family, 'With this present we stop your ears, that you may not listen to any proposals that may be made by others for this girl' (p. 214).

permission for her to marry him. The ceremony is arranged after both the families have approved the marriage of a young couple.

On the evening of the event the parents, relatives, friends, near neighbours, and usually the parson, gather in the home of the bride-to-be. Food and drink are served to the guests as they sit awaiting the arrival of the groom's family. The entrance of the house is tightly closed and secured.[22] After a time a knock is heard at the door. An older member of each family group acts as their spokesman and the dialogue of the ceremony is intended to be highly entertaining. Spokesmen are chosen for their skill in being original and in making everyone laugh. The following is an example of the dialogue which follows the knocking at the door:

Bride's spokesman: 'Who is there?'

Groom's spokesman: 'We are friends from a far-off land.'

Bride's spokesman: 'What do you want?'

Groom's spokesman: 'We have been sent with a message from our chief.'

Bride's spokesman: 'What sort of a message and who is your chief?'

Groom's spokesman: (A name of a fictitious chief is offered) Our chief has sent us to say that when he was passing through this town the other day he saw a lovely white rose in your garden. He is anxious to obtain this beautiful rose to grow in his own garden.'

Bride's spokesman: 'We do not believe you, you are spies.'

Groom's spokesman: 'Truly, Sir, we are not spies.'

Bride's spokesman: 'But if you are not spies, what guarantee do we have?'

Groom's spokesman: 'If you will open the door to us, you will see that we are honest and true men and women

22. I am very much indebted to Mrs. Molaki Taylor, Mrs. Zainabu Kamara, and Mrs. Enid O'Reilly-Wright for discussing the meaning of the ceremony and providing me with written accounts. One of these accounts was prepared by Mrs. Kamara for her son's wedding and she closed it with the following paragraph: 'The above is the African custom in connection with the engagement ceremony between a couple. We, the mother and relatives of Alex, do not intend to minimize the importance of Western custom[s], but feel as Africans we must uphold our traditions and therefore the foregoing ceremony. Greetings and God's blessings we pray on the lives of our children' (14th April, 1968).

who have come to do real business with
you.'

Bride's spokesman: 'Very well, we are going to open the door
halfway to see who you actually are and if
you are not worthy people you will be beaten
up and driven away.'

The spokesman's skill at prolonging the period before the door is
opened and still keeping his audience amused is one measure of
success. At one engagement party I attended, the groom's spokesman
employed the imagery of space and space travel, announcing they had
just arrived from another planet. His speech included a number of
Latin words richly mixed with Krio, much to everyone's amusement.

When the door is finally opened the bride's family are consulted in
whispers as to whether or not they think the people outside look
respectable. Finally, when they agree, the door is flung wide open and
the visitors are admitted. After entering, they are formally welcomed
by the bride's family's spokesman, offered seats and served food and
drink. Then, once again, the dialogue between the two spokesmen
continues. The groom's spokesman brings greetings from the family
and informs the group once again of their mission; he refers to the
'rose' they have come for and are hoping to transplant to their own
garden. The serious nature of their mission is emphasized and then
gifts are presented to the bride's family. These, the spokesman points
out, are to prove the sincerity of their mission. Two little girls, each
carrying a calabash wrapped in satin on her head, step forward, and
these calabashes are handed to the most senior female member of the
brides' family. Several of the relatives of the bride retire to a bedroom
(which is sometimes decorated with white and blue ribbons) to
examine the contents of the calabashes. I shall list the items which
should be included and explain what each is meant to symbolize.

1. The Bible: token of affection and goodwill to the betrothed
   and a guide to the couple's future.
2. Engagement ring: the first step in binding the partners together, and a symbol of love.
3. Kola nuts: symbol of unity. (Kola is widely used on all
   kinds of ceremonial occasions. They are often offered as a
   symbol of friendship. They are used in divining and, traditionally, were one of the first gifts the suitor offered a girl's
   family.)

4. Something gold and something silver: symbolize a wish for the couple's wealth and prosperity.

5. Attaray or alligator pepper (a local spice): this spice has a very sharp taste and is a warning to the couple to refrain from having quarrels.

6. Needle and thread: this is to remind the bride that she will be expected to mend the family's clothing.

7. Pins: it is said that wives in the heat of bad temper may say to their husbands, 'You never even gave me a pin' (*'Pin sef ee nor gie me'*). By presenting a pin in this calabash, the husband avoids such an accusation.

8. Bitter Kola: it is medicinal and symbolizes long life, good health and vitality. It may also be a warning that sometimes you may encounter bitterness in your married life.

9. An envelope containing money: this money is for the bridal outfit and is called 'the married clothes copper' (*'Marrade close coppoh'*).

10. Bottles of brandy or other spirits: the drink may be used to pour a libation to the ancestors and to entertain the guests.

11. The calabash container: symbol of the womb and given with the prayer that the marriage will be fruitful and bring forth many children.

12. A white lappah[23] used to wrap the calabashes: a gift to the bride's mother to remind her of the lappahs in which she carried her daughter on her back when she was a baby. This gift is a token of compensation for carefully training her daughter.

13. A white lace cloth used to wrap the calabashes: said to symbolize 'the beauty of peace'.

14. Blue ribbon tied around the calabashes: symbolizes love and also a wish for a son and heir.

After all these contents are carefully examined by the bride's family, they return to the waiting guests and announce they have found the gifts acceptable. After this the dialogue begins once again. The groom's spokesman asks if they may now see the 'rose'. A number of women from the bride's family are brought out one at a time and

---

23. A lappah is a piece of cloth approximately two yards long which is used as a skirt in traditional dress. Lappahs are also used to wrap around the mother's back to support the baby.

presented as the 'rose'. Each time the groom's family compliment the quality of the 'rose' they have been shown but remark that this is not the 'rose' they have come for. Often an old woman or an obviously ugly old woman will be brought out and represented to the groom's family as the 'rose' they are seeking, much to everyone's amusement. Each time the groom's spokesman will tactfully explain that although this 'rose' is lovely it needs a bit more time in the garden and that they are sure there is still another rose in this garden which is more lovely and desirable than this. Finally, the bride is brought out and everyone shouts out 'Yes, this is the one' (*'Ebi! Ebi! Hurah!'*). The parson or some elderly person then offers prayers asking for God's blessing on the couple.

The calabashes are brought out of the bedroom, rewrapped, containing a gift for the groom's family. Usually this gift includes a bottle of brandy and rice cake, which is a sweet served on special occasions. At this point in the ceremony the date for the wedding may be discussed and set.[24] Then the groom's representatives leave, dancing and singing 'The bride's mother has said yes' (*'Yaewo Mammy dɔn answer yes oh'*). Music at these occasions is often played on a guitar accompanied by a triangle but sometimes by goombay drumming (goombay, however, is usually reserved for weddings).

When the groom's representatives leave the bride's house they return to a party at the groom's house. When they arrive they tell the groom and all the others who have been waiting what transpired at the bride's house. They go over the details: how long they were kept waiting, how many 'roses' were presented before finally they saw the bride, etc. The groom is obviously very interested and keeps asking for more details.[25]

24. The bride is given a lot of attention by the members of the groom's family who are present. At one engagement party I attended one of the older women pulled the girl into her lap, fondling her breasts and remarking on their small size but promising they would give her good care so that she would develop fully.

25. At one party I attended the old women present began making obscene jokes with some old men who were looking in at the window. One woman joked about how she was big enough now so that she no longer wet her bed. Another woman went outside briefly and all the rest laughed, explaining she had gone to have intercourse with one of the old men. When she returned they told her their joke and asked her how she was. She replied that she was 'fine now'. A young man, sitting beside me, explained all the jokes which were told in Krio. He admitted to me that he thought all this engagement ceremony was un-

Marriage ceremonies

Creole weddings have always been important and expensive social events. Most of the wedding expenses fall on the groom and as a result, as noted earlier, many a young man gets deeply into debt.

The wedding continues to have great social significance for both men and women, and they prefer to make it as lavish a display as possible.

On the day before the wedding relatives of the bride begin to assemble at her home to assist with the preparation of the food. Friends begin dropping in with gifts. On the night before the wedding a party, called the 'Bachelor's Eve', is held. There is a Krio saying about this party, 'You can tell how the marriage will go by the success of the bachelor's party (*'Mared we go sit na from di batchɛlɔs iv fɔ tek no'*). A good bachelor's party will last until the dawn of the wedding day.

At dawn on the day of the wedding special prayers are offered and libations to the ancestors may be poured. The bride is supposed to be the first person in the household to have her bath. She may be assisted on this day by an elderly relative. She spends most of the time before the ceremony in her mother's room. She wears a long white dress and veil, which may have been made locally, but is often an imported article. When the time for the ceremony arrives, she is escorted to the church by her father, brother, or some other male relative. The wedding party includes bridesmaids, ring-bearers and attendants for the groom. The ceremony is the traditional Christian one and the parson gives a short sermon exhorting the couple on the responsibilities of Christian marriage. After this the couple retire to a small room to sign the register. Parents and godparents are also called forward to sign it. The signing of the register after the ceremony is an opportunity to honour important persons in the family and in the community. While all the guests remain seated in the church, people are called forward, one by one, to sign it. Since weddings are such an important social event everyone dresses in their very best attire.[26]

---

necessary; in fact, he thought it was a bit silly. He preferred the 'English way'. However, he did say that it was good to see how Africans could enjoy themselves and he remarked on their 'sexiness' and how they knew how to enjoy sex in contrast to the English.

26. Although women in Freetown rarely wear nylon stockings, it is almost mandatory to wear them at weddings.

After the wedding ceremony and the signing of the register, the guests go directly to the reception. This may be held in the bride's home or in some rented hall. The bride and groom are seated before the guests, and individuals from both families make extended speeches. Speakers are chosen for their gift of oratory. They elaborate on the family backgrounds of the two young people who are marrying, describing the events leading to the marriage and generally amusing the audience with anecdotes about the bride's and groom's childhood and their romance. The groom must also make a speech, thanking all those who have assisted with the wedding preparations. The wedding cake is cut and served and toasts are offered, for which the guests have been provided with champagne. At the end of the reception the bride tosses her bouquet in the direction of her bridesmaids and the guests throw rice on the couple as they depart. The groom escorts the bride to her home, leaving her there after telling her what time he will come to take her 'home'. Either at this time or when the couple finally depart for their honeymoon there is another small ceremony. The bride's mother or some other older woman in the family offers a sip of water to the bride and groom from a small glass, and makes a speech full of advice about the rules for a happily married life. This ceremony is regarded as very serious and sometimes, if a bride's mother is dead, the woman who is giving the speech will remind the bride of her mother's tender care and her high expectations for her daughter. Often the bride is reduced to tears before the speech is over.

After the reception most of the guests return to their homes to change their clothes to something more comfortable for the parties that follow. The bride and her female relatives usually wear the '*ashobe.*' '*Ashobe*' is the practice of the bride's close relatives wearing dresses made of the same material which the bride has chosen and purchased for them. It is a custom of Nigerian origin and one woman described how it first came to be observed in Sierra Leone.

'It was first introduced into Sierra Leone in the twenties by the May family, formerly of Maysville, Ascension Town, Freetown. The late Mrs. Nettie May was a Lagosian who married a Sierra Leonean, the late Mr. Cornelius May. When their daughter, Isa, was to get married to a Dr. Prince Williams, relations from Lagos travelled to Freetown for the wedding. On that occasion the immediate relations of the bride put on the same dress material at home after the wedding and reception. This was the introduction of "Ashoebe" [Ashobe] into Sierra Leone. Its purpose was for immediate relations of a bride to put on the same dress material after the wedding and reception, and wear it during the wedding jollification at the home of the bride.'[27]

If a wedding is large and the families are well-known, there may be several parties going on simultaneously in the homes of the bride, the groom, god-parents[28], and friends. Enormous amounts of food and drink are provided, and there is dancing. The bride and groom must make an appearance at all these parties. Finally, late in the evening, they are allowed to go off on their honeymoon. Ideally, arrangements have been made for them to go to a country or seaside bungalow. Friends may accompany them, although today many couples prefer to keep the location of their honeymoon a secret. The bride is not allowed to cook during the first three days of married life, and so her mother provides the couple with a hamper of food and replenishes it during that time.

On the Sunday following the wedding the couple, together with the entire wedding party, attend the groom's church in their wedding attire. This is called 'churching the bride'. The parson offers a special prayer for the couple. After the service they go to the bride's home for a meal and then to the couple's new home where guests are entertained for the remainder of the day.

The right of the individual to make his own choice of a marital partner and the importance of love as the basis for marriage appears to have been thoroughly incorporated into the values of young educated Sierra Leoneans. Most studies of change in family patterns emphasize the way the choice of a mate has become an individual rather than a family matter. Goode (1963) has noted how the idea of 'romantic love' as the basis for marriage has become almost universally accepted,

27. Today the use of *ashobe* is not limited to relatives of the bride; she may request any number of her girl friends whom she wishes to honour to wear it. The practice of *ashobe* is no longer restricted to weddings. *Bundu* girls who are celebrating their graduation from the society may wear it. Dancing groups may practise this custom and sometimes women in political organizations wear *ashobe* when they are participating in some public demonstration.

28. There are sometimes two sets of god-parents, one set appointed at the birth of a child, who participate in the christening ceremony, and another appointed when a couple marry. These latter god-parents are supposed to be persons to whom the couple may go when they have problems. The practice is, however, rapidly dying out.

but we have seen that educated Sierra Leoneans are still very concerned with such things as family background. Little (1966b) has pointed
out that the emphasis upon love for a single partner provides a
'rationalizing function' for the individual caught between the traditional demands of his extended family and his individualistic economic
motives. It appears that the persistence of traditional attitudes about
marriage choices affects women more than it does men. Women continue to be assessed by traditional criteria despite the fact that educational and occupational opportunities are open to them. A woman's
status is still very much bound up with her family background and her
marriage. On the other hand, a man may achieve a social position far
above his family's through his own educational and occupational
achievements.

Courtship as it is now practised among educated Sierra Leoneans is
a dramatic innovation. Long years of education have interrupted the
traditional pattern of early marriage for women. Traditional culture
provides no guidelines for the behaviour of physically mature young
people who are not married. The western institution of courtship is
a solution for such young people. However, the freedom allowed unmarried young people permits them to behave in ways which are often
in contradiction to traditional values. For example, when they have
passed the usual age for marriage in traditional society many young
people assume the right (and have increased opportunities) to engage
in premarital sexual relations. But, since men continue to be con-
servative about the kind of girl they wish to marry, girls, in their
ambition to achieve a good marriage, are faced with serious conflicts
about their conduct.

There is a Krio saying, 'If the first child is a girl it is good luck for
the Daddy' (*'If yu fus pikin nar gial nar luck en daddee'*). Families
are said to tend to treat girls with more favour, and mothers too may
be quite indulgent with their daughters. Even after marriage a girl's
relationship with her mother remains very close and the mother assists
her in every possible way. The favoured position of a girl growing up
in the family and her special status during courtship are, as we shall
see in the next chapter, in some contrast with her role as a wife.

8

The organization of domestic life and family relationships

'Nɔ tɛk to mi lɛk yu wɛf' [1]

Any description of the organization of domestic life or of the structure of relationships within the household must suffer from the methodological limitations involved in an examination of such an intimate institution as the family in contemporary society. And, as mentioned earlier, such research is also handicapped by the biases and value judgements implicit in the concepts and theories used in most family studies. Obviously the first problem can never be completely resolved: the very nature of modern family life for the most part restricts the investigator's observations to situations which the subjects are able to control. Other information gathered comes from inferences drawn from conversations, attitudes elicited in response to questions, and the good fortune of happening to be present at some critical moment in family life.

The problems of theoretical biases built into the research design of this and most studies which attempt to provide data for cross-cultural comparisons of marriage and family life have also been discussed. The approach of this study is to describe the family in terms of the manner in which it organizes its day-to-day maintenance, secondly, (in Chapter Nine) to examine the conflicts which occur in the course of daily life and the way these are resolved. Out of these data some general statements about the roles of husbands and wives and the functions of the family in relation to the wider social structure in Sierra Leone will emerge.

In the last chapter it was noted that courtship behaviour with its emphasis on romantic love as it was observed among young people in

1. 'Don't talk to me as if I were your wife'. This phrase may be used in any situation where one person takes a superior or patronizing attitude towards another and expects a subservient, docile or submissive reaction or response.

Sierra Leone is an innovation; nothing analogous exists in traditional society.[2] It was also suggested that the favoured role of the daughter within the family while she is growing up and the attention given her during courtship are in considerable contrast to her role as a wife. Young men may adopt the behaviour of the suitor which they believe is characteristic of western patterns during courtship, but their expectations and values with regard to marriage continue to be largely 'traditional'. Suttner (1969) says of traditional relationships between husbands and wives in Africa, 'There was no competition between men and women. They never compared their positions, since they fulfilled distinct, though complementary roles.' Whether or not we accept this as a completely accurate statement of traditional male-female relationships, we can agree with Omari's (1960) description of the situation today, 'Attitudes of educated women and girls seem to be more anti-traditional than those of men.' The lack of agreement between men and women about the roles of husband and wife are often the source of conflicts which occur within the family.

The organization of domestic work

Many studies of marriage relationships measure the degree of segregation of conjugal roles by examining the extent to which husbands and wives share household tasks. (For some examples see Bott 1956, 1957; Mogey 1956; Rosser and Harris 1965.) Questions posed by such studies are often slanted so as to measure the degree to which men assume the duties usually thought the responsibility of the wife, and neglect to investigate the extent to which women might be undertaking those tasks typically thought to be the province of the husband (Harrell-Bond 1967, 1969). Although questions about the extent to which husbands assisted in household tasks were included in this study, it was very clear from the outset that the responses had very little to do with concepts of conjugal roles among Sierra Leonean professional husbands and wives. The men appear to take an extremely practical view of such matters. I had many opportunities to observe professional couples living abroad with their children and without servants. Under

2. In traditional society men were more constrained to please and impresse the girl's family than the girl.

these circumstances husbands help their wives with cooking, cleaning, washing-up, purchasing food, and caring for children. However, in Sierra Leone households are organized in quite a different manner, which usually makes a husband's direct assistance unnecessary.

Most of the professional households employ servants. Often these servants live on the premises and are on more or less twenty-four hour duty. Moreover, the households of professional families include not only their own children but relatives' children and wards. All these persons are engaged in household work. It is the wife's responsibility to direct the activities of the household but usually she does very little of the actual work herself. Tasks are 'stratified' and relegated to all members of the household according to their age and position in the family. Most of the more arduous work is done by the younger members of the household. Children usually rise very early in the morning to sweep and tidy the house and do other work around the kitchen before they leave for school. Boys have the responsibility of cleaning the family car as well as helping with tasks in the house. Children learn to launder clothes and iron them when they are quite young. Generally if there are relatives' children or wards in the home they will be required to do more work than the other children of the family. The following is one wife's description of how housework is allocated in her home. Her two children were both under four years old.

Task	*Person(s) responsible*
Marketing	Boy[3] and wife
Store shopping[4]	Wife
Cooking for husband	Wife
Laying the table	Boy
Washing-up	Boy
Cleaning floors	Boy and wife's sister
Tidying living room	Wife's sister

3. Paid servants in African households in Sierra Leone are usually referred to as 'boy'. In this case the 'boy' was actually a distant relative.
4. Although this will be discussed more fully later, it should be noted that distinction is made between buying in the market and shopping in stores. Imported foods are mainly available in supermarkets while local fresh foods are sold in the market.

Task	*Person(s) responsible*
Cleaning bedroom of husband and wife	Boy and wife
Cleaning children's rooms	Wife's sister
Laundry	Boy and wife's sister
Washing the car	Driver
Care of small children (bathing, dressing, changing nappies, plaiting hair, etc.)	Wife and her sister
Buying clothing for children	Husband and wife

Another wife, a primary school teacher, describes how she managed her household work:

> 'I do the marketing and go to the store. I also cook the meals for my husband, that is, I do it on Saturday and Sunday and I prepare breakfast. Other days my niece does the cooking. In my home we eat together. One of the children sets the tables. The children wash the dishes and clean the floors. At the moment we have no boy so they do everything. They must do it because the work has to be done. Sometimes you aren't going to be able to have a boy so the children must get used to it. The children clean the windows, but when we have a boy he does it. One of them does our [the parents'] bedroom and they all clean their own. I wash my husband's shirts, but he prefers his own ironing so he irons them. I do the washing unless we have a boy. The children make their own beds and my son washes the car. We all do the garden together – not my husband though. We have a schedule for the children which tells them when to take baths.'

Another wife who had eight children (the oldest was fourteen) describes her routine:

> 'I do the marketing although sometimes my husband takes me in his car, otherwise I go by bus. I cook the meals for my husband. The older boys set the table and wash the dishes. My cousin also helps me do it. The children and my cousin clean the floor. I sort of share the cleaning with the children. The elder boy is in charge of the sitting room. The other children clean the windows and our bedroom. My cousin washes most things. The oldest boy does my husband's shirts and the boys wash the car. I used to do the gardening before I got sick. I used to bath the children but

now I tell them. My husband never did do that. Sometimes he helped me make milk for the baby and helped feed and dress them when they were small, if we were going out. He takes them to school. I used to wash the children's clothing but now they do it themselves. I buy their clothing and plait their hair. Sometimes I ask the barber to cut the boys' hair. The boys polish all the shoes. They know that every morning they do it.'

Although some professional families spare their children from taking such heavy responsibilities for household work, many parents feel that children should learn to do everything for themselves. After all, one never knows when circumstances may make it necessary for them to be self-sufficient.

One example illustrates how the assignment of tasks symbolizes status relationships within the family. I was a guest for some time in the home of a professional family. Two of the three children in the household were relatives. Each morning these two arose before six a.m., apparently without being awakened by anyone. They cleaned the kitchen and laid the table for breakfast. At seven a.m. one of them brought a cup of tea to my bed. About fifteen minutes later the other child who belonged to the family came down to eat breakfast with the others and they all went off to school. This household employed a number of servants so the wife's responsibilities during the day were restricted to organizing their work. As far as I could observe during my visit, the only time the daughter of the family did any household work was when she assisted her mother in serving meals. However, the other two children continued to have regular duties when they returned from school.

One informant told me of her experiences when she was a teenager still living at home with her parents. She became pregnant and for several reasons it was not possible for her to marry the father of the child. Her parents were extremely angry about this disgrace and she described their method of punishing her. For several months she was given all the menial jobs in the house usually thought to be the responsibility of the younger children. She had to rise at five a.m., light the fire, pound the rice, sweep the house, do the washing, clean the windows and get the breakfast.

The presence of children, other relatives and servants in the household may largely relieve the wives of doing actual household work, but there are some tasks which are primarily their responsibility and are seldom delegated to anyone else. The wife is expected to spend her time mainly in the house, to be primarily responsible for the cooking (even if most of the preparations are made by others, it is the wife who does the final combining of ingredients), and to supervise the children. Her position is analogous to that of the head wife in the traditional polygamous household. She has the authority to allocate the most difficult work to others and can often spend her free time in some other occupation from which she earns money.

As we have seen, when wives were asked to describe their daily household routine they rarely mentioned participation by their husbands. I asked the professionals about the extent to which husbands assisted in particular household tasks. Although one might have expected variations between the responses of men and women in describing the amount of work the men did around the house, in fact there were no significant differences. One can conclude that their responses more or less approximate to the actual tasks with which the husbands on

Table 19. *Husband's assistance in household tasks*[a]

	Creole		Provincial	
	Yes	*No*	*Yes*	*No*
Making beds	52	48	48	52
Gardening	39	61	57	43
Tidying-up	75	25	84	16
Washing-up	40	60	66	34
Store shopping	84	16	91	9
Shopping in the market	35	65	45	55
Buying children's clothing	62	38	82	18
Dressing children	63	37	58	42
Bathing children	52	48	42	58
Laying the table	30	70	43	57
Cooking	46	54	39	61

a. The respondents were asked about the tasks listed in the table. They were given the following choices for their responses: 'never', 'occasionally', 'usually', 'more than half the time', and 'previously, but not now', (as for example, when the couple lived abroad without servants but not while living in Sierra Leone). For the purpose of this table 'never' and 'previously, but not now' were combined as 'no'. Most of the responses shown as 'yes' were actually 'occasionally' and, on the basis of observation, could have been described more accurately as 'very seldom'.

some occasions do assist their wives rather than represent some ideal model of the husband's role. Table 19 shows these responses.

Although some of the differences in the table suggest that marriages where the husband is Creole have moved more towards the so-called western model of 'joint conjugal roles' (Bott 1957) than have marriages where the husband is a Provincial, there are enough exceptions to challenge such an explanation. For example, 66 per cent of the Provincial husbands compared with only 40 per cent of the Creole husbands help their wives with washing dishes. Mogey (1956) took such willingness of men to wash-up as the critical indication of 'joint conjugal roles' in his study.[5] The willingness of Sierra Leonean husbands to assist occasionally with certain domestic chores is better explained in terms of their interest in westernizing their style of family life. This is particularly the case in those areas of family activity which are open to observation by outsiders. Most professional men, particularly Provincial men, have had considerably more experience abroad than have their wives. These men are concerned that certain patterns they observed while abroad should be introduced and maintained. Often the only way for them to accomplish this is to instruct their wives and also to assist them. For example, a majority of both Creole and Provincial husbands help with the tidying of the house, but this usually means they help tidy only the *living room*. This is the room in which guests are entertained and a good deal of emphasis is placed on its furnishings and care. One wife confided that she would be frightened for the husband to come home and find the living room in a mess. Children are taught to respect this room as well and they usually sit very quietly if they are allowed to remain when guests are being entertained. Many households have television sets and record-players which are part of the furnishings of the living room. Usually decorations are in western style although in a few homes one can find various pieces of African art on display as well. One can almost predict the attitude of a couple towards traditional life – whether they are proud of it or not – by the manner in which they have decorated their living room. For example, one couple had systematically collected all kinds of masks, drums, carved figures, basketry, decorated cala-

5. I also used this measure in a study of Irish and English husbands and tried to show that even if husbands were willing to do such work in the household it told us very little about the character of the marriage relationship (Harrell-Bond 1969).

bashes, paintings of African scenes, ivory carvings, animal-skin rugs, etc. The husband had arrangèd to have these displayed in glass cases in the living room. He explained that he did not want his children to forget their African heritage.

As shown in Table 19, most men did store shopping for the family, although the majority did not go to the market. These men have acquired a taste for imported food and they have observed that it is quite customary to find men shopping in supermarkets in the West; the local market is quite another matter. Selling there is usually done by women and they definitely do not welcome men as customers. Men are thought to drive a harder bargain than would their wives. So marketwomen naturally prefer to sell to women and they will often abuse men who come to the market with the Krio phrase, 'Daddy, go sit down, won't you? It is not a man's work to come to the market' (*'Daddie go si dɔn na ya. Nɔ to man wok fɔ kam maket na wuman wok'*). Such a taunt embarrasses men, reminding them they are overstepping the bounds of traditional concepts of the women's role. One husband related his experiences with the women in the market. His wife was an American and when they returned from overseas he was determined they would eat local food because it was more economical. Since his wife was unfamiliar with local products he decided he would shop for the food. Once the marketwomen started to recognize him they began to insult him. They asked if he was one of those 'stingy but greedy men' (*'He wan got man'*). He found the situation intolerable and very quickly handed the task over to his wife.

Although the responses recorded in Table 19 show a majority of men assisting their wives with the purchasing of children's clothing, this does not mean that they usually take this responsibility. Often their participation is limited to stocking up on clothes for the family when they are travelling abroad. Those men who do help their wives with bathing the children usually only bath the little boys. Laying the table is another task which more Provincial than Creole men said they did but again, this assistance is usually only offered when there are to be guests.

In the traditional household the primary responsibility for the care of the children rests with the wife. When a child becomes ill in such a family the mother may be accused of having broken some taboo or of having neglected the child. Although men do not usually take an active role in the physical care of their children, they are intensely concerned about their well-being. Sometimes if a child merely falls and slightly injures himself, the father may severely beat his wife for neglecting the child. The mother is held responsible for the training of young children, and, if the child is a girl, for protecting her virginity until she is married. If she succeeds in this she is highly honoured, but is she fails she is the one to be disgraced. Although professional husbands do assume considerably more responsibility for the actual care of their children than their traditional counterparts the pattern of expecting wives to assume the major role continues. Most fathers do keep a very watchful eye on how well their wives are attending to the care and training of their children. Almost all the married persons admitted they argued over some aspects of bringing up their children, for example, whether or not the wife is spending enough time caring for them, questions of discipline, or other decisions concerning their welfare. If a wife works, as many do, disputes over the care of the children are often intensified. While there may be other relatives in the household who can supervise the children while the mothers are away at work, few fathers liked this arrangement.

A tremendous emphasis is laid upon children's success in school. While it may be the mother's responsibility to see that the children do their homework, many of the fathers in the professional group also give a lot of attention to this matter. Many fathers require their children to show them their completed work.

Although usually physical punishment of young children is meted out by the mother, in most households it is the father who is more feared. Mothers rely on his final authority and can almost always get instant compliance by promising to report any disobedience to him. Children are taught to show respect to parents and their behaviour before all adults is usually very restrained. Even the smallest child who has just learned to walk is taught to greet guests and shake their hands.

When a woman marries she is expected to assume the responsibility for managing the work of the household, to bear the children and care for them. According to their responses to the questionnaire administered to primary school children, (see Appendix A), those boys and girls from professional families who were living with both parents confirmed that in their households it was the mother who took the major responsibility for directing domestic work. They also reported that it was the mother who was primarily concerned with taking care of the children. According to them their fathers usually saw to it that their children had good table manners and that they ate all the food they were given. Father was also described by these little children as the parent who took them for outings and gave them their pocket money. This description of the roles of father and mother was similar to that given by the university students when asked about their own childhood experiences. Two-thirds of them said their mothers were responsible for most of their 'discipline' when they were children. In personal interviews with them it was clear that they interpreted 'discipline' very broadly to include most aspects of child care. Students favour the idea that fathers should assist with the care of their children, although most of them assume that the primary responsibility rests with the mother. They see a very real problem for the woman who tries to combine her role as a mother with a career. About one-third of both the men and women students feel that a mother should give up her career and remain at home, while the rest of the students thought it would be possible to allocate some of the care of the children to another person. However, no-one ever suggested that the other person should be the father. Students were asked other questions about their attitudes towards the role of husband and their responses suggest that young people expect that husbands will share more in household work and child care when they are married than is normative in the households I observed. However, the notion that husband and wife should participate *equally* in domestic tasks has certainly not been incorporated into their view of marriage.

Bott, in her study of London married couples, argues that the greater participation of the husband in the household tasks was related to the break-up of close-knit networks of kinsmen and resulted in a couple's increased 'mutuality' and a greater emotional investment in the marriage: 'They must get along well together, they must help one another in carrying out familial tasks, for there is no sure external source of material and emotional help' ((1957, p. 95). Elsewhere I have argued that the joint organization of household duties is, by itself, an unsatisfactory way of measuring the amount of emotional investment partners may have in one another or of assessing the degree of 'mutuality' in marriage relationships, if such terms can ever have any precise meaning anyway (Harrell-Bond 1969). However, it is clear that there has been a tremendous change in the organization of domestic work in these professional households as compared with the traditional pattern discussed earlier. As one man put it:

'I have had the experience of Christian marriage where we feel that the wife is equal. Sometimes people laugh when they see me doing all these things. They think I am being too good to the wife and that she will use me as a puppet.'

The respondents in the professional sample were asked to respond to the statement, 'I (or, My husband) give(s) more assistance with domestic work and child care than my father gave my mother.' Just over half the Creoles and 86 per cent of the Provincials agreed and, of course, the greatest changes have come about in the Provincial households. The question of how much assistance can be expected of a husband is a source of at least some conflict in some marriages. Respondents in the professional sample were asked if they would try to think what was the most usual thing over which they and their spouse disagreed. Using this open-ended question, only six mentioned arguments over things relating to the organization of household work and one mentioned they argued over what were the wife's duties. However, later in the interview I asked respondents to indicate whether they and their spouses diagreed over a series of specific issues and one-quarter indicated that the sharing of household tasks was a source of conflict.

The organization of family finances

Creole families have always depended mainly on the monthly earnings of employed husbands, although it has also been very common for the women to contribute to the family income through trading or other means. However, for the professional Provincial, very significant changes have taken place in the financial role of husbands compared with his traditional counterpart. To understand these changes it is necessary to examine briefly the financial arrangement of the traditional household. The economy of village life in Sierra Leone is primarily based on subsistence agriculture. Women, as well as men, play an important role in providing food for the family. They tend the gardens which are the source of the day-to-day vegetable needs of the family. They also catch the fish, the main source of protein in the diet. Once a man has ensured the family has a sufficient quantity of rice for the year most of the proceeds from any cash crops may be spent in ways which will strengthen his position in the community and increase his status and prestige. Such expenditure may include the costs of making marriage payments for an additional wife, assisting a young male relative with such costs, contributing to the funeral expenses of some relative, giving 'dashes' or gifts of money to dancers and musicians on festive occasions, and fulfilling obligations to his own and his wife's kinsmen. Generosity is an important attribute of a 'big man' in the village and so it is important to have sufficient resources laid by to be able to give at least token assistance when it is requested. Men may also be called on to pay school fees for their own children as well as for those of their relatives. Having a zinc roof on one's house is also an important sign of wealth and importance and requires an outlay of a man's cash, but the house itself is built out of local products with the assistance of other village men.

In the modern professional marriage all this has been radically altered. Husbands are expected to be responsible for providing the family with a place to live, supplying money for food and clothing, paying the children's school fees, buying petrol for the car, and generally keeping up with the expenses of running the household. For those who are paid by the government some of these expenses, such as the rent for the house and payments on items which may have been purchased through a loan, are automatically deducted from the husband's salary cheque. At the same time, particularly if the individual is of Provincial origin, the husband continues to have the series of traditional obligations to his own and his wife's relatives. How well he honours these latte obligations contributes to his image as a good husband. Moreover, the professional feels compelled to spend his money in conspicuous ways which enhance his prestige in terms of modern values. These involve owning a car, spending money on girlfriends, building a house in Freetown and, for a Provincial, also building a house in one's home village. If a husband has any children born outside the marriage (and the evidence suggests that a great many have) he has the additional financial burden of supporting them. At the same time, modern ideas about the roles of husbands largely free women from any direct responsibility for any of these expenditures, even if they are earning an income.

Interestingly, in response to the open-ended questions about conflicts in marriage cited earlier, only 17 of the respondents in the professional sample mentioned money matters as a source of conflict in their marriages. Even more interestingly, when asked specifically whether or not they ever disagreed about family finances, *no-one admitted they ever did*. However, one-third of the married respondents conceded they did disagree 'at times' over the question of financial obligations to relatives. Decisions about the use of the family's economic resources involve a convergence of very dynamic issues. There are often extreme conflicts of interest between husband and wife and some of these are related to the different demands of the traditional and the modern family system and the changes in the ideas about economic responsibilities of husband and wife. It appears that arguments over financial matters are extremely threatening to the stability of the marriage relationship and most couples have completely separated their finances to avoid such disagreements.

Financial obligations to relatives

The obligation to share what one has with the members of one's family is a value taught early in the life of the child. The custom of distributing the whole of one's first month's salary to the relatives which is described by one informant reinforces the idea that the individual's primary obligations are to his relatives:

'When a boy has his first job and he is getting paid at the end of the month, that is his first salary, he comes home with it and shows it to his parents. His parents say, "You give auntie two shillings, give Uncle Tom two shillings, and so on". And you give to the friends of the family. You give to as many people as you can. The boy is willing, he feels happy. He learns to keep up the habit (of sharing his earnings with his relatives) with the next month's salary. The relatives say, "Thank you, God is going to bless you" (*"Tank yu, Gɔd go blɛs yu"*).'

Sometimes a young man or woman may simply turn over the entire first month's salary to one old relative who takes charge of distributing coins to the other members of the family. But, however the matter is handled, the message is the same: the fruits of the individual's labours do not belong to him alone. He not only has an obligation to remember the members of his family and to share with them, but they have a *right* to expect him to do so.

It is impossible to understand the way professional couples manage their finances without considering the profound conflicts which the individual must resolve in moving from this kind of traditional value-system, where prestige is gained by sharing, into an economic system based upon individualistic motives. As shown earlier, Africans writing or speaking of the traditional marriage system often express disgust with the economic aspects of customary marriage, which involve marriage payments. The wife is often described by them as simply a chattel purchased by her husband. However, to emphasize this aspect of the marriage transaction is to miss the very essence of the meaning of the relationship in economic terms to the relatives, and particularly to the wife's relatives.

I have already noted that the members of the professional group may receive financial assistance from a large number of relatives during the years of their education. Although only 12 per cent of the professional sample indicated that they felt it was necessary for them to repay this money directly, almost all of them expected they would be repaying it indirectly through giving assistance to other relatives now that they were earning an income. Most Sierra Leoneans say that it is impossible to refuse flatly a relative's request for financial help. Even though very few of them are currently benefiting from the system of family obligations, there is always the possibility that at some time they also may be in need of help. Moreover, they are also subject to a number of powerful moral sanctions which enforce kinship obligations. While some professionals are beginning to question this system, many feel considerable conflict over the matter. Here are some of their comments:

'The African system makes people lazy. I work for myself but they don't seem to think about that.'

. . .

'I try to limit it. It depends on the character of the relatives mainly. Some Africans are overdoing this [responsibility of kinsmen].'

. . .

'I don't mind, but I think it is possible. My husband has his sister who is not married but has all those children all dependent on him.'

. . .

'Sierra Leone is faced with different problems than in the west. You *must* acknowledge responsibility. Most of the relatives are poor.'

. . .

'You shouldn't encourage it, but if they are in need I would help. I don't believe in encouraging laziness.'

. . .

'It is part of the traditional set-up. I feel some kind of satisfaction having to support my brothers and sisters.'

. . .

'I don't think it is desirable but I am forced to do it.'

. . .

'If I were not willing my relatives could call me names, they would call me a "black white man".'

. . .

'This practice is spoiling marriages.'

. . .

I strongly disapprove of it. I don't want to be indebted to my relatives. Men are hindered by the extent of the family system. Your income is just not sufficient to meet all their demands.'

. . .

'I believe in helping relatives so long as it is not detrimental to one's first obligations.'

. . .

About a third of professionals and students agreed with the statement, 'The African idea of financial responsibility for one's relatives is out of date'. More of those agreeing were women, suggesting that they are more concerned than men with the financial drain these obligations impose. On the other hand the professionals were asked to state how they felt about the practice of relatives assisting each other in financial ways, and 89 per cent indicated they approved (over half of them said they 'strongly approved'). So, whether 'out of date' or not, the practice continues. Many pointed out the necessity of discriminating between deserving relatives and those who were willing simply to be 'parasites'. It was discouraging to keep on financing a young relative who continually failed his examinations and showed no academic promise. A Krio saying sums up this problem, 'Snakes have no feet and so if you try to get a snake to stand up, you are just labouring in vain' ('*Snek nɔ get fut fɔ tinap, so if yu want am fɔ tinap, yu go leb fɔ natin*'). Despite such risks and the hardship which may be involved, most people continue to feel that kinship obligations are a necessary part of life. Over half the students agreed with the statement,

'If necessary I would lower my standard of living in order to be able to give financial assistance to my relatives.' Most Provincial professionals are already doing this.

One of the traditional incentives for having large numbers of children is to provide security for one's old age. As already noted, women in traditional societies are highly dependent upon their sons for support when they are old. By honouring their own obligations to their relatives, parents set an example for their children, enabling them to understand just what their own obligations will be when they are grown up. I wanted to know if the professionals or the students looked forward to the time when they could depend on their own children for support, thus perpetuating the system of family obligations. Table 20 shows their responses to the statement: 'When I am old I expect my children to provide financial assistance for me'. The wide differences of opinion between the students and the adults may be explained in terms of the immediate life experiences of the two groups. The students are at present receiving assistance from their relatives and, in view of their immediate dependency on the traditional system, would be unlikely to dismiss it lightly. The professionals, on the other hand, are no longer benefiting financially from the system of kinship obligation. Rather they are in the period of life when the demands of their relatives are heaviest. None of them believed they could ask any of their relatives for the kind of help they were now giving others. The following response was typical: 'I could really get no help from *any* of my relatives. I could not go to them because first they don't have it. Perhaps one day in an extreme emergency I could go to the three boys; I have been responsible for their schooling. But now they have only just begun working and have very little.'

Some professionals observed that it would be unrealistic to expect

Table 20. *'When I am old I expect my children to provide financial assistance for me' (Percentages)*

		Professional	Student
Agree		32	60
Other (no response, 'Only if necessary')		65	38
Disagree		3	2
Totals	%	100	100
	No.	157	229

children to support them in the future. They are aware of how difficult it is for them to finance their own parents now and see such responsibilities as becoming even more difficult in the future. Moreover, most of them have retirement schemes as part of their employment benefits and many have savings, investments, and insurance programmes. Some are investing in property and most build houses. Such persons expect to be able to provide for themselves in their old age. However, there are still those who feel they are investing in their personal future security through paying the educational costs of their children who they fully expect will be supporting them in their old age. Women in general are more likely than men to expect their children to support them when they are old. An analysis of Table 20 by sex and tribe shows more Provincials than Creole men expected their children to support them (44 per cent as against 21 per cent), but about one-third of *both* Creole and Provincial women expected their children to take responsibility for their support.

To neglect one's parents, particularly one's mother, is a matter of great shame. I have already noted how co-wives may deride the mother whose son is studying overseas (something which generally they envy) and forgets to send her money regularly. Even if a mother doesn't actually need financial assistance, most professionals continue to send token amounts of money to her. Among those whose mothers were alive, 88 per cent of the men in the professional sample gave them money at regular intervals, usually monthly. Among those whose fathers were alive, only 39 per cent of the professional men gave money to them either regularly or irregularly, showing the greater importance attached to supporting one's mother. It is understandable, in view of the structure of relationships in the traditional household, that the child's feelings of responsibility for his mother are stronger than for his father. One informant explained it very well:

> 'If I have a bulk of money and give it to my father, he doesn't let my mother know. So what can I do? I have to take the money and give it to my mother. Then I give some to my father and say it is for *both* of them. If I give it to my father he doesn't care. He doesn't give it to her. I also give her gifts and don't tell my father. That is what they always do, these fathers. Daddy has so many wives and he has to see to all of them the same.'

In short, the head of a polygamous household is required to share equally with all his wives, and children are not usually inclined to support all their father's other co-wives. A son who forgets his responsibility to his mother may be reminded, 'You are not remembering that it was out of my belly you were born' (*'Na mi bɛlɛ cum out, but yu no no that'*). Obligations to take care of one's mother (and to obey her wishes) are also reinforced by the belief that a mother can curse her child and thus bring bad luck on him for the rest of his life.[6] 'The results of your actions will follow you' (*'Yu go se am'*) is a curse or threat which a mother can pronounce, and it is to be avoided at all costs. Another Krio phrase that a mother may use is, 'Unless I was not the one who gave you breasts, the curse will follow you' (*'Pas nɔ to mi gi yu bɔbby'*). To swear on his mother's breast or his mother's milk is the most sacred oath a person may utter. Such intense feelings of respect and fear influence relationships between children (particularly sons) and their mothers. These beliefs and attitudes towards mothers are widespread and provide a strong incentive for men and women to follow the advice of their mothers and to fulfil their obligations to them all through their lives. While it is also possible for a father to curse his children it is thought very unlikely that he would do so. A man's position and economic support are secured by virtue of his membership of the extended family. The father is not dependent on his son for support, but the son is dependent on being favoured by his father in order to be named as his heir. Sons look to their fathers for their blessing. Mothers, on the other hand, are never able to rely with any sense of security on the support of their husband's family for, once he has died, they may easily neglect their responsibilities towards her. She must secure herself through impressing her son with his obligation to support her. In a collection of Mende stories, Marion Kilson (1961) found that while it is generally assumed that children will obey their parents, there was no example of a child disobeying his father. On the other hand, there were several stories giving instances in which a child disobeyed his mother. 'In one of the latter disobedience led to the death of the offending child, which suggests the strength of the sanction governing respect for one's mother.' She concludes that:

> 'Although there are a number of examples of children disobeying
> their mother, the affective bond between mother and child ap-

6. A prominent lawyer died during my stay in Sierra Leone. Several unfortunate events in his life were recounted in the local press and explained as having resulted from his mother's curse.

pears to be stronger than that between father and child. For example, in one story when a woman's only son died, she grieved so intensely that her son returned to life' (1961).

Both students and professionals were asked to respond to the statement, 'The fear of my mother's curse is something I feel very deeply'. Eighty-two per cent of the students agreed, with no differences between the responses of either the men and women or of Creoles and Provincials. Although the number of persons in the professional sample agreeing that they still fear their mother's curse was smaller, 51 per cent, the differences by sex and tribe show the greater importance of this belief to Provincials and to the men generally. These comparisons are shown in Table 21.

Table 21. *'The fear of my mother's curse is something I feel very deeply' (Percentages)*

| | | Men | | Women | |
		Creole	Provincial	Creole	Provincial
Agree		50	73	36	52
Disagree		48	27	60	43
Other		2	0	4	4
Totals	%	100	100	100	100
	No.	48	37	48	24

As we have seen, family obligations are not limited to parents. Sierra Leoneans sometimes refer to their extended family system as the 'elastic family' because so many people are able to claim kinship ties with other. Professionals complain that the size of the family seems to grow in direct proportion to their advances in income, so that they are never able to save any money. I asked the university students if they expected to give financial assistance to certain other categories of relatives, in addition to their parents, after they leave university and are earning an income. These responses are shown in Table 22. It appears from the results shown in Table 22 that these students expect to be giving most financial assistance to younger relatives who will be of school age. The most acceptable request a relative can make is for the educational costs of some child in the family. Paying for the education of a younger relative is viewed as an investment in the future of the entire family.

Table 22. *'Which of these relatives do you expect to assist financially when you leave university?'*

	Creole	Provincial
Brothers and sisters	52	79[a]
Nephews and nieces	30	53
Aunts and uncles	32	47
Grandparents	21	33
All who call themselves relatives	1	17

a. All figures are given in terms of the percentage of 'yes' answers.

While this question did not include all categories of relatives who may lay claims of kinship on these students once they begin earning an income, it does show quite clearly that their sense of responsibility to relatives is strong. These data also indicate that the Provincials feel the sense of duty to relatives more strongly than Creoles do. We can only sympathize with the 17 per cent who expect to help *all* those who call themselves relatives. Both groups complain about the problem of limiting the number of relatives who come to them for assistance, but one Creole claimed, 'Among we Creoles, we don't have the extended family.' Although many Creoles may have been successful in limiting the number of relatives who can demand direct financial help from them, quite a lot of mutual assistance among them continues.[7]

In addition to the obligations a man has to his own family, a husband must also give money to his wife's family. When a man marries, he becomes involved in a lifetime of obligations to his in-laws. Among the students 54 per cent of the men expected that they would be providing financial assistance to their wives' families. Of course, in addition to the direct gifts of money which the professionals make to their own and their wives' relatives, there are other indirect ways in which the family's financial resources can be used in fulfilling kinship obligations. As noted before, many couples have relatives' children living with them and almost half of these children are the wife's relatives. As one man put it, he didn't mind so much having to send

7. Abner Cohen (1971), in his paper entitled 'The Creole way of Death', has emphasized the way in which poorer members of Creole families use the general attitude of respect for ancestors as a means of identifying themselves with their higher-status, wealthier relatives, thus obtaining a certain amount of assistance from them.

money to his parents, but he had such a difficult time getting his relatives to stop sending children to him to educate in Freetown. When a husband or his wife visit either of their home villages it is necessary for them to take gifts commensurate with their status as professionals to all their relatives. This is a matter of great importance to the village family enhancing their own local status and position. Whenever a kinsman comes to the city he expects to receive unlimited hospitality and assistance during his visit.

The wife's family stands to gain a great deal of advantage from the marriage of their daughter to a professional, particularly if she is also earning her own income. Nearly all married couples keep their financial accounts strictly separate and so at the same time that a husband is making contributions to his wife's relatives in one way or another, his wife may also be giving regular amounts of money to them. Among those professionals whose parents were alive, 75 per cent of the women were giving regular amounts of money to their mothers and 31 per cent of them were contributing to the support of their fathers. Many wives told me they were investing their incomes in building houses in their parents' village. (According to customary rules of inheritance the wife may not inherit from her husband but in some cases she can claim from her father's estate.) One wife described how her family had arranged to care for her father:

'In my own case I am doing it for my father because he is poor and doesn't have enough so we have to help him. I give him allowances every month. We decided amongst ourselves, the children. Myself and my youngest sister decided to send him money at the end of every month. It comes out of my salary. For the past two years I have been sending not less than £8 a month because he has to put up a house so sometimes we spend up to £10. He is still a trader, but not so much [not so active]. He is the only relative I am responsible for now. Earlier I had my sister's daughter from the age of four up to fifteen. I took her as my own right from the start when I had no children.'

I asked this woman about her husband's family obligations. Was he supporting anyone? She responded that she *supposed* he was supporting his mother, but she didn't know. They never discussed such matters. Avoiding the subject reduces the chance of disagreements over this continual financial burden as well as keeping hidden the additional amounts of money a wife may be giving her relatives.

It is impossible to ascertain just how much money is spent monthly on relatives. Most people claim they do not keep account of how much they give their relatives since they never expect it to be repaid anyway. One doctor discussed his own heavy commitments to relatives, 'But,' he said, 'it is not just the *regular* expenses. At the last forty-day ceremony for one of my relatives who died, I contributed £50'. There is a general concern, especially among Provincial couples, for the large number of their relatives who are in real poverty. One woman said:

'We don't give money to relatives every month, but when we have money to spare we send it. Relatives ask when they need it. Anybody, a cousin, somebody that can't afford it, if we have it, we give. By doing this it is not easy to save money. It is the custom. If we don't do that, they will feel otherwise' [in other words, the relationship between them will be strained].

Since it is almost impossible to refuse a relative's request for money, many try to avoid situations where they will be asked for help. For example, many of the professionals stated they preferred to live in a part of town which made it more difficult for their relatives to drop in on them. Geographical distance helps to minimize the amount of contact with relatives. Most men say they spend their leisure time with 'friends' rather than with relatives and that they prefer this pattern. But, since the number of relatives who request financial assistance increases with the degree of disparity between the economic position of the professional person and the rest of his family, setting limits on such claims becomes more and more difficult. Some professionals choose to take a direct approach to the problem as in the following case of a young professional who was employed as a lecturer at a teacher-training college:

'I manage to avoid most involvements with my relatives because I live in Goderich [a small village several miles from the centre of Freetown]. It is very difficult for anyone to get in contact with me, but I do keep two of my relatives' children. They are small so it isn't a problem, otherwise transportation to school from Goderich is too expensive. When I began working I went to see my mother and told her about my income. I pointed out all the expenses I would have so she would know exactly just what I can afford and so there would be no unpleasantness about it. Those people who have difficulty with relatives are those who hide the amount they earn and don't discuss their finances freely with their relatives. My mother is very sympathetic with the additional expenses I have since I have taken up this job.'

The segregation of financial matters

We have already seen that many married couples consider it most advisable to avoid discussions of how much money they give to their respective families. This is a particular advantage to the wife's family since, if the wife is working, she can contribute to them without its influencing the amount of money her husband gives them. Strict segregation of financial accounts is not, however, limited to the handling of the monies given to relatives. It is a general pattern among professional couples. Husbands are responsible for the upkeep of the home. Wives who are earning are, ideally, free from any direct involvement in financial obligations to the household.[8] A good husband is one who supports the home entirely, without expecting his wife to contribute any of her income. In practice, of course, the situation is quite different. Women do contribute, usually by taking responsibility for purchasing their own clothes, buying things for the home, and supplementing their housekeeping allowance from time to time. However, such contributions are to be made entirely of their own free will and no husband has a right to expect his wife to supplement their budget with her earnings. It is regarded as humiliating for a husband to have to borrow money from his wife or ask her to assume some expenses.

Only 12 per cent of the professional couples had joint current bank accounts and 19 per cent had joint savings accounts. Since these cases were the exception, I asked several who had joint current accounts how it came about that they had decided upon this arrangement. One husband replied that they had three accounts. One was his, one was hers

8. One husband told me he didn't know how much his wife had in the bank until he was called before a commission of inquiry and had to produce their bank accounts. He said he was astounded to discover how much she had managed to save. Another couple discussed the matter with me after hearing a radio broadcast which had promoted the idea of husbands and wives contributing equally to the upkeep of the household. This couple found it an extremely objectionable idea. Both of them contended that any man who expected his wife to contribute equally to the family expenses only did so because he wanted to spend his money on other women.

and the third they shared! He always deposited the housekeeping money into that account! Another said that his wife was so suspicious of his spending habits that he decided a joint account was the only answer. Some of the couples having joint accounts had stated the practice when they were living overseas and one husband said that since he had insisted that his wife should not have a job he had 'extended this facility to her to see that she doesn't feel slighted'. But the most general attitude of men was summed up by one husband who said, 'It is better to keep finances separate because if you don't it becomes almost like competition in marriage'. As we saw in the discussion of the choice of a spouse, men view women's ability to earn an income as an open threat to their authority in the home. Being willing to take full responsibility for the expenses of the household even when their wives do earn an income is one means of protecting that authority.

Women, on the other hand, wish to keep finances separate largely as a means of safeguarding themselves and their children should the husband fail to maintain them. Many of them have their money in savings accounts. One woman invested her money in gold jewellery. As one wife put it, 'You can't have a joint bank account in this society. We are afraid of our men.' Or as another wife, who did not share her money with her husband, said, 'If my husband is nice with me, we will join our money together, share the money. But if my husband won't love me, I will *never* share my money.' Women resent the amounts of money they suspect their husbands spend on other women. If they know their husbands have responsibilities for children born outside the marriage, the problem is even more serious. Women usually claim they have no idea how much their husbands earn. As one explained:

'Well it is common for our men to go around with other women and if they tell their wives how much they earn then they must explain the way their money has been spent and it would be impossible to conceal the fact that they are spending money on other women. Most women, if they are working, are not particular about what their husbands are doing with their money if they get enough for the necessities in the home.'

The students were asked to respond to the statement, 'The reason a man does not tell his wife how much he earns is usually because he is spending his money on another woman', and, although only one-quarter of the men agreed with this statement, 57 per cent of the women agreed.

There does seem to be a growing feeling among the university students that husbands and wives should co-operate more in financial matters. Eighty-seven per cent of the women and 69 per cent of the men agreed with the statement, 'In money matters a wife's opinion should carry as much weight as her husband's.' There also appears to be considerably less enthusiasm for completely separate financial arrangements. Only 29 per cent of the men and 35 per cent of the women agreed with the statement, 'If a husband gives his wife a house-keeping allowance, she should not expect to know how he spends the rest of his money.' While most agree that wives should be able to scrutinize the husband's income, many of the women students continue to feel that a wife has the right to keep her earnings separate. When asked to respond to the statement, 'It is preferable for a working wife to keep her salary separate from that of her husband and to spend it as she thinks best', 46 per cent of the women compared with 28 per cent of the men agreed. Because women continue to feel high-ly insecure about financial matters they see it as highly desirable that their husband should include them in decisions about spending their income. However, at the same time, because of this continued insecuri-ty, they wish to be allowed to continue to use their own income as they see fit. As one student explained:

'This [not knowing the husband's salary] is what usually brings dissension. For example, if the woman does not know the salary of the man then she suspects that maybe he has so much money and he doesn't want her to know. Probably the man is not having that much, but because he has kept his salary from her she suspects, probably unnecessarily . . . if the woman knows that this is so much that the man earns and this is so much that the woman earns then maybe if he doesn't give enough for the running of the home then she will understand that it is not much or that he has put it towards the repairing of the car or using it for lighting or buying petrol. Knowing this you will not argue too much. But you start to suspect when you don't know how much he earns and he doesn't give you sufficient. Then you say he is misusing it.'

In addition to their fears about men spending money on other women, the insecurity of women regarding financial matters is no doubt related to traditional attitudes towards ownership of property. Traditionally, if a woman decides to leave her husband or is sent away, she leaves with only her most personal possessions and even those could be claimed by her husband if he wanted to be difficult. It is still generally believed that all the possessions of the household belong to the husband. Forty per cent of the professional sample and 42 per cent of the university students agreed that if a woman leaves her husband she also leaves behind her the property they have accumulated during the marriage. The following case from my field notes describes how one wife feels about the way decisions about spending and purchasing are made in her marriage:

> We discussed their financial arrangements and Doris said that she was only given money for food and that she usually had to ask for it. She claimed she had no idea how much he earned and wouldn't want to know more about their finances. He, she said, made all such purchases as the furniture for their new house. Now that he had bought it he didn't like it and wanted to change everything. I asked if she liked having him choose the furniture and she responded that she felt like a stranger in her own house. She repeatedly emphasized that she was sorry that she had been educated for so many years in England as it did not prepare you for life in Africa. Your ideals and expectations, she said, were completely different. I reminded her that her husband had also been educated in England. She replied that made absolutely no difference because it was a man's world in Africa. The moment any African returned to Sierra Leone he changed completely.

Often when I asked wives about ownership of property, they would point to certain items in the house which belonged to them, things they had purchased out of their own incomes. In one divorce case the wife's personal property came up for discussion. The wife asked either to have it handed over to her or to be compensated. The judge ruled against her:

> 'With regard to the petitioner's prayer relating to the recovery of her personal belongings left in the matrimonial home or their approximate value, I am not satisfied that the petitioner has proved this claim. It is true that she was pushed out of the matrimonial home by the respondent. Although she said in her evidence that she went with her mother subsequently to the respondent at No. 7 Upper Easton Street, there was no discussion about the petitioner's things left behind. She also swore that her mother went to the respondent after that. There is no evidence of her having claimed any of the petitioner's things left behind. Further-

more, the petitioner swore that the respondent later visited her regularly at No. 23 Patton Street for some time and ate with her. She said she asked the respondent for her things but the respondent said she should wait. She continued to cook for him. In this regard I prefer the story of the respondent that the petitioner left the matrimonial home with all her belongings. This prayer is therefore refused' (Decker v. Decker, *The African Law Reports*, Sierra Leone, 1964-66, p. 338).

Food and eating practices have complicated symbolic meanings. Here the judge is assuming that since the husband came to visit his wife, ate her food and, despite his refusal to return her things immediately, she continued to cook for him, she must have accepted that his refusal was justified.

The husband who fails to support his family properly may be reminded of his responsibility when his wife or one of his relatives says to him in Krio, 'Put your eye down so that you can see your nose' (*'Put yu yai dɔn mɛk yu si yu nos'*) meaning that the person addressed should be serious and attend to his first responsibilities. Or a wife may sarcastically remark, 'The cow that has no tail still has God to help her drive away the flies' (*'Kau we nɔ gɛt tel nɔ gɔd de drɛb in flai'*) meaning someone who has no one to help him in times of difficulty still has God as a defender. Open conflicts over the maintenance of the family usually indicate that the marriage is in serious trouble. We shall now turn in Chapter Nine to an examination of other areas of conflict between husbands and wives.

9

Marital conflicts and their resolution

Observations of married couples and intensive interviews with those included in the pilot group (see Appendix A) revealed a number of areas of potential conflict between spouses. Later the students were asked to rank these topics in the order in which they thought they were most likely to cause problems between married couples. Table 23 shows these results by sex and tribal affiliation.

Table 23. *Students' ranking of possible sources of conflict between married couples*

Source of conflict (Rank order)	Mean rating			
	Men	*Women*	*Creole*	*Provincial*
				(both sexes)
Unfaithfulness of the spouse[a]	1.9	2.5	2.2	2.1
Interference from husband's mother	3.6	2.5	2.7	3.5
Interference from wife's mother	3.6	3.7	3.3	3.8
Disagreement over money	3.9	3.6	3.7	3.8
Disagreements over children's discipline	4.5	4.8	4.7	4.5
Husband's leisure habits	4.3	5.2	5.0	4.4
Religious differences	5.9	5.8	6.2	5.7
Total numbers	142	87	90	136

a. Although the term 'spouse' was intended to apply to either the husband or the wife, in fact all respondents interpreted this to mean 'husband'.

The professionals were asked open-ended questions about the most usual topic of disagreement between themselves and their spouses. The order of the main topics of disagreement in terms of the number of times mentioned by the professionals are as follows:

1. Jealousy
2. Interference from relatives
3. Money
4. Children
5. Organization of the household.

There was a remarkable congruence between the responses of the students shown in Table 23, this list provided by the professionals, and my own observations of the behaviour of married couples. In addition to these topics of disagreement which were mentioned most often, some told me they argued about the quality of the wife's cooking, her working, or her wanting to work. A number of persons would only say they argued over 'petty things' and five informants said they 'never argued'. When asked if they argued about specific items a similar picture, shown in Table 24, emerged.

Table 24. *Topics over which professional couples sometimes argue*

Topic of disagreement	No. of respondents
Faithfulness of the husband	123[a]
Caring for children	61
Friends	56
Discipline of children	53
Recreation	49
Demonstration of affection	46
Obligations to relatives	40
The way food is prepared	38
Politics	32
The wife working or wanting to work	32
Sharing household tasks	32
Religious matters	21
Table manners	18
Faithfulness of the wife	17
Family finances	0

a. These figures represent the number of persons who admitted 'sometimes' arguing over the topic mentioned. There were 125 extant unions.

Reference to such things as the husband's leisure habits, recreation, and demonstration of affection are euphemisms for the central issue in most marital conflicts, the question of the husband's sexual fidelity. It was noted before how the publicity surrounding the bill to equalize the position of the children born outside marriage has resulted in a greater sense of insecurity among married women.

The problem of a husband's extra-marital affairs is highly complicated and multi-faceted. While women may more or less accept the inevitability of their husbands' sexual infidelity, the belief that the law equalizing the inheritance rights of illegitimate children was passed has exacerbated their anxiety over the matter. In the next chapter a number of attitudes towards sex which influence men to have extra-marital affairs will be considered. Here we shall concentrate on how a husband's unfaithfulness is either accommodated within the marriage or finally leads to its breakdown. It was noted that a woman may overlook her husband's infidelity so long as his behaviour does not endanger the economic security of the family or threaten the prestige associated with her status as a married woman. The minimum requirement is that the husband shall mask his affairs in a pretence of absolute secrecy. The rules of the game are highly intricate. A husband who does not want an open argument with his wife must regulate his schedule so that the hours he spends away from the home can be rationalized. Usual excuses are late office hours, and many husbands 'return to work' after a meal and a rest in the late afternoon. It is also acceptable for men to spend evenings in the company of other friends. If these absences do not occur too often or become too obvious to neighbours, friends, or relatives who frequent the house, so that they begin to make open comments about the husband's whereabouts, the wife will ignore them. Some men may precipitate an argument with their wives so as to enable them to storm out of the house. In such a situation a wife, suspecting her husband's intent, may pointedly remark, 'The bird wanted to fly, but it was just waiting for someone to shake the tree' (*'Bɔd wan flai yu to tɔch tik'*) or 'Before the bird flies, I know how many eggs are in his belly' (*'Bifɔ bɔd flai a nɔ ɔmɔs eg de na im bɛlɛ'*), (in other words, 'I know exactly what you have on your mind, I am up to your tricks'). Much conflict over this problem can be avoided by the husband who, on every public occasion, shows his wife the greatest respect. He must fulfil certain obligations such as being present at all family gatherings, performing as a good host when guests are present, and being available to attend social functions to which he and his wife are invited. So long as he is careful about these matters and carries out his other responsibilities as a husband, the wife may be quite prepared to ignore what he is doing at other times.

A highly critical factor in this matter of extra-marital affairs is the social position of the other woman with whom the husband is involved. Wives always prefer their husbands to be having affairs with women whose status is about the same as their own in terms of education and social background since such a woman will be as concerned as the wife with matters of reputation and the importance of behaving discreetly. Of course, if a girl-friend's social position is too high compared to the wife's, the marriage may be endangered, since the husband may eventually come to prefer her to his wife. But it is considered a most dangerous matter if a husband is involved with a woman of lower status than the wife. As one professional woman who was a lawyer said:

> 'If my husband is unfaithful, I prefer it is with a woman who is an equal. I would, of course, be jealous, but if it is with a woman of lower status, I would feel humiliated because she would say, "With all her education, I have got one over on her. She's got the ring, but I've got the man". It makes you feel you are lacking something. No woman of equal status would make such a remark.'

It is quite common for such girls to approach the wife in some public place and abuse her openly. The thought of such encounters fills women with terror for they cannot be ignored and almost inevitably lead to separation. Almost any indignity or amount of neglect from their husbands is preferable to such a confrontation. In one divorce case the couple had been separated for fourteen years, but the wife did not sue for divorce until one day her husband's girl-friend provoked the action by challenging her in public (Decker *v.* Decker, *The African Law Reports*, 1964-66, pp. 334-41).

The superiority of the wife over a girl-friend depends to a very large extent on her having been married by statutory law. A woman who has been married only according to customary law feels especially insecure if she is confronted by a girl-friend of her husband. One such case I encountered in the course of my fieldwork is typical of what can happen. I was invited along with another couple to have lunch with a family. We arrived to find the household in absolute chaos. There were a number of bundles lying just outside the door and the wife's female relatives living in the house were shouting all kinds of abuse directed at the husband (who was absent) and rushing about packing the wife's belongings. The wife, in her ninth month of pregnancy, was wandering dazedly around the house without saying anything to anyone. The husband, we were told, was at his office, but he had left the telephone receiver off the hook so that he could not be reached. No-one attempted to explain anything else to us, and after a few minutes it became obvious we were not going to be offered lunch so, to save them embarrassment, we left. I returned the next day to find the husband all alone in the house with only one small girl to cook for him. Everyone had moved out, including his wife and small children. They had gone to her father's house. The story came out that the husband's girl-friend had come to the house to show the wife her new baby boy.The insult was intensified because up to that time the wife had only given birth to girls. The husband told me he had scolded his girl-friend for daring to trespass in their home, but she had said that she had as much right in his house as his wife since he was only married by customary law. This event, the husband admitted, had convinced him that eventually he would have to have a church wedding.

It appears that such confrontations are on the increase. It may well be that the widespread belief that the law eliminating the idea of illegitimacy has been passed has reduced the stigma attached to women who form such attachments to married men. Certainly, as we have seen, they are increasingly taking advantage of the greater financial benefits available to them under the maintenance law. The following excerpt from the local press illustrates the kinds of situation married women dread and which may be on the increase:

> 'HENGANDAY,' [*Hengande*] FACES WIFE.[1] This world is becoming a very uneasy place for some of [us] to live. And all the blame we must accept is ourselves.
>
> Call it what you wish but the Bench begins to wonder how now this earth is becoming very not for people who one time or the other pledged their freedom to stay with their husbands. They now begin to contend their rights with sweethearts. "Hengandays" now begin to challenge lawful wedded wives on their rights.

1. '*Hengande*' comes from a Krio phrase meaning 'to hang on the nail' and is very similar to our own reference to clothes 'bought off the peg'. It was used by tailors to refer to very cheap dresses which they displayed in the open market, hanging on nails outside their shops.

Last week at Fourah Bay Road, it was at night and the time was 11 p.m. A car was parked along Fourah Bay Road between Magazine Cut and Bombay Street. A young lady was inside the car mouth-rocketing some heavy words against a wild woman outside the car who had become furious because of an information that led her to trace her husband's car.

The woman inside refused to alight and the woman outside rejected all plea to allow the car to move.

As passers-by came grouping by the car, the owner, the lawful husband before God and Man, of the woman outside sat tightly to the steering wheel.

There were rains of insult and abuses between the wife outside the car and the woman inside the car.

All efforts to get the woman inside the car to alight failed. She contended she would not leave the car and she had all rights to be there.

This is not kiding, the Bench[2] was present, heard and saw it all. The wife got to know that a woman who had long been associated with her husband unlawfully was inside her husband's car. She left a wedding arrangement[3] – and was engaged in chasing the car. On approaching the car, she demanded that the "Henganday" drop down but the other woman refused.

For full three hours crowds gathered around in gossip finding who was right. Housewife or "Henganday". Others around blamed the husband, who refused to say anything, as being foolish and did not respect his wife.

At one stage the wife climbed the car's bonnet and refused to move.

Relatives and friends of the wife joined in and demanded that the "Henganday" to alight. Still this was fruitless.

Other people joined in and forced the husband to ask the other woman out.

After some hot exchanges the "Henganday" yielded, alighted and took a taxi home.

At last the wife had the sweet end. She entered the car and her

2. It will be recalled that 'The Bench' is the name of a regular editorial column in the Sierra Leone *Daily Mail*.

3. Apparently the wife had left some household where she had been helping with the preparations for a wedding.

husband drove home. Whatever happened at home was purely domestic.

But the time has now come for the "Henganday" to challenge wives. Therefore housewives must now be prepared to meet force outside their homes.

Ah, these career Hengandays, how long would they last?' (Sierra Leone *Daily Mail*, June 22, 1968).

Some wives feel that the best way to deal with a woman who is getting involved with the husband is to approach her directly. Such a wife may go to the woman she suspects and tell her in no uncertain terms to stay away from her husband, 'Come out from behind my man' ('*Kɔm ɔt bihɛn mi man*'). The following article from the same issue of the Sierra Leone *Daily Mail* discusses the position of the 'other woman' with a certain amount of understanding but emphasizes her inferiority as a 'spinster' with few if any chances of ever getting a husband:

'HOW DO YOU FEEL BEING THE OTHER WOMAN? The Association with married men – the sweet honey and the gall. Our world is filled with sweet honey and gall and many of us women find ourselves in one of these laystack that make us happy or sad.

Perhaps when we look into the sweets and gall of life, we would sit back as women and take responsible positions in life. The question of being another woman to a married man has been a subject for discussion today among many people, especially young girls. The question of falling in love and holding on to a married man with wife and children at home has been querried here and there.

Most of [us] see gains in holding to married men when we young girls, are not married. It might be of interest to look into the asociation between an unmarried woman and a married man and how does this woman shape up with the married man. What is the sweet honey and gall of the association? The interest there in and whether these women don't have any hope of being led to the altar or the Mosque.

Let us first discuss here the case of Moslems who are said to have rights to marry more than one wife. But in this our developing country, I would not wish to come in whether it is applicable nowadays. Perhaps I would ask whether a man's love could be shared equally and whether he would give equal treatment to each woman. Excuse me poking my nose in such an elastic subject. Coming back to my subject of being another woman, how far does the association between a married man and for once I wish to call the woman, a spinster, started varied and interesting.

To the many young people I spoke to I got to know how they fell in the hands of married men when some of them confessed that they fell victims to love at first sight.

Others said they knew the men were married and had nothing else to do but fall in line and love them.

Of course many of them forced me to believe that though the exercises are difficult being another woman, there are always in-roads where by they can have their ends.

Some of them say they find pleasure and respect in loving married men as they are Careerists with no hope of joining hands in the altar or Mosque but others who really think of their future say "It's a means to an end."

Most of the second group believe that during their early stages they need to start life by cutting right in the middle and by holding on to a respectable married man they can build a good strat [sic: start?].

How true this is it is definitely questionable because the question poses itself, who do you wish to follow you on after your association with the married man. Would a bachelor decide to group with a woman who has played the role of a second woman[?]

The all majority of women or girls who hold on to married men have very little to complain to make. They assured me that except when in a case where the association had been long, the men only under strain endeavour to discuss their wives; and this they say gives them more confidence. If the man does not discuss his wife, it is very unlikely he discusses her.

All well and good but how far this would run. The problem of where and how and when these women meet these men I did not bother to follow through; but most of them agree and seem to understand that whatever they do, the men must have some time to look after their wives and children.

A young woman told me that she always shows some sympathy to the wife whenever the man is around and on most occasions she asks the man to go home when it is getting late.

This makes me begin to wonder whether this woman sincerely loves her man. As far as I know a woman who agrees to play the game of a second woman always considers herself unselfish and has been deprived of the meaning of the words "jealousy and pride".

Some of us are prone to believe that each woman should have her own man but when a woman agrees to be a second wife or in other words to be an Henganday, everything that pride carries has been buried in the grave.

Perhaps whenever the man is around and he is silent on the subject of his wife this proves that all is not well at home. And therefore the second wife thinks she has a chance.

If on the reverse all is well, what do these married men offer when they think of their wives and children (Sierra Leone *Daily Mail*, June 22, 1968).

The topic of the 'other woman' comes in for a great deal of attention in the press, suggesting it is a growing problem. For example, one article was entitled 'School for would-be wives' or 'Lessons for Husband?' (Sierra Leone *Daily Mail*, March 23, 1968). It discussed one couple who were convinced by their relatives that they should reconcile their differences. The husband agreed on condition he was allowed to see his mistress at week-ends:

'On the first weekend under the reunion arrangement there was a row when the husband complained he would be late meeting the other woman because his lunch was not ready. When his wife heard this, she got annoyed. Abused the husband, threw hot water on him and pushed him out of the house.'

The article continued by asking how it would be possible for such a couple ever to 'be joined together again?'. Another article was headed: '3 HENGANDAS VIE FOR HUSBAND' and it described a 'shameful' situation where three women were brazenly pursuing a married man at his office and fighting over him:

'Perhaps the wife of the foolish man may learn of her husband's disgraceful association with snubs outside their matrimonial home. The drama confirms the saying that "women have lost their blessed pride" and it seems as if things are [so] difficult for our girls and they now fight for married men with wives at home.

Excuse the Bench to ask – MAN DON DON NAR TOWN?[4']
(Sierra Leone *Daily Mail*, May 17, 1969).

One more example from the local newspaper describes an amusing situation which reportedly occurred shortly after the *coup* in 1968 when the curfew was in force. One night the news went out that the curfew was lifted and then, only 25 minutes later, it was announced that the . . . curfew had been reimposed and "everybody must keep off the streets and anyone who contravenes this order will suffer serious consequences".

> 'Then there was panic. Husbands and wives were alarmed. Boy and girl friends had to give up their wonderful escapades. And "hengandas" had to suffer more because they had to abandon their entertainment. One unfortunate man had to abandon his car and fled home forgetting he had a vehicle.
>
> This man had settled down somewhere he was not expected to be that evening. And the interest was that his wife and children were worried when they heard the disturbing announcement. As the wife and children looked over the window in expectation to see daddy drive home, they noticed him running home almost breathless. As he entered the house, the children gave him a poser, "where is the car, daddy?" '

According to the editorial, the next day the wife discovered the car near the house she had 'suspected her husband had been visiting for sometime. The Bench has to stop here because of the scandal':

> 'But such incidents have given cause to a new bill to be introduced in Texas, U.S.A. The new law will permit women to shout their husbands' lovers "Hengandas" if they catch them in act of adultery.
>
> In this Texas state, husbands already have the right to shoot their wives' lovers and so the wives are to be given the corresponding right.
>
> For sometime Texas women had wanted to repeal the law altogether but the State representative said he wants to give the men the right to protect their homes. This just give[s] them [the wives] equal shooting rights: that's all.

4. A Krio phrase usually employed when a woman is rejecting a man's amorous advances meaning 'Even if all the men in the town were gone, I wouldn't want you.' Here the writer is probably asking, 'Are all the good men in the town gone?'

Perhaps wives here are safe when curfew is imposed but husbands, boyfriends and girlfriends, including "Hengandas" will have it hard under curfew' (Sierra Leone *Daily Mail*, April 22, 1968).

Some of the evidence, including all the publicity, suggests that the stigma attached to being the 'other woman' has been reduced, with a resulting intensification of marital conflict over the problem. Furthermore, today married women are not so prepared to countenance the situation. As one professional woman noted,

'Men feel they have a right to go out and our old mothers and grandmothers said you must accept this. But [today] the longer women are married, the less they are prepared to put up with it. Most women were not economically independent but *now they are*. That's why you get more divorces. It used to be that women became ill, nervous or died, but they just *had* to stick it out. Two-thirds of the homes in Freetown are arguing over this question.'

As shown in Table 23 there is an important difference between the rating of unfaithfulness as a source of conflict by men and women. The same is true of the rating of the husband's 'leisure activities'. Men see these two items as even greater sources of conflict than do women. Clearly wives are becoming very effective in making their husbands aware of how much they are disturbed by these outside relationships and the men are not embarrassed to admit this. For example, I had dinner one evening with a professional couple. After the meal the wife urged me to stay on for a while to continue our conversation. She looked at her watch and announced it was only 9.45 p.m. so there was plenty of time. 'Besides', she said, 'as long as you are here he [pointing to her husband] won't go out. This is the first night for weeks that he has stayed in so long. Of course, whatever time you leave he's going to go out afterwards anyway.' It is possible that such open remarks and conflicts about the question of his infidelity further aggravate the problem and lead a man to seek refuge from a nagging wife in the arms of another woman. Married women tend to band together and inform one another about each other's husbands' affairs. A husband may object to his wife spending too much time with other women and warn her with the Krio phrase, 'I don't want this friendship business' ('*A nɔ want padi biznɛs*'). As one man put it, 'Any time we see women gossiping together we know they are talking about some husband's sweetheart'.

Relatives

After the question of a husband's fidelity, interference from relatives, particularly from the mothers-in-law, is the problem that causes most disagreements between married couples. Mother-in-law problems come in for considerable publicity. One panel discussion which was broadcast over the local radio station considered the many ways mothers-in-law affect the happiness of married couples. It was concluded that in Africa it was impossible to sever connections with parents completely after marriage, but that it was far preferable for mothers, and particularly the husband's mother, to try to keep out of their married children's affairs. An article in the local press entitled, 'Those Conflicting Mothers-in-law' referred to them as 'controversial people in marriage'. Immature husbands were given the large share of the blame for the problems which develop:

> 'One fact which brings a mother-in-law into direct conflict with the wife is the attitude of some men towards their wives. Many men still cling to their mothers as if they are hoping for another round of sipping Cow and Gate from the feeding bottle. This naturally provokes the wife to become jealous and to form the impression that [it] is the mother-in-law who is the enemy' (Sierra Leone *Daily Mail*, August 3, 1968).

As shown in Table 23 men were inclined to rate interference from their own and their wife's mother as equal sources of conflicts in marriage. I asked the students two other questions at different points in the questionnaire, to compare their attitudes towards each of their mothers-in-law. In response to the statement, 'Generally it is the wife's mother who causes trouble between married couples', 22 per cent of the men and 15 per cent of the women agreed. When asked to respond to the same statement about the husband's mother, 28 per cent of the men and 72 per cent of the women agreed! Observations of relationships between married couples and their mothers-in-law support this view that it is the husband's mother who is most likely to be a source of conflict between the couple, but, of course, most of the tension she creates is felt by the wife.

On the other hand the relationship between a wife and her mother is usually very close. As mentioned, girls tend to be favoured when they are growing up. Mothers may be especially indulgent with them since, as one woman put it, 'Girls will only be women anyway'. Part of the reason girls continue to join the *Bundu* society stems from the close relationship between daughters and their mothers. There are special duties which ideally only a daughter should assume at the death of her mother and can only do if she is a member. One informant told me about his mother who was mourning the loss of his sixteen-year-old sister who had died in an accident by being electrocuted. He described his mother as

'... sitting around the village crying and not being able to work. It takes a long time for a mother to get over the death of a daughter. It is different when a son dies. A daughter is responsible for taking care of her mother at death, washing her and having the responsibility for various funeral ceremonies. If a mother loses her only daughter, there is nobody to take care of her when she dies. So, when they think about all these things, they mourn all the more about the death of a daughter. Even when the mother is sick the daughter would be allowed to do certain things that I would not be allowed to do.'

I asked this informant who would take the daughter's place when his mother died. He responded, 'Except my cousin. She has a sister who has given birth to females. So perhaps she will get one of these.'

The close relationship between daughters and their mothers continues after marriage. An often-quoted Krio saying points out that a mother takes all the responsibility for her daughter and it is only after a mother dies that a daughter knows that she is a married woman with no place to turn for help (*'Gial pikin nɔ ba no se i mared tete iŋ mami dai'*). When there is trouble in a marriage from a wife's mother it usually results from her objections to the way the husband is treating her daughter, or her concern with the health of her daughter or the grandchildren. Of course, interference in such matters may be highly irritating to the educated wife of a professional man, particularly if the mother tries to insist that certain traditional approaches to household management or child-care should be employed. However, perhaps women are more able to cope with problems caused by their mothers, for as we saw in Table 21, significantly fewer women were afraid of their mother's curse than were men. Moreover, it is very much in the interest of the wife's mother to keep up a good relationship with her daughter and son-in-law. A husband is not likely to be the model of generosity with his wife's family if his mother-in-law is a source of trouble in his marriage.

The relationship between a son and his mother is quite another matter. I have already alluded to the dependence of women on the patrilineage for support in the event of the death of their husbands. There is considerable uncertainty regarding inheritance and succession, resulting in often bitter rivalry between co-wives in the polygamous household.[5] And, as mentioned before, if a man has received the necessary education to achieve professional status, it can be assumed that in the background there has been a highly ambitious mother totally committed to his success. There is a general absence of trust in most relationships, especially with persons who might stand to gain economically from another individual's downfall or death. The one person a man can always trust is his mother. After all, she is one of the few persons who cannot conceivably gain by his death. We have already discussed the special fear and respect sons feel towards their mothers. Men often refer to the strong emotional relationship which exists between them and their mothers. One provincial lawyer brought up the topic in conversation. We were discussing the differences between the traditional and the western way of caring for babies. His wife was about to give birth to their first child and he was troubled about the question of which was the best way to bring it up. His comments illustrate how many men feel about their relationship with their mother:

'But there is a sentimental attachment that does not obtain in the West. Like now, I am sitting here, there is no day I do not think of my mother, how is my mother feeling, is she happy, and so forth. I probably started getting that feeling in childhood. Because in western homes you just don't breast-feed your children so much. Here sometimes after three years he is still being breast-fed by the mother. Well the child grows with the mother. You sleep with her in the same bed. With you now [in the West] you have to get a separate bed. Well, from the time he is born until probably five or six years he is sleeping with his mother. So there grows a

5. Customary laws of succession and inheritance are highly ambiguous. Ideally, the oldest son of the first wife should succeed his father but in practice this rarely happens. Heirs are not named until after the death of the father and then appointed by elders to whom he has indicated which son should succeed him. Often the father will have chosen the son of a favourite wife and this may well be the youngest woman to have joined the household. Since a woman's security in her old age is very dependent upon her son, co-wives are always competing to improve the position of their male children.

greater attachment between the child and the mother than when you put your child in the bed and you have to give her this or that. But the African mother has the breast to feed the child all the time, you can even have it in the bath! This grows with the child when the mind is pliable.

I still think of the time when my mother used to put me on her back, even when I was big. At five or six years you must remember certain things. And I was still sleeping with her when she got my sister. It is a physical thing. So this is the difference when I said there is a greater attachment to the child in the African home than the mother in the western way.'

One old Creole gentleman describes his childhood memories:

'I can remember how my mother used to wake up and come to me in the early hours of the morning and wake me up. She would ask me to read to her from the scriptures. Especially if it was near to the time of examinations. Then she would pray for me. After a while she would say "Go lie down now" and I'd go to sleep feeling so lifted up. She put life into me, strength, especially at exam time. I'll always think of how she used to come. "Bobo, my son, are you sleeping, come now wake up."

My wife still does this for our children. My wife is like a mother to me. A *good* wife takes the place of a mother. If my wife sees I don't eat well at night when we sit down, she asks what is the reason don't I like the soup or was something troubling me.'

As noted before, men often describe a good wife as being like a mother. In a letter included in one of the caseworkers' files in the Department of Social Welfare, a husband begged his wife to return to him and be 'as a mother to him'. One husband told me that when he is angry with his wife he refuses to eat her food and goes to his own mother to be fed, 'My wife's food is nice, but my mother's is better, nicer.' A similar relationship often grows up between a little boy and his older sister who may assume much of the mother's responsibility in caring for him. The following excerpts from a letter used in court as evidence of a man's cruelty to his wife expresses the need of one husband to establish the kind of close relationship with his wife that he had had with his sister:

'The contents of the letter you sent with driver Bockari are not at all pleasing to me, especially when you stated that you had entirely decided not to come back to me. I am writing this letter with contrition, and full repentance of the past and with eyes full of tears. You know Kate, I am very haughty, it is not wickedness that had led me to maltreat you: it is jealousy and it is because I love you. To be outspoken, your absence has left my heart bleeding with worries. At present my position is rather pitiful and require your forgiveness. I was looking up to you in place of my late sister Laura who was my all in all. Who then must I look up to now that you have almost deserted me? I have now realised the evil that lies in beating. Since I left Tiama, I have been filled with care and worries so much that I scarcely find time to sleep when I got to bed ... Please forgive me for the sake of only Ken and Chris, I am praying daily so that God will change my evil ways and create in me a clean heart. Now I make this solemn promise as I did when we first got to Bo that I never again will ill-treat you and further promise to co-operate with you in everything whatsoever. Therefore I am asking that you change your mind and resolve to come back with the hope of meeting your husband a thoroughly changed person' (Williams, (C.C.) *v.* Williams (V.E.S), *The African Law Reports*, Sierra Leone, 1964-66, pp. 122-23).

Many men gave as their reason for marrying the need to have someone who would assume the role of their mother in their life. As one man put it, 'I got married mainly for a cook and to have children -- a steady place to eat. I thought it was time to stop depending on my mother to cook for me and to start looking around for a girl.' Food has a highly symbolic meaning and to eat the food someone cooks for you implies a relationship filled with trust. David Gamble, in a study of family life in Kenema, asked men the classic question, 'If you were in a canoe with your mother and your wife and it capsized and you could save only one of them, which would you save?' Almost always the respondent chose the mother. After all, as many said to him, 'You can always get another wife, but you can never get another mother' (Personal communication). The most serious abuses which can be spoken are obscene references to the mother. A Krio phrase emphasizes that one's very humanity is connected with one's mother, 'After all my mother bore me' ('*Afta ɔl na mami bɔn mi*'). It means, 'Don't treat me poorly, I am also a human being, I am not a dog. I was borne by my mother.'

In view of the closeness of the relationship between a mother and her son, and the tendency for husbands to look to their wives to assume her role in their lives, it is not surprising that sometimes competition and jealousy develop between the husband's mother and his wife. I was often told that the husband's mother becomes more jealous and troublesome if her son's marriage is too happy. If the son fails to fulfil his traditional obligations to her in terms of giving her regular gifts of money, or neglects visiting her, it is the wife who is blamed. Interestingly, in this traditional patrilineal society, it is the husband's mother who represents and is able to impose forcefully the traditional obligations on the professional family. The wife, on the other hand, in the modern monogamous marriage, symbolizes to the husband's mother and his family his break from traditional patterns and the commitments he has assumed *vis-à-vis* contemporary urban life. As we have seen, prestige and status in town require him to drive an expensive car, entertain, dress himself and his wife and children in western clothing, eat imported foods and attend social functions.[6] And, as we have also seen, even the wedding requires an enormous outlay of money by the husband. Sometimes a man is able to explain these expenses to his relatives and sometimes they accept his explanations, particularly if they are wealthy and his obligations to them can be fulfilled by token gifts. More often the husband is forced to attempt to pacify his relatives, particularly his mother, with small amounts of money, and he tries to avoid all but the minimum of contact with them. Professional couples definitely favour maintaining separate residences from their parents. Not many persons could foresee a situation which would necessitate bringing a mother or father into the household to live. Most men felt they could provide for their parents' care in some other manner. Over three-quarters of the professionals (and more of the Provincials than the Creoles) agreed that it is likely to spoil a marriage for a married couple to have either of their parents living with them. Eighty per cent of the students also said they would prefer not to live close to their parents after they married. Geographical distance makes it easier to control the amount of contact with relatives, and lessens the likelihood of open conflict.

The kinds of disputes which arise between a wife and her mother-in-law emphasize how these two women represent the opposing de-

---

6. During the dry months, October to May, many dances are held which require formal dress and may cost as much as £6 per couple.

demands of traditional and urban values. Wives might be accused of not caring properly for the house or for the children, but they are much more likely to be criticized for their expensive tastes and western ways. While in traditional society a husband's first loyalties were very clearly defined – they were to his own relatives – today, when open conflicts occur between his wife and his mother, his role is ambiguous. In the traditional family, the wife has little recourse in an argument with her in-laws except to return home and complain to her own kin group, and such a drastic step would require that her case be extremely well-supported. Today, when such a dispute arises, the husband no longer 'naturally' or unquestioningly supports his own family's interests as represented by his mother. Nor, at the same time, in view of his profound psychological dread of displeasing his mother, can he side openly with his wife. When the students were faced with the statement, 'If a wife and her husband's mother quarrel, the husband should side with his wife' only 8 per cent of the men, compared with 29 per cent of the women, agreed. Among the professionals, in response to a similar statement, 'If the wife and her mother-in-law quarrel, it is to be expected that the husband should side with his wife whether or not he thinks she is wrong' one third of the women and 17 per cent of the men agreed. More of the men who agreed were Provincials than Creole. Perhaps the great disparity between traditional standards held by the mothers and the modern ideas held by professional couples make it necessary, in at least some cases, for the Provincial husbands openly to support their wives when they are under attack by their mothers. After all, the husband, as well as his wife, is interested in maintaining these new standards to which his mother is opposed. Most men, however, assured me that the safest plan was to remain absolutely neutral and objective so that they could mediate in arguments between the two women. Understandably, some wives resent their husband's attempts to remain aloof in such conflicts and they often feel themselves caught between the traditional demands and expectations of their husband's mother and the new way of life which they and their husbands are trying to live.

The role of the wife and the authority of the husband

Both students and professionals mentioned other sources of disagreement in marriage. Arguments over the way food is prepared and over the wife's working or wanting to work are often part and parcel of the same problem, conflicts over the wife's role and the question of the absolute authority of the husband in the home.

There are definite conflicts between the educated woman's role in the society and her role as a wife and mother. When asked to respond to the statement which included a reference to the dual role of the educated woman ('If a woman has a university education she has a responsibility to help the country by working, whether she has young children or not'), 68 per cent of the men and 54 per cent of the women students agreed. (I could find only two women in the country who had a university degree who were not employed.) Although among students 61 per cent of the men and 80 per cent of the women agreed that it should be the wife's decision whether she wanted to stay at home or work outside the home, only a quarter of them could agree that a wife should have the prerogative to choose *between* having children and having a career. I shall discuss the general importance of children in the next chapter, so it is sufficient to say here that they are considered an absolute necessity for a happy marriage, and as already noted, that many couples find it difficult to employ persons who care satisfactorily for their children when the wife works away from home. But more important, in terms of the marriage relationship, it is nearly impossible for a man to maintain his traditional role of authority over the wife when she works and earns her own income. Many couples argue over whether or not it is the wife's sole responsibility to care for the children even if she does work, in other words, whether or not the husband should assist her with some of her household responsibilities. Clearly, if a wife is spending her money as she chooses and not contributing to the household budget, the husband will have even less reason to encourage her.

Women are also answerable to their husbands regarding their whereabouts whenever they are away from the house. Almost all the students (93 per cent of the men and 96 per cent of the women) agreed that a woman must ask her husband's permission if she wants to go out alone at night. One wife had a very serious argument with her husband over the fact that she had even accepted a lift from one of his male friends on her way home from teaching at school. He had to explain to her, since she was not a Sierra Leonean, what this implied about her relationship with the other man (that she was his mistress) and that it was a matter which could cause him extreme embarrassment with his family if they heard about it. He told her that if she could not walk home then she should leave her job immediately.

The following excerpts from the local press have less to do with the question of wife-beating than with the problem of the change in the woman's role which challenges the husband's authority in the home:

'DO OUR WOMEN PREFER BEATING TO PETTING? What is wrong with you? Your face is squeezed and swollen up? My husband beat me up last night. And this is all what happens every day in many homes.

Every corner in this country we hear of stories like these. Recently, two housewives had prayed the courts to grant them divorce on the grounds that their husbands beat them even in public places. Why should this kind of treatment be meted to women even in this day and age? Are wives generally beaten because they are weaker sex and therefore can be physically dealth with in any disagreement? Or, is it because they are incorrectible and mouthy hence need to be taught good manners by beating them?

Or is it because they – women – persist like goats in doing what they are asked not to do by their husbands and therefore need to be taught a lesson by some sort of cudgeling? In short why is it necessary to beat one's dear own wife.

... Mr. Samuels a Trade Unionist sees nothing bad in beating a wife. He said, "Nothing is more effective as a disciplinary measure than beating your wife provided it is not excessively done." He said this attitude was passed down from generation and therefore "it can be said to be so old as man. It is not peculiar to Africans." Mr. Samuels continued: "Most people who claim sophistication think wife beating is rather crude or un-civilized. But they have yet to envisage an alternative method of bringing their misbehaving wives under control. Again I know of women who actually expect to be beaten by their husbands once in awhile; It is an interesting experience they say. They also say it is manifestation of love. "I certainly would not support any 'ban wife beating movement' if anybody were to plan it."

A prosperous trader at Fisher Street market will never under any circumstances support violence between husband and wife, "Instead they should reason and discuss amicably any matter that could result in violent argument. It is not only that the man is disgracing himself but also lowering his personality. Neighbours look down on such couples and have no regard or respect for them. What is the marriage for if the husband resorts to beating his wife anytime there is misunderstanding? . . ."

A student thinks that women at times push their husbands to a point where they cannot resist beating them. Besides, he claims, it is necessary to give one's wife some spanking once [in] a while. But he believes there are other alternatives to beating. For example: "I can boycott my wife's bed and if she is reasonable she will come to beg me. If it happens that I am at fault I will honestly apologise to her if she calls me to reason instead of pushing her right to the extreme." In a matrimonial home it is a question of give and take. But there is a saying that "When democracy is misused a dose of autocracy should be applied."

A housewife, Mrs. Adama King who has been married for almost fifteen years and never been beaten once says: "It is very wrong to beat one's wife. If there is love, there will be no question of beating." It is true a man is the master of the house, but that does not give him any licence to be brutal to his wife.

A wood contractor who is alway[s] bitter about the attitude of women, says he beats his wife anytime she does anything wrong and fails to give reasonable explanation. "Again she will get thoroughly beaten if I should see her with other men. He asks: How can a wife I married with my own sweat be going about with other men and I turn a blind eye[?]".

Don't you go about with other women, I asked? To this he flew into a rage. Pointing to me, he said: "I am the master in my house. I am free to do anything I like. Naturally, men are not bound to and cannot be satisfied with only one woman. That is the work of nature. Women should not compare themselves with men in this case . . ." ' (Sierra Leone *Daily Mail*, July 13, 1968).

I included the question as shown in Table 24 regarding arguments over table manners because in my initial interviews with couples I found that when they argued over table manners it was no longer an argument in which the husband had the upper hand. In all cases when couples reported arguing over this topic, it was the wife who was criticizing and correcting the husband!

Resolving conflicts

As the quarrels which occur between married couples often reveal the conflicts between traditional and contemporary values, the manner in which they are resolved often displays the way in which individuals manage to manipulate both systems in their own interests. Traditionally, even the most trivial quarrels are resolved by the involvement of other members of the family. Husbands and wives rarely discuss a problem between themselves. For example, if a husband is displeased with his wife, he refuses to eat her food or goes to a relative to be fed. If a wife is angry for some reason and wants to let her husband know about it she may refuse to cook for him. By the time the actual reason for a married person's anger is known to the spouse, the fact that there is some disagreement between them is already known to their relatives who immediately take action. When a wife has a grievance against her husband she may take the problem to her relatives who will try to talk the couple into resolving their differences. Similarly, the husband's relatives also get involved when a couple quarrel.

The students were asked to respond to the statement, 'When a quarrel or dispute arises between a married couple, they should turn to their relatives to help them settle it.' Only 13 per cent of the Creoles compared with 54 per cent of the Provincials agreed this was a good approach to conflict resolution. The professional couples were asked who helped them resolve conflicts between them and their spouses. Among the Creoles 79 per cent of the men and 86 per cent of the women said that 'no one' helped them; they relied on discussions between themselves to work out their problems. Among the Provincials 50 per cent of the men and 45 per cent of the women gave this response. Clearly, Provincials are more likely than Creoles to prefer traditional methods of coping with marital disputes. Those couples who did admit to relying on outside assistance mentioned the wife's parents, the husband's parents, other relatives on either side, their godparents, 'any relative who can help' and their friends.[7]

7. As noted in Chapter Seven, children often have godparents appointed when they are christened and it was often common, at least among the Creoles, to have different godparents appointed when a couple married. These people were usually very close friends of the family who were older and who would be able to give objective guidance to the young couple. This is not a common practice today.

Even among those who did admit that they sometimes relied on other persons to help them resolve their problems, most indicated they were loth to involve their relatives unless the problem was extremely serious. Many professionals avoid putting their problems before older relatives since they are unlikely to understand the modern situation. There is also the matter of traditional attitudes of absolute respect for the authority of elders. Serious problems could arise should an older relative give advice which for some reason the couple could not follow. One husband described how another young couple, friends of theirs, often assisted him and his wife in working out their difficulties, and that they did the same for these friends. Couples living far away from relatives may even consult politicians from their home area to help them sort out their differences.

Although traditionally wives do not usually make complaints about their husbands to the husband's relatives, this seems to be a common practice today among professionals. One husband told me how embarrassing it was for him to have his wife call his father at night if he failed to return home at a respectable hour. Invariably the next day his parents would have him round for a lecture on the responsibilities of a good husband. In another case, since the wife was not a Sierra Leonean, she had no other family than her husband's to rely on, and took every complaint to his father. Although sometimes the father tried to work out the problem alone with his son, usually he brought the matter before the entire family. This practice became less than satisfactory to the wife because she found her sisters-in-law usually siding with their brother, since they resented his marrying an outsider.

In the case described earlier in which the wife had left the house after the husband's girl-friend appeared with their new baby boy, representatives of the wife's family intervened. Twice they came to the house to talk with the husband and then they arranged a meeting with the wife present. Since the husband readily admitted he was at fault, the wife's relatives encouraged her to return home. The wife took no active role in the discussion. It was clear that she and her husband had not come to any actual understanding, rather that she was simply returning to the household because, as she said, 'they told me to go back'. Although the involvement of relatives in such matters may bring about such a solution to the immediate problem, in this case at least it was hardly a means of promoting 'mutuality' between the husband and wife.

The Department of Social Welfare provides family caseworkers and there is a growing tendency for married couples to bring their problems to them. Here the traditional approach to settling family disputes is employed. First both the partners are called in together to present their problem and then relatives may be asked to join the discussion. The relatives, together with the caseworker, decide on the case and if the couple agree to follow their advice, the case is considered to have been successfully concluded.

Although there are still relatively few actual divorces, as noted before, many women take their problems to a lawyer hoping such drastic action will influence their husbands to change their ways. Once again, as with the social workers, these lawyers often attempt to bring about the couple's reconciliation by discussing their problems with them and advising them. Of course, some married couples are not able to resolve their differences and many decide simply to take up separate residence.

The following paragraph was taken from an essay written by a university student on the topic, 'Marriage in African Society is different from Marriage in Western Society'. In his view, in traditional African family life the woman

'... is the chattel of her husband and once a woman has got children in a house, she becomes a real slave because she is required to please her husband in every inch or else her children will not be blessed. They will become riff-raffs or Teddy Boys and will always be in trouble. Our poor mothers had to obey our fathers and in my own home I have never seen anything like equality between my father and my mother. My father is the absolute boss of the house and nobody dares flaunt his orders. Nobody questions him. Whenever he quarrels with any of his wives, he drives them out at any time of the night and usually they sleep outside the verandah. They dare not leave the confines of the house and sleep elsewhere.'

I have included this illustration here not because I think it represents an accurate or general picture of traditional relationships between husband and wife; rather, the interesting point is that in this young man's mind the most salient feature of traditional conjugal relationships in comparison with western ones is the absolute authority of the husband. This view of the husband's role is in some contrast to the position of the husband in the following illustration. Here a husband finds himself helpless to control his wife and has written a letter to the family caseworker in the Department of Social Welfare:

'Dear Sir:

Report against my legal wife

I am making the following complaints against my legal wife.

1. She had from [for a] long time neglected cooking in the house at the appropriate time, letting the children to suffer.
2. She does not clean the house and she is more inclined to her self market making, leaving the children abruptly. She goes to Bo almost everyday buying ice[d] fish.
3. She never tells me in my presence when [she is] going anywhere in this District.
4. She does not respect me even in the presence of the people or before my fellow men. She gives me an open defiance and can't apologise. She feels she has more right than I and can control the house.
5. She is always depriving my children and I from our meals and leisure in the house.

Sir, I am appealing to you to warn this lady to stop all these malpractices and maltreatments and let us cooperate and work as a team. Let her remember that we have children and we all hail from the same town.

Yours faithfully,'

Although people perceive great differences in modern ideas about the roles of husband and wife compared with traditional patterns, the stress throughout this discussion has been on the manner in which persistence of traditional values continues to influence marriage relationships. It is undeniable that there are sharp conflicts between the structure of traditional family life and the contemporary urban structure. Although they are willing to conform outwardly to urban standards of prestige and status, it appears that men very strongly retain traditional attitudes towards the wife's role: a good wife is docile, obedient, discreet, well-mannered, able to cook and entertain guests (now according to western standards), a dedicated mother, and sexually faithful. Ideally, when a woman marries she should devote herself to her household and her children. Women, on the other hand, have been quick to accept what they view as the advantages of the western concept of the role of a wife which include freedom from economic responsibilities for the upkeep of the household. Their ideal-ized version of the western husband includes the expectation that he should assist with household duties and involve himself directly in the care of the children. And, as we have seen, the conflicts between traditional and contemporary structures are not expressed simply in opposition between husband and wife, but involve considerable internal conflict in each partner as well. This is particularly clear in regard to the employed wife's dual role.

Courtship is a radical innovation. This new pattern of courting leads girls to expect that the relationship with the husband after marriage will follow the romantic image they have of western monogamous marriage. Although men have accepted many aspects of this idealized version of the husband's role, most of them continue to behave in a more traditional fashion once they have married. They expect to spend their leisure time away from the household and that, as in the traditional village, their chief concern will be with their position in the community. Although they hope their marriages will enhance their prestige, they do not apparently think it is necessary for them to direct much of their energy into family relationships. Traditional attitudes towards sex roles produce a situation much like that described in a study of a Yorkshire mining town:

> '. . . the sharp cultural division between the sexes, and the atti-tudes consequent upon it, run right through the community and produce tension within the family itself. The demands made on behaviour by this division are in conflict with the demands of the life of the family as a unit' (Dennis, *et al.* 1957, p. 249).

Conflicts between the expectations of husbands and wives lead to considerable tension within the relationship and are reflected in the nature of the disputes which occur. Acceptance of the importance of romantic love, with its emphasis upon the couple's relationship during courtship, does not necessarily mean that there will be a similar emphasis after marriage. In Marion Kilson's (1961) analysis of Mende stories she found:

> 'The relationship between spouses, which is pivotal in 12 per cent of the stories told by men, is marked by ambivalence. On the one hand, the economic interdependence of husband and wife is stressed; on the other, the fear of impermanence and deceit is reflected. Many stories note the wife's economic roles as cook and farm worker. Nearly all reflect a general lack of trust of the

spouse. Several stories emphasize that a man can depend upon neither the affection nor the fidelity of his wife ... Moreover, a man's wife not only may deceive him, but may work against his best interests. In one tale a man almost lost his life, because he revealed some of his hunting secrets to his wife, who related them to his enemies. Thus the relationship between spouses is marked by doubt and fear as projected in these stories ... Although the relationship between husband and wife may often be characterized by fear and doubt, nevertheless, it is one which should be characterized by reciprocity of affection and trust as well as economic interdependence.'

Clearly, the idea that marriage should be marked by mutual trust, loyalty, fidelity and affection between partners is not entirely a western innovation.[8] Traditional ideas about the family also rated such qualities highly. Although probably only rarely achieved in any society, it appears that the present structure of society in Sierra Leone with its conflicting values and expectations makes the realization of such an ideal even more difficult and unlikely.

In this chapter we have seen how the manner in which various marital disputes are resolved, like the nature of the conflicts themselves, reveals the way in which the conventions and values of the traditional structure and those of the contemporary urban structure collide, and how individuals seek to adapt themselves to the demands of both systems. The trend is unquestionably towards the nuclear family unit, increasingly isolated from extended family involvements, but the slow-moving economy keeps many professionals deeply involved in responsibilities for their kinsmen. It is interesting to observe that the individual concerns, social status, prestige and economic security, which lie behind the troubles of married couples which we have been discussing in this chapter, are in large measure only transferred from the traditional to the urban context. Perhaps these concerns contribute more widely to marital dissatisfactions and conflicts than those of us who have been reared in a society committed to the 'romantic model' of companionate marriage have always clearly recognized.

8. Little (1967) refers to the extra privileges associated with being the 'love wife' among the Mende (p. 144).

10

Attitudes towards sex, family limitation and the use of contraceptives

The problem of limiting the size of families and the use of contraceptives is of quite general concern among Sierra Leonean professionals. Investigating the opinions individuals held regarding these matters provided considerable insight into attitudes towards sex and their influence upon relationships between husbands and wives. Traditionally, in Sierra Leone, high prestige was accorded to the person who could acquire a large number of wives, children and dependants. If a man in the village was asked how many children he would consider ideal he would respond, 'as many as possible'. Today professionals are aware that they are unable to support and educate large numbers associated with prestige, a whole pot-pourri of attitudes, children are associated with prestige, a whole pot-pourri of attitudes, beliefs and practices has grown up to support and maintain that association. These beliefs, attitudes and practices, often having intense emotional content, stand in the way of widespread adoption of methods of birth control. The exploration of these hindrances to ready acceptance of contraception also revealed many obstacles in the way of achieving the ideals of monogamous companionate marriage.

Attitudes towards limiting the size of the family

Most of the professionals and the students indicated that they would prefer to have four or fewer children. Table 25 shows the range of their responses to the question of what they thought was the ideal number of children.

Table 25. *'Ideal number of children'* (Percentages)

		University Students	Professionals
One - Three		21	31
Four		62	49
Five or more		15	13
Other ('according to circumstances', no response, and one in each group responded, 'as many as possible')		2	7
Totals	%	100	100
	No.	229	139[1]

Professionals think that limiting their families to four children represents an enormous departure from the traditional ideal of 'as many as possible' and if everyone followed their example the population would decline. The evidence suggests that they are incorrect. The mothers of two-thirds of both the professionals and the students had borne four or fewer children. Moreover, not all these children had survived childhood. Among the professionals 83 per cent had three or fewer brothers and sisters still alive, and 23 per cent were now only children.[2]

Although professionals may indicate a preference for limiting the number of their children to four, it is very difficult to collect accurate information on the actual number of children born to them and whom they are supporting. Only 10 per cent of the married couples said they had more than four children. But the evidence suggests that people tend to under-report the number of their children.[3]

Although education usually delays marriage, it is not unusual for

1. See Appendix A, page 309, for an explanation of the difference between the total of responses in this table and the number of interviews.

2. Of course, any changes which favourably affect infant mortality would immediately alter this situation. In a fertility study among women living in Freetown and in other tows and villages, Dow (1971) found that women between the ages of 40 and 49 had an average of 7.5 live births with an average of 3.9 surviving children.

3. It is also not possible to predict the size of completed families of these professional couples, since most of them are still of child-bearing age (two-thirds were under 40 years of age). Moreover, 65 per cent said they wished to have more children and 15 per cent of the wives were either pregnant or 'not sure' if they were at the time of the interview.

men to have fathered several children before contracting a 'formal' marriage. As one informant put it:

> 'Sometimes before a man gets married, you have left school. You have got an ambition to become a doctor, lawyer or anything. You are still struggling to get a scholarship or to raise enough funds for you to go overseas to study but you are already full grown. You have gone to college and finished but you decide to work and save money. During that period you don't want to commit yourself by marrying, but still you have got girl-friends. [Perhaps] one of them is impregnated and you get issue from her. You accept the children as your òwn children although the woman is not your wife. So by the time you get married, after your professional training you will have four or five children outside. This is what happens in the majority of the cases. Before you decide to choose a wife you will already have four or five children.'

Married men also establish relationships with women outside marriage, and, as we have seen, sometimes these women have children. (I have already noted that it was not advisable to ask people *how many* outside children they had.) The following case study illustrates the problem:

> 'This informant had had two children by two different women before leaving Sierra Leone to study in Britain. One of these unions had been regularized by the payment of bridewealth. One child was being cared for by his parents and the other was with its mother. While he was in Britain, this man lived with an Irish girl and they had two children. Upon his return to Sierra Leone, he married and he and his wife had four children. During my fieldwork this man had another child with a girl-friend. In addition he supported two other women who had children by him. His wife had also had a child before this marriage and it was being cared for by her father. Nevertheless, in the interview, this couple only reported the *four* children living in the household.'

The professionals were asked 'open-ended' questions about their attitudes towards large families. Table 26 shows their responses to these questions. These answers reveal changing attitudes towards having many children and show that the expense involved in rearing them is the chief reason for family limitation. People often said that they would prefer to invest in the education of a few more of their relatives' children rather than to have more than three or four of their own.

Table 26. *'What would you say was the best thing about having a large family?' (Percentages)*

Responses		Males	Females
'Nothing good'		52	56
'Mutual financial assistance'		11	4
'Companionship'		11	37
'Security in one's old age'		4	1
'A better chance that some will survive and make good'		6	1
'Better preparation for life to grow up in a large household'		1	1
'Perpetuate Creole group'		1	–
'Status'		8	–
'Preserve family name'		5	–
Totals	%	100	100
	No.	82	59[1]

'What would you say was the worst thing about having a large family?' (Percentages)

Responses		Males	Females
'Financial costs' (respondents specifically mentioned educational costs)		19	20
'Finances'		50	58
'Too much responsibility'		4	1
'Individual child not well cared for'		10	12
'Burden on the mother's health'		4	3
'Loss of privacy'		4	1
'Nothing bad'		1	1
Other (no response, 'Don't know')		6	3
Totals	%	100	100
	No.	82	59

4. See Appendix A, p. 308 for explanation for differences betwee total responses in this table and the total sample.

A small group of professional people in Freetown have taken the initiative in establishing a Planned Parenthood Association which is quite active. In 1969 they presented a play entitled, '*I de inɔ du*', which is a Krio phrase meaning, 'There is some, but not enough for anyone else'. This phrase is usually employed when a relative's request for financial assistance cannot be met. The play was very successful and performances were repeated by popular demand. It emphasized the constant problem of insufficient money to pay school fees and buy food and clothing for large numbers of children. A Krio song was part of the presentation and became very popular in Freetown:

> 'Who is there now that doesn't know the world had become difficult for us?
> Who is there now that doesn't know the world has turned upside down?
> Who is there now who doesn't know money is finished in town?
> Money is finished.
> It is there, but it is insufficient.
> Some people are better off than their mates.
> Like our little children in their different homes.
> Some have few children others have many.
> It is there, but it is not enough.[5]

The use of contraceptives

The approval of limited families, of course, implies the need for employing some method of birth control. The majority of the professionals, 85 per cent, said that they approved of the use of contraceptives. They were asked to state what methods of contraception they had ever used at any time in their lives. These responses are shown in Table 27. As shown, only 22 per cent indicated they had never used

---

5. *U de nao wey nɔno se wɔl dɔŋ trɔŋ paŋ wi*
U de nao wey nɔno se wɔl dɔn tɔn oba
U de nao wey nɔno se kɔpɔ dɔn
Kɔpɔ dɔn na tɔŋ
I de inɔ du
Sɔm man yu kin bɛtɛ pas in kɔmpin smɔl
Lɛkɛ dɛn wi lik pikin dɛn na dɛn difrɛn om
I de inɔ du

any method of contraception. However, when these people were asked what methods of contraception they were using at present, quite a different picture emerged, as shown in Table 28. Sixty-four per cent were not using any method although 50 per cent of these indicated they did not wish to have more children.[6] It was also clear from discussions with many married men that the method of contraception they reported was the method they were using in their extra-marital relationships and they were using no methods of birth control with their wives other than abstinence. Despite the fact that professionals claim to approve the use of contraceptives and indicate that they wish to limit the size of their families, very few of them are actually making use of any method of birth control in their marriage.

Table 27. *Methods of contraception ever used (Percentages)*

Sheath		32
Foam tablet		2
Jelly		2
Diaphragm		5
Rhythm method		3
Coitus interruptus		7
'The pill'		17
Surgery (either male or female)		2
Abstinence		4
I.U.D.		12
Douche		0
'Nothing'		12
Totals	%	100
	No.	184[a]

a. n > than sample because some respondents indicated they had used more than one method at some time.

6. Although 14 per cent of these persons said that they planned to use some method of contraception in the future, we cannot rely very much on these responses. The respondents were provided with a list of contraceptives which included an opportunity for the respondent to indicate, if he was not using any method, why not. The choices for such response included: 'Not using any method because wife is pregnant', 'Because more children are desired', 'Because of religious convictions', 'Not using any now, but plan to in the future', or, 'Not using any and do not plan to in the future'. Respondents would be less likely to admit they never planned to use contraceptives because of their already-stated firm commitment to family limitation and the very obvious inconsistency such a response would involve.

Table 28. *Methods of contraception currently used (Percentages)*

Sheath	9	
Foam tablet	0	
Jelly	0	
Diaphragm	1	
Rhythm method	2	
Coitus interruptus	0	
'The pill'	9	
Surgery (either male or female)	2	
Abstinence	2	
I.U.D.	10	
Douche	1	
Not using any method because the wife is pregnant or because more children are desired	14	
Not using any method now, but plan to in the future	14	
'Nothing' and 'not using any method and never plan to do so'	36[a]	
Totals	%	100
	No.	140[b]

a. Included two persons who were not using any method of contraception for religious reasons.
b. See Appendix A, p. 308 for explanation of differences in total number responding to this question and the size of the sample.

Beliefs and attitudes influencing the use of contraceptives

Certain beliefs and attitudes, which are part of the traditional background of most Sierra Leoneans, complicate the ready acceptance and the practice of contraceptive techniques even though most professionals wish to limit the size of their families. To begin with there are practically no traditional methods of contraception, and such as do exist are highly disapproved of.[7] Because of the high mortality of infants

7. Some traditional medicine-men supply women with special cords to tie around their waist to prevent conception, and Freetown women have access to them. The Temne have a practice called 'turning womb' ('*ka lafthi aŋ pɔru*'). Certain manipulations are performed by old women who have acquired the skill, and afterwards a woman is said to be incapable of conceiving. There is said to be a medicine made of herbs or roots which is drunk and, although it is not always effective as an abortifacient, it has been known to be lethal! Some-

and the high value placed upon children, very few women in the traditional family would be interested in terminating a pregnancy. The idea of artificially limiting the number of children born to a family is still highly disapproved of by older women. They will say, 'God who separates the mouth at birth will put food in it' (*'God we plit yu mot go put it di'*), or 'God is not going to give you a load you are unable to bear' (*'God no de gi yu lod we yu no go ebul tot'*).

Although abortion, in traditional society, is practically unknown and certainly disapproved, today it is thought to be quite common among educated single girls and married women in towns. One informant discussed the difference in attitude:

'Abortion is very rare in villages. Most villagers are afraid of committing artificial abortion. This abortion is actually committed with girls going to school. They are unmarried girls and they don't want to have issue ... Abortion is very common in the larger towns and it is mainly amongst school-girls and young girls who have left school and are working. They are not engaged and so it is socially wrong for them to have issue when they have not yet married. It would spoil their chances of getting married. But for the married woman [in the village] the happiest thing that can happen to her is to get children. A woman can get twenty! They are able to send them to school by and large, or they can send them to work on their farms, so there is not fear [of having too many to support].'

Fifty-five per cent of the professionals thought abortion was very common today but, according to them, it occurred only among the educated. Respondents were asked if they had any objections to married couples using abortion as one means of limiting their families. Over one-third of the men and a quarter of the women indicated they had *no* objections. Among those who disapproved of abortion as a method of family limitation, very few gave 'religious' reasons and only two mentioned the idea that abortion was murder. Most of the objec-

---

times the bark of a certain tree is ground up and, in the form of a pad, is inserted in the vagina. It burns and is extremely painful but is supposed to be effective as an abortifacient if the pregnancy is less than two months. Women who wish to induce a miscarriage must find an old woman who has the appropriate knowledge and pay for her assistance. However, abortions in the traditional family are, as one person said, 'terribly frowned upon and a serious crime'.

tions centred on the fear of possible ill-effects of abortion on the future fertility of the woman.

It is impossible to get an idea of how extensively abortion is practised as a means of birth-control or family limitation. Among the women in the professional sample who reported having miscarriages, 20 per cent admitted they were induced. Since respondents were being asked to admit to having committed an offence, (abortions are illegal in Sierra Leone) we can be quite sure these figures do not exaggerate the numbers who try to abort a pregnancy. Moreover, since both husbands and wives were being asked this question, it is quite likely that the 20 per cent figure under-represents the number of wives who have tried to induce an abortion. Men are more adamant than women in their objections to various methods of birth-control, so they would be less likely to report (or, perhaps, even to know) that their wives had induced a miscarriage. For example, one wife found she was pregnant just before she and her husband were to leave for an overseas assignment. She induced a miscarriage but, as she said, she would 'never dream of telling him about it'. Several admitted they had attempted it more than once. After telling about one abortion she had induced, one woman remarked, 'I always say I won't try any more to dissolve a pregnancy after three months'.[8]

Although abortions are illegal, no doctor in Sierra Leone has ever been charged with committing this offence. It is said to be relatively easy to arrange for a medical abortion.[9] There is one nursing home which is known for catering mainly for abortion cases. After the law regarding abortions was liberalized in Britain, there was some discussion of the need for such revision of the law in Sierra Leone. One editorial in the local press suggested that the government should look into the subject and 'take all necessary action to keep our country up-to-date with the modern precept of the subject' (Sierra Leone *Daily Mail*, June 1, 1969). It appears likely that if abortions were legalized,

8. It is also difficult to determine whether the abortions result from the methods women claim they use or would have occurred naturally. There are a variety of things which they believe to be effective abortifacients: laundry blue mixed with gin, quinine, and of course, the native medicines mentioned earlier. Doctors report that some women often try all these methods together and that others resort to inserting an instrument to induce bleeding. However, many doctors discount the possibility that any of these methods except the last would be effective.

9. The cost is about £25.

and people were assured such operations would be conducted with adequate medical safeguards, most would cease to have objections. However, under the present circumstances, the growing number of abortions, particularly among young girls, is a matter of alarm, as is illustrated in the following excerpt from a college newspaper:

'*Abortionists in our Midst*. The rate of abortion in the campus is increasing every term. I am not trying to be biased against anyone but to say the truth regardless of who gets hurt.

Right now in campus, three girls are suffering abortion. What pains me most is that these people have once suffered abortion, they have not got any steady boy-friends, only the usual froys.[10] Some abortion leads to sterilization and one cannot tell which one will lead to that. Many people suffered abortion more [than] once since they came to college, and if the percentages of abortionists to non-abortionists is calculated, one would be surprises [sic]. Does this mean that our girls are more sexually inclined? I can only advise them to control their sexual feelings.

Statistics show that girls who go steady suffer abortion more frequently than other girls' (Fourah Bay College mimeographed newssheet, 1968).

That educated girls resort to abortion is largely a result of their fears of contraceptives. University students, unlike the majority of the population, have easy access to contraceptive devices through the college medical services. Some may fail to make use of them simply because they lack information about contraceptives and others may be too embarrassed to ask the doctor for them, but many fear that *any* contraceptive device could lead to sterility. Students repeatedly told of cases where a sheath had come off during intercourse and had gone, irretrievably, up inside the uterus, causing infection and sterility. Oral contraceptives are also avoided because it is feared they could have the same effect on fertility. Students often told me of friends and acquaintances who were the 'kinds of girls who used such things' or of those who had 'dissolved' pregnancies, who found, once they were married, that they were unable to conceive. However, the student who finds herself pregnant is in a desperate situation. Unless she manages

---

10. 'Froy' is the term for a casual girl or boy-friend and refers disparagingly to individuals who go from one person to another with no permanent attachment.

to terminate the pregnancy her hopes of finishing her education (to say nothing of her chances of marrying) will never be realized.

The high rate of infant mortality in the village is a constant reminder of the importance of children. Moreover, people who do not have children are considered abnormal. Traditionally, sterile persons are even accused of being witches.[11] Most mothers hesitate to allow a person who is childless near their children and they do not allow them to be responsible for their care. There are several related beliefs among the various tribes in Sierra Leone but perhaps the most common among all of them, including the Creoles, is the belief in the witchbird or '*kaka*'. When the very distinctive call of this bird is heard, everyone knows that the bird belongs to someone who is about to kill a child. When the bird is heard, all the people from the village or the neighbourhood mass to drive the bird away, to identify the guilty person and to force him to leave the area immediately. Invariably the person identified as the owner of the witchbird is a sterile man or woman. The following excerpts from two issues of the local press illustrate the kind of reactions this bird's calls elicit even in Freetown:

> '*WITCHBIRD AT POLICE STATION* A large crowd of about 300 people stormed the Eastern Police Station yesterday, as word went round that the police had detained a witchbird – local[ly] known as korkor.
>
> Accompanying the bird to the police station was a middleaged woman from Blyden Lane at Gingerhall; in Freetown's east end, who is helping the police in their investigations.
>
> Residents around the area, particularly suckling mothers, had complained that they were terrified by the frequent cries of the bird which started shortly after the woman in question moved to the area recently.
>
> A number of children are also reported to have died in the area recently at the rate of one almost every day.
>
> Also being questioned yesterday was a jujuman from Kenema; alleged to have found the bird and named the woman as the owner.
>
> The woman had to be rescued from an angry mob of women as

11. Among the Mende such persons are called *ndelei*, which means they have evil spirits. An *ndelei* is a python (or, in West African vernacular, a boa-constrictor) whose spirit sucks the blood of children.

they fell on her. An army officer had to intervene to save the woman from molestation.

Police later released the woman but the bird was left in a bucket of water at the police station. The juju man was also released' (*Unity*, May 12, 1969).

. . .

'*FIRE FORCE ALERTED AS "WITCH TREE" BURNT DOWN*
A bid by unknown persons to destroy a "witch tree" in the West end of Freetown, nearly caused a major disaster at the last week. The Freetown Fire Brigade had to be called out and the fire was brought under control.

It happened that for several days some residents of Bolling Street, King Tom, were molested by cries of a bird locally known as 'koko' and believed to be a witchbird.

On Wednesday evening some people in the neighbourhood decided to burn the tree and get rid of the bird. Efforts to drive it away on previous nights failed. So stones and sticks were hauled [hailed] at the tree but the bird did not move. Dried grass and leaves were piled at the foot of the tree and set ablaze.

The fire was immediately greeted by a violent wind and sparks of fire went flying in all directions and threatened wooden houses in the area. The threatening blaze and the wind were also interpreted by the people in the neighbourhood as a sign of anger as the witch bird flew off.

The Fire Force was immediately alerted and there was a sigh of relief as the fire was brought under control and a serious disaster averted.

There was also a sigh of relief that the 'witch' bird has been silenced and the residents in the area can now sleep in peace' (Sierra Leone *Daily Mail*, April 6, 1968).

One of the most serious abusive terms which can be applied to a man is to call him impotent (impotency being equated with sterility).[12]

Similarly, one of the worst things a man can say to his wife or any woman is 'I have a cockerel in my house' ('*Kak na me os*') or, 'You are a cockerel' ('*Yu na kak*'). A young man may be warned against marrying a girl who is sterile with the Krio phrase, 'Make sure you don't put a cockerel in your house' ('*Mek si yu nɔ put man kak no*

12. The Krio word for impotent is *okobo*, the Temne is '*aŋ hɔrɛ*' or '*aŋ bɔrk*' and in Mende it is '*barrkeh*'.

yu os'). It is a common belief that it is better to have three at the altar than two, or, in other words, it is best that a woman's fertility be established *before* marriage. In response to the statement, 'It is preferable for a girl to be pregnant by her boy-friend before they are married so that they know that they are able to have children', 42 per cent of the university men agreed. A young couple may be reminded at the birth of their first child that 'One child is really not a child' (*'Wan pikin nɔ to pikin'*). After all, you must certainly have more than one child since if you have only one and it dies, you will be left with an empty house.

Although a wife's adultery is considered a very serious offence, the husband may be forced to overlook her behaviour if it proves that their childlessness was the result of his sterility. This attitude is summed up in the Krio phrase, 'The sterile or impotent man cannot frighten the pregnant woman' (*'Okobo man nɔ de skia bɛlɛ wuman'*). In short, her adultery has proved him to be guilty of the far more serious offence of being sterile.

Two Sierra Leonean men discussed with me this matter of the vital importance of having children and the extremes to which people will go to get them. They cited an example of one couple who had been childless for a long time:

> 'This couple went to England and while they were abroad they reported back to their relatives that the wife was pregnant and that they would remain in England until she delivered. They have now returned with a small baby that is 'whiter than you with straight hair and both of the parents are as black as the two of us sitting here'. These people were so desperate they would do *anything*.'

The implication of their story was that the husband had been willing to arrange that his wife have an affair with an Englishman so that they could have a child. One bachelor told me that he had 'helped several childless couples' by getting the wives pregnant. He told about one such relationship with a married woman who had no children. The wife kept telling him how much she wanted a child. Finally she did get pregnant and had a little boy. He said that after this he stopped all sexual relations with the woman and became more friendly with the husband. The husband was informed about the paternity of the child but there was no trouble over it. Of course, he said, the woman was now very happy. 'Why not, a woman with no child in Africa is always unhappy!' Examples of the extremes to which people will go to get a child could be multiplied.

With such concern about fertility it is little wonder that young married couples do not wish to delay having a child. In response to the statement, 'It is preferable for married couples to wait for two years before having their first child,' 80 per cent of the university students disagreed. In no case was it thought possible to maintain a happy marriage relationship without any children. It is common for young married couples to have one or two relatives' children living with them in their home from the beginning of their marriage. All those professional couples who had no children of their own were raising some relatives' children. One prominent professional couple had had no children but had raised two of the wife's nieces as their own, but in my interview with the wife she did not admit they were her nieces, she claimed that they were her *own* daughters. Although, as mentioned before, a lot of marital strife results from a husband's extra-marital relationships, they are still considered to be a legitimate recourse where the couple are childless.

There is a traditional practice regarding the disposal of the after-birth which illustrates the importance of fertility and reveals the extreme anxieties women feel about it. It is believed that when the placenta is buried it must be laid in a special way or the mother of the newly-born child will never conceive again. One wife of a professional described this practice:

'The placenta is buried near some landmark in the compound. Mine is buried in my grandmother's compound. It is always done by aged people. They bathe it with palm oil. There is a very special way to lay it otherwise you will never have another child. So if after the first birth you don't conceive you may have been bewitched by the relative who buried it. People know who can be responsible for bewitching. Mummies then have to collect certain leaves and bathe the persons. They wash you up and then they charge you for it. After the placenta is buried you have to keep an eye on it so no one digs it up, like a rival for the husband or a mate [co-wife]. If it is dug up it will make you sterile so if a woman wanted to stop having children she would ask the mummies to turn it over the other way.'

The belief in the importance of the correct handling of the placenta continues. Women who have their babies in nursing homes now often ask the midwife for the placenta so that it can be properly buried. Otherwise, to ensure that it is not used to endanger the mother's future fertility, it is destroyed by throwing it into the sea.

Attitudes towards women's sexuality and their influence over men

Certain traditional attitudes towards women and their sexuality serve as more subtle complicating factors influencing marital relationships and the use of contraceptive devices. Some of these could be loosely described as the belief in the supernatural power of women. While all these beliefs are not directly related to the use of contraceptives, they have a definite impact upon relationships between men and women.

To begin with, there is the belief that mothers have the power to render their baby sons impotent.[13] If a nursing mother accidentally gets some of a baby boy's urine in her mouth the baby will become impotent. Mothers are warned to avoid letting the baby boy's urine spray into food which they later might inadvertently eat. Students were asked if they believed that mothers, if careless, could make their sons impotent, and 37 per cent of the men and 44 per cent of the women agreed this was possible.[14]

The question is not so much that urine could get into the mother's mouth by accident. After all, most women can quite easily take the necessary precautions to avoid this happening. The importance of the belief is that it is thought that a mother might deliberately decide to do this thing to her son. As it was explained, a woman may have been deserted by her husband or widowed, or her older sons may have forgotten their responsibilities to her. Such a mother might decide to make her youngest son impotent so that when he grew up, instead of marrying and leaving her, he would remain at home and take care of her.

The belief in the mother's curse has been described. It is also believed that wives may curse their husbands if they are driven to it by

13. The Krio word for impotent is *okobo* and is equated with sterility, weakness, or applied to a man with feminine characteristics.
14. One informant, underlining the danger, told about a relative whose eight-year-old son accidentally urinated near some meat. After this had happened, his mother would not cook this meat; she gave it all away. The informant emphasized, 'Whether suckling the boy or not, as long as it is her son, she wouldn't risk it.'

their behaviour. It is also believed that a girl-friend or wife can make a man impotent. If, after having intercourse with him, a girl discovers her lover is not sincere she can arrange with a *mori* man to perform a ritual which will render him impotent. His condition is incurable unless the girl in question arranges for another ritual by the *mori* man. Men are often warned against getting themselves into such situations with the saying 'The leaf that the goat finds sweet will give him diarrhoea' (*'Lif wey swit got mɔt na im go rɔn in bɛlɛ'*). Following your appetite rather than reason or sound advice will lead you into trouble.

There is also the very common belief in the danger of menstrual blood. Intercourse during menses is forbidden and menstruating women should not prepare food for their husbands. One man described the dangers:

'A man should have no contact with a woman during her period. In Temne there is no name for menstrual blood but a man would ask "Have you seen your moon?" or a woman would say, "I have seen my moon" (*"I nɔnk aŋ of ami"*). A man would not sleep in the same bed as a menstruating woman. The woman would not cook for her husband, it is believed to be a curse and any contact would be inviting the curse. Creoles can't cook certain foods because it is said they won't hold together or they will spoil quickly.'

It is also regarded as dangerous for a man to see the cloth a woman uses during her menstrual period. Today this can easily happen because, after washing them, women tend to hang them in the toilet; in the village men and women had separate toilet areas. And, of course, a woman could do this purposely if she wished to harm a man. A man who trespasses in the secret bush of the *Bundu* society is also in danger of losing his potency or being struck with elephantiasis of the testicles. The sanctity of the women's organization is preserved by such fears of the power of women to destroy the potency of men.

There is also the belief that under certain circumstances intercourse may be dangerous for a man. Many college students told me that they had been warned that each time a man has intercourse he loses a 'small quantity of blood'. Intercourse with a woman who is much older is regarded as especially dangerous. No one pretended that such fears acted as an effective deterrent, and most adults who spoke about the matter claimed it was simply a way mothers used to persuade their sons not to be promiscuous. Adults, however, would often emphasize the dangers of having intercourse too often. Too frequent intercourse is said to 'drain a man's strength and sap his energy' and to result in a 'weak mind'. I was often told that it was possible to recognize someone who was promiscuous by such physical symptoms as a bad complexion and general weakness. I attended a funeral with a young man. After the service he remarked to me, 'I would go off my head if I lost my mom'. I asked him what about his feelings if his father died. He replied, 'I *expect* to lose my dad at any time, because he is promiscuous. Promiscuity is dangerous to the health, especially in a man.'[15] However, there certainly was no evidence that professional men took such fears about the physical dangers of intercourse very seriously except perhaps as an explanation when someone became ill.

There is a definite disapproval of the open display of affection between men and women. As noted before, Westerners are accused of being insincere in their expressions of affection because they hold hands or kiss in public. I had dinner with one professional family on New Year's Day. After the meal we retired to the sitting room for a drink. The host proposed a toast and wished us all a Happy New Year. Then he kissed his wife on her cheek and proceeded to comment to me and the other guest, a Sierra Leonean, on how 'anglicized our life is'. He referred to the fact that his wife was allowed to eat with him and his guests and that he had even kissed her before us. The two men continued to discuss how they had never seen their parents exchange any signs of affection. I have personally been present when a couple met for the first time after a very long separation. They simply greeted each other very formally and shook hands. Relationships between husbands and wives in public were always very restrained. Displays of affection between them before their children are also disapproved of.[16]

Not only is the public display of affection disapproved of, but it is

15. Traditional society imposes many rules about the time and place for sexual intercourse. For example, it is forbidden during the daytime or in the bush. Persons who break one of the many rules about the approved time and place may suffer serious illness. In one man's opinion these rules not only attempted to prevent illicit sex, but were aimed at reducing the frequency of sexual intercourse.

16. Among the students 49 per cent of the provincials and 33 per cent of the Creoles agreed that this was not a good thing and all the married couples said they avoided it.

believed that deep feelings of emotional attachment are not to be trusted and in any case not to be expressed. Husbands often reminded me that it was not good to let your wife know you liked her too much because she could take advantage of your feelings. It is quite generally accepted that women can influence the behaviour of a man by putting a medicine called *ɛfodi*, a love-potion, in his food. It is believed that if this medicine is fed to an unsuspecting man, he will fall hopelessly in love. Husbands who are very indulgent with their wives or young men who ignore their own male companions and spend an 'unnatural' amount of time with their girl-friends are understood to be suffering from the results of such medicine. A Krio song goes 'He has eaten *ɛfodi* so he should sit down quietly' (*'ɛfodi, ɛfodi, i dɔn eat ɛfodi, sidɔn saful'*). Such husbands are described as rushing home to be with their wives even when their friends ask them to go out. They are accused of being so passive that they even allow their wives to go out with other men. I was told of a divorce case in Freetown where the man had re-married within three months. Such behaviour could only be explained, according to the informant, as resulting from the man being the victim of *ɛfodi*. Hence a young man is very careful not to eat in the house-hold of any girl-friend whose mother may have designs on him for a future son-in-law!

Married men also avoid eating food cooked by their girl-friends. Even if the efficacy of the medicine as a love-potion is discounted (as it usually is among the married professional men) the mere fact that a girl-friend might be adding some unknown herb or substance to their food could be dangerous. Wives, aware that their husbands are having affairs with other women, plead with them not to expose themselves to the added threat of having their affections stolen away by eating food prepared by their sweethearts. Girl-friends of a different tribal back-ground from the wife are often more feared because wives believe these tribes may have knowledge of more effective *ɛfodi*.[17]

The students in the university sample were asked if they believed that women are able to influence men's behaviour by adding certain things to their food and 40 per cent of the men compared with 27 per cent of the women agreed. It may be that the belief in the efficacy of love-potions is declining among the educated but it certainly is a topic

17. When girls graduate from the *Bundu* society a special meal of red rice is prepared and girls may send some to their boy-friends as well as offering it to important men in the village. This meal is also said to contain a love potion.

which elicits considerable amusement, as illustrated in the wollowing Krio song:

'One woman went to a medicine man
To ask for something which would make a man like her
This man gave her one medicine to lick
And one medicine to rub.
The woman licked the one which was for rubbing
And she rubbed the one for licking. [18]'

The idea that it is unbecoming for a man to act too devotedly to his wife or girl-friend continues to be supported by derisive references to the effects of *ɛfodi*.

There are other attitudes towards women's sexuality which directly affect the use of contraceptives by married women. In traditional society, as in many parts of the world, women are regarded as basically promiscuous. One of the perpetual problems facing the polygamous husband in the village is the control of the sexual behaviour of his wives. 'Woman damage' cases (women accused of committing adultery) are the most frequent problem brought before the local courts. The most popular explanation or rationalization of the practice of clitero-dectomy in the *Bundu* society is that it reduces a woman's sexual desire and makes the husband's problem of controlling his household easier. As one woman explained to me, 'Circumcising a woman does-n't completely take away sexual desire. It just makes it easier to control oneself.' While it is not possible, of course, to account completely for the continued practice of female circumcision as resulting from men's fears of women's potential promiscuity, we have seen that a very high premium is placed upon the good character of a girl who marries a professional man. Both the student and the professional men agreed that a wife's infidelity is unforgivable. As one man put it, 'A husband's affairs with his sweethearts don't threaten the marriage, they only disturb the peace in the home, but if a wife is unfaithful the only possible outcome is divorce.' [19] Doctors find that one of their main

18. '*Wan wuman go to wan mɛrɛ sin man,*
Ɛɔ ask fɔ somtin wey go mid in man lɛk am
Di man gi wan mɛrɛ sin fɔ lik,
En wan fɔ rɔb
Di wuman lik di wan fɔ rɔb
En rɔb do wan fɔ lik.'

19. Modern monogamous marriages lack the traditional institution of 'woman damage' which provided a convenient mechanism for dealing with a wife's adultery without divorce.

difficulties in getting women to use contraceptives is the belief of husbands that their use gives rise to promiscuity. Fear of pregnancy is thought to be the best deterrent to women's extra-marital relations:

'The way I see contraceptives affecting married life is that say the wife had a friend, she could go on having relations with him when her husband was away without fear of being pregnant. If the husband returned and was told about it or got to know about it in some other way, he could get a divorce. But, except the husband is told, he wouldn't know about his wife's sex relations. That is the way birth-control aids affect one's married life.'

Seventy-two per cent of the university men and 45 per cent of the women agreed with the statement, 'Women who use contraceptives are more likely to be unfaithful to their husbands.'

It appears that Sierra Leonean men view women as generally divided into two groups: those who are controlled and discreet in their relationships with other men and completely faithful to their husbands, and those who are promiscuous.[20] As one man put it, 'Women are supposed to have no appetite for sex. It is frowned upon.' A woman who does reveal her sexual interest in men might be referred to in such abusive terms as 'the whole world's wife' (*'Ol wɔl wɛf'*) or a 'man's mattress' (*'Man matras'*).

Another practice affecting marital relationships is the continued practice of the traditional post-partum sex taboo. Traditionally women are forbidden to have sexual intercourse during the time they are breast-feeding, a period which may continue as long as two or three years, and if a child becomes ill the mother is accused of having broken this taboo. Although one effective means of spacing births in the traditional polygamous family, its continued observance among monogamous couples gives rise to problems. Obviously, it interrupts normal sexual relations in marriage and may account for the recent and quite general trend towards a shortened period of breast-feeding.[21] Both samples were asked to respond to the statement, 'Intercourse during the time a mother is breast-feeding her child is harmful to the

20. Rodman (1971) observes that where there is a double sexual standard it '... can best be maintained where the significant group of women are revered while some other group of women are sexually available to men' (p. 61).
21. The longest time recorded in this research that a professional wife nursed her child was six months, but usually the time is very much shorter. Some never do breast-feed their babies. Today village women are also shortening the period of breast-feeding, at the expense of their infants' diet.

child.' More of the students than the professionals agreed, 63 per cent compared with 28 per cent. However, those professionals who did not believe intercourse could harm the child still refrained if a woman was breast-feeding an infant. As one man said, 'Medical theory proves that it is not harmful, so what can I say? *But I don't do it.*' Some men described the idea of sexual intercourse when a woman was breast-feeding as 'revolting' or 'disgusting'. Even those men who had over-come their own feelings about the matter said their wives would never agree.[22] It is understandable that the tendency to avoid intercourse when a woman is pregnant and the continued observance of the post-partum sex taboo serve to justify men's extra-marital affairs. As one man put it, 'It is the time when most men slip up. That is the only time I ever slipped up during that period.'

Attitudes of men towards sexuality

Throughout the discussion of marriage among the professionals in Sierra Leone, aspects of the problem of husbands' extra-marital affairs have come up for consideration. This matter must also be considered in terms of men's attitudes towards sexuality and in relation to their position in male society. As we have seen, a number of factors en-courage men to develop relationships with women outside marriage. There is the overriding importance of having children, particularly if the marriage is childless. Further, there is the inconvenience of long periods of sexual abstinence surrounding birth which increase the tendency for men to seek sexual gratification outside marriage. We have also seen how, although professional couples prefer to limit the number of children they have to four or less, men object to the idea of their wives using contraceptives because they associate the possibi-lity of promiscuity with their use.

There are more complicated psychological factors which are in-volved. As we have seen, men associate the qualities of a good wife with those of a mother or a sister. Good women, like mothers, sisters and good wives, do not openly manifest evidence of their sexual feel-

---

22. Among the students there was a greater tendency for women than for men to agree that the practice was harmful (56 per cent of the men as compared with 74 per cent of the women).

ings and they are not available for sexual relations with anyone other than their marriage- partner. An unfaithful wife is intolerable. As noted, it appears that men categorize women into two groups: those who are good (e.g. like their mothers and sisters and good wives) who are unavailable for illicit sex, and those who are available for sexual relations outside marriage. It is permissible for the women in this latter group to show interest in sex and to use contraceptives. Although men would hesitate to describe such women as 'bad', they would certainly regard them as unmarriageable.

Moreover, we have seen that men distrust the expression of strong emotional feelings towards their wives. In view of all these considerations, it is easier to understand why once a couple have had four children there is a tendency for men to abstain from sexual relations with their wives. Most men who admitted that abstinence was the method of birth-control they employed in their marriages rationalized the practice as necessary in order to be absolutely certain there were no more children conceived. The evidence suggests that to a large extent men view sexual relations in marriage primarily as a means of getting children rather than as a way of expressing love or affection. As a result one suspects they are blocked from developing or enjoying a satisfactory relationship with their wives which provides mutual sexual gratification.

Although these factors may to a large extent explain the tendency for men to seek sexual satisfaction in extra-marital affairs, it is also necessary to consider the effect of illicit affairs on a man's relationships with his male friends and his association of his manhood with his potency. As we have seen, a man's position and prestige in traditional society is measured largely in terms of the number of wives, children and other dependants he could acquire. The prestige associated with his procreative powers continues to act as a strong motive for a man to beget as many children as possible. Today, as noted before, a wife's discovery of her husband's illegitimate child is the occasion for intense conflict within the marriage. She moves out of the household and all the conciliatory resources of the extended family are required to persuade her to return. But at the same time as the husband is involved in such an unpleasant palaver within his household, outside he is being heartily congratulated by his male friends. They sympathize with him over the trouble his wife is causing him, but another birth evokes their sincere and enthusiastic approbation. Men know about each other's affairs and their outside children and these are an important measure of prestige among them.

I was repeatedly reminded (and it is generally believed) that there are more women than men in Sierra Leone and that this problem is especially acute in towns. Since these surplus women have no hope of marriage now that people are tending to marry only one wife, men argue that these women can get children only through having affairs with married men. Not only are extra-marital affairs justified in this way, the practice of polygamy is similarly explained in demographic terms. However, the evidence from the population census does not support these notions. In Freetown there are between 18 and 20 per cent more men than women in the age-groups between fifteen and thirty-four years (*1963 Population Census of Sierra Leone*). Clarke (1968) found an overall surplus of 10,543 men in Freetown and he found that the pattern of excess men is also found in most other urban settings in the country (p. 276). The total population of Freetown is 127,917 (*1963 Population Census of Sierra Leone*). Women prefer to marry men of higher social and economic status. If they cannot marry them they may be willing to establish sexual liaisons with them. In the case of the professional men so many women are eager for their attentions that they get the impression there is a vast surplus of women.[23]

The desire to beget children (or to assist the imagined excess of unmarried women to bear them) is only one aspect of the attitudes of men towards sexuality which lead them to indulge in extra-marital affairs; proving sexual prowess is another. In the polygamous household wives take turns sleeping with the husband. It is the responsibility of the husband to get these women pregnant. As one paramount chief who had more than twenty wives commented, 'After a while it becomes a duty, not a pleasure!' The importance of being successful in keeping one's wives pregnant is emphasized in the following comments about the traditional marriage:

> 'Sterility worries them [the husbands] to death. In the native
> homes, especially when you are married in a polygamous family,
> the main reason why your parents sent you to be married to the

23. Many girls are blatant in their approach to men. Dressed in their best, they often 'visit' professional men in their offices; sometimes they ask for money, making it quite clear what they will offer in return.

chief is to get issue. Because the only benefit they can get from
you, from that marriage, is issue.'

Failure to impregnate one's wives can be the occasion for public
humiliation. Easmon (1967) describes a chief who had failed to impregnate any of his wives and describes the extreme public humiliation
he had to endure as a result. At one ceremonial occasion a performer
sang the following song to a large gathering of the chiefdom:

'Chief Briwa beds with many a girl –
But what does he all through the night?
Keeps he the bedlight burning bright,
Or snores his wives into a fright?
His name is known through all the land,
His word is good as gold band.
But Briwa, Chief, your Chiefdom wants
For other things than roads or grants.
It would not have your sires forgot,
Their fame and power decline and rot.
So pray, O Chief: Let down your pants,
Bring forth, O Chief, a boy or girl!
All else is good but this most worth:
Bring forth, Briwa, bring forth!' (p. 117)

The stress on the husband's sexual performance as measured by
resulting pregnancies is so great that the ability to perform sexually
may become a matter of intense anxiety among men. Complaints about
impotence are a very frequent reason for men to seek medical advice.
One epidemiologist who ran a clinic in the Provinces as part of his
research, said that impotence was the most frequent complaint men
brought to him. He referred to these common fears about impotence
as a kind of 'type anxiety' of the society. I discussed this problem
with several doctors who confirmed his findings.[24] These fears are not
limited to men in traditional families who must have sexual relations
with more than one wife; professional men have similar concerns.
Many consult doctors to receive injections of testosterone (male
hormone) which they believe will increase their sex drive.[25]

24. During the short time I spent in a remote village almost all the men at
one time or another came to me privately asking me if I had an injection for
them because they were suffering from impotence.

25. The fear of impotence has been observed in other parts of Africa. For
example, Levine (1966) found '... a widespread and intense preoccupation with
impotence. Many married men report experiencing impotence, others fear it, and

Men desperately fear situations which will expose their sexual limitations. Wives may use this knowledge to punish them for their extra-marital affairs. When a husband comes in late and the wife is aware that he has been out with a girl-friend, she may demand to be satisfied sexually. The husband is loth to refuse since the wife has full right to report this failure to his family. Men joke about this problem and describe how they try to stay out as late as possible in the hope that their wives will have gone to sleep and not wake up when they come in.

There are other intense social pressures on men to participate in extra-marital liaisons. Groups of married men have informal clubs and their only activity is to organize parties to which they bring their girl-friends. Relationships with girl-friends are, after politics, the chief topic of conversation when men get together for drinks. Married men who attempt to be faithful to their wives do so against almost impossible odds.

Because of the resentment felt toward someone who marries outside the ranks, more pressure is placed on the professional man who has married a non-Sierra Leonean woman. One such husband thought he would make his position very clear. He had just returned from studying abroad with his new wife, who was an American. He was invited to one of these parties and instead of taking a girl-friend, he took his wife. She was embarrassed because she found all her friends' husbands there with their girl-friends and she was the only wife. The other men were furious because of the possibility she would expose them to their wives. This couple told me that after this event their friends never invited them to *any* social gathering and for more than a year they were practically socially isolated until they found a few couples who felt as they did.

Men who are known not to have extra-marital affairs are derided

---

it is an extremely common topic of conversation. Medical practitioners are besieged by impotent men seeking cures.' Levine also cites Leighton *et al.* (1963) who conducted a psychiatric study in western Yorubaland and found that a large proportion of the men included in their investigations reported suffering from impotence. Levine comments, 'The lack of comparable figures for other groups and of evidence that the potency problems were psychogenic in origin restricts the drawing of definite conclusions from these data; at this point all we can say is that this epidemiological survey appears to confirm independently the present author's impression that impotence is a distinctively serious source of concern for Yoruba men.'

by their male friends. Even women may express scorn and derision.[26] Men compare notes regarding one another's girl-friends. They co-operate with each other in securing places where they can take these girls, and protect each other from exposure to their wives. Men claim absolute loyalty to one another, as far as women are concerned, in that they would never try to take another's girl-friend or wife. How-ever, in reality a great deal of this kind of competition between men over women does take place.

Most interestingly, in these extra-marital affairs there is beginning to be a greater emphasis on the sexual experience itself rather than simply on the production of children. This may be due, in part, to the change in attitude towards illegitimate children since they have become an increasing financial burden and such a major source of marital discord. A great deal of conversation goes on among men about the art of love-making. They compare notes on the relative attractiveness of the girls they admire and make guesses about their skill in making love. They argue about whether or not certain tribal girls are more passionate than Creole girls, or whether, because Creole girls have not been circumcised, they are the more interested in sex. Such preoccupa-tions are in considerable contrast to the traditional view of sexual relations as one informant described them:

'As far as the native man in the village is concerned he is not particular about sexual education. All he requires is to satisfy himself. It is only by education, you have been to school, you read about sex and that women also had the same desire as you do and that there are certain areas of a woman that excite her, give her maximum feeling and so forth. But the man in the bush doesn't know that. They do not even *know* whether the existence of the clitoris gives a woman extra sensitivity. It is only by process of education ... And, in fact, in native homes, the people in the village, they don't have to caress a woman, to play with her, to excite her. All he does is go to the room straightaway and go to bed with her. When a woman expresses desire, a man feels that she is immoral.

Nowadays with the advent of education, young boys read about

26. One man said that hardly a day passes but someone makes a sarcastic remark about his probable impotence because it is known he does not have girl-friends. It was fortunate, he remarked, that he already has four children by his wife to prove his manhood.

it, in love stories, and they see film stars. This generation of school-children, boys and girls, they are taking rapidly to western ways of making love – caressing and so forth. Whereas to the average native man all that is unnecessary. It is not part of what he wants. He is more direct in his love-making. He only wants to have his sexual satisfaction.'

As a result of the diminished value associated with having children and the greater emphasis upon the sexual relationship itself, men are beginning to use contraceptives in these outside relationships sometimes long before they would ever think of using them with their wives. Some of these married men have been known to help girlfriends arrange an abortion and to pay for it. They are also known to encourage their girl-friends to use oral contraceptives.

The research data collected and this discussion of attitudes about sex only represent minute aspects of this very complicated area of human behaviour. However, even such meagre insights into the topic suggest that to ignore its investigation altogether in a study of marriage would unnecessarily limit understanding of a set of dynamic factors influencing conjugal relationships.

The traditional practice of polygamy has largely been rejected and today most professionals state that they prefer the monogamous form of marriage. At the same time the acceptance of the ideology of the companionate monogamous marriage system is in dramatic conflict with many traditional attitudes towards sex. We have seen how they regard it as impossible (and perhaps even 'unnatural') for a man to limit his sexual relationships to one woman.[27] The resolution of the contradiction between the rejection of polygamy and the notion that men cannot limit their sexual relations to one woman is summed up in the Krio saying, 'It is better to have sweethearts in the street than to have two women in the house' ('*Fɔ get switat na trit bɛtɛ pas fɔ get tu wuman na os*'). Such a solution brings with it another host of problems which, together with the persistence of certain other traditional attitudes which tend to maintain the segregation of sex roles, militate against the development of mutual trust within marriage.

27. Catholic priests are often described as hypocrites since it is thought impossible for a man to remain celibate. Those who believe that priests actually do practise celibacy explain that they must take some 'medicine' which enables them to avoid sexual relations with women.

The economic burdens of the professional make family limitation desirable but having only a few children conflicts with the traditional way in which a man gains prestige. Moreover, beliefs about the nature of women (which are in opposition to the view of the idealized behaviour of the wife of a professional) make men loth to allow their wives to use contraceptives. Such a conflict of motives encourages the tendency of men to seek sexual gratification outside marriage, especially once they have produced enough children within the marriage. As a result of the increased pressure on married men to support their illegitimate children, together with the newer emphasis upon mutual gratification in sexual relations, the use of contraceptives in *extramarital* relationships has become more common.

The awareness of both the immediate and long-range effects of worldwide population growth has prompted an enormous investment in promoting population control. A particular emphasis has been placed on this problem in the so-called underdeveloped parts of the world where food shortages create imminent crises. Since the success of such efforts usually demands acceptance of certain radical changes in values and attitudes, considerable stress has been placed on research on this topic in such countries. It has almost reached the point where the *willingness* of individuals to make use of contraceptives and of national governments to invest in family-planning programmes has become a kind of index of modernity. [28] In this discussion the emphasis has not been on problems of population control. However, I have tried to point out that such measures or statements about the ideal family size, at

28. Certain governments have devoted large amounts of their overseas aid expenditure to promotion of research and applied programmes, sometimes out of proportion to the degree of success so far achieved. Some of these countries, investing heavily overseas in population control programmes, have not even begun to solve their own population problems. While the political and ideological implications of these efforts have not gone unnoticed by leaders in Africa and other places, this problem and the more complicated issue of what constitutes over-population have not concerned us in this discussion. Although doubtless family-planning programmes should continue to have priority in development plans in such countries as Sierra Leone, much of the present approach to research and application fails to inform adequately those who are responsible for organizing family-planning programmes. Even the most 'scientific' approaches to research continue to be limited by ideological assumptions which are usually unexamined. For example, although abortion would probably be accepted in Sierra Leone as one approach to the problem of family limitation, given adequate medical facilities, it is highly unlikely that abortion will be officially promoted by those international agencies dispensing population control guidance.

least in Sierra Leone, may be misleading if they are taken as indications of a downward trend in the birth rate. We have seen that the economic burdens associated with traditional kinship obligations are a strong incentive for professional people to limit the number of children they produce. Furthermore, professionals have radically changed their attitudes from the traditional ideal family size, 'as many as possible' to 'four or less'. But, judging from the size of their families of orientation, if these professionals succeed in rearing four children to adulthood, such 'planned families' will actually contribute to a population increase. Moreover, other problems which persist continue to expose many more women than just wives to the possibility of pregnancy. Ironically, the recent laws which increase and enforce a man's financial responsibility for illegitimate children benefiting unwed mothers may even encourage these women to produce 'as many as possible'.

Despite the avowed aim to limit births, we have seen how certain traditional attitudes and practices complicate the ready acceptance of birth control. I have traced the manner in which it appears that the emphasis formerly placed upon procreation has gradually been modified to an emphasis upon sexual performance and upon the sexual relationship itself. Perhaps these data suggest a different approach to population control.

Educated Sierra Leoneans read modern magazines and see films. They have come to emphasize the importance of romantic love (as against the traditional pattern of the family choosing one's partner) as the basis for marriage. There is an emphasis on erotic symbols and love-making. Most certainly the revolution in sexual attitudes is not confined to the western world. In this process of changing attitudes, some of the former negative reactions towards the use of contraceptives, at least in relationships outside marriage, have been reduced, and birth-control methods seem to be gradually becoming more acceptable.

11

Prospects for marriage among the professional group

The emphasis of this study has been on providing a detailed ethnographic description of marriage among the professionals in Sierra Leone. It was observed in Chapter One that we cannot automatically predict trends regarding marriage relationships and family structure for the society as a whole from the findings of a study of this elite group. This is especially the case because of the unique set of conditions which have given rise to the western-educated professional group as we find it in Sierra Leone today. All that can be done is to make some comment tentatively about the possibilities of the emergence of the nuclear family as a domestic unit in its own right within the professional group.

One basic assumption has guided both the focus of the investigation and the methods that have been employed to collect the data. This is that marriage relationships cannot be understood without examining them in relation to the wider society in which they are embedded. Thus it was first necessary to trace the history of the country since first European contacts. Through this exercise it became obvious that some of the most dynamic factors shaping values about marriage as this institution is found today among professionals have arisen during the period of colonialism. It was thus found useful to employ Balandier's (1951, 1970) concept of the 'colonial situation' and to examine the special set of conditions resulting from imperialism. We have seen how the particular history of the development of the Colony for repatriated slaves in Freetown led to the formation of the Creole group.

The special relationship of near-equality with the British who founded the Colony and who provided the Creoles with the opportunities for educational and economic advance encouraged them to assume an attitude of superiority towards the indigenous tribesmen. The stage was set for competition and rivalry between the Creoles and the tribal groups, which persist today. For as we saw, during the nineteenth century the Creoles were allowed to participate in the administration of the Colony to such an extent that they came to believe the political destiny of Sierra Leone would soon be placed exclusively in their hands. Then, after the turn of the century, their privileged position was suddenly and radically challenged. The British began to develop the Protectorate in their own economic interests, and began extending education among the indigenous groups. The Creoles had come to constitute a threat to colonial domination, and so the British employed a number of strategies to preserve their own power. Not only did the British encourage the development of the indigenous population but they also began to adopt a different and more negative attitude towards the Creoles, and colour increasingly came to be the basis for social discrimination by the British. They also reduced the numbers of Creoles in the civil service, and highly educated Creoles found it increasingly difficult to get employment. During the years following the turn of the century many of them were forced to leave Sierra Leone to seek jobs in other West African countries. Moreover, the British encouraged the Lebanese and Syrians to assume a major role in trading activities, making it more difficult for the Creoles to compete in this field. Economic motives brought Lebanese and Syrians to Sierra Leone in the first place, but they remained and built their homes; today many regard the country as their home. Nevertheless, the attitudes which one might have thought would have been provoked by political and economic domination have been directed almost completely against the Lebanese and Syrians rather than the British. This is explained no doubt by the fact that the economic competition between the Lebanese and Syrians and the Africans was much more direct. Even today the belief in the superiority of British culture remains almost unchallenged.

In his explication of the concept of the 'colonial situation' Balandier (1951, 1970) accuses anthropologists of paying too little attention to the problem of race relations and to the effect on the individual of the racial basis for social groupings, when they examine societies which have undergone colonial rule. He says this can in part '. . . be attributed to the more or less conscious desire on the part of these anthropologists to avoid questioning the very foundations (and ideology) of the society to which they belong, the society of the colonial power' (p. 53).

Admittedly colonial domination was associated with an ideology having a racist foundation, and the acceptance of subordinate status by the colonized certainly made (and, in some parts of Africa, still makes) the task of political control much simpler. However, while it is relatively easy for the anthropologist to chart the structure of relationships between racial groups and to determine the extent of segregation and discrimination in a society, it is far more difficult for him to measure psychological factors, as Balandier seems to be suggesting, or, in other words, the psychological effects on the individual of acceptance of inferior status. Some inferences about such effects might be drawn from observing the often unquestioning and uncritical acceptance by Africans of the superiority of the ways of the white man (although, of course, in some cases to appear uncritical and un-questioning may have been just common sense). We have seen how to-day the Creoles are in an extremely uncertain position because of their numerical minority. Even though they continue to have significant political influence and to dominate the professions, the rise of the Provincials profoundly threatens their security. The Creoles as a group cannot hope to be able to maintain indefinitely their favoured position in the country, and many express extreme anxiety about the fuure.

On the other hand, Provincials feel considerable ambivalence in their relationships with the Creoles. We have seen how the Creoles, like their colonial rulers, have assumed a position of superiority towards the Provincials. Although the latter may represent a numerical majority, they continue to form, as Balandier expresses it, a 'socio-logical minority'. That is, the Creoles have managed to maintain a remarkable hold on power within Sierra Leone by asserting the superiority of their mode of life as compared with the 'native's'. Provincials have in large measure accepted that Creoles are superior, and their way of life has become the model of 'western civilized behaviour'.

The predominant ideological influence of the early period of the Colony was Christian. It has been emphasized that the chief concerns of the missionaries were to introduce western education and to reform the family, eliminating polygamy. Western education and religion became the new standards for assessing prestige and status, and largely superseded the traditional ones. Acquisition of educational qualifica-tions, adoption of monogamous marriage and the European mode of life became the hallmarks of being 'civilized'.

Finally, in addition to considering the influence of traditional values and attitudes towards them, the historical factors leading to the present composition of the professional group and affecting relationships between persons from the various ethnic categories, and the impact of racial and religious ideologies on behaviour, it was necessary to consider the results of the imposition of a foreign legal system. The colonial government introduced a legal system based upon British law. They intended that it should apply mainly to the Creoles and cover those problems of administration which were beyond the scope of customary law. By recognizing Islamic and customary family law, the colonial government aimed to honour their policy of non-interference in the domestic sphere. But, as we have seen, the vested interests of the missionaries made it expedient to extend some of the provisions of marriage law to the 'natives'. More important, the three groups for which these laws were intended did not remain separate and distinct. Intermarriage between groups has resulted in a series of legal problems for which no solution is readily apparent.

The discussion of family law in Sierra Leone, and in particular the findings regarding the status of the child born out of wedlock, seriously challenge the 'consensus' view of law as held by many social anthropologists. Although Fallers (1970) has implied that the legal problems of post-colonial countries are somehow unique, the data suggest that legal institutions may often be available for manipulation of power by small groups of persons within society. And, as Goode (1963) has noted, 'Nowadays, in the more revolutionary countries, new legal codes become a major lever for initiating changes' (p. 20). He also points out that the legislation and court decisions in recently independent colonies have '. . . generally pressed towards some conjugal form of the family and have been in advance of actual family behavior' (p. 20). In such countries the law can hardly be described as representing the consensus norms of the population.

Particularly relevant in this connection is the question of the status of the child born out of wedlock. Although this problem has very wide social ramifications, its analysis exposes a number of dynamic issues which affect the relationships between husbands and wives. The woman married under statutory law enjoys a status far superior to that of unmarried women or those married according to customary law. One reason married women tolerate their husbands' extra-marital affairs is that the children born to such illicit relationships do not have equal legal or social status with children born to the married couple. The proposal to introduce a law equalizing the status of illegitimate and legitimate children understandably produced a violent reaction from married women and from others who were concerned with the preservation of the status of marriage under statutory law. Such a law would effectively undermine the security of the married woman. As we saw, the belief that this law was passed has radically influenced marital relationships. Women are not so prepared now to countenance their husbands' relationships with other women, and conflict over this problem within marriages has increased. The law requiring fathers to maintain their illegitimate children has also been stiffened and as we saw, paternity disputes are becoming common. These data regarding the status of children born out of wedlock suggest an important area for further and more precise investigation of the relationship between law, social practice and the manipulation of power through the appeal to an ideology.

We noted also that the requirement of obtaining a western education has interrupted the traditional practice of early marriage for girls. Western ideas of courtship behaviour have been adopted to fill the gap of these years in school and university. Viewing themselves as adults and having considerable freedom of movement, young people are exposed to the temptation and possibility of premarital intercourse. Traditional values about the importance of virginity at marriage have been tempered, but the good character of a girl as well as family background is still a critically important consideration affecting her chances of marriage. As a result girls face conflicting standards relating to behaviour during courtship, since they aspire to marry a man of high social status. The practice of premarital intercourse is complicated by traditional values attached to having children. Both men and women fear and avoid the use of contraceptives because it is believed that their use may interfere with a woman's future fertility. As a result many girls get pregnant and, since a child born out of wedlock would jeopardize their chances of marriage, abortions have become very common among unmarried educated girls. Married women also practice abortion as a method of family limitation.

Young Sierra Leoneans have wholeheartedly accepted the western emphasis on romantic love as the basis for choosing marriage partners. However, as we have seen, the traditional authority of relatives over the choice of a mate still exists. Few young people want to marry someone of whom their parents disapprove. We have also seen that girls are often favoured within the family, especially by their mothers, and suitors are also required to pay special attention to the whims and wishes of the girls they are courting. These experiences of girls may set up expectations about their future role which are far from consistent with the experiences of wives. McGinn (1966) found a similar pattern in a study of marriage and family among the middle-class in Mexico. He pointed out that in Mexico the inconsistency or 'discontinuity' between the experiences of childhood and courtship in this group is reflected in the way mothers rear their children and that, in turn, these practices lead to and perpetuate a 'cycle of male-female role dichotomy'.

Although western ideas about courtship have been assimilated, we have seen that traditional attitudes and values still have a very strong influence on marriage relationships. Extended family obligations continue to have importance, although these have largely been translated into modern terms. That is, professionals are willing to invest in the education of relatives' children, but they are less willing than they were to make their resources available to any relatives who might request assistance. Economic obligations to relatives are a source of serious conflicts of interest between husband and wife and so, as we have seen, the spouses' finances are kept strictly separate. Other factors influence the segregation of household moneys. Ideas about the financial responsibility of husband and wife have radically altered from the traditional pattern. Formerly men spent their money in a manner which would build up their prestige in traditional terms, and women carried a major share of the responsibility for the upkeep of the household. Today ideas about the husband's role in monogamous marriage require men to support the household, relieving wives, in theory at least, of economic responsibility. A 'good husband' will not rely on the fact that his wife is contributing to the maintenance of the home, but will make it clear that she is free to spend her own earnings as she chooses. However, since most men spend money on their relatives, on women outside the marriage, and incur financial obligations for the support of illegitimate children, wives often feel it is necessary to insure their own security by investing their money outside the marriage, in their own families, or by saving it.

As has been shown, the mother-son relationship, as observed in so many parts of Africa (Lloyd 1967; Goode 1963), continues to have a profound influence upon the behaviour of men. Interestingly, the husband's mother has become the representative of traditional obligations and influences, and her interference constitutes a major source of marital conflict, because the husband is afraid to offend her. As a result, the pull of traditional obligations is felt more strongly by men than by women and produces antagonisms within marriage which perpetuate the segregation of interests of husband and wife. Cohen and Spain (1970) in a discussion of woman's role in Africa hypothesized '. . . that the roles of women by their very nature (i.e., inferior status and restricted access to societal activities) can be expected to produce a constant tendency in human society for female dissatisfaction.' They also suggest that this dissatisfaction will be '. . . manifested in subversion of male authority where possible in traditional society, and easy acceptance of change when it is afforded to them by the social context.' In Sierra Leone women have been quick to recognize certain advantages offered them by marriage under statutory law, and have accepted the values implicit in the notion of companionate marriage. However, as we have seen, few couples realize these ideals, and marriage relationships are rarely characterized by mutual trust.

Traditional values and attitudes regarding sex have a continuing impact upon marriage relationships. We noted that traditional attitudes towards women's sexuality make men reluctant to agree to the use of contraceptives by their wives but, at the same time, professional couples prefer to limit the number of their children. The apparent tendency to avoid conception through abstinence from sexual relations in marriage, after a couple have the desired number of children, exaggerates the tendency for men to seek sexual satisfaction outside marriage. Anxiety about their sexuality as shown by fears of impotence are manifested among the men in the professional group as well as in traditional society. The pressures from the male peer group and traditional ideas about the importance of sexual potency encourage extramarital liaisons. But today the financial requirements of supporting both legitimate and illegitimate children have begun to make it less attractive to men to have children outside marriage. Men are beginning to approve the practice of methods of birth control, at least in their relationships with women outside marriage, and we have seen how the emphasis on procreation in these 'outside' relationships has given way to a greater concern with the quality of sexual relations and with mutual satisfaction. However, as yet, this change in attitude has not, for the most part, had an appreciable effect upon sex in marriage. These data, indicating how gradually the approval of the use of contraceptives comes about among these professional men, point to important areas of investigation for those concerned with population control. As has been observed, much of the emphasis on family planning has been directed towards women rather than men. It is suggested that the attitudes of men are more crucial to the acceptance of methods of birth control than those of women. These findings support those of Stycos (1969) who showed that in many countries fertility declines have historically been accomplished by means of male contraceptive techniques and, since men are usually more accessible to new ideas than women, they may also be the more effective disseminators of these ideas.

Because this has been a study of marriage relationships among the professionals, we have not dealt extensively with the particular role of the professionally qualified woman. Nevertheless, she cannot be completely ignored because her status in the society has an effect on attitudes towards the education of women and marriage. A large number of these women have remained unmarried, and marriages where the wives are highly educated are regarded generally as unstable. Men prefer to marry women with less education than themselves. As a result the role of the professional woman in society is highly ambiguous. Since every woman prefers to marry, these professionally qualified women stand as a constant reminder to other women of the dangers attending high educational achievement.

We have seen that professionals in Sierra Leone are faced with two quite separate systems of prestige and status, the traditional and the contemporary urban. By virtue of his having gained high qualifications in terms of western education, the professional has achieved a position of respect in both spheres. Maintaining his prestige in the urban sphere requires his conforming to the pattern of monogamous marriage. At the same time, maintaining his position generally in the society means he must fulfil numerous traditional obligations which may clash directly with the requirements of achieving a successful relationship with his spouse. Before considering these problems further, let us first examine just what are the advantages of monogamous marriage for the professional man and for his wife.

The first benefit which comes to the professional man who marries one wife according to statutory law is the tremendous prestige associated with this type of marriage in comparison with marriage by customary law. During the colonial regime the monogamously married man gained the approval of his peers, and, more importantly, of the white administrators upon whom he depended for any educational or occupational advance he might hope to make in the future. Moreover, he established an unquestioned position of superiority *vis-à-vis* the rest of the society.[1] (It should be remembered that statutory marriage, educational achievements and reasonable financial resources are associated. It would be impossible to undertake such a marriage without sufficient financial resources, since weddings are usually very expensive social events.) Secondly, by assuming the right to choose his own spouse the professional man does gain a degree of autonomy from the authority of his extended family. However, it should be recalled that no one likes the idea of marrying a person their family has not approved and so at least some tacit consent is usually extracted from relatives.

Although these matters are all very much a matter of degree, monogamous marriage does provide some rationalization for more individualistic attitudes towards the spending of money. As we have seen, professionals now attempt to limit their more general financial obligations to kinsmen and try to fulfil their obligations by raising one or more of their relatives' children and/or helping with the school expenses of the 'more promising' young people in the family. For Creoles, whose personal law is based upon English law, monogamous marriage allows for the building up of a family estate which will be inherited by only the wife and the legitimate children. Due to their misunderstanding of the law, many Provincials believe that the English rules of inheritance which they see as advantageous, also apply to them once they have undergone statutory marriage.

Harris's (1969) discussion of whether or not the conjugal family is a cause or effect of industrialization is relevant to the question of change in Sierra Leone. He says that one of the conditions which are

---

1. In one notorious case a Sierra Leonean cast off his customary wife and married another woman in a registry office in Britain. When the legality of his action was questioned, he was reported as saying that he had been married to the first woman by a form of marriage recognized neither in his own country nor in Britain. Had he said that his customary marriage was not 'socially recognized' amongst the professional group he might have been somewhat more accurate.

necessary for autonomous industrialization to occur is that there must be a surplus of capital which can be employed in industrial uses. He observes that 'the extent to which capital is dispersed among a large number of individuals as opposed to being relatively concentrated will depend to a great extent on the system of inheritance that prevails' (Harris 1969, pp. 116-117).

The relation between inheritance rules in a society and attitudes towards family limitation and the definition of illegitimacy should also be noted. Harris observes that one of the effects of inheritance rules is that the more children one produces under a system of equal division of inheritance, the more one's property will be divided. As a consequence, there may be a tendency to limit the number of children born. As we have seen, in Sierra Leone the tendency to limit the number of rightful heirs has also resulted in the continuation of inheritance laws which exclude illegitimate children.

What about the advantages of monogamous, statutory marriage for women? Most importantly, it provides them with an unquestioned superior status in the society. The importance of having achieved this status is underlined by drawing attention to the very limited possibilities for women to marry under statutory law. In Chapter Five, Table 12 shows the number of marriages registered under statutory law between the years 1961 and 1968. Banton (1957) collected the same statistics of registered marriage for the years 1941 to 1952 inclusive (p. 209). Over the twelve years between 1941 and 1952 there was an average of 42 registered Mohammedan marriages per annum compared with an average of 41 such marriages per annum between 1961 and 1968. Over the same period Banton reports an average of 311 marriages per annum registered under Christian and Civil statutory marriage law. I found that between 1961 and 1968 there was an actual *drop* in the average number of such registered marriages to 264 per annum. It should be pointed out immediately that these figures do not take into account the number of Sierra Leoneans who marry while living out of the country; many do contract their marriages in some other country. However, the evidence certainly underlines the exclusiveness of the group of statutorily married women and explains to some extent why women are so willing to endure the disparity between their expectations for marriage and their subsequent experiences.

A further advantage that statutory monogamous marriage affords a woman is her superior position *vis-à-vis* not only the society at large, and almost all other women, but, most vitally, it ensures her unrivalled superiority *vis-à-vis* the (inevitable) other women in her husband's life. She is not forced to get on with co-wives or share her home with them. And, of course, related to this, is the security which statutory marriage affords (or in the case of the Provincial wife, which she thinks it affords) her legitimate children as far as inheritance rights are concerned. In view of the dependence of women on their grown children for support in their old age, the importance of this security cannot be over-emphasized.

Furthermore, statutory marriage frees the wife from the authority of the husband's relatives. Upon marriage she moves into her own home and is not under the authority of her husband's mother as she would have been in most cases in traditional family life. Moreover, upon his death, she is not financially dependent on her husband's relatives. (Although it must be once again emphasized that this is largely a misconception in the case of women whose husbands are Provincials.)

Moreover, during a couple's lifetime together, both the law and general social values about the role of the husband in the monogamous marriage support the idea that the husband should be the sole provider for the family. (Even the wedding vows include the husband's pledge '... and with all my worldly goods I thee endow').[2] This allows the wife considerable economic freedom if she is lucky enough to have a husband who conscientiously provides for the home. And, as we have seen, the general anxiety women feel about this matter leads them to exercise their financial independence by securing themselves through investing their money outside the home, often in their own relatives' estate.

Does the nuclear family 'fit' Sierra Leone society?

Goode (1963) has observed that social science has developed only one comprehensive theory of family change, which was based upon nineteenth-century evolutionary ideas. This theory, as he points out, was intended to explain both the observable differences among the world's family patterns and their history. The theory asserted that

2. The extreme reversal of the economic status of the wife, as represented by the marriage vows, must be emphasized. Under customary law the wife was part of the estate to be inherited.

the family has progressed from the primitive sexual promiscuity of the semi-animal horde, through group marriage, matriarchy, and patriarchy in some polygamous form to '... culminate in the highest spiritual expression of the family, Victorian monogamy' (p. 3). Although, as Goode notes, science had evolved beyond that theory, a substitute one has not been developed. Although it is generally accepted that there is a relationship between technological systems and changes in family patterns, as Goode observes, '... no specific family form seems to be correlated with specific "states" of the economic and technological evolution' (p. 4). It has been observed that wherever the economic system expands through industrialization family patterns change, extended kinship ties weaken and '... a trend toward some form of the conjugal system generally begins to appear – that is, the nuclear family becomes a more independent kinship unit' (Goode 1963, p. 6).

In Chapter One reference was made to some observers of African urban marriage who have concluded that marriages there fashioned on the western monogamous model encounter so many difficulties just because the model does not 'fit' the African situation. The emphasis of some of these observers has been on the inability of urban Africans to cope with an institution with which they have not had sufficient experience or familiarity. In other words, it is frequently implied that these individuals have not been sufficiently socialized in western values for them to make a success of the nuclear family as an independent unit 'rather than a mere cog in the kinship wheel' (Little 1973, p. 169). Oppong (1973, as quoted by Little 1973, p. 169) found that second and third generations of educated people were more successful in avoiding some of the problems which threaten their marriage' (p. 168). Longmore takes a similar view, that it is the in- that 'What does seem to emerge ... is that the new marital norms are actually followed more closely when both husband and wife have in their childhood received a degree of preparation for partnership in marriage' (p. 168) Longmore takes a similar view, that it is the incomplete preparation for the demands of the western model of marriage that is the cause of the problem: 'Western monogamy, without its accompanying values and ideals, is meaningless and ineffective ...' (1959, pp. 15-16). Such conclusions about the present state of urban African marriage not only imply a degree of paternalism towards the new generation of educated Africans who are struggling to achieve new standards for their families, but also fail to constitute a sociological explanation for the troubles which these marriages encounter. Our explanation takes us back to an emphasis on some of the characteristics of the society in which marital roles are lived out.

The problem of many studies of African urban marriage has been an over-emphasis on the extreme type of the isolated nuclear family which Parsons (1952; 1956) argued was most adapted to the structure of industrialized societies. Numerous studies of family life in Britain and elsewhere have shown that in fact many different forms of the family exist within an industrialized society and, moreover, that the nuclear family is anything but isolated (for example, see Young and Willmott 1957; Bell 1968; Sussman 1959; and Sussman and Burchinal 1966). As Harris (1969) points out, the important question is just what Parsons meant by 'isolated'.

> 'What Parsons means is quite clear. Because the American kinship system is in his words an "open, multilineal, conjugal system" – that is to say because there are no rules prescribing or favouring marriage with particular relatives or categories of relatives ("open"), and no single line of transmission is preferred ("multilineal") – there are no principles which by *themselves* can lead to the formation of kin groups wider than the nuclear family. Hence the nuclear family is *structurally* isolated. That is to say the rules governing behaviour of individuals provide for the formation of nuclear family groups only. . . . What they do in this situation is another matter. They may use the family process to form all sorts of extended family groups, but they get no help from the rules which govern it. Structurally, the nuclear family, based on the marriage bond between husband and wife ("conjugal"), is the basic unit and *structurally* it is isolated' (pp. 98-99).

In this nuclear family the duties of the husband are primarily to his spouse and young children, these obligations being more stringent than any obligations to parents or other kinsmen. Obligations to the descendant generation always take precedence over those to the ascendant generation. Goode (1963) describing the conjugal (or nuclear) family said that the ideal family is characterized by neolocality, primacy of the husband-wife relationship, emotional intensity, and the relative exclusion of wider kin.

But what of the characteristics of the industrial society which Parsons indicated correspond to the situation in which this structurally isolated nuclear family fits best? First of all, such a society must have an economy characterized by occupationally induced mobility. Furthermore, as Harris (1969) has summed them up:

'The basic requirements of industrialization ... are a surplus of capital, the requisite financial institutions, willingness to employ capital in productive uses on the basis of maximizing its return, enough people and/or good enough communications to constitute a mass market and provide a labour force, an educated *élite* capable of technological innovation, a set of ideas which will legitimize the activities of control and co-ordination of productive processes, and a surplus of agricultural produce' (p. 113).

Further, Parsons' theory includes the assumption that there is a conflict of values between those of the family and those of the economic institutions in an industrialized society. The values of the family are based upon *particularism* and *ascription* while those of the economic institutions are based upon *achievement* and *universalism* and are also characterized by *affective neutrality*. This conflict of values is best resolved, according to Parsons, by the restriction of the family group to the nuclear family. As Harris explains:

'Major conflict is therefore avoided by two types of segregation. The nuclear family is cut off from wider kin in the sense that the most stringent ties are confined within it, and because its members do not perform economic roles opposite one another. It is also segregated from the economic system except for the husband. In this way intrusion of family values into the sphere of work is avoided and work values do not disrupt the solidarity of the family' (1969, p. 102).

Returning to our setting, Sierra Leone, we can see that the requirements of an industrialized society as listed above are certainly not fulfilled by the present economy of Sierra Leone or probably any other post-colonial and 'developing' country. Generally economic relations in the society are not based upon universalistic and achievement values. Decisions regarding occupational or political advancement are made most frequently on the basis of favouritism derived from some kinship or ethnic tie, or a relationship based upon reciprocal favours, or between members of some interest group see A. Cohen 1971). The professional in Sierra Leone is enmeshed in highly competitive relationships with his fellows. The limited number of opportunities for occupational advancement and the fluidity of the political situation intensify the insecurity of the professional and make the establishment of a solid network of highly personalized relations a crucial requirement if he is to fulfil his ambitions.[3] This is not to suggest that any industrialized society fulfils completely the requirements set down by Parsons. It would be more accurate to argue that in an industrialized society the dominant values of economic relations are based upon universalism and achievement. In Sierra Leone, the dominant values which characterize economic relations are based upon particularism and ascription. Thus we see that it is not simply a matter of the persistence of traditional attitudes towards marriage and family organization which hamper the emergence of the nuclear family as an independent domestic unit. The very nature of relations in the wider society coalesce with these traditional attitudes and clash with the aims of the nuclear family.

So it is clear that it is necessary to extend the scope of our examination to include the character of relations in the wider society in addition to considering such matters as the persistence of traditional norms and values regarding marriage, if we are to find an answer to the question regarding the 'fit' of the nuclear family to this urban African society. Let us look now at some of the requirements of the nuclear family as described by Parsons (1952; 1956) and Goode (1963) to see if they conflict with the successful pursuit of the professional's career. (There can be no doubt that the professional in Sierra Leone is highly motivated to achieve success.) First of all, the nuclear family had been described as one where the stress on obligations to the descendant generation are most stringent. As we have seen, the professional may try to limit his obligations to relatives either of the ascendant generation or to his collateral relatives in either direction or to their descendants, but he may not eliminate them. All those persons who can establish the remotest kinship tie may assume the right to make demands upon him. It has also been observed that although in principle such obligations to kinsmen in the extended family are reciprocal, in practice, as far as the flow of money is concerned, these obligations operate in only one direction, from the professional to his

---

3. A Krio saying, often used during political campaigns, emphasizes the importance of personal influence. 'You want something, a job or assistance? You say you have been to grammar school? Well, you show me your educational qualifications and I'll show you *my* connections' (*'As fɔ yu ed yu se yu go grama skul'*).

relatives. Not many professionals expect any financial assistance from their relatives. The resulting financial pressure on the professional's income increases his motivation to augment his income to cover these obligations and to secure his own personal needs for the future. However, given the limited economic potential of the country, many find it extremely difficult to improve their income significantly. Since whatever he earns has to be apportioned between all his obligations, his wife and children will certainly feel the pressure on the household budget.

Moreover, the time required by both the normal demands of his work and by the building up and maintaining of a wide network of personalized relations with his peers militates against his fulfilling another requirement of the nuclear family: spending his leisure time with his wife and children and strengthening the bonds of affection between them. Further, the monogamous nuclear family implies commitment to sexual fidelity within the marriage. But, as we have seen, the values of the wider society, represented especially by his male companions, place considerable pressure on a man to involve himself in extra-marital liaisons. Although the professionals subscribe to the value of limiting the size of the nuclear family, the tendency for men to increase the number of their dependants through these extra-marital relationships continues. As a result of stiffer maintenance laws pertaining to illegitimate children, these extra dependants place added strain on the professional man's already over-subscribed income. All these factors, the time a husband spends away from home, the necessity to spread his income over a wide number of obligations, the loyalty to kinsmen, which often appears to take precedence over his family commitments, his sexual relations with other women, diminish the possibilities of his developing a strong relationship with his wife based upon shared interests and mutual confidence. The results, as we have seen, in that the wife takes measures to secure herself, are often in opposition to the requirements of the nuclear family as an independent domestic unit. Finally, the demands of occupational advance require the professional to be geographically mobile. As has been shown, both the process of obtaining professional level qualifications and making occupational advance may necessitate frequent moves. Couples are often separated for long periods of time, either because of study abroad or because the husband has been posted to some part of the country where schools for their children are regarded as inadequate.

The emphasis which has been placed on the relation between the family and the structure of the wider society should not be taken to imply that influence flows in only one direction – from the society towards the family. It is within the family that children are socialized to the values of the society. Therefore, in order to predict a change in family structure, it would also be necessary to examine the values which are being taught to children within the family. Although this investigation did not examine that problem, it was observed, for example, that many, especially the professional men, did not expect their children would be supporting them in their old age and were making provision for themselves.

In conclusion the question as to what type of family structure will finally emerge in Sierra Leone cannot be answered. The lesson of this investigation is that the form of the family varies with the character of relations external to itself. We have seen that the character of marriage relationships of professionals in Sierra Leone reflects the clash of traditional values with modern ideas. The intensity of these conflicts suggests some resolution involving change is required. But the direction of that change will depend to a large extent on factors outside the control of individual men and women.

Appendix A

Methods

The investigation of an elite or professional group in a developing country presents some particular methodological challenges. It becomes even more difficult when one seeks to investigate such an extremely sensitive topic as marriage in a situation where people have imbibed certain western or Christian values regarding marriage, and where status considerations lead them to make a pretence of outward conformity. In Sierra Leone these problems were exacerbated by the very nature of the professional group, which included persons from several tribal groups who form factions. Moreover, this research was done during a period of military rule which followed two *coups*. Another *coup* occurred while I was there and, in most of the later period, a state of emergency was in force.

Anthropologists have been notably reluctant to describe the methods they use in their research. A careful study by Jongmans and Gutkind (1967) of monographs published over the past forty years showed that only twenty per cent of the authors provided their readers with a clear idea of how they collected their data. Freilich, commenting on anthropologists' commitment to the method of participant observation, notes that 'Strangely enough, they are often loath to write about it in a personal way ... they only rarely publish accounts of their own experiences as participant observer' (1970 p. 4). Doubtless most of the personal experiences of the fieldworker have a bearing on the kind of data collected but a complete report would be voluminous and, as Beattie implied (1969), an impossibility. As with reporting the research itself, one must attempt to select those aspects of the field experience which seem to have immediate relevance for the evaluation of the results. Such reporting should also be complete enough to provide guidance for someone embarking on similar research.

Festinger, *et al.* (1950), discussing their work (which may be considered a model for social research), remark on how the very nature of a group in its natural setting indicates the need for a diversity of methods:

'... In different field studies the techniques of informal interviewing, using informants, participant and non-participant observation, field experimentation have all been used in a variety of combinations. The necessity to employ such a multitude and apparent confusion of diverse techniques is, of course, inherent in the extreme complexity of the subject matter of the field study... These various techniques supplement one another. They gather data on different aspects... and it is only the combination and integration of these diverse data that permits us to construct a coherent and insightful picture of the group under study' (1950 p. 1).

In Sierra Leone the research methods developed and changed as I learned more about the situation and became aware of aspects of the problem which could only be tackled by applying some new approach.

Elite studies in Africa are faced with other problems besides methodological ones. Among educated Africans antagonisms are ever increasing towards Europeans treating Africa as a kind of laboratory for their academic pursuits.[1] Furthermore, there is the necessity to explain the nature of an investigation and the aims of the research to persons of varying levels of educational background. A fair amount of discussion took place among colleagues on the question of how this research should be described to the professionals in Sierra Leone. Realizing that they were likely to be highly sensitive about the topic of marriage, one suggestion was that I should conceal my true aims and behave as a kind of light-hearted academic tourist.[2] The approach that I took was to describe my research as part of a wider comparative study of marriage and family organization which the University of Edinburgh was launching in a number of countries. Usually, I made reference to the common assumption in sociological literature that the

1. See the discussion of this problem following the crises in the African Studies Association during their 1969 Annual Meeting in Montreal, *African Studies Newsletter*, 1969-70.

2. Indeed, a letter of introduction, for which I was not responsible, pointed out that, although I would be doing a study of marriage, I would not be including the Creoles, implying they were far too sophisticated to permit such research to be conducted in their midst.

extended family would not survive the process of industrialization. This study was, in part, an attempt to test this notion by finding out to what extent patterns of the family life of professionals have changed from the traditional mode.

In Sierra Leone, the problem of interpreting one's research aims to others is not limited to contacts with Africans. I inevitably met expatriates who were part of the same social circle as the professionals and who were curious about the research. I tried to limit the information I gave them by saying I was studying family organization but my remarks were often deliberately misinterpreted. Frequently, the response was, 'Oh, you're doing a Kinsey report'. On several occasions individuals joked about this in the presence of Sierra Leoneans and one asked my assistant if I was finding out how many times a week Africans copulate. More than once expatriate men were embarrassed in case I discovered their relationships with Sierra Leonean women, so that they were understandably loth to let me find out too much about the social life of Freetown for fear for their own reputations. One such man asked his Sierra Leonean colleague to avoid talking too much to me.

Some expatriates are openly critical of the anthropologist fraternizing with Africans. It is interesting that this objection would probably not have been raised had I been doing a 'proper anthropological study' in a remote village. For those for whom racial considerations are a problem, the educational, economic and social equality of the professionals give rise to considerable ambivalence. Certain clubs remain almost totally segregated and, for the most part, social relations between expatriates and Africans are formalized and official or only developed in the interest of securing the expatriate's place in the community.

Learning the language

Traditionally, learning the language of the people studied was a *sine qua non* of British anthropology. The use of interpreters was a sign of weakness and to be discouraged and dispensed with at the earliest possible moment. In Sierra Leone the problem of language was both simplified and complicated by the particular history of the country. The professional group is made up of persons from several tribal groups, each with their own distinctive language. Krio, a language based on English, French, Portuguese, Yoruba, and other African languages, has become the *lingua franca* and there are few places in the country where it is not possible to communicate in this language. However, the official language of the country is English. Many of the educated in Sierra Leone almost make a fetish of their ability to speak perfect English. In some schools children are punished if they are caught speaking to one another in Krio.[3] Families of Provincial background claim that they only speak their tribal language or English at home, never Krio. They maintain they do not want their children to learn Krio, to which they often refer as corrupted English, or patois.[4] Thus, the original design of this research assumed that the investigation would be conducted in English.

Although English was the official language and many Provincials pretended they would prefer altogether to avoid the use of Krio, the reality of the situation was quite different. Almost without exception, daily informal communication between Sierra Leoneans is conducted in Krio. Data regarding situations, relationships and content of conversation and the shifts between English, Krio and tribal languages would doubtless provide rich insight into the structure of relationships. However, to have begun working in Krio, despite its common use, undoubtedly would have been unfavourably received. In fact, it might have bordered dangerously on being insulting. Fanon examines this matter in the context of the problem of the relationships between white and black. Although his views developed from his personal experience in the Antilles, the situation he describes is painfully similar to that in Sierra Leone.

'To speak pidgin to a Negro makes him angry because he, himself, is a pidgin-nigger talker. But, I will be told, there is no wish, no intention to anger him. I grant this; but it is just this absence of wish, this lack of interest, this indifference, this automatic manner of classifying him, imprisoning him, primitivizing him, decivilizing

3. My son was auditioned for a part in an educational broadcast. He did not get the part because, as it was apologetically explained to me, 'David doesn't have a perfect British accent.'

4. One Mende husband, married to an American, strongly objected to her efforts to learn Krio. He stated that it would ruin her English and 'in the social group we belong to she must be able to speak good English. If we are at Abu's house, for example, how is it going to sound if she starts mixing up her English with patois?'

him, that makes him angry ... to talk pidgin-nigger is to express this thought: "You'd better keep your place" ' (1970, p. 24-25).

Of course, it was necessary to try to learn to understand the conversations going on around me in Krio. Krio proverbs and idioms are a rich source of data concerning certain beliefs and attitudes and I made an extensive collection of these. When I travelled in the Provinces, I used an interpreter who could communicate in the appropriate language or Krio. In a sense, success at building rapport could be gauged by the growing tendency of individuals to continue speaking in Krio when I was included in the conversation.

Use of local resources

Sierra Leoneans are often vocal about their disapproval of most researchers who ignore the assistance available to them through persons in the country often equally well trained and interested in the subject they are investigating. Often, these Africans are not themselves engaged in actual research because of lack of funds or the press of professional commitments such as teaching. It is frustrating to have research interests and not be able to pursue them. It is more frustrating and discouraging to know that you may be as well qualified to conduct a particular investigation as the outsider who has suddenly appeared with the necessary resources to proceed. But the situation becomes intolerable and antagonistic when the outsider goes about his work as though his African colleagues did not exist. The researcher who appears condescending towards his African professional colleagues aggravates a situation which will probably lead to official policies against foreign researchers. Moreover, he also loses opportunities to enrich his own work, which these persons are often willing and able to provide.

During the time this research was being conducted, only a few persons with qualifications in anthropology or sociology held academic posts, but I found many with such training and interests working in education and social welfare work. The extent to which my work progressed was very much a result of the many conversations we had together. They were completely unselfish with their time and knowledge. There were those who, without funds, had quietly gone about collecting data which they often discussed with me. Since my study led me into legal matters, I depended a great deal on the counsel of people trained in this field. In fact, the importance and relevance of the problem of law to my investigation only became clear through such conversations. Other facilities offered by the university included seminars conducted by the Institute of African Studies, where research could be discussed with staff members and students.

Data collected
Case studies of pilot families

It is seldom that the anthropologist has the opportunity to choose his first informants once he has decided upon the location for his research. Usually they choose him, in the sense that they are the first to show friendliness or the willingness to talk about what interests him. The dangers of relying on these persons as long-term or exclusive sources of information has been discussed over and over again among anthropologists. Sometimes they are marginal characters whose own position in the society is not well defined. Still, it is quite obvious that the anthropologist conducting a traditional study is initially completely dependent on the assistance of these first willing individuals.

My own situation was quite different. I was faced with the necessity of enlisting the help of informants who would be willing to admit me into one of the more obscure areas of society, family life. Since I had chosen to make a direct approach, I could not slip into the households of these people under some guise and observe behaviour. My aim was to find a sufficient number of couples who would form a pilot group of persons willing to endure prolonged intensive interviews. They were to be selected so that they, to some extent, represented the composition of the professional group as I had come to know it.

I secured names of possible candidates for this pilot group from doctors, welfare workers and a lawyer. I called on these people and was able to secure the agreement of fourteen families. After introducing myself to these people, sometimes showing letters of introduction, I explained my research and how I would like them to help me. I told them that, although I was to study family life in Sierra Leone, this being my first visit to Africa, I really knew nothing about it. In order to begin this difficult task I would like to have permission to come to see them, either together or individually, at least four times to ask questions and to learn from them. It appeared necessary to limit the request to only four formal appointments because of the general wariness many revealed. This caution was not unrelated to the political situation of the moment.

In the usual anthropological approach, the investigator is able to sit around chatting informally before finally getting down (and then indirectly) to a discussion of his research interests. Because I was a stranger and had asked to visit four times, it was necessary to give more shape to these sessions in order to rationalize my visits. It is just not possible to ring the doorbell of a professional family in Africa, any more than anywhere else, and, as a stranger, simply sit down and observe behaviour. I hoped that, after the first contracted and more formal interviews had been completed, I would be well enough acquainted to drop in informally. And, of course, it was later when I was more trusted and during the course of the more informal relationships that followed that I obtained the most valuable data.

After the four interviews were completed (most of them tape-recorded) I was able to drop in on almost all the households at any time of the day. These families invited me for meals and some visited me for social occasions. I tested the questions for the interview schedule by administering them to this group. I know many of them felt very much involved and responsible for the adequacy of this instrument. The seriousness and sincerity with which they approached the study was the most gratifying aspect of the first months' experience in the field.

I will list some characteristics of these families as they were when we met.

Family One – The husband was a lawyer in a high position with the government. The wife had been a teacher but was not now working. They had four children. He was a Kono and she was a Susu. They lived in government quarters.

Family Two – The husband was a lecturer in the Civil Service Training College. The wife was a teacher in a primary school. They had eight children. Both were Mende and they lived in government quarters.

Family Three – The husband was an Education Officer. The wife had never been employed. They had seven children. Both were Mende and they lived in government quarters.

Family Four – The husband was a printing engineer and worked for the local press. The wife was a primary school teacher. Both were Creole and they had two children. They lived in a rented appartment.

Family Five – The husband was a lecturer in the Civil Service Training College. The wife had been a primary teacher but had not been employed since marriage. They had six children. He was a Kono and she was a Mende. They lived in government quarters.

Family Six – The husband was a town planner. His wife was a primary school teacher. They had two children. He was a Mende and she was an American. They lived in government quarters.

Family Seven – The husband was a magistrate. The wife was not working, although she had worked as a secretary before marriage. Both were Mende and they had two children. They lived in government quarters.

Family Eight – The husband was a civil servant. The wife was a primary school teacher. They had two children. He was a Mende and she was a Sherbro. They had two children and lived in government quarters.

Family Nine – The husband was a civil servant. He had formerly worked in the Ministry of Education. The wife was a secondary school teacher. They had no children. He was a Temne and she was a Sherbro. They lived in government quarters.

Family Ten – The husband was a civil servant. The wife was an office worker. They had one child, having lost an infant just before we met. Both were Creole and they lived in government quarters.

Family Eleven – The husband was an official in a bank. The wife was not employed. They had three children. Both were Temne; she was a Muslim and he was a Christian. They lived in a residence provided through his employment.

Family Twelve – The husband was a civil servant. The wife was a primary school teacher. They had four children. He was a Mende and she was a Sherbro. They lived in government quarters.

Family Thirteen – The husband was a lawyer. The wife was not working, although she had worked as a television announcer and had trained in catering and hotel management. They had no children. The husband was a Creole and the wife was Ghanaian. They lived in a private residence.

Family Fourteen – The husband was an officer involved in the education programme provided for the army. The wife was unemployed. They had three children and both were Mende. They lived in army quarters.

Over the two years I knew them, rather dramatic, and even in some cases, tragic changes occurred in the lives of most of these families. Two of the men were imprisoned following the *coup*. Both their wives were forced suddenly to vacate their homes. One wife, with her children, moved into the already crowded household of another family in the pilot group. Her husband was released after a few months but the other man was released only after a prolonged trial two years later. Another family parted with their only daughter, by giving her to a relative who had had no children. Later, the husband of this same family, hoping to get a scholarship to study overseas for four years, moved his wife and family to a Provincial town. Although he didn't receive the scholarship, they maintained this arrangement of separate residence as he continued to live and work in Freetown. Later he was selected a member of Parliament and appointed a minister.

Several men were transferred from Freetown to Provincial towns or changed their occupations. The magistrate resigned as a result of political pressure and began a private law practice in a distant town, which necessitated his being away from home most of the time. This family had to give up their government house when he resigned. Later, as a result of political tension, he and his family left Sierra Leone. Another civil servant was transferred and became permanent secretary in another ministry. Later, he was made secretary to the Cabinet. Another civil servant was appointed a District Officer, necessitating the family's move from Freetown to a Provincial town. This man's wife died during this time. One husband, a civil servant, was transferred to another ministry and the next year he and his wife spent a year in Britain where he attended a study course. Another husband was appointed ambassador to a European country.

Three of the pilot group couples separated, two of them for just a few weeks and one for much longer. Babies were born to three of the couples and a childless couple adopted a child. One wife began a study course in addition to her teaching job, which necessitated her being away from home all day and every weekday evening for over a year. Another wife received a grant to study for several months in England. Several husbands went overseas on trips of varying lengths. One of the couples, who had previously been married by customary law, travelled to Britain, where they were married in church and subsequently had a honeymoon in Europe.

The case studies of these families were intended to provide the basis for the construction of a questionnaire. The changes which occurred in their family life were not atypical for the professional group. Clearly it would be impossible to understand marriage and family relations from the use of a questionnaire alone. Other more serious problems emerged from these intensive studies. The problem of formulating questions which will elicit reliable responses obviously must receive considerable attention, especially in the construction of a standardized interview schedule. Care must be taken to ensure comprehensibility in terms of the particular social context, and it is possible to build into a series of questions certain checks for inconsistencies in responses. However, in survey research, such matters as collecting accurate information on household or family composition are usually regarded as straightforward matters. Despite the almost optimum conditions for my intensive interviews with these people in the pilot group, even such usually unproblematic material was subject to error.

Although it was possible to list the number of relatives, wards and other unrelated persons living in a household, it was not always possible to know if the numbers and relationships reported represented the facts or what the informant wanted you to believe. For example, I called a number of times on one wife in the group. She often had to change the time of our appointment because of her obligations to a relative who was ill. Then I had an appointment alone with her husband. He told me that his brother had died and so, in the traditional pattern, he had inherited one of his brother's wives. Recently, he had returned to his home village and, while he was there, he observed this woman was ill. He informed her that as his wife he required her to come with him to Freetown for medical attention. He remarked how fortunate he was to have a wife who understood the traditions and accepted this woman in their home. Nevertheless, the wife had concealed the fact that this woman was actually residing with the family even though she must have been in the house most of the times I was there. In another case, a five-year-old child living in the home was described as a ward, the child of a relative this family was educating. The child was the only boy in the household. Much later, during an interview with the wife, she admitted to me that the child was really her husband's child by another woman. When I returned the second time to Sierra Leone I found this couple had had a new baby boy of their own and the older boy was no longer living with them. After this, I always saw this couple together and I never found a way to ask the delicate question of where the other boy had been sent.

In another case, an illiterate woman living in the household was first described as the nanny but it turned out that she was a second wife. This information was only divulged to me in a very painful session with the wife, who was considering leaving her husband (and later did) because she could not tolerate the situation. And, in another home, two small girls appeared during Christmas holidays. I discovered they were offspring of the husband and wife respectively through other relationships before their marriage, although they were now being supported by the husband and considered part of their family.

Such information emerged only after long and intimate contact with these families. If it is necessary to spend such a long time getting accurate details of household and family composition, then we can assume that more complicated topics will present even greater difficulties to research. One is led to conclude not only that interpretations of data collected by formal survey techniques are highly suspect but that even the intensive methods anthropologists have relied on may be subject to wide error.

Questionnaires administered to university students

The university students were included in the study for several reasons and some of these have been discussed in Chapter One. There were also some more practical considerations which led me to include them. The students' questionnaire was tested three times before administering it to the university sample and the overall exercise helped in framing the questions that were finally used for the professional group. I also discovered that it was often possible to discuss certain topics quite freely with students, which often seemed to create resistance in conversations with adults. Students are more familiar with the methods of social research and were able to complete the questionnaire with relative ease.[5] Finally, all these data from the students were processed, tabulated and were available for preliminary analysis before devising the final questionnaire for the professionals.

An interval sample was drawn of twenty-five per cent of all Sierra Leonean students enrolled in Fourah Bay College and Njala University

5. A copy of this questionnaire and the one administered to the professionals may be found in Appendix B.

College. Because the number of girls enrolled was small compared with the men, I doubled the number of girls in the Fourah Bay sample. At Njala University College I included all the girls who were enrolled. Table 29 shows the composition of the samples. The response rate was as follows:

| Njala University College | 100 per cent |
| Fourah Bay College | 99.4 per cent |

Table 29. *Composition of the university sample*

College	Males	Females	Total
Fourah Bay College	78	55	133
Njala	64	32	96
Totals	142	87	229

After the administering of the questionnaire, every fifth student on the list was interviewed to check for ambiguous items in the questionnaire and for accuracy in the interpretation of their responses.

Questionnaires administered to the professionals

A sampling frame of all professional persons who were living and working in the country at the time of the research was drawn up. Since no list of such persons existed, it was necessary to obtain lists of all occupational groups which included professionals. The sampling frame, as finally completed, included 754 persons who were graduates or professionally qualified, who were living and working in Sierra Leone. Of these, 602 were men and 152 were women. Since it was not possible to know the marital status of persons listed before the interviews were conducted, a 20 per cent random sample of all the professionals was drawn in order to have a sufficient number of extant unions to provide data for the study.[6] Furthermore, there was an advantage in sampling the entire population of professionals as the interviews would provide some general descriptive information on the composition of the professional group as a whole. Originally it was

6. Table 1, p. 37 showns the representation of marital status groups in the sample.

planned to divide the list of married professional men, interviewing the wives of every second man on the list. In view of the lack of advance information about marital status and because of the greater difficulty of locating the women, this was not possible. As far as possible, the women interviewed were selected in the manner originally planned but, in the end, the number of wives interviewed form a quota sample. In summary, the statistical data describing the professional group were gained from interviews with professional men randomly selected from the sampling frame, and from interviews with a quota sample of the wives of the professional men. All the never-married professional women were interviewed. Table 30 shows the marital status and sex of those persons interviewed.

Table 30. *Sex and marital status of persons selected for interviews*[7]

Married male	64
Never-married male	11
Divorced male	1
Widowed male	1
Married female	61
Never-married female	19
Divorced female	0
Widowed female	0
Refusals	3
	160

The sample was drawn in April, 1968. The interviews were begun the following November and completed during the following four months. I personally conducted each interview. Although the sampling frame was complete (only seven out of 160 persons listed as professionals were found not to hold university degrees as indicated in the following table) and fairly accurate and the sampling done by means of a random number table, the nature of the political situation during the period and other factors made it necessary to replace a number of persons in the sample. Table 31 shows the reasons for these replacements.

7. The numbers in Table 30 naturally differ from those in Table 1, as Table 30 shows the number of persons interviewed from whom data describing the professional group as a whole were drawn.

Table 31. *Reasons for replacing persons included in the sample*

Out of the country (political reasons, study leave, etc.)	25
Retired (after sample was drawn)	1
In prison	2
Deceased	1
Errors (did not hold qualifications for inclusion)	7
Other (wife recently deceased, could not be located)	3
Total	**39**

It was possible to make appointments for many of the interviews by telephone. During this first meeting I offered letters of introduction, described the research, explained how I had got their name and asked them if they would be willing to be interviewed. Sometimes they allowed me to administer the questionnaire in this first meeting but, in a great many cases, it was necessary to arrange another time. Although the interview schedule required only about fifty minutes to administer, with all these preliminary arrangements and time spent in discussions before and after the interview, it was necessary to devote about three hours to completing one. It was also difficult to locate the addresses of many who had no telephone or who had moved since I had first obtained their names. Sometimes I only knew the approximate part of town and would have to begin by asking people in the street if they knew the whereabouts of a certain person.

All these problems were multiplied in the interviews with the wives. Sometimes, when I did finally locate them, they considered it necessary to ask their husband's permission before being interviewed. In many cases it was necessary to make two or three visits before the interview was completed. Of course, all these difficulties made it possible to become much better acquainted with the respondents than it would have been if the interviews had been conducted under easier conditions. Hence one ought not to conclude that the difficulties encountered in survey research always lead to poorer data. In the sample, only three individuals, all men, refused to be interviewed.

In considering the statistical tables it should be noted that the total percentages do not always equal one hundred due to rounding off numbers. It will also be noted that in some of the tables the total numbers of responses differ. This is because in some interviews it was not possible to ask informants to respond to certain questions. If an interview was interrupted by someone, a thing which frequently happened, I sometimes dropped a question, since it might be embarrassing for the respondent to discuss it before someone else. In a very few cases, women were unable to comprehend a question so it had to be explained in such detail as to influence the response. These were not included. Such problems are common in sociological interviews, but, comparing my experiences in previous research in Britain, I believe conditions for interviewing were no more difficult in this African setting than there. As far as possible, questions were asked exactly as they appear on the questionnaire.

Questionnaires administered to primary-aged children

A short questionnaire was administered to the upper two classes of four primary schools in Freetown (ages 9 to 11). These schools charged higher-tha-average fees and were attended by children of the professional group. The questionnaire replicated a study done by Oeser and Hammond (1954) in Australia and questions were designed to examine the way children perceived the organization of domestic work in their households. The children were also asked to indicate the number of persons living in their household and whether or not they were living with parents or other relatives. These data provided interesting checks on the other household composition information collected from the interviews with the professionals. A total of 142 questionnaires was administered.

Essays by secondary school pupils

Early in the research I collected essays from secondary school students, aged 16 to 19, who had been assigned to write on the topic, 'Compare traditional African marriage and family life with western marriage and family life'. These proved to be an effective way of gaining insights into the attitudes of students towards the two systems and how they perceived the differences. Later, 241 such essays were collected from the students in the fifth and sixth forms of ten secondary schools located in Freetown and Bo. They were usually written as a regular assignment in English classes.

Attitude scale

The interview schedule administered to the professional sample had included a scale which respondents were given the opportunity to indicate their approval of certain qualities of marriage and family life which they thought were distinctly western in contrast to traditional African patterns. The scale was constructed from statements elicited from informants during the first period of research. This same scale was administered later to a group of 70 university students. (See question 100 in Appendix B.) The respondents had the opportunity to indicate first if an attribute was more typical of the West than of traditional African patterns and then to evaluate it. If the respondent indicated the attribute was western and that it was a good thing, his attitude was scored as positive towards the western image. If he responded that it was more western than African but not a good thing, his attitude was scored as positive towards African patterns. If the respondent indicated an attribute was not more typical of western than of African patterns and that it was a good thing, his attitude was scored as neutral. The fourth logical possibility was that a respondent would indicate that an attribute was neither African nor western and that it was a bad thing. The last possibility never happened and the third possibility only occurred three times in all.

Interviews with experts

Sellitiz *et al.* (1964) describe a method they refer to as the 'experience survey'. By this they mean interviews with persons who, by virtue of their profession, have frequent contact with the population or problem being studied. I conducted many such interviews with lawyers who handle divorce cases, educators, members of the judiciary concerned with family law, doctors, clergymen and social welfare workers. These people were often able to provide insights into aspects of marriage and family life. The interviews also resulted in a kind of 'census' of important problems to be followed up and many suggestions how to go about investigating these areas.

In a sense, these interviews were made more difficult by the fact that the very persons discussing the problems were themselves part of the group under examination. Some of them, later, appeared in the sample. Nevertheless, in almost all cases, these persons were so concerned with the problems we considered that they were willing to talk about the matter, not only objectively from the perspective of their particular professional insights but also with reference to their own personal situations.

Official records and other statistical data

I gathered information on all divorces granted in the country under the general law between 1961 and 1968. These data indicated whether the petitioner was the husband or wife, the grounds upon which the divorce was sought and finally granted, and to whom it was granted. Proceedings of many divorces were also made available for me to read and record.

The statistics on numbers of women who had sued for child support under either the Married Woman's Maintenance Act or the Bastardy Act were collected, and case material studied and recorded for the same period, 1961 to 1968. These data were very incomplete. Record books for certain months were missing.

The birth statistics for the years 1961 to 1968 were collected. The information available included all babies born whose births were registered in the Western area only. The importance of these data relates to the problem of children born out of wedlock. The registration reveals the marital status of the parents of the child and, for several years, also revealed the tribal affiliation of both parents.

Details of all marriages contracted under the Acts between 1961 and 1968 were collected, which totalled 2472 records of marriages. This material was available through the Registrar's office in Freetown but covered the entire country. Information included occupation, age, marital status and birthplace of the spouses, as well as the occupations of their fathers. Although customary marriages are being registered in some chiefdoms, the records were not complete enough to merit collection.

The Ministry of Social Welfare in Freetown and some Provincial towns maintain a family case-work programme. Many persons involved in marital problems make use of these services. I read and recorded all such case record material from 1961 to 1968 from the Freetown Office and two other Provincial towns.

The emphasis throughout this research was on the collection of qualitative data to be checked and, wherever possible supported by quantitative data. These statistical results were then to be rechecked by further qualitative approaches. In the interviews with the sample of professionals, a number of cases were encountered which would not easily have been found through observational methods alone (e.g. widowed and divorced persons, persons born out of wedlock, 'outside' wives, estranged married couples, etc.) As has been noted, the 'outside' wife is the term for a woman who has entered into a more or less permanent relationship with a man who is married to his own wife according to statutory law. The social position of an 'outside wife' is ambiguous and it is extremely difficult to make contact with such women under ordinary research conditions. Similarly, 'outside' or illegitimate children form a category of persons who are more or less stigmatized. No one ever admitted they were illegitimate outside the more formal interview situation.

Research and surveys are often undertaken in more familiar cultural contexts without the benefit of preliminary intensive observations because the investigator thinks he knows the relevant domains and categories to be researched. Most family research starts from assumptions drawn from certain myths about the nature of the 'normal' family. One of the very distinct advantages of a family study in another society is that the investigator is forced to discard most of these assumptions and think again. In such a situation it becomes very obvious that the research must employ as eclectic an approach as the investigator's skills and opportunities allow.

Questionnaires administered to samples of students and professionals

Note: The manner in which the interview schedules were administered has been described in Appendix A. The questions are reproduced here. As will be recalled, the students filled in their own questionnaires and every fifth person was interviewed afterwards. I interviewed the professional sample and filled in the questionnaire form. The questionnaires were laid out to simplify the process of coding. However, in the case of the professionals, because I was asking the questions, very few required 'forced choice' responses. Those that did are indicated here and the responses are given. An explanatory letter was attached to each questionnaire. Copies of these letters are included. It should be noted that the student questionnaire was devised after five months of intensive interviews with the fourteen pilot group couples. The professional questionnaire was written after a preliminary analysis of the results of the student data and further observations.

1. University Student Questionnaire

(i) Explanatory letter

This set of questions is part of a study of the family and of attitudes towards marriage which is being sponsored by the University of Edinburgh and associated with the Institute of African Studies, Fourah Bay College. The purpose of the research is to attempt to discover the direction that the changes in family structure may be taking. The investigation is limited to families of the professional class and university students. It is assumed that these people are the 'pace-setters' for the society as a whole. Your co-operation, as members of this group, will not only be greatly appreciated, but will significantly contribute to the scope and accuracy of the study in its attempt to assess the extent to which family life will be changing from traditional patterns in the future. Thank you.

THIS IS NOT A TEST: There are no right or wrong answers. The purpose of the questions is to gain insight into *your* opinions. Please *do not* write your name on this paper. The study is completely confidential and no names are needed. You do not have to answer any questions you do not want to answer. However, it is sincerely hoped that you will co-operate to make this a good scientific study by answering all the questions as frankly and honestly as you can.

(ii) *Questionnaire*

I. *Directions*: Please fill in the blanks or circle the number of the answer which best anwers the question.

1. How many years have you spent in this University? 1 2 3 4 5.
2. Did you come to university straight from secondary school? 1. yes 2. no.
3. If NO, how long were you employed before coming to the university? ....
4. In what district did you receive your primary education? ....
5. What was the name of your secondary school? ....
6. How old were you when you first left the care of your mother?

    ....
7. How many years did you spend in boarding school? 1. .... 2. None.
8. Did you ever live in the home of a family other than your own parents?

    1. yes
    2. no

    If YES, where did you go? .... Was this a relative? 1. yes 2. no.   **(Town)**

    Which term would most closely describe your role in that household?

    1. son
    2. steward
    3. ward
    4. daughter
    5. student
    6. other .... (specify)

When comparing yourself with the other children in the household did you receive: (Circle *all* the answers which apply)

    1. same food
    2. same sleeping arrangements
    3. different food
    4. different sleeping arrangements
    5. more work
    6. same amount of work
    7. less work
    8. there were no other children
    9. other? .... (specify)

9. How many relatives besides your own father and mother contributed to your support up to now? That is, in terms of providing for your housing, food, or money.

    1. .... (number of relatives)
    2. No one other than my own parents

10. What is your national grouping? (tribe) ....

11. What is your age? .... Your sex? 1. Male 2. Female

12. What is your present marital status?

    1. married
    2. single
    3. separated
    4. engaged
    5. widowed
    6. divorced

13. What is the national grouping of: Your father? ....
                                        Your mother? ....

14. Please circle the answer which describes your parents' present living arrangements.

    1. Both alive, living together
    2. Both alive, living separately
    3. Father not living
    4. Mother not living
    5. Neither father nor mother living

15. Did your father ever have more than one wife at a time?

    1. If YES, how many? ....
    2. No, only one wife

16. How many full brothers and sisters have you (by the same mother and same father)? ....

17. How many half brothers and sisters have you on:
    1. Father's side? ....
    2. Mother's side? ....
18. What was the usual occupation of your father and mother while you were growing up?
    1. .... father
    2. .... mother
19. What is your father's present occupation?
    1. ....
    2. Deceased
20. What is the religious affiliation of your:
    1. self? ....
    2. father? ....
    3. mother? ....
21. Where were you born? ....
                             (Town)   (District)   (Province)
22. For what occupation are you now preparing yourself? ....
23. Do you have any children? 1. no 2. yes. If YES, how many ....
24. Please indicate the amount of schooling the following persons have had:

	None	Primary	Secondary	University	Other (Specify)	Don't know
Your father	1	2	3	4	5............	6
Your mother	1	2	3	4	5............	6
Your father's father	1	2	3	4	5............	6
Your father's mother	1	2	3	4	5............	6
Your mother's father	1	2	3	4	5............	6
Your mother's mother	1	2	3	4	5............	6

25. What do you think determines status and prestige in the village?
....
....
....

26. What do you think determines status and prestige in the city?
....
....
....

27. Would you circle all the answers which would describe your father and/or your father's family in their hometown?

1. poor		9. a politician	
2. just average wealth		10. large number of dependents	
3. wealthy		11. owned houses	
4. very wealthy		12. a civil servant	
5. part of chief's household		13. none of these	
6. leader of a secret society		14. has influential relatives	
7. highly respected		15. member of ruling family	
8. owned land			

28. What do you consider the ideal age for marriage of a university-educated man or woman?

        1. Man ....

        2. Woman ....

29. What is the ideal number of children for the educated family?

....

30. What type of marriage did the following people have?

	Customary rites	Muslim	Christian (civil)	Other
Own parents	1	2	3	4
Father's parents	1	2	3	4
Mother's parents	1	2	3	4

31. Please check which relatives you will expect to give financial assistance when you leave university.

....	1. Both parents regularly
....	2. Both parents, only irregularly
....	3. Mother only regularly
....	4. Father only regularly
....	5. Mother irregularly
....	6. Father irregularly
....	7. Neither mother nor father
....	8. Both parents deceased
....	9. Mother is deceased
....	10. Father is deceased
....	11. Brothers and/or sisters
....	12. Nephews and/or nieces
....	13. Uncles and aunts
....	14. Grandparents
....	15. No relatives will be given assistance
....	16. All who call themselves relatives

32. Below are some items that could be important to consider in the choice of a marital partner. Please indicate the degree of importance you would give each.

		Very Important	Important	Not Very Important	Not Important
a.	Same tribal background	3	2	1	0
b.	Good-looking	3	2	1	0
c.	Being in love	3	2	1	0
d.	Educated, same level as myself	3	2	1	0
e.	Good family background	3	2	1	0
f.	Being a virgin	3	2	1	0
g.	Willing to leave Sierra Leone	3	2	1	0
h.	Educated, but not as much as myself	3	2	1	0
i.	Same leisure-time interests	3	2	1	0
j.	Same religion as mine	3	2	1	0
k.	Is at least moderately wealthy	3	2	1	0

II. *Directions*: Below are some duties of husbands and wives. Would you rank the following statement in order of their importance, numbering from one to five – one for the most important and so on? *Do it for both the husband and the wife.*

.... To support the wife financially

.... To be faithful and loyal to the wife

.... To be a good companion to the wife

.... To be a good father to the children

.... To love the wife

.... To cook and keep a nice house

.... To obey and respect husband

.... To be a good companion

.... To be a good mother to the children

.... To love the husband

III. *Directions*: Below are some possible sources of conflicts between married couples. Would you rank them in the order which you think they are most likely to cause problems between married couples? Number them in the order of their importance, numbering from 1 to 7 – one for the most important and so on.

.... Interference from husband's mother
.... Disagreements over money
.... Unfaithfulness of the spouse
.... Religious differences
.... Disagreements over discipline of children
.... Husband's leisure-time habits
.... Interference from wife's mother

IV. *Directions*: Listed below are a number of statements. Each represents a commonly held opinion and there are no right or wrong answers. You will probably disagree with some and agree with others. Read each statement carefully. Then indicate the extent to which you agree or disagree by circling the appropriate letters after each statement.

Strongly agree	– SA
Agree	– A
Disagree	– D
Strongly disagree	– SD

1. If I love a person, I shall not be concerned whether or not my family approves my choice of a marital partner.
2. If a wife and her husband's mother quarrel or disagree, the husband should side with his wife.
3. When I am married and have children I would prefer to live as close to my parents as possible.
4. Such things like laundry, cleaning, child care are 'women's work' and a husband should take no responsibility for them.
5. A man's inheritance should be divided equally between his legitimate and his illegitimate children.
6. When I am married I would prefer that my spouse and I each have an equal part in making family decisions.
7. My way of life is based more upon 'western' ideas than upon traditional African ideas.
8. A married woman has the duty of helping her husband to earn a living for the family.
9. The reason a man does not tell his wife how much he earns is usually because he is spending his money on another woman.
10. It is preferable for a working wife to keep her salary separate from that of her husband and to spend it as she thinks best.
11. A couple may love each other sincerely, but if their marriage is not blessed with children it is bound to be unhappy.

12. It is preferable for a couple to wait at least two years after marriage before having children.

13. If a woman has a university education she has a responsibility to help the country by working whether she has young children or not.

14. A husband should be willing to take care of the children and do some housework in order for his wife to take an active part in community affairs.

15. A wife should not object if her husband's leisure time is spent mainly with persons other than herself and their children.

16. A married woman with children should be able to decide for herself whether she wants to stay at home or work outside the home.

17. In money matters, a wife's opinion should carry as much weight as her husband's.

18. If a husband gives his wife a housekeeping allowance, she should not expect to know how he spends the rest of his money.

19. Any display of affection between a husband and wife is not suitable before their children.

20. A man should not take sides with his wife if she quarrels or disagrees with his mother.

21. The people with whom I spend most of my leisure-time are my relatives.

22. My mother was responsible for most of the disciplining when I was a child.

23. If I thought it would better my child's educational opportunities, I would send him to a relative to be reared.

24. Telling a child you do not love him when he misbehaves is a better form of punishment than the use of the cane.

25. My father was responsible for most of the disciplining when I was a child.

26. The relative in whom I usually confide is my mother.

27. When choosing a mate the approval of one's family is as important as the love a couple might feel towards each other.

28. Women who use contraceptives are more likely to be unfaithful to their husbands.

29. Generally it is the husband's mother who causes trouble between married couples.

30. The African idea of financial responsibility to one's relatives is out of date.

31. Generally, it is the wife's mother who causes trouble between married couples.
32. It would be preferable for the government rather than the family to provide homes and support and care for old people.
33. I would prefer that my children are initiated into a secret society (e.g. Bundu, Poro).
34. African wedding traditions are unimportant to me, I would prefer to have a simple ceremony in the Registrar's office.
35. It is preferable for a girl to be pregnant by her boy-friend before they are married so that they know they are able to have children.
36. If a wife wants a career and does not want children, she should have the right to make that decision.
37. It is preferable for a wife to have no more than a secondary school education.
38. When a mother has children under school age she should give up her work outside and remain at home to care for the children.
39. When a quarrel or dispute arises between a married couple, they should turn to their relatives to help them settle it.
40. Adultery should be grounds for divorce for both men and women.
41. If my parents strongly disapproved of the person I chose to marry, I would not marry that person.
42. In my marriage I expect to provide for my in-laws.
43. It is unfair for a wife to expect her husband to have sexual relations only with her.
44. The western idea of a family, one man, his wife and children living on their own will never be accepted in Sierra Leone.
45. When I am old I expect my children to provide for me.
46. If a marriage does not produce children, a wife should be understanding and permit her husband to have children outside.
47. It is almost impossible for a woman to be a good mother and wife and have a career.
48. It is preferable for married couples to limit the number of children born to them.
49. The best number of children for an educated couple to have is four or less.
50. If a wife wants to go out alone at night she should ask her husband's permission.
51. I find I usually can trust persons of my own sex with secrets more than the opposite sex.

52. Responsibility for disciplining children should rest mainly with the father.
53. It is more important to teach a child obedience and respect for authority than to teach him ambition and the desire to get ahead.
54. The fear of my mother's curse is somehing I feel very deeply.
55. I would prefer to rear my children the way I was brought up.
56. Isolating a child in a room is generally a better form of punishment than the use of the cane.
57. Intercourse during the time a mother is breast-feeding her child is harmful to the child.
58. A husband should expect his wife to take the entire responsibility for the care of the children while they are babies.
59. After I am married, I would be willing to have some of our relatives' children living in my home with my family.
60. A husband should manage his time so that he is able to share in the care of the children.
61. I would prefer a system which allows a man more than one wife.
62. If necessary I would lower my standard of living in order to be able to give financial assistance to my relatives.
63. I see no reason to make a special effort to teach children about traditional customs.
64. Women are able to influence a man's feeling of love for them by adding certain things to the food they give him.
65. Mothers, if they are careless, can make their baby sons impotent (*okobo*).
66. If a wife leaves her husband, she also leaves behind her the property they have accumulated during the marriage.

Thank you very much for your assistance.

2. *Professional Questionnaire*

(i) *Explanatory letter*

I am wondering if you would consider assisting in a study of the family which is being conducted by the Department of Social Anthropology, Edinburgh University, under the direction of Professor Kenneth Little, and which is also associated with the Institute of African Studies, Fourah Bay College? Your name was selected in the following manner: a list of all graduates and other persons with professional qualifications in Sierra Leone was compiled. From this list every fourth name was chosen.[1] If the results from this sample are to be worthwhile, it is essential for there to be a hundred per cent response and we would therefore be very grateful for your co-operation.

The purpose of the research is to attempt to discover the direction and the extent of change which may be occurring in the organization of family life in several countries. In Sierra Leone the study is limited to families of professional people because it is thought that these are the 'pace-setters' for the society as a whole. Your help would be deeply appreciated and would make a significant contribution to the understanding of family life in Sierra Leone.

The questionnaire asks for certain factual information about education, birthplace, numbers of persons living in your household, the extent to which you presently assume responsibility for your own relatives, etc. It also provides the opportunity for you to express your own attitudes and opinions. There are no right or wrong answers, but if the results of the investigation are to reflect, in a balanced and objective manner, the actual behaviour and attitudes of professional people in Sierra Leone, it is essential that the answers be well thought out.

Thank you so much for your kind assistance.

(ii) *The questionnaire*
1. Would you kindly state the birthplace of yourself, your spouse, your father? Would you indicate the year they were born? [Respondents were asked to give the village or town, district, Province.]
2. In what place(s) (town or village and district) did you attend primary school?
3. In what place(s) did you attend secondary school? Please name the school(s).
4. How many years, if any, did you spend in boarding school as a boarder?
5. Please list the educational institutions you attended after leaving secondary school, the country located, the degree or qualifications received, if any, and the number of years spent there.

1. It will be recalled that the sample was drawn by means of a random number table. However, it seemed appropriate to make only this simple explanation which showed the respondent his name was selected by chance.

6. Please state the highest qualifications you now hold.
7. In all, how long have you lived out of Sierra Leone?
8. In all, how long has your spouse lived out of Sierra Leone?
9. Please indicate your present marital status.
10. If MARRIED, what year were you married?
11. What is your present occupation?
12. What is your spouse's present occupation?
13. How many years did your wife (you) work before she (you) were married, if any?
14. How many years has she (have you) worked since you have been married?
15. Is she (are you) presently earning an income in any way?
16. Please tell me the number of years of education attained by the following persons. (Yourself, father, mother, father's father, father's mother, mother's father, mother's mother, your spouse.)
17. What type of marriage ceremony did the following persons have? (Yourself, your parents, your father's parents, your mother's parents.)
    [Responses offered included: 'customary rites', both customary and Christian rites, Christian or civil, Muslim, other – about half-way through the interviews I learned to say 'not married' as one alternative for the respondent.]
18. Please indicate the religious affiliation (church membership) of the following persons. (Yourself, your father, your mother, your spouse.)
19. Do you attend church regularly (i.e. at least twice a month)?
20. Please indicate the national grouping (tribe) of the following persons. (Yourself, your father, your mother, your spouse.)
21. What was your father's usual occupation while you were growing up?
22. What is his present position?
23. What was your spouse's father's usual occupation?
24. How many brothers and sisters have you had by the same mother and same father?
25. How many are still alive?
26. Would you state your position in the family (i.e. oldest child, third child, etc.)?
27. How many half-brothers and sisters have you had on your father's side?

28. How many half-brothers and sisters have you had on your mother's side?
29. Would you state which person had the major responsibility for your care as a child before you began school?
30. Were you ever placed as a ward in the household of a family not related to you?
31. On reflection, could you say which of the following you would rate as having had the *greater* influence upon the formation of your attitudes towards marriage and family life and most specifically towards your idea of your role as a married person?
    [Responses offered included: parents, other relative, school, church, European individuals, other non-relatives, western ideas, spouse, none of these, please specify any others.]
32. Would you tell me all those relatives who have helped you complete your education either by paying school fees or providing for you in some other way?
33. If you have received actual financial assistance, do you expect to have to repay this assistance?
34. How do you feel about the practice of relatives assisting each other in financial ways?
    [Responses offered: strongly approve of it, mildly approve of it, mildly disapprove of it, strongly disapprove of it, other.]
35. Would you indicate the regularity with which you and your spouse give financial assistance or token gifts to the following relatives? (Your mother, your father, your spouse's mother, your spouse's father.)
    [Responses offered included: regularly, irregularly, only rare token amounts, never, except gifts on festive occasions, or relative deceased.]
36. Before you were married did you think about how many children you would like to have?
37. How many children did you want?
38. Have you changed your mind about how many children would be the ideal number for you and your spouse to have?
39. If you were just getting married now and could have just the number of children you wanted, how many would you consider ideal?
40. What would you say was the best thing about having a large family?

41. What would you say was the worst thing about having a large family?

42. Since you have been married, has it been necessary for you and your spouse to live apart temporarily for any reason?

43. If YES, how long was this separation?

44. Would you indicate the birth date, sex, and present residence of your children, beginning with the eldest?

45. Have you had children that have died?

46. If YES, how many?

47. Are you (is your spouse) pregnant now?

48. If there are other persons living in your household, would you please indicate their approximate age, sex, their relationship to your family, whether or not they are considered a permanent member of the household and the extent to which you are financially responsible for them, or indicate if you pay them a salary.

49. Are you (or your spouse) financially responsible for any children born to either of you outside this marriage?

50. Do you and your spouse wish to have more children?

51. Nowadays some married couples use some method of contraception to either space their children carefully or to keep them from having too many children (or more than they want). Generally speaking, do you approve or disapprove of the use of contraceptives?

52. Would you please circle the number(s) of those methods listed below that you (and/or your spouse) have used?
[Here the questionnaire was turned towards the respondent to allow him to see the choice of response offered. These included: durex, foam tablet, jelly, diaphragm, rhythm (safe period), coitus interruptus (withdrawal), the pill, surgery (either the husband or the wife), other method (please specify).]

53. If you are presently using a method of contraception, please indicate which of these it is.
[Respondents were offered the following choices if they were not using any contraceptive: not using any method because the wife is pregnant; not using any method because more children are desired; not using any method, now, but plan to in the future; not using any method and do not plan to in the future.]

54. Have you (has your wife) ever had a miscarriage?

55. Have you (has your wife) ever found it necessary to induce a

miscarriage because of an unwanted pregnancy?

56. In your opinion is abortion common in Sierra Leone?

57. What do you think about the idea of the father being present at the birth of his children?
[Responses offered included: good idea in principle; good idea, but not for me; *not* a good idea.]

58. Would you indicate the extent to which you (your husband) assist(s) with the following tasks? [These included making beds, gardening, tidying up, washing dishes, store shopping, buying children's clothes, marketing, dressing children, bathing children, setting the table, and cooking.]
[Respondents were asked to respond in terms of frequency. Responses offered included: never; occasionally, more than half the time, usually, previously, but not now.]

59. How many persons are employed by you for domestic services (including driving, gardening, or watchmen responsibility) who do not live in your household?

60. Do you have a joint current banking account with your spouse?

61. Do you have a joint savings bank account with your spouse?

62. Would you say that most of your leisure-time, other than that which you spend with your immediate family, is spent with relatives or friends?

63. Would you try to think what it is that is the most usual thing over which you and your spouse disagree?

64. In the event that you and your spouse argue, to whom do you usually turn for help in resolving the conflict?

65. Married couples agree and disagree about a variety of subjects. Would you try to estimate the extent to which you and your spouse agree or disagree about the following topics which are part of every married life? [Topics mentioned included: handling family finances, matters of recreation, religious matters, demonstration of affection, the way food is prepared, friends, table manners, politics, wife's working, obligations to relatives, faithfulness of the wife, caring for children, faithfulness of the husband, discipline of children, sharing of household tasks.]
[Responses offered were: almost always agree, occasionally disagree, frequently disagree, almost always disagree, always disagree.]

66. When problems arise about such matters as bringing up children,

disagreements about relatives and friends, financial problems, and the like, does thinking about how your parents (relatives) might handle the problem help you in deciding what to do?

67. Would you say that interference from relatives is a source of conflict between you and your spouse?

68. Would you try to think back over the activities of the past week and try to remember the people who visited you at your home and the visits that you made to other homes? Would you try then to indicate the number of such visits? (Number of relatives visiting you at your house, number of friends visiting you at your house, number of relatives you visited at their house, number of friends you visited at their house.)

69. Would you say that the amount of visiting which took place last week between you and your friends and relatives was about the same as usual?
[Reponses offered included: more visiting occurred than usual, less visiting occurred than usual, about the same amount of visiting occurs each wetk.]

70. Would you list the organizations and associations or clubs to which you belong? Please indicate whether you consider yourself an active member or not.

71. Are you a member of a secret society?
Instruction: I will read out a number of statements now. Would you indicate the extent to which you agree or disagree with each? You may find that you agree with some and disagree with others. You may indicate if you strongly agree, agree, disagree, or strongly disagree.

72. It is likely to spoil a marriage if a couple have either of their parents living with them.

73. A man's inheritance should be divided equally between all his children whether born inside the marriage or not.

74. My way of life, as far as marriage and family is concerned, is based more upon 'western' ideas than upon traditional African ideas.

75. A wife should not object if her husband's leisure-time is spent mainly with persons other than herself and her children.

76. The African idea of financial responsibility for one's relatives is out of date.

77. If I thought it would better my child's educational opportunities

I would send him to a relative to be reared.

78. It would be preferable for the government rather than the family to provide homes and support and care for old people.

79. I would prefer that my children are initiated into a secret society (e.g. Bundu, Poro).

80. It is unfair for a wife to expect her husband to have sexual relations only with her.

81. It is preferable for husbands and wives not to discuss the amounts of money that they give their own relatives.

82. The approval of one's family of one's choice of a marital partner is as important as the love the couple felt for each other before they were married.

83. If a wife and her mother-in-law quarrel, it is to be expected that the husband should side with his wife whether or not he thinks she is wrong.

84. I see no objection to married couples using abortion as one means of limiting the numbers of children born to them.

85. The western idea of a family, one man, his wife, and children living on their own without relatives will never be accepted in Sierra Leone.

86. When I am old I expect my children to provide financial assistance for me.

87. If a marriage does not produce children a wife should be understanding and permit her husband to have children outside.

88. The fear of my mother's curse is something I feel very deeply.

89. I would prefer to rear my children the way I was brought up.

90. Having intercourse during the time a mother is breast-feeding her child is harmful to the child.

91. My husband and I are willing to have some of our relatives' children living in our home with our family.

92. It is preferable for this society to have a system which allows a man more than one wife.

93. I see no reason to make a special effort to teach children about traditional customs.

94. If a wife leaves her husband she also leaves behind her the property (other than personal possessions) they have accumulated during the marriage.

95. I (my husband) give(s) more assistance with domestic work and child care than my father gave my mother.

96. I would prefer to live in a location which would make it easy for relatives to get together.
97. I want a house with enough room for our parents to feel free to move in.
98. A husband should be careful not to tell unpleasant things to his wife for fear of upsetting her.
99. Here are some generalizations which have been made that compare African and Western family life and attitudes towards marriage. Would you state whether *generally* you agree or disagree with each of the following statements by circling either 'yes' or 'no'. (Please make your observations of Sierra Leone society today as the basis for your own comparison.)

    1. In Africa marriages are generally more stable than marriages in the West.
    2. Western young people have freer choice than Africans in the selection of a mate.

       It is a good thing to have freer choice in the selection of one's mate.
    3. Western husbands are generally more faithful to their wives than are African husbands.
    4. Relationships with relatives in the West are more formal than those of African families.

       It is a good thing to have relationships with one's relatives more formal.
    5. Western husbands share more in the actual housework than do African husbands.

       It is a good thing for husbands to share in the actual housework.
    6. Western families plan and spend more of their leisure-time together as families than do African families.

       It is a good thing for families to plan and spend their leisure-time together.
    7. African husbands often use physical punishment to control their wives more than do western husbands.

       It is a good thing for husbands to use physical punishment to control their wives.
    8. Western husbands and wives display more love and affection than do African husbands and wives.

       It is a good thing for husbands and wives to display

love and affection.

9. African children fear their parents more than do western children.

It is a good thing for children to fear their parents.

10. Western couples settle their disagreements without interference from relatives more than do African couples.

It is a good thing for couples to settle their disagreements without the interference of their relatives.

11. Western husbands treat their wives more as equals than do African husbands.

It is a good thing for a husband to treat his wife as an equal.

12. Western husbands prefer their wives to have a career more than do African husbands.

It is a good thing for a husband to prefer his wife to have a career.

References

Afreh, K. 'Ghana's Legal Muddles', *West Africa*, May 18 and 25, 1968.
Aldridge, T. J. *The Sherbro and its Hinterland*, London, 1901.
— *A Transformed Colony*, London, 1910.
Allott, A. N. *Essays in African Law*, London, 1960.
Ardener, E. A. *Divorce and Fertility*, Nigerian Social and Economic Studies No. 3, Oxford, 1962.
Baker, T. 'Woman elites in western Nigeria', unpublished MS. Department of Anthropology, Edinburgh University, 1957.
Baker, T. and Bird, M. 'Urbanization and the position of women' in Special Number on Urbanism in West Africa, ed. K. Little, *Sociological Review*, Vol. 7, No. 1, New Series, 1959.
Balandier, G. 'The colonial situation: a theoretical approach', in *Social Change: The Colonial Situation*, ed. L. Wallerstein, New York, 1951.
— 'Sociologie des Brazzavilles Noires', *cahiers de la Fondation Nationale des Science Politiques*, No. 67, Paris, 1955.
— *The Sociology of Black Africa*, London, 1970.
Bangura, J. 'Born to be outcasts'. *Flamingo*, Sierra Leone, Vol. 4, No. 11, August, 1965 Edition.
Banton, M. *West African City*, London, 1957.
Barnes, J. A. 'The Politics of Law', in *Man in Africa*, ed. M. Douglas and P. Kaberry, London, 1969.
Beattie, J. Review of *Anthropologists in the Field*, (ed. Jongmans, D. J. and Gutkind, P. C.), *Bijdragen*, December 1969.
Beetham, T. A. *Christianity and the New Africa*, London, 1967.
Bell, C. R. *Middle Class Families*, London, 1968.
Bird, M. 'Social changes in kinship and marriage among the Yoruba of Western Nigeria'. Unpublished Ph. D. thesis, Edinburgh University, 1958.
— 'Urbanization, family and marriage in Western Nigeria', in *Urbanization in African Social Change*, Centre of African Studies, Edinburgh University, 1963.
Birdwhistell, R. L. 'The American family: some perspectives', *Psychiatry*, Vol. 29, August 1966.
Blood, R. O. and Wolfe, D. M. *Husbands and Wives*, New York, 1960.
Bott, E. 'Urban families: conjugal roles and social networks', *Human Relations*, 8, 1955.
— *Family and Social Networks*, London, 1957.
Campbell, D. T. and Levine, R. A. 'Field Manual Anthropology', in *A Handbook*

of Method in Cultural Anthropology, ed. R. Narroll and R. Cohen, New York, 1970.

Clarke, J. I. 'Sex Ratios in Sierra Leone', *The Journal of the Sierra Leone Geographical Association,* No. 9, 1965.

— 'Population distribution in Sierra Leone', in *The Population of Tropical Africa,* C. Okonjo *et al.,* London, 1969, *Sierra Leone in Maps,* London, 1966.

— 'The Creole way of death', paper presented at the Sierra Leone Symposium held at the University of Western Ontario, London, Ontario, 1971.

Cohen, A. 'The politics of ritual secrecy', *Man,* Vol. 6, No. 3, September 1971.

Cohen, R. *Dominance and Defiance,* Anthropological Studies, No. 6, 1970.

Cohen, R. and Spain, A. 'Feminism, divorce, and the role of women in Africa', unpublished manuscript, Northwestern University, Chicago, 1970.

Collier, G. *Sierra Leone – Experiment in Democracy in an African Nation,* New York, 1970.

Crabtree, A. I. 'Marriage and family life among educated Africans in the urban areas of the Gold Coast', unpublished M.Sc. Thesis, London University, 1950.

Daniels, W. C. E. *The Common Law in West Africa,* London, 1964.

Deen, R. I. 'Informal education among the Aku tribe', unpublished dissertation, Milton Margai Teachers' Training College, Freetown, Sierra Leone, 1967-68.

Dennis, N., Henriques, F. and Slaughter, C. *Coal is our Life,* London, 1957.

Dollard, J. *Caste and Class in a Southern Town,* New York, 1937.

Dow, T. E. 'Fertility and family planning in Sierra Leone', *Studies in Family Planning,* Vol. 2, No. 8, August 1971.

Dynes, R. R., Clarke, A. C., Dinitz F. 'Levels of occupational aspiration', *American Sociological Review,* Vol. 21, No. 2, 1956.

Easmon, R. S. *The Burnt-out Marriage,* London, 1967.

Edgell, S. 'Spiralists: their career and family lives', *British Journal of Sociology,* Vol. 21, 1970.

E'ias, N. and Scotson, J. F. *The Established and the Outsiders,* London, 1964.

Fallers, L. G. *Law Without Precedent,* Chicago and London, 1969.

Fanon, F. *Black Skin White Masks,* London, 1970.

Festinger, L., Schachter, S. and Back, K. *Social Pressures in Informal Groups,* New York, 1950.

Freilich, M. *Marginal Natives: Anthropologists at Work,* New York, 1970.

Fyfe, C. H. *A History of Sierra Leone,* London, 1962a.

— *A Short History of Sierra Leone,* London 1962b.

Gamble, D. P. 'Occupational prestige in an urban community (Lunsar) in Sierra Leone', *Sierra Leone Studies,* New Series, No. 19, July 1966.

Goldthorpe, J. E. 'Educated Africans: some conceptual and terminological problems', in *Social Change in Africa,* ed. A. Southall, London, 1961.

Goode, W. J. 'Industrialization and family change', in *Industrialization and Society,* ed. B. F. Hoselitz and W. E. Moore, UNESCO, 1963.

Goody, J. R. (ed.) *Developmental Cycle in Domestic Groups,* Cambridge, 1966.

Goody, E. N. 'Conjugal separation and divorce among the Gonja of Northern Ghana', in *Marriage in Tribal Society,* ed. M. Fortes, Cambridge, 1962.

Grama, M. and Graham, K. 'Some changes in Thai family life' (preliminary draft), Institute of Public Administration, Thammosat University, Bangkok, Thailand, 1958.

Gutkind, P. C. 'African Urban family life', *Cahiers d'Etudes Africaines,* Vol. 3, No. 2, 1962.

Harrell-Bond, B. E. 'Blackbird Leys: a pilot study of an urban housing estate', unpublished B. Litt. thesis, Oxford University, 1967.
— 'Conjugal role behaviour', *Human Relations*, Vol. 22, No. 1, 1969.
— 'Survey research in a study of marriage', *Solving Problems of Survey Research in Africa*, ed. O'Barr, Spain and Tessler, Chicago, 1972.
Harris, C. C. *The Family*, London, 1969.
Henriques, F. *Family and Colour in Jamaica*, London, 1968.
Izzett, A. 'Family life among the Yoruba in Lagos, Nigeria', in *Social Change in Modern Africa*, ed. A. W. Southall, London, 1961.
Jahoda, G. *White Man*, London, 1961.
Jellicoe, M. Unpublished London University Diploma in Social Anthropology thesis, 1955.
Joko-Smart, H. M. 'Inheritance to property in Sierra Leone', *Sierra Leone Studies*, No. 14, January 1969.
— 'Sierra Leone', in *Allott's Judicial and Legal Systems in Africa*, ed. A. Allott, London, 1970.
— 'Inheritance to property in Sierra Leone', unpublished manuscript (n.d.).
Jongmans. D. G. and Gutkind, P. C. W. *Anthropologists in the Field*, Assen, 1967.
Jordan, R. S. 'The place of the Creoles in the bureaucracy of Sierra Leone with special reference to the civil service' paper presented at the joint meeting of the African Studies Association and the Canadian Committee on African studies, Montreal, October 1969.
— 'The place of the Creoles in the bureaucracy of Sierra Leone with special reference to the civil service' paper presented at the Sierra Leone Symposium held at the University of Western Ontario, London, Ontario, 1971.
July, Robert. 'The Sierra Leone legacy in Nigeria: Herbert Macaulay and Henry Carr', in *Freetown Symposium*, ed. C. Fyfe and E. Jones, Freetown, 1968.
Kilson, M. de B. 'Social relationships in Mende *Domesia*', *Sierra Leone Studies*, N. S., December 1961.
Kilson, M. *Political Change in a West African State: A Study of the Modernization Process in Sierra Leone*, Cambridge, Mass., 1966.
Koroma, J. S. 'The Gratuities Committee: a partial appraisal of the duties of the Administrator and Registrar General', unpublished manuscript, Afrika-Studiecentrum, Leiden, Holland, 1972.
— 'The administration of Islamic law in Sierra Leone', unpublished manuscript, Afrika-Studiecentrum, Leiden, Holland, 1973.
Koelle, S. W. *Polyglotta Africana*, London, 1851.
Krapf-Askari, E. *Yoruba Towns and Cities*, Oxford, 1969.
Kup, A. P. *A History of Sierra Leone 1400-1787*, Cambridge, 1961.
Leighton, N. C. 'The Lebanese Committee in Sierra Leone', Paper presented at the 15th annual meeting of the African Studies Association, Philadelphia, Pennsylvania, 1972.
Levine, R. A. 'Sex Roles and Economic Change in Africa', *Ethnology*, 5 (2), April 1966.
Little, K. L. 'Some patterns of West African marriage and domesticity', in 'Urbanism in West Africa', ed. K. L. Little, *Sociological Review*, Vol. 7, No. 1, New Series, 1959.
— 'The political function of the Poro', *Africa,* Vol. 35, No. 4, October 1965; Vol. 36, No. 1, January 1966.
— 'Attitudes towards marriage and family among educated young Sierra Leoneans', in *The New Elites of Tropical Africa*, ed. P. C. Lloyd, London, 1966a.

— 'The strange case of romantic love', *The Listener*, April 7, 1966b.
— *The Mende of Sierra Leone* (First Edition 1951), London, 1967.
— *African Women in Towns*, Cambridge, 1973.
Little, K. L. and Price, A. 'Some trends in modern marriage among west Africans', *Africa*, Vol. 37, No. 4, October 1967.
— 'Urbanization, Migration, and the African Family', An Addison-Wesley Module in Anthropology, No. 51, 1974.
Litwak, E. 'Geographical mobility and extended family cohesion' and 'Occupational mobility and extended family cohesion', *Amer. Sociol.* 26, 1961.
Lloyd, P. C. ed. *The New Elites of Tropical Africa*, London, 1966.
— *Africa in Social Change*, London, 1967.
Lockwood, P. *The Black Coated Worker: A Study of Class Consciousness*, London, 1958.
Longmore, L. *The Dispossessed*, London, 1959.
McCulloch, M. *Peoples of Sierra Leone*, Ethnographic survey of Africa, London, 1964.
McGinn, N. F. 'Marriage and family life in middle class Mexico', *Journal of Marriage and the Family*, August 1966.
McKinley, D. G. *Social Class and Family Life*, Glencoe Illinois, 1964.
Mair, Lucy (ed.). *African Marriage and Social Change*, London, 1969.
Massally, A. J. 'Questionnaire on points of customary law', mimeographed pamphlet, Kenema, Sierra Leone, December 1964.
Mercier, P. 'Aspects de la Société Africaine dans l'agglomeration dakaroise: groupes familiaux et unités de voisinage', *Etudes Senegolaises*, No. 5, 1954.
Mogey, J. M. *Family and Neighbourhood: Two Studies in Oxford*, Oxford, 1956.
— *Sociology of Marriage and Family Behaviour* 1957-1968, The Hague, Paris, 1971.
Moore, S. F. 'Law and anthropology', in *Biennial Review of Anthropology*, ed. B. J. Siegel, Stanford, 1970.
Murdock, G. P. *Social Structure*, New York, 1949.
Nadel, S. F. 'African elites', *International Social Science Bulletin*, Vol. 3, No. 3, 1956.
Nicol, D. 'West Africa's first institution of higher education', *Sierra Leone Journal of Education*, Vol. 1, No. 1, 1966.
Noble, M. 'West African marriage study', mimeographed description of a research project presented to a seminar on social networks, Department of Anthropology, University of Edinburgh, 1968.
Notes and Queries on Anthropology, Sixth Edition, Committee of the Royal Anthropology Institute of Great Britain and Ireland, London, 1951.
Oeser, O. A. and Hammond, S. B. *Social Structure and Personality in a City*, London, 1954.
Omari, T. P. 'Changing attitudes of students in West-African society toward marriage and family relationships', *British Journal of Sociology*, Vol. 11, No. 3, September 1960.
— 'Role expectations in the courtship situation in Ghana', *Social Forces*, Vol. 42, No. 2, December 1963.
Oppong, C. *Marriage among a Matrilineal Elite*, Cambridge, 1974.
Parsons, T. *The Social System*, London, 1952.
— *The Family*, London, 1956.
Peterson, J. *Province of Freedom*, London, 1969.
Phillips, A. 'An introductory essay', in *Marriage Laws in Africa*, ed. Phillips, A. and Morris, H. F., London, New York, Toronto, 1971.

Porter, A. T. *Creoledom. A Study of the Development of Freetown Society,* London, 1963.

Rodman, H. *Lower-Class Families,* New York, 1971.

Rosser, C. and Harris, C. *The Family and Social Change,* New York, 1965.

Rudolph, L. I. and Rudolph, H. S. *The Modernity of Tradition,* Chicago, 1967.

Saario, U. U. 'A study of discrimination against persons born out of wedlock'. Sub-commission on Prevention of Discrimination and Protection of Minorities, United Nations, New York, 1967.

Sawyerr, H. 'Graveside libations in and near Freetown', *The Sierra Leone Bulletin of Religion,* Vol. 7, No. 2, 1965.

— 'More graveside libations in and around Freetown', *The Sierra Leone Bulletin of Religion,* Vol. 8, No. 2, 1966.

— 'Two short libations', *The Sierra Leone Bulletin of Religion,* Vol. 9, No. 1, 1967.

Selltiz, C., Jahoda, M., Deutsch, M. and Cook, S. W. *Research Methods in Social Relations,* New York, 1964.

Sinclair, J. S. 'Perceptions of social stratification among sub-elite of Sierra Leone', paper presented at the Sierra Leone Symposium held at the University of Western Ontario, London, Ontario, 1971.

Spitzer, L. 'The mosquito and segregation in Sierra Leone', *Canadian Journal of African Studies,* Vol. 2, No. 1, 1968.

— 'The Sierra Leone Creoles', in *Africa and the West,* Madison, Milwaukee, London, 1972.

Stephens, W. N. *The Family in Cross-Cultural Perspective,* New York, Toronto, London, 1963.

Stycos, J. M. 'Problems of fertility control in under-developed areas', in *Population Evolution and Birth Control,* ed. G. Hardin, London, 1969.

Sussman, M. B. 'The isolated nuclear family: fact or fiction', *Social Problems* 6, 1959.

Sussman, M. B. and Burchinal, I. G. 'Parental aid to married children: implications for family functioning', in *Kinship and Family Organisation,* ed. Farber, B., London, 1966.

— 'Kin family network: unheralded structure in current conceptualisations of family functioning', in *Kinship and Family Organisation,* ed. Farber, B., London, 1966.

Suttner, R. S. 'The legal status of African women in South Africa', *African Social Research,* 8, December 1969.

Turay, A. K. 'Loan words in Temne', Ph. D. thesis, School of Oriental and African Studies, London University, 1971.

Turnbull, C. M. *The Lonely African,* London, 1963.

Van der Laan, H. L. *The Sierra Leone Diamonds,* London, 1965.

Van der Laan, H. L. 'Syrians or Lebanese: which name is correct?', *Kroniek van Afrika,* No. 2, 1969.

Watson, W. 'Social mobility and social class in industrial communities, in *Closed Systems and Open Minds,* ed. Clevons, E. and Gluckman, M., Edinburgh, 1964.

Webb, E. J., Campbell, D. J., Schwartz, R. D. and Sechrest, F. *Unobtrusive Measures: Nonreactive Research in the Social Sciences,* Chicago, 1970.

Whiting, J. W. M. and Child, J. L. *Child Training and Personality,* New Haven, London, 1953.

Wilson, G. 'An essay on the economics of detribalization: *Rhodes-Livingstone Papers,* 5, Part I, Livingstone, Northern Rhodesia, 1942.

Young, W. C. E. *Statistics of Education 1964-65*, Research Bulletin No. 2, Department of Education, Fourah Bay College, 1966.
Young, M. and Willmott, P. *Family and Kinship in East London*, London, 1957.

MISCELLANEOUS

Administrative Postings, 1st September 1969, Freetown, Sierra Leone. An ordinance to promote a system of administration by tribal authority among the tribes settled in Freetown. 31 July 1905.
Answers to the United Nations Questionnaire. Persons considered to be born out of wedlock. Typescript copy. Supplied by Atterney General's Office. No date.
African Studies Newletter, 1969-70.
Composite Report for period 1960-65. Typescript report for circulation within Ministry of Social Welfare. No date.
Directive on Customary Law. April 27, 1963.
Household Survey of the Western Province, November 1966-January 1968. Central Statistics Office, Freetown, Sierra Leone.
Household Survey of the Western Area, November 1966-January 1968. Final Report. Central Statistics Office, Freetown, Sierra Leone.
Household Survey of the Northern Province, March 1968-December 1969. Final Report. Central Statistics Office, Freetown, Sierra Leone.
Household Survey of the Eastern Province – Urban Areas, March 1968-January *1969*. Central Statistics Office, Freetown, Sierra Leone.
Household Survey of the Southern Province – Urban Areas, March 1968-January 1969. Central Statistics Office, Freetown, Sierra Leone.
Laws of Sierra Leone. 1960 Edition.
Legislation of Sierra Leone, 1961, 1962, 1963.
Outline for the Collection of Information on Persons considered to be Born out of Wedlock. United Nations. Typescript Copy supplied by Attorney General's Office. No date.
Report of the Customary Law Advisory Panel, April 1963.
Supplement to *Sierra Leone Gazette*. Vol. XCVII, No. 71, 15th September 1966.
Sierra Leone 1963 Population Census: Vol. 1, 2, 3. Central Statistics Office.
1960-61 Sierra Leone Law Reports, Vol. 1. Street and Maxwell, 1966.
1962 Sierra Leone Law Reports. Vol. 2. Street and Maxwell, 1966.
The African Law Reports. Sierra Leone. 1964-66. Oceana Publications, New York, 1969.
Sierra Leone Gazette, 23 January 1969. Government Printing Office, Freetown, Sierra Leone.
1963 Population Census of Sierra Leone, Vol. I and II, Central Statistics office, Freetown, 1965.

COURT RECORDS.

George *v*. George and Four Others. Sierra Leone Court of Appeal, 13 March 1967 (Civil App. No. 20/166).
Div. C. 25, 1966. C. No. 2 Supreme Court of Sierra Leone. Divorce Jurisdiction. Cummings *v*. Cummings, November 1, 1968.
Div. C. No. 27/66. Supreme Court (Cole, Ag. C. J.): January 4th, 1967, Macaulay *v*. Macaulay.
Div. C. No. 28/65. Supreme Court (Browne-Mark, J.): May 4th, 1967. Navo V. Navo.

NEWSPAPERS

Sierra Leone Daily Express, 23 July 1969.
The Truth, Freetown, Sierra Leone. 9 May 1969.
Sierra Leone Daily Mail. 17 May 1961; 31 August 1965; 3 September 1965; 6 January 1968; 3 March 1968; 9 March 1968; 23 March 1968; 16 April 1968; 22 April 1968; 25 May 1968; 22 June 1968; 13 July 1968; 17 July 1968; 3 August 1968; 17 May 1969; 1 June 1969.
Clarion Weekly (college newspaper, no date).
Fourah Bay Newssheet, 1968.
Unity, 12 May 1969.

Index

References to tables are given in italic

abortion:
  among educated single girls, 257, 259-60, 283;
  arranged for girl-friends, 270;
  as a means of family limitation, 257-8;
  cost of, 258n9;
  extent of, 257, 258;
  illegality of, 258;
  induced miscarriages, 258;
  medical, 258;
  reasons for resorting to, 259;
  traditional attitudes to, 257
acknowledgements, iii-v
administration:
  British in, 27, 28;
  Creoles in:
    colonial, 25, 27, 28, 280;
    percentage of, 27;
  of the Protectorate, 26
adoption:
  absence of legal provision for, 118;
  children 'given' to relatives, 119n39;
  inheritance and children by, 148;
  law:
    attitudes to, 121-2;
    question of, 118-9;
  of orphans, 118n38;
  practice of rearing children:
    as wards, 119;
    with others, 119;
    with relatives, 119-121;
  ties of kinship and, 120n40, 121
adultery:
  as grounds for divorce, 97;
  attitudes of university students to, 102;

husband's, attitudes to, 102;
  in customary law, 101-2;
  wife's:
    attitudes to, 102, 262-3;
    excusable in cases of sterility, 262-3;
  woman damage, 101-2, 268;
  see also sexual infidelity
affection, expression of:
  disapproval of, 266-7;
  professionals' attitudes, 266n16;
  stereotypes of, 73
African:
  personality, growing appreciation of, 83;
  self-confidence, 10
age:
  as a prestige factor in villages, 51, 52;
  at marriage:
    of professional group, 39;
    university students' view of ideal, 39;
  of professional group, 36
aged, the:
  in traditional society, 211;
  in urban setting, 51, 57-8;
  stereotypes of care for, 79-80, 81;
  see also old age
agriculture:
  at Njala, 35-6;
  as occupation of fathers, 50;
  development of, 29;
  employment prospects in, 35-6;
  traditional households and subsistence, 206
All People's Congress (APC):
  composition of, 33;
  Creoles in post under, 31;

Creole support of, 30, 32;
victory in 1967 elections, 30
ancestors:
appeal to respect for, 215n7;
role of, 63, 192
Anglicanism:
of professionals, 39;
prestige of, 39
appendix:
A. methods, 296-313;
B. questionnaires, 314-32
Arabic, use of script, 13n10
ashobe, 193-4
associations, *see Bundu, Poro,* secret
societies
attitude scale, 311
attitudes:
and values, 16-17;
behaviour and, 16-17;
Creoles as reference group for, 33-4;
towards:
contraceptives, use of, 254-64, 268-
70;
emotional attachment, 266-7, 271;
family limitation, 250-4;
husbands' extra-marital affairs, 139-
44;
sexuality, men's, 270-6;
women's influence over men, 264-
70;
women's sexuality, 264-70;
see also abortion, adoption, adultery,
etc.
Bai Bureh, 26
Bar Association, 152
Bastardy Act:
cases tried under, *114*, 114;
obligations on putative fathers, 128;
provisions of, 94, 114;
unwed mothers suing under, 128
behaviour, values and attitudes, 16-17
beliefs:
and social change, 125, 154;
and the legal status of illegitimacy,
19-20, 145, 153-4, 225, 282-3;
influencing the use of contraceptives:
dangers of menstrual blood, 265;
Bundu secret bush, 265;
love potions, 267-8;
mother's power to make son impotent, 264;
post-partum sex taboo, 269-70;

promiscuity of women, 268-9;
supernatural powers of women,
264-5;
the witchbird, 260-1;
times of intercourse, 265-6;
treatment of the placenta, 263-4;
women's power to make men impotent, 264-5;
responses on, 270
bigamy:
absence of charges of, 91;
definition of, 90;
law, 90
'Big Men':
urban, 141-2;
village, 207
birth control, idea of, 19, 20;
see also contraceptives, family limitation
birthplace of professional group, 36-7
births:
analysis of, from mixed unions, 113;
registration of:
by midwife, 126;
by mother only, 126, *127*;
by parents making marriage payments, 126-7;
by putative father, 126-7, *127*, 128;
in Provinces, 126;
in Western Area, 126;
method of, 126-7;
number of illegitimate births in
Western Area, *127*, 128
Bo, school at, 26
breast-feeding, shortening periods of,
269-70
bridewealth, attitudes to, 68-9
British:
founding of the Colony, 22;
in administration, 27, 28;
policy in Protectorate, 27, 59, 280;
relations with Creoles:
demoralization of Creoles, 28n5,
280;
during colonial period, 23;
under the Protectorate, 27-8, 59;
settlers, increase in, 27;
trading activities:
early, 21;
in Protectorate, 26;
Bundu:
age of joining, 165;

attitudes to:
    fathers', 166-7;
    mothers', 166;
    Muslim Creoles', 157n2;
    Provincials' 166-7;
cultural syncretism through, 62;
dangers of men trespassing secret
    bush, 265;
emphasis on virginity, 164-5;
girls' desire to join, 165-6;
graduation from, 159n7, 267n17;
increase in number of village soci-
    eties, 166;
initiation, 157, 164, 165, 167;
male attitudes to female sexuality
    and 165, 265, 268;
mother-daughter relationship and,
    234-5;
operation of:
    present, 157-8, 165;
    traditional, 157, 164-5;
period of seclusion, 157, 164-5;
special meal at graduation, 267n17
Catholicism, Roman, 39, 276n27
change in the future:
    influence of professionals on, 6;
    influence of sub-elite on, 6;
    question of role of elite in, 8-10;
    prediction of, 8-9;
    prospects for marriage among profes-
        sional group, 279-95;
    university students and predicting
        trends, 35-6
chiefs:
    education of sons of, 26;
    families of paramount, in professional
        group, 50;
    government through cooperative, 26;
    membership of household as prestige
        factor, 51, 53;
    succession question, 151, 236
child-bearing, importance to women
    131n3m, 143-4
child-family relationships, stereotypes
    of, 76-8
childlessness:
    distrust of childless people, 260-1;
    extra-marital affairs and, 143-4, *144*,
        263;
    fear of, 262-3;
    wife's adultery justified in cases of,
        262-3

children:
    allowances for, under maintenance
        law and Bastardy Act, 115, 128;
    as belonging to father, 104, 138;
    born before marriage, 15, 135, 251-2;
    born during cohabitation, 15;
    born outside marriage *see below*
        children born out of wedlock;
    born to inherited wives, 91;
    buying clothes for, 199, 201, 203;
    care of:
        in professional households, 204, 205;
        in traditional households, 203-4;
        small, 199, 205;
        university student responses on,
            205;
    custody of, 104, 147-8;
    disciplining of, 204, 205;
    disputes over rearing, 204;
    domestic duties of, 198, 199, 200;
    employed wives and rearing of, 204;
    essential to happy marriage, 263;
    failure to support in desertion cases,
        114-5;
    fear of father, 204;
    haste for married couples to have,
        263;
    high value placed on, 257;
    importance of, 143-4, 257, 260, 262,
        263;
    number of:
        'as many as possible', 250, 251, 278;
        born before marriage, 251-2;
        born outside marriage, 252;
        expense of large, 252, 253, 254;
        four as ideal, 250, 251;
        ideal, 250-1, *251*;
        in professional families, 251;
        in professionals' parents' families,
            251;
        prestige associated with large, 129,
            130, 140-1, 250, 277;
        professional attitudes to large, 252,
            253;
        traditional attitudes to large, 130,
            252;
        under-reporting, 251;
    raising of relative's, 263;
    relationship between parents and,
        76-8, 211-14;
    sex relations in marriage and, 271;
    success at school, emphasis placed on,

204;
supervision of, as wife's duty, 201;
to provide for old age, 211-12
  see also daughter, son
children born out of wedlock:
  as a major social problem, 124;
  bill to equalize position *see* illegit-
    imacy bill;
  colonial background and, 124-5, 130;
  defined, 130;
  distinction between those born before
    and after marriage, 135;
  legal status of:
    absence of surname, 147, 149;
    consensus theory of law and, 124;
    Creole women's fear of change in,
      142;
    custody, 147-8;
    customary law position, 148;
    discrimination, 132, 144, 147;
    domicile, 147;
    impossibility of legitimization, 127,
      146-7, 149;
    inheritance and, 144-5, 148, 149;
    liabilities of mother, 148;
    liabilities of putative father, 147,
      148;
    nationality, 147, 149;
  scope of the problem:
    birth registration, 125-7;
    fathered by married men, 129-30;
    maintenance responsibilities, 128-9;
  number of illegitimate births, *127,*
    128;
    paternity disputes, 129, 147;
    professionals' parents with outside
      children, 55-6;
    professionals with outside child-
      ren, 129-30;
    putative fathers, 126-7, *127, 128*;
    threat to monogamous statutory
      marriage, 130, 144, 145, 154;
    unwed mothers, 128-9;
  social position of:
    abusive language reflecting atti-
      tudes, 139;
    concealing illegitimacy, 134;
    denial of discrimination, 146, 149,
      154;
    effect on educational and occupa-
      tional opportunities, 134;
    effect on girl's chances of marriage,

134;
    illegitimate girls becoming outside
      wives, 134;
    mothers losing children to married
      home, 137-8;
    psychological damage, 132;
    rearing in married home, 135-7,
      139;
    relationship with:
      father, 134-5;
      father's wife, 135;
      half-brothers and sisters, 134;
      outside wife, wife, and outside
        child, 138-9;
    religious discrimination, 139;
    social stigma, 115, 132-3;
    traditional background, 130-1;
    unwed mother's position, 131-2;
    unwed mothers with other illegit-
      imate children, 135;
    wives' attitudes to rearing outside
      children, 135-7;
    see also illegitimacy
choosing a marriage partner, 157-95;
  see also courtship, marriage partner
christenings:
  cost of, 139;
  discrimination against illegitimate
    children at, 139;
  social importance of, 95n22
Christian, Christianity:
  as predominant ideology, 281;
  attempts to convert indigenous peo-
    ple to, 21, 26;
  Creole propagation of, 29;
  discrediting of polygamy, 3, 130;
  education and, 9;
  indoctrination, 26, 40;
  influence of:
    family organization, 1;
    monogamous marriage, 1, 3, 9, 10,
      64, 88-9, 130, 282;
  Muslim resistance to, 26, 40;
  prestige of, 40;
  social importance of education, statu-
    tory marriage and, 54-5;
  superiority of, 23;
  suppression of colonized under, 9n7;
  values, colony based on, 9;
    see also missionaries
church:
  attendance, 39;

Creoles in the, 25, 28;
discrimination against illegitimate
children, 139;
organizations, reaction to illegitimacy
bill, 152
civil service:
British in, 27;
Creoles in:
colonial, 25, 27, 28, 280;
under independence, 30-1
'civilized being':
Creole code of official behaviour and,
29;
monogamous marriage as, 3, 10, 34,
63, 130, 281
colonial:
influences:
attitudes to illegitimacy and, 124-5;
family organization and, 1, 4;
monogamous marriage and, 14,
279;
on marital relations in Sierra Leone,
3, 9, 10, 279;
patterns, conformity with, 9;
situation, Balandier's concept of, 3-4,
279, 280-1
Colony, the:
education in, 22-3;
founding of, 21-5;
history of, 21-34;
independence and, 31-4;
legal system in, 84;
Protectorate and, 25-6
colour discrimination, 27, 280
commerce *see* trading
communications:
ease of, and cultural uniformity, 62;
in Sierra Leone, iii
comparative studies:
and the Sierra Leone situation, 5;
limitations of, ii
composition of professional group *see*
professional group
conflict, marital, *see* marital conflict
conjugal roles:
changes in, 205-6;
question of equal participation, 205;
responses on, 204-5;
western model of 'joint', 204
constitution of 1951, 29-30
contraceptives:
attitudes towards sex, family plan-

ning and use of, 258-78;
attitudes towards sexuality and, 268-
70;
beliefs influencing use of, 256-64,
283;
conjugal relations and, 250, 255;
native abortifacients, 256-7n7;
native methods of contraception, 256-
7n7;
use of:
associated with women's promiscuity, 268-9, 270;
attitudes influencing, 254-64;
by outside wives, 153, 271, 285;
by wives, 153, 154-5, 255, 268-70,
277;
illegitimacy bill and, 19, 153-4;
in extra-marital affairs, 255, 276,
277;
infidelity and, 268-9;
methods ever used, 254, 255;
methods used at present, 255, 256;
need for propaganda among male
population, 286;
professionals' approval of, 254;
reluctance to use:
female, 259;
male, 277, 286;
response on, university students,
269
cooking:
husbands assisting with, 201;
quality of, as source of conflict, 224;
wife's responsibilities in, 198, 199,
201
courts:
colonial, 84;
illegitimacy and the, 146-7;
legal decisions and social conditions,
122;
native Protectorate, 84;
tribal, 85n2
courtship:
acceptance of western ideas of, 158;
adolescence and, 158, 195, 196;
as an innovation, 195, 196-7, 248, 283;
attention to girls during, 181;
attitude of Creole families to, 178,
179, 181;
behaviour of young men during, 178-
80, 197;
engagement, 187-92;

expectations and marriage, 248, 282-3;
giving of presents, 181;
letter-writing, 181-7;
of a Creole-Provincial couple, 178-80;
period of, as normal prerequisite to marriage, 171;
permission to visit house, 178;
pleasing the family, 181;
stereotypes of, 67;
waits outside the house, 178, 181
co-wives, jealousy among, 46-7, 119, 212, 236
Creole(s):
ambivalence in attitudes, 29;
among the professionals, 9;
as reference group for:
attitudes, 33-4;
social behaviour, 33-4, 281;
ascendancy, period of, 40;
background:
colonial, 279;
pre-colonial, 62;
social, 53,
traditional, 62-3;
childhood experiences of, 45-6;
concern with personal advancement, 23;
defined, ii-iii, 22;
difficulties of legal definition, 88;
education:
abroad, 36;
achievement in, value placed on, 40;
control of educational institutions, 29, 31;
higher, in Britain, 25;
history of, 41;
of grandparents, 41;
of professionals' parents, 41-2, *41*, *42*;
of students' parents, 41, *41*, *42*;
opportunities for, 59;
preference for overseas, 36;
propagation of British, 29;
relatives paying for costs of, 44;
residence during, 44-5;
scholarships awarded to, 33, 36;
standard of, 9, 22-3, 24;
students, percentage of, 35;
working to pay costs of, 43;
emigration of, 27, 280;

family:
background, importance of, 161;
expectations of children providing for old age, 212;
financial obligations in, 215;
half-brothers and sisters, 55-6, *56*;
involvement in extended, 63;
life, as a model, 34, 58, 59, 63;
future of the, 281;
households, one-parent, 99;
illegitimacy controversy, attitudes in, 142, 145, 154;
in administration:
colonial, 25, 27, 28, 280;
percentage of, 27;
in civil service:
numbers of, 25, 27, 28, 30, 280;
under independence, 30-1;
in professions:
dominance of, 29;
professions entered by, 25, 28, 29, 30-1;
percentage of, in professional group, 35;
intermarriage:
Creole women marrying Provincial men, 38, 178-80;
extent of, 38, 113;
inheritance problems, 109-13;
position of Creole husband, 110;
position of Creole wife, 109-10;
with indigenous people, 62, 88;
marriage:
age, 39;
as a model, 34, 59;
attitude to educated wives, 163;
attitude to economic independence of women, 49, 174;
behaviour of young women, 157, 159, 178-81;
Christian monogamous, 54-5, 63, 130;
courtship, attitudes to, 178, 179, 181;
evaluation of love and family approval, *172*, 173;
girls' attitudes to sexual fidelity, 142;
partners, choice of, 38;
polygamous, attitude to, 91;
prestige equated with monogamous, 124;

relationships in, attitudes to, 10;
types of, of professional parents, *54*, 54-5;
types of, of students' parents, *54*;
vested interest in monogamous, 124;
Muslim, 40, 157n2;
nationalism among, 27-8;
number of, 33;
occupations of fathers, 50;
origin of, 22;
part in:
  developing hinterland, 24;
  Hut Tax wars, 26;
passing as, 24-5, 45, 88;
patronage of, 24, 28, 34, 58, 279;
politics:
  dependence of Provincials on, 34, 281;
  influence of, 31-2;
  manipulation of ethnic groups, 32, 34;
  opposition to 1951 constitution, 29;
prestige role in society, 29;
Provincials' attitudes to, 31-2, 34, 281;
psychological conflicts in position of, 29;
relations with:
  British:
    demoralization of Creoles, 28n5, 280;
    during colonial period, 23;
    under the Protectorate, 27-8, 59;
  indigenous groups, 23-4, 62;
  Mende, 30-1;
  Protectorate people, 28-9, 34, 281;
  Temne, 24;
religion:
  attitudes to affiliation, 39;
  emphasis on, 161;
  missionary activities of, 23;
  propagation of Christianity, 29;
standard-setting role of, 33-4;
status, social:
  associated with being Creole, 85;
  evaluation of, 51-3;
  view of father's attributes, 53;
stereotypes of:
  careers for women, 76;
  equality for women, 76;
  physical violence, 72;
  western patterns, 83;
superiority, attitude of, 24, 28, 58, 279;
trading activities of, 23, 24, 25, 27, 28, 58, 62, 174, 280;
view of role in Sierra Leone, 29;
ward system, 24, 45;
western culture of, 23, 28, 29, 33;
western values of, 9, 28, 29, 58-9
cruelty:
  as grounds for divorce, 97;
  interpretations of, 102-4, 122;
  psychological, 103-4, 122
culture:
  British, acceptance of superiority of, 280-1;
  Creole attitudes to western, 23, 28, 29, 33;
  traditional:
    appreciation of, 10;
    as indigenous, 14;
  uniformity of:
    between tribes, 61-2;
    sharing patterns of, 62;
    syncretism through secret societies, 62;
    through intermarriage, 62
currency, 116n34
custody of children, 104, 147-8
daughter:
  death rites performed, 131n3, 235;
  mother relationship:
    after marriage, 235;
    fear of mother's curse, *214*, 235;
    mother's duty to train, 161;
    mother's indulgence towards, 234-5
death rites, 131n3, 235
demographic data:
  Creole, 29, 33;
  heterogeneity of population, 22, 62;
  Protectorate, 29;
  Sierra Leone, ii-iii
dependants, number of, as prestige factor, 51-2, 53
desertion:
  as grounds or divorce, 97;
  maintenance of children, 114-5
developmental cycle, in2, 14-15
diamond mining, 29-30
divorce:
  attitudes to, 98;
  causes of, 99-101;
  child custody in, 104;
  decrees absolute, *97*, 97, 98;

decrees nisi, 97, *97*;
divorcees in sample, 37;
grounds for:
  adultery, 97, 101-2;
  cruelty, 97, 101, 102-4, 122;
  desertion, 97, 101;
  in customary law, 101-2;
  in Islamic law, 85, 97;
  in Kanuri society, 11-12;
  in statutory law, 97-104;
  magistrates' attempts to prevent, 99;
  petitions filed and decrees granted,
    97, 98;
  position of women after, 107;
  property settlement in, 104-7;
  remarriage after, 107;
  separation preferred to, 98;
  stigma attached to divorcees, 107;
  uncommonness of 55;
  women's difficulties in winning suits,
    102;
  see also separation
domestic work:
  allocation of duties, 198-200;
  care of children, 203-4;
  changes in organization of, 205-6;
  children's duties, 198;
  education of children, 204;
  husbands' assistance in, *201*, 201-3;
  in Sierra Leonean households living
    abroad, 197-8;
  of disgraced children, 200;
  professionals' views on sharing, 206;
  school children's views on, 204-5;
  status relationships and assignment
    of tasks, 200;
  stratification of tasks, 198;
  tasks not delegated by wives, 200-1;
  tidying the living room, 198, 202-3
dress:
  adoption of western, 21;
  emphasis on fashionable, 159;
  press views on, 160;
  worn at weddings, 192
Dutch traders, 21
Eastern Province:
  average number of persons per house-
    hold, 57;
  education in, 33
economic:
  change, influence of, 1;
  exploitation, 27;

independence of women, 49, 174, 175;
security as problem in marriage, 249
educated, defined, 13n10
education:
  abroad, 9, 25, 46-7, 50;
  achievements, value placed on, 40-1;
  as criterion of elite studies, 5-6, 281;
  as criterion of professional group,
    i, 5;
  childhood experiences of, 45-6;
  Christian, 9;
  costs of:
    anxiety about, 46;
    fathers given credit for paying,
      43n7, 44;
    met by employers, 43;
    met by mother's relatives, 44;
    met by relatives, 43-4, 209;
    obligation on parents to meet, 42-3,
      46;
    students working to meet, 43;
  Creole, 9, 22-3, 24, 61;
  Creole propagation of British, 29;
  family organization and, 1, 59-60;
  female, opportunities for, 7, 26;
  higher:
    indigenous, 10;
    under independence, 33;
  history of:
    Creole, 41;
    Provincial, 41-2;
    Sierra Leone, 6-7;
  importance attached to, 47;
  indigenous, for trading purposes, 21;
  indoctrination through, 40;
  institutions of, Creole control of, 29;
  in the colonial situation, 4, 9;
  in the Protectorate, 26, 28;
  in the Provinces, 29, 33, 40;
  length of time to acquire qualifica-
    tions, 47-8, 177-8;
  living away from home, 119;
  marriage partners and levels of:
    attitudes of:
      Creoles, 163;
      men, 162-3;
      Provincials, 162-3;
      secondary school students, 163n9;
      university students, 162-3;
      women, 161;
    education as potential threat to
      marriage, 163, 286;

Muslim, 13n10, 40n6;
of professional group:
  children of professionals, 47;
  comparison of Fourah Bay and
    Njala students, 35-6;
  parents of professionals, 41-2, *41,
    42*;
  percentage with Sierra Leone de-
    grees, 36;
  professional wives, 48;
of sub-elite, 6;
of the Mende, 28, 31;
of university students, 9-10;
opportunities:
  Creole, 59;
  Provincial, 44;
  Western Area, 45;
residence during, 44-5;
sacrifices made for, 40, 43, 46;
scholarships, 33;
school fees, 42;
schools:
  boarding, 40;
  effects of mission, on pupils, 46;
  for sons of chiefs, 26;
  girls, 26;
  influence of African teachers, 59;
  missionary, 9, 24, 26, 46;
  Muslim, 40n6;
  numbers attending primary, 33;
  numbers attending secondary, 33;
secular, 10;
social:
  change and, 5-6;
  importance of Christianity, monog-
    amous marriage and, 54-5;
  mobility and, 5, 6-7;
  status, monogamous marriage and,
    67n10;
  stratification and, 6;
teacher training college, 28;
under independence, 33;
wardship system and, 45;
western:
  acceptance of, 40-1;
  marriage and, 1, 9, 66, 130;
  missionary emphasis on superiority
    of, 23;
  prestige of, 51, 52, 281;
  values in, 9;
  see also university
elite:

and the professionals, 5-6;
corporate feeling of, 5-6;
defined, 6;
education and, 5-6;
manipulation of values in own interest, 124-5;
special characteristics of Sierra Leonean, 9-10;
standard-setting role of, 8-9;
studies, problems of, 297-8;
sub-elite and, 6;
university students as new, 9-10
emotional attachment, attitudes towards,
  266-7, 271
employment:
  husbands' attitude to wives', 49-50;
  of married couples, *49,* 49-50;
  type of wives', 49
engagement:
  ceremony, 'The Gage', 187-92;
  party, Creole, 180;
  practice among the Mende, 187n20
English law:
  as informal basis for colony, 84;
  conflict of tribal and, 85;
  formalized, 84n1;
  problems of applying, 84-5
equivalency of siblings, 120n40
estrangement:
  leading to separation, 98;
  'one-parent' households and, 99;
  percentage admitting, 39;
  percentage of professional women
    estranged, 50;
  study abroad and, 47;
  unwillingness to admit, 15
ethnic:
  composition of professional group,
    35;
  composition of Sierra Leone, ii-iii;
  tensions in professional group, 34
ethnographic studies, need for, ii
Europeans, use of term, iiin7
exclusiveness of professionals, 6, 10
expatriates:
  defined, iiin7;
  problem of, in research, 298
expectations:
  of girls on marriage, 142, 248, 282-3;
  of students in marital relationships,
    16;
  of young men, traditional nature of,

197
extra-marital affairs:
    as greatest source of marital con-
        flict, 15, 139, 153;
    association with potency, 271;
    attitudes towards:
        Creole women's, 142;
        general, 139-44;
        men's, 141, *144*;
        Provincial women's, 142;
        university students', *144*;
        wives', 225-6;
        women's, *144*;
    'Big Men' and, 141-2;
    childlessness and, 143-4, 263, 270;
    children born from *see* children born
        out of wedlock;
    conflict between Christian monog-
        amous marriage and, 276-7;
    confrontations with other woman,
        226-9;
    delicacy of subject, 55;
    desire to beget children, 271-2;
    emphasis on sexual experience in,
        275-6;
    factors encouraging, 270;
    good wife as mother image, 270-1;
    husband's observance of social obli-
        gations, 225-6;
    influence on family organization, 139-
        40;
    of Creole parents, 55-6;
    polygamous nature of man, 140, 141,
        142, 276;
    position in male society, 270, 271-2;
    post-partum sex taboos, 269-70;
    prestige from large numbers of chil-
        dren, 140-1, 271-2;
    proving sexual prowess, 272-4;
    publicity on, 231-3;
    ratio of men and women, 272;
    rules of the game, 225;
    sexual abstinence and, 270;
    sexual fidelity question, 142;
    sexual gratification from, 277;
    social ambitions of unmarried girls,
        141, 272n23;
    social position of other woman, 226;
    social pressures underlying, 274-5;
    use of contraceptives in, 255, 276,
        277
family:

adaptation to urbanism, 1-2;
attributes of father's, 53;
background and choice of marriage
    partner, 134, 161;
-centred theoretical network, 2;
change, theory of, 289-90;
conjugally- based, 12, 15;
developmental cycle, in2, 14-15;
extended:
    brotherly love in, 81;
    Creole involvement in, 63;
    households and obligations to, 55-7;
    nuclear, and society, 2;
    obligations and education, 44;
    obligations, continuing importance
        of, 284;
    professionals belonging to, 105;
    role in modern marriage, 172-3;
finances, organization of, 206-8;
law:
    question of reform of, 86;
    transformed under colonialism, 124;
    uniformity of tribal, 85n3, 87;
life:
    attitude of university students, 10;
    Creole as a model, 34, 59;
    in English coalmining community,
        3;
    problem of idealized concepts of,
        14-15;
    stereotypes of:
        child-family relationships, 76-8;
        desire for change in traditional,
            83;
        married couples and relatives,
            79-81;
        practice of eating together, 71;
    'the sentimental model', 11, 15;
    urban African marriage and future
        of, 12;
limitation:
    abortion, 257-60;
    as index of modernity, 277-8;
    attitudes towards, 250-4;
    beliefs hindering acceptance of, 250;
    concern among professionals for,
        250;
    conflict between traditional values
        and, 277;
    conjugal relationships and, 250,
        276;
    expense as chief reason for, 252,

253, 277;
fears of sterility, 259;
inheritance laws and, 287-8;
kinship obligations and, 278;
Planned Parenthood Association, 254;
professional attitudes to large families, 252, *253*;
size of professionals' and parents' families, 251;
traditional attitudes towards, 256-7
nuclear:
and Sierra Leone society, 289-95;
as domestic unit in own right, 12, 279, 281;
Christian ideology and, 281;
colonial influences and, 1;
geographical mobility and, 294-5;
kinship obligations obstructing development of, 249;
nature of Sierra Leone society and, 292-3;
possibilities of emergence of, 249; 279;
question of isolation, 291-2;
requirements for establishing, 293-4;
social values inculcated within the family, 295;
values of the wider society and, 294-5;
organization:
and the individual, 2-3;
effect of extra-marital affairs on, 139-40;
from children's viewpoint, 15;
influence of colonialism on, 1;
literature on, 4-5;
retention of rural characteristics, 1-2;
traditional, 13, 61-2;
uniformity of principles in, 62n3;
patterns, changing economic conditions and, 290;
planning:
Planned Parenthood Association, 254;
stereotypes of, 76-7;
world programmes, 277-8;
relationships:
colonialist factor and, 4;
organization of domestic life and,

196-222;
society and the form of, 3-4;
structure, 63;
studies, methodological problems in, 196;
traditional, disintegration of, 1, 2;
types, variation in, 15;
fashion, interest in, 159
fathers:
attributes of, 53, *53*;
family, attributes of, 52, *53*;
financial assistance to, 212;
occupation, 50
female, education, 7, 26;
see also wives, women
fertility:
beliefs regarding, 263-4;
importance of, 259, 260-3
finance(s):
as source of marital conflict, 207-8;
changes in Provincial professional households, 206, 207;
Creole, 206;
in traditional households, 206-7;
money spent for prestige, 207;
responsibilities of professional husbands, 207;
segregation of, *see* financial matters;
support of outside children, 207;
use of resources, conflict over, 208
financial:
arrangements in divorce, 104-7;
assistance:
expectation of, from children:
professional responses, 211, *211*;
student responses, *211*, 211-2;
for educational purposes, 214;
indirect, 215-6;
in professional group, 212-4;
mutual, among Creoles, 215;
professional attitudes towards, 214;
professionals supporting fathers and mothers, 212;
Provincial students' sense of duty, 215, *215*;
received from relatives, 209;
repaying of, 209;
to parents, 211, 212;
to relatives, 214, *215*;
to young relatives, 214;
matters, segregation of:
attitudes to:

husband's 218-9;
students', 219-20;
wives' 219;
husbands:
  earnings of, 219;
  responsibilities of, 218;
  spending money on other women, 219;
  joint accounts, 218-9;
  laws of property and ownership and, 220-2;
  monies paid to relatives, 218;
question of co-operation in, 220;
  reasons for, 105, 208, 218-9;
  wives':
    feeling of insecurity, 220;
    ignorance of husbands' earnings, 219;
    interest in safeguarding children, 219;
  obligations:
    ambivalence on, 210-11;
    as source of conflict, 208;
    conflict between communalistic and individualistic motives, 208-9;
    distributing first month's salary, 208;
    extent of, 217, 284;
    gifts on visits home, 216;
    hospitality to kinsmen, 216;
    in traditional society, 212-3;
    keeping relative's children, 215;
    marriage payments, 209;
    means of avoiding, 217-8;
    moral sanctions enforcing, 209-11;
    to wife's relatives, 215-6;
    wives meeting, 216;
    women's attitudes to, 210;
  stresses in professional marriages, 105-7
food:
  imported, in stores, 203;
  symbolic meaning of, 238;
  see also cooking
Forster, Mrs Hyde, 7
Fourah Bay College:
  affiliation with University of Durham, 7;
birthplace of students of, 37;
  collection of data from, 16;
  Creoles on staff of, 31;
  employment prospects of students, 35;
  founding of, 24;
  tribal composition of students, 35
Freetown:
  Albert Academy, 26;
  average number of persons per household, 57;
  demographic data, ii, 272;
  heterogeneity of population in 19th century, 22;
  Hill Station, 27;
  origin of, 22;
  professionals born in, 36, 37;
  professionals living in, ii;
  schools in, 47
French traders, 21
future change, *see* change
Gage, The, 187-92
Ghana:
  conflict of laws in, 85;
  students attitudes to polygamy, 123;
  study of stereotypes in, 66
girl-friends:
  making men impotent, 265;
  money spent on, 207, 219
god-parents, 194n28, 244n7
group:
  defined, 12;
  use of term, 12-13n9
hair styles, western, 159, 160
half-brothers and half-sisters, 55-6, *56*, 134
health conditions, 27
hengadays, 2277-33
Hill Station, Freetown, 27
hinterland:
  contact with, 24;
  declared a Protectorate, 25-6
historical background, 21-34
history of:
  Colony, 21-5;
  Protectorate, 25-30;
  Sierra Leone since independence, 30-4
house(s):
  building of, in village, 216;
  owning:
    as prestige factor, 51, 52, 53;
    in Freetown, 207;
    in village, 207;
    zinc-roofed, 52, 207
households:
  of married professionals:

age structure, 58, *58*;
aged relatives in, 57-8;
average number of persons per, *57*;
children of relatives in, 57;
Creole values and, 58-9;
entertainment of relatives, 57;
ideal, 56;
in Freetown and the Provinces, 57,
57;
obligations to extended family,
56-7;
paid servants, 57;
role of education and pattern of,
59-60;
'one-parent', 99
organization of:
allocation of duties, 198-200;
assignment of tasks and status relationships, 200;
as source of conflict, 224;
changes in, 205-6;
children's role in, 198, 200;
emotional investment in, 205;
financial arrangements in traditional, 206-7;
husband's assistance in, *201*, 201-3;
relative's children working in, 198,
200;
servants in, 198;
Sierra Leonean abroad, 197-8;
wards in, 198;
wife's exclusive duties, 200-1;
polygamous, headwife in, 151, 201
husband(s):
assistance in household tasks, *201*,
201-3;
concept of conjugal role of, 197, 204;
concern for children, 203-4;
financial:
responsibilities of professional, 207;
role of professional, 206, 207;
role of traditional, 206-7;
influence of experience abroad, 202;
interest in westernizing style of
family life, 202;
London, 205;
market shopping, *201*, 203;
role of:
school children's view, 204-5;
traditional, 241-2;
university students' view, 205;
store shopping, 203;

tidying the living room, 202-3;
traditional values regarding marriage,
197;
wife's challenge to, 242-3
Hut Tax, 25-6
illegitimacy:
bill:
belief that bill was law, 19-20, 145,
153-4, 225, 227, 282-3;
conflict of interest groups, 154-5;
debate on:
attitudes to monogamous marriage an ' 10, 124;
exclusiveness of the professionals
and, 10, 124-5;
influence of Christian ideals, 10,
124;
power of the elite, 10, 19-20, 124-5;
decrease in number of illegitimate
children, 153;
effect on marital relationships, 153,
282-3;
effects on society, 155-6;
feeling of insecurity produced by,
156, 283;
judiciary's views, 145-6;
not to be retroactive, 149;
object of, 149-50;
opposition to, 151-2, 154;
political issues involved, 145;
reaction of:
Bar Association, 152;
church organizations, 152;
wives, 145, 151-2;
Women's Federation, 151;
publicity surrounding, 115, 125,
145, 153-4, 227, 283;
support for, 150, 154;
use of contraceptives and, 19, 153-4;
decided in law courts, 147;
declared by act of parliament, 147;
defined, 125-6, 146-7;
in traditional society, 150-1;
notion of, as western concept, 150;
perpetuating, 134;
succession and inheritance rights and,
151;
United Nations Sub-Commission on,
146
impotence, impotent:
disgrace of, 272-3;
distrust of impotent people, 261, 262,

264n13;
fear of, 273-4, 285;
mothers making sons, 264;
women making men, 265
income per capita, 42
independence:
Creoles as reference group under, 33-4;
education, 33;
ethnic tensions, 34;
government under, 31-3;
grant of, 30;
political influence of Creoles, 31-2
indigenous people:
antagonisms between Creoles and, 23-4, 28-9, 62, 279-80;
attempts to convert to Christianity, 21;
Creoles as reference group for, 33-4;
education of, 21, 24, 280;
employed in Freetown, 24;
passing as Creoles, 24-5;
political power of, 25;
trading activities of, 25;
see also Provincials
individual, the:
colonialism and, 3-4;
importance of, 2-3
infant mortality, 251-2, 256-7, 260
inheritance:
administration of laws, 112-3;
complications arising from, 110-12;
concern over, 151;
customary law of:
ambiguity in, 236n5;
adopted children under, 148;
children's rights, 148;
conflict of systems, 108-9;
flexibility of, 112-3;
inherited wives, 109-10, 111;
mother-son relationship and, 236;
'personal' law of wife, 108;
provisions of, 107-8;
step-children under, 148;
syncretism of practices, 109;
tribal variation in, 108-9;
division of, responses on, *152*, 153;
family limitation and, 287-8;
illegitimacy and, 144-5, 151, 225;
intermarriage and, 113;
'personal' law:
administration of, 107;

belief that statutory marriage changes, 109;
in native-non native marriages, 109-13;
Muslim law and, 109;
position of Creole wife in mixed marriage, 109-10;
prevalence of tribal practice, 108;
under different types of marriage, 108;
plurality of laws, 19, 107-8;
problem in polygamous households, 236;
publicity on, 145, 153, 225;
statutory law:
belief that statutory law alters 'personal' law, 109;
Christian marriage and, 108;
in native-non native marriages, 109-13;
Provincial respect for, 112-3;
testacy and, 113, 144-5;
under Muslim law, 109
intermarriage:
analysis of births from, 113;
and the legal systems, 85, 282;
attitudes to, 170-1;
Creole-Provincial, 38, 62, 85, 109-13, 171;
degree of tribal, 62;
extent of, 113, 170-1;
inheritance problem arising from, 109-13;
promoting cultural uniformity, 62
Islam, impact of, 62-3;
see also Muslim
judiciary, views on illegitimacy, 145-6;
Kanuri society, divorce in, 11-12
Kenema, study of family life in, 238
kinship:
attitudes to obligations, 210-11;
behaviour towards categories of, 121, 122;
networks and the individual, 2;
obligations and finance, 209-10;
obligations as necessary, 210-11;
system:
rearing of relative's children, 120n40;
supporting children under education, 43n7
Krio, 299-300

labour force in Freetown, indigenous, 24

land-ownership as prestige factor, 52, 53

languages, tribal, 22

law:
consensus theory of, 124, 154, 282-3;
conflict of, 85, 282;
failure to represent values of society, 154;
graduates in:
Creole, 25, 28;
Provincial, 28;
Sierra Leonean, 6-7;
personal:
absence of courts for, 85;
of professionals, 86;
problems of determining, 87-8;
reform and political power, 154, 283;
serving interests of elite, 124-5, 154;
students at Njala, 36;
see also family, inheritance, maintenance, marriage, property

Lebanese:
attitudes to, 280;
immigration of, 28, 280;
in Freetown, iii

legal:
institutions and values of society, 124-5;
pluralism:
colonial, 85;
effects of, 86;
problems of, in marriage law, 87-9;
profession, Creoles in, 31;
setting of marriage:
adoption, 118-22;
divorce, 97-104;
inheritance law, 107-13;
marriage law, 86-97;
maintenance law, 114-18;
need for culturally sensitive body of law, 122-3;
property settlement, 104-7;
status of children born out of wedlock, 144-8;
systems:
and the consensus theory of law, 124;
British, 19, 38, 84, 282;
conflict of, 85, 282;
customary, absence of body of law, 85;
English law as basis, 84;
history of, 84-6;
in Colony, 26, 84;
in Protectorate, 26, 84, 85;
in Sierra Leone, 84-6;
intermarriage and, 85, 88;
Muslim, 19, 38, 84, 85;
plurality of, 84-6;
traditional, applied by missionaries, 84;
traditional attitudes and, 86;
tribal, 19, 38, 84-5

liberated Africans:
assimilation of, 23;
defined, 22;
Muslim, 22n2

living room:
descriptions of, 202-3;
significance of, 202-3;
tidying, 198, 202

living together without marriage, 38

love:
as criterion in marriage, 159, 160, 194-5;
compared with family approval, *172, 173*;
courtship based on romantic, 158, 159, 160, 173, 178, 194, 196, 278, 283-4

love potions, 267-8

maintenance law:
allowances for children, 115, 128;
Bastardy Act:
amendment to, 115;
cases tried under, *114*;
increase in cases under, 115;
provisions of, 114, 128;
desertion, claims for, 114;
disputes over maintenance, 117-8, 128;
effects of stiffening, 15, 154, 283;
Married Woman's Maintenance Act:
attempt to amend, 116;
cases tried under, *114*; 114;
provision of, 94, 114;
maximum payments under, 115;
non-support, claims for, 114;
paternity disputes, 116-7, 128, 283;
problem of conflict of traditional and western values, 118;
scope of problem, 114-5

Margai, Sir Albert:

as prime minister, 30, 31;
educational qualifications of, 28;
role in illegitimacy debate, 145
Margai, Sir Milton:
as leader of the SLPP, 29;
educational qualifications of, 28;
period as prime minister, 30-1
marital conflict(s):
affection and trust in marriage, 249;
conflict:
between expectations of husband
and wife, 248-9;
of traditional and modern ideas of
conjugal roles, 247-8, 249;
of values and expectations, 249;
disagreement, topics of:
demonstration of affection, 224;
finances, 222;
friends, 224;
household tasks, 224;
table manners, 224, 243;
wife's fidelity, 224;
husband's:
acceptance of idealized urban version, 248;
behaviour in traditional fashion,
248;
concern with position in community, 248;
traditional attitude to authority,
246-7;
traditional attitude to wife's role,
247;
investigation of 15-16;
relatives and, 234-40;
resolving:
by Department of Social Welfare,
246;
by lawyers, 246;
by manipulating traditional and
contemporary values, 244;
by others, 245;
by relatives, 244;
disadvantages of relatives mediat-
ing, 245;
intervention of wife's family, 245;
Provincials' resort to traditional
methods, 244;
responses on, 244;
traditional role of relatives in, 244;
wives complaining to husband's
family, 245;

sources of:
children born out of wedlock, 19;
children's discipline, *223*, 224;
extra-marital affairs, 15, 139, 153;
fidelity of husband, *223*, 224, 225-
33;
finance, *223*, 224;
leisure-habits of husband, *223*, 233;
mothers-in-law:
husband's mother, *223*, 234;
wife's mother, *223*, 234;
professional responses, 224;
relatives, *223*, 234-40;
relative's interference, *223*, 224;
religious differences, *223*, 224;
students' ranking order, *223*, 224;
wives working, 224, 241;
wife's:
idealized version of western husband, 248;
role, and the authority of the husband, 240-3, 246;
sense of insecurity, 225;
western attitudes, 247-8
marital relationships:
and the wider society, 279;
colonial influence on, 3-4, 10;
Creole attitudes to, 10;
disputes and their causes, 99-101;
influence of attitudes to sex and
family limitation on, 276-8;
society and the form of, 3;
stereotypes of, 70-5;
traditional ideas about, 249;
university students attitudes, 10
tradition, persistence of, 247-8;
university student's attitudes, 10
marital roles, social environment and,
2-3
marital status of the professionals:
at time of marriage, 92, *96*;
estranged couples, 39;
extant unions, 38;
married male and female, percentages
of, 37
separated couples, 39;
sex classification, 37, *37*;
unmarried men and women, percentages of, 37
market:
buying in:
as wife's duty, 198, 199;

by husband, *201*, 203;
distinction between buying in store and, 198n4
marriage(s):
abroad, 95;
and family life, 12;
and the individual, 2-3;
attitudes towards:
compared with behaviour, 16;
of university students, 10, 16;
background to:
historical, 297-81;
legal, 282-3;
social, 283-6;
by customary law, 38;
by Muslim law, 38;
by statutory law, 38, 39n5;
ceremonies:
description of *see* weddings;
stereotypes of, 69-70;
children born out of *see* children born out of wedlock;
Christian:
influence, 3, 9, 10, 64, 88-9;
monogamous, 12, 64-5;
colonialist influence, 1, 4, 281;
Creole, as a model, 34, 59;
customary:
Chiefdom Councils Act, 92-3;
Customary Law Advisory Panel, 93;
followed by statutory marriage, 94-5;
law *see* marriage law;
Married Woman's Maintenance Act and, 94;
parents married under, 54-5;
payments under, 126-7;
registration of, 92-3;
rituals observed by Provincials, 92;
widow inheritance under, 90-1, 93;
ideas about:
traditional, 284-5;
western, 283-4;
Kanuri, instability of, 11-12;
laws *see* marriage laws;
legal setting of, 84-123;
monogamous:
advantages of:
for husband, 286-8;
for wife, 288-9;
as 'being civilized', 3, 10, 34, 64,

130, 281;
as status symbol, 12, 54-5, 64, 154, 281;
as superior, 64;
as the 'sentimental model', 15;
as western, 13-14;
Christian influence and, 3, 9, 10, 64, 88-9;
Christianity, as hallmark of conversion to, 9, 64, 88-9, 130, 281;
colonial influences and, 1, 3, 130;
Creole background and, 9, 54-5, 130;
emphasis on, 54;
ideology of, 64-5;
illegitimacy and, 10, 130;
lack of 'fit' in, 1, 12, 64, 291-2;
myth of conforming to, 15;
reasons for preference for, 95;
Sierra Leoneans views on, 14, 64-5, 123;
status and prestige of, 65n8, 123, 130, 281;
status of professional wives and, 17;
student attitudes to, 10;
threat of illegitimate children to, 130;
traditional attitudes to sex conflicting with, 276-7;
Muslim:
marriages, 54, 85;
marriage law *see* marriage law;
ordinance/statutory *see* statutory;
preparation for, 290-1;
problem of maintaining dual systems of prestige, 286;
professional wife's need to make success of, 17;
prospects for, among professional group, 279-95;
registered in 1941-52, 288;
registered in 1961-68, *96*;
social environment and, 2-3;
statutory/ordinance:
attitudes to:
men, 122-3;
women, 122;
law, *see* marriage law;
parents married by, 54;
position of men and women under, 122-3;
prestige of, 151;

reasons for preferring, 94;
social importance of, 55;
stereotypes of:
    patterns of, 15-16;
    relationships under, 70-5;
    types of marriage, 67-70;
traditional:
    disparagement of, 64-5;
    rituals observed by Provincials, 92;
    trends in, 123;
types of, of parents, *54*, 54-5;
urban African, as a predictor, 12;
western, as a predictor, 13-14;
    see also marital, marriage law,
        partner, payment, married
marriage law:
Christian Marriage Ordinance/Act:
    amendment to, 89-90;
    customary union under, 89-90;
    inheritance and, 108;
    marriage under, 95, *96*;
Civil Marriage Act:
    amendment to, 89, 90;
    inheritance and, 108;
    marriages under, 95, *96*;
customary:
    attempts to reform, 92-4;
    Chiefdom Councils Act, 92-3;
    Christian Marriage Act and, 89-90;
    defined, 86-7;
    disadvantages of marriage under,
        94;
registration under, 92-3, 126;
    statutory marriage subsequent to,
        91;
    types of union under, 90-1;
    widow inheritance under, 90-1;
minimum age of marriage, 89;
Muslim:
    marital status of persons at time of
        marriage, 92, *96*;
    number of marriages under, 95, *96*;
    provisions of, 91-2;
    scope of, 87;
    statutory provision for, 86;
'native', defined, 86;
'non-native':
    defined, 87;
    problem raised by term, 87-8;
problems of:
    determining 'personal' law, 87-8;
    interpretation, 88-90;

plurality of systems, 87;
Sierra Leonean, 86-97;
systems, 86-7;
marriage partner, choice of:
assessment of women by traditional
    criteria, 158;
conflict of traditional and western
    ideas, 158
courtship, 158, 178-81;
criteria:
    behaviour, 161-2;
    dress, 159, 160;
    educational standard:
        of men, 161;
        of women, 162-4;
    family:
        approval, 171-4;
        background, 38, 134, 161, 195;
        harmony, 173-4;
        love compared with approval of,
            172, 173;
        opinion in modern setting, 158,
            171-4;
        opinion in traditional society,
            157, 157n4, 171;
    love, 158, 159, *172*, 173;
    physical attractiveness, 159, 160;
    religion, 161;
    tribal background, 170-1;
    virginity, 164-70;
female aspirations and, 158, 177-8;
freedom of choice, 158, 171, 194;
roles of husband and wife and, 158;
scarcity of professional men and, 158,
    178;
stereotypes of, 67-8;
traditional:
    element of choice, 157n4, 171;
    family role in, 157;
    girl's preparation for marriage,
        157-8;
    ideas, persistence of, 158, 172-3,
        195;
    role of the *Bundu*, 157-8;
youth relationships, length of western
    education and, 157, 158
marriage payments:
attitudes to, 68-9, 209;
refundable in divorce, 93-4;
refundable in cases of repeated adul-
    tery, 102;
status of children born before com-

pletion of, 126-7
married couples:
  attitude to children's education, 47, 50;
    occupational status and employment of, *49*, 49-50;
  stereotypes of relatives and, 79-81
Married Woman's Maintenance Act, 94, 114-5
medicine:
  as a profession:
    Creoles in, 30-1;
    Sierra Leoneans practising in Britain, 47n8;
  graduates in:
    Creole, 25;
    Provincial, 28;
    Sierra Leonean, 6, 7;
  students of, at Njala, 36
Mende:
  attitude to Creoles, 30;
  betrothal ceremony, 187n20;
  Creole manipulation of, 34;
  educational achievements of, 28, 31;
  government under independence, 30;
  percentage of professional group, 35;
  -Temne antagonisms, 34;
  -Temne uniformity of culture, 61-2
methodology:
  adaptation of original scheme, i-ii, 14-15;
  additional data, 15-17;
  anonymity of informants, 17;
  attitude scale, 311;
  composition of university sample, 307;
  consistency checks, 17;
  lata collected, 301-13;
  described, 296-313;
  diversity of methods, 297;
  eliciting the truth, 17-18;
  essays by school pupils, 310;
  expatriates, problem of, 298;
  fieldwork, ii, iii-iv;
  group and sample, 12-13;
  interpreting aims to others, 297-8;
  interviews with experts, 311-2;
  issues raised by surveys, in3;
  learning the language, 298-300;
  limitations in studies of family life, 196;
  official records and other statistical data, 312-3;

persons selected for interviews, *308*;
pilot group, 301-6;
political conditions during research, 296;
problem(s):
  encountered, 2-6;
  of elite studies, 297-8;
  of investigator's bias, 11-12;
  of theoretical biases, 196;
  questionnaires to:
    primary school children, 310;
    professionals, 307-10, 323-32;
    university students, 306-7, 314-23;
reasons for replacing persons in sample, *309*;
sampling frame, 307;
sources of data on stereotypes, 66n9;
use of local resources, 300-1
Mexico, study of marriage in, 284
missionary, missionaries:
  activities of Creoles, 23;
  education, 23, 26, 30, 281;
  emphasis on superiority of Christianity, 23;
  enterprise as factor in colonial situation, 4;
  founding of boarding schools, 40;
  influence on monogamous marriage, 3, 9, 34, 88-9, 130, 282;
  influence on attitudes to polygamy, 3, 281;
  part in wars, 26;
  policy, 9n7;
  schools, 9, 26, 40
mistresses, 141
modernity, concept of tradition and, 63-5
monetary economy, 4
monogamy *see* marriage
morality of young women, 176-7
mother:
  -daughter relationship:
    after marriage, 235;
    fear of mother's curse, *214*, 235;
    mother's duty to train, 161;
    mother's indulgence towards, 234-5;
  disobedience to, 213-4;
  good wife described as like, 237-8;
  role in marriage of:
    husband's, 172n16, 239-40;
    wife's, 195, 235;
  -son relationship:

emotional character of, 236-7;
fear of mother, 236, 240;
fear of mother's curse, 214, 236;
mother's ambitions for son, 236;
mother representing traditional
    values, 284-5;
nature of, 213-4;
respect for mother, 236;
succession and inheritance laws
    and, 236
mother's curse, fear of, 172, 213-4, *214*
methers:
and education of their chillren, 43,
    44;
educational levels of, *42*, 42;
reasons for sons' sense of responsibil-
    ity to, 212-3;
son's traditional duties to, 211, 212-3
mothers-in-law:
as source of marital conflict, *223*;
husband's mother:
    compared with wife's mother, 234;
    representing tradition, 239-40;
husband's role in event of disagree-
    ment between wife and mother,
    240;
publicity given to, 234;
rating of problem, *223*, 234;
separate residences for, 239;
types of dispute between wife and,
    239-40;
wife representing western values,
    239-40
Moyamba, school at, 26
Muslim(s):
among Provincials, 40;
background of university students, 9;
Creole families and the *Bundu*,
    157n2;
Creoles, 63, 87n6;
education, 13n10, 40, 40n6;
identity with traditional life, 40;
inheritance law, 109;
law:
    divorce, 97, *97*;
    in Sierra Leone, 19;
    parents married by, 54;
    statutory provision of marriage,
        divorce and devolution of prop-
        erty, 85;
liberated Africans, 22n2;
marital status of men and women at

time of marriage, 92, *96*;
Mohammedan Marriage Act, 38, 95,
    109;
polygamy, 92;
resistance to Christian indoctrination,
    26, 40
nationalism among Creoles, 27-8
nationality:
of illegitimate children, 147;
United Nations definition of, 147n14
'native':
and inheritance law, 107-13;
and marriage law, 86;
defined, 86;
marriage under:
    Christian Marriage Act, 108, 109;
    customary law, 108;
    Muslim law, 109;
problems of inheritance in native-non
    native marriages, 109-13
Ngoni native courts, 154
Njala, educational institutions founded
    in, 28
Njala University College:
birtplace of students of, 37;
collection of data from, **16;**
curriculum, 35;
educational status of, 35;
employment prospects of students,
    35-6;
occupations aspired to, 36;
tribal composition of students, 35
non-literate:
defined, 13n10;
people as traditional, 13
'non-native':
defined, 87;
-native marriages:
    extent of, 113;
    inheritance problems in, 109-13;
problems in inheritance law, 107-8;
problems in marriage law, 87-8
non-Sierra Leoneans:
among professionals, 36, 37;
as marriage partners, 38;
child custody of separated, 104
norms shared by group, 13n9
Northern Province:
education in, 33;
average number of persons per house-
    hold, 57
occupations:

and social status, 48-50;
fathers', 50;
occupational status of married couples, *49*, 49-50;
of:
Creoles, 24, 25;
professional men, 48;
professional women, 48;
wives of professional men, 48-9,
48
opotho, defined, 31n8
old age:
children providing for parents', 211-2;
dependence on sons in, 151, 211, 289;
expectation of children providing for:
analysis of responses by sex and
tribe, 212;
the responses, *211*, 211-2;
paying education costs as investment
for, 212;
provision for one's own, 212, 294
other woman:
confrontation with legal wife, 226-9;
married women's fight against, 233;
position of, 229-30;
press attention to, 231-3;
social position of, 226
outside children *see* children born out
of wedlock
outside wife:
defined, 98n23, 130;
examples of husbands taking, 98;
female attitudes to, 131;
illegitimate girls becoming, 134;
losing children to married home,
137-8;
origin of practice, 130;
question of stigma attached to, 131;
relations with legal wives, 138-9
parents:
children's view of roles of, 15;
educational levels of, 41-2, *41*, *42*;
meeting costs of education, 42-3;
separate residences for, 239;
type of marriage of, *54*, 54-5
participant-observation, i, 11, 296
paternity:
absence of procedures for disavowal,
147;
denial of, 129;
disputes:
increase in, 116-7, 129, 154;

reasons for, 129;
order assigning, 129;
putative fathers acknowledging, 126,
128;
tendency to dispute, 129
patronage, Creole, 24, 28, 34, **58**, **279**
personal qualities, as prestige factor,
51, 52
physical attractiveness:
as criterion for marriage, 159, 160;
in traditional society, 159n7
physical violence, 72
placenta, disposal of the, 263-4
political:
circles, colour discrimination in, 27;
parties *see*
All People's Congress,
Sierra Leone People's Party,
United Democratic Party;
position, as prestige factor, 51, 52;
power:
as a prestige factor, 51, 52, 53;
law and, 154;
of indigenous people, 25
politics:
dependence of Provincials on Creoles,
34, 281;
influence of Creoles in, 31-2;
manipulation of ethnic groups, 32, 34;
tribal affiliations and, 30-1
polygamy:
as prestige factor in villages, 52;
attitudes to, 91;
attitudes of Ghanaian students to,
123;
discrediting of, 3, 130;
extent of, 92;
linked with venereal disease, 70;
Muslim law and, 91-2;
of Provincial students' fathers, 55;
rejection of, 123, 176;
stereotypes of, 70;
urbanization and, 92
Poro:
membership of, as prestige factor,
51, 52;
percentage of professionals in, 166;
promoting cultural syncretism, 62
power:
of professional group, 6, 10, 19;
political *see* political
practices:

and beliefs influencing use of contraceptives, 256-64;
traditional:
  defined, 13;
  shared by Creoles and Provincials, 63;
western marriage, as viewed by professionals, 14;
  see also stereotypes
prestige:
  as problem in traditional and urban marriage, 249;
  colonialism and emergence of symbols of, 1, 130;
  dual systems of:
    in villages and towns, 51-3, 286;
    Provincial students' awareness of, 51, 53;
  factors determining, 51-2;
  father's or father's family's attributes, 53, *53*;
  in traditional and western society, 207;
  marriage partners and, 38;
  of:
    Christianity, 40;
    large number of children, 129, 130, 140-1, 250, 277;
    monogamous marriage, 65n8, 123, 130, 281;
    statutory marriage, 151;
    university degree, 7, 8;
    western education, 51, 52, 281;
  role of Creoles in society, 29, 34;
  see also status
professional group:
  age, 36;
  birthplace, 36-7;
  common goals of, 13n9;
  composition of, 35-48;
  defined, 12;
  education, 40-8, 163;
  households, 56-60;
  marital status, 37-9;
  monogamy and social status, 54-6;
  nature of, and methodology, 296;
  occupation and social status, 48-50;
  questionnaires to, 307-10, 323-32;
  religious affiliation, 39-40;
  sample used, size and significance of, 12-13;
  sense of:

    superiority, 64;
    unity, 13n9;
  shared norms, 13n9;
  size of, 12;
  social:
    background, 16, 48-60;
    status, monogamy and, 54-6;
    status, occupation and, 48-50;
    status in village, 51-3;
  stereotypes:
    effects of experience on, 66-7, 73;
    of child-family relationship, 78;
    of choice of marriage partner, 68;
    of equality of women, 76;
    of expressing affection, 73;
    of physical violence, 72;
    of settling disputes, 81;
    of sexual fidelity, 74-5;
  tribal:
    composition, 35-6;
    tensions in, 34
professionals:
  and the elite, 5-6;
  defined, i;
  educational qualifications as criterion of, 5-6;
  exclusiveness of, 6, 10;
  power of, 6, 10, 19;
  relationship to rest of society, 6, 9;
  special characteristics of, 9-10;
  university students as new, 9-10, 16
progress, idea of, 3
property:
  acquired during marriage, 104-5, 221;
  attitudes to ownership, 105, 221;
  husband's control of, 104;
  inheritance of, 107-13;
  law in regard of women, 220-2;
  Muslim law of, 85;
  ownership:
    legal decision on, 221-2;
    responses, 105, 221;
  rights in traditional society, 104;
  settlement on divorce, 104-7
Protectorate:
  administration of, 26;
  creation of, 25;
  development of, 40-1, 280;
  education in, 26, 28, 280;
  graduates from, 28;
  history of, 25-30;
  legal system, 26, 84;

1951 constitution, 29-30;
rebellions in, 25-6;
trading activities in, 26, 40-1, 280;
  see also hinterland, indigenous people, Provincials
Provinces:
  creation of, 29;
  people of *see* Provincials
Provincials:
  acceptance of inferior status vis-à-
    vis the Creoles, 34, 281;
  appreciation of African personality
    among, 83;
  attitudes to:
    adultery, 102;
    children supporting old age, 212;
    Creoles, 31-2, 34, 281;
    educational qualifications of
      women, 162-3;
    extra-marital affairs, 142;
    family life, 24, 281;
    marital conflict, 223, 240, 244;
    marriage, 34, 130;
    marriage partners, choice of, 162-
      3, *172*, 173;
    mother's curse, 214;
    polygamy, 91;
    secret societies, 166-7;
    sexual fidelity, 142;
    statutory law, 122-3;
  defined, 30n6;
  educational qualifications of, 30;
  in professional group:
    education:
      anxiety over costs of, 46;
      appreciation of western, 41;
      childhood experiences, 45-6;
      feeling of inferiority, 46;
      fellowship of suffering, 46;
      financing of, 46-7;
      influence of African teachers,
        59;
      of families, 41;
      of parents, 41-2, *41*, *42*;
      problems of acquiring, 59;
      residence during, 44-5;
      sacrifices made for, 46;
      study abroad, 46-7;
      value placed on, 40-1;
      ward system, 45, 46;
    family organization, 206, 207;
    father's occupation, 50;

half-brothers and sisters, 56, *56*;
households, *201*, 202, 203;
marriage age, 39;
marriage of parents, types of, 54-5,
  54;
marriage partners, choice of, 38;
  Muslim, percentage of, 40;
  polygamy of fathers, 55;
religious affiliation, 39-40;
  wives earning, 49;
  wives' parents, type of marriage,
    54-5;
marriage with Creoles, 38, 62, 88,
  113, 178-80;
Muslim, 40;
political control exercised by, 34;
political dependence on Creoles, 34,
  281;
relatives, concern for, 217;
role in illegitimacy controversy, 154;
stereotypes of:
  economic independence of women,
    76;
  equality of women, 76;
  physical violence, 72;
  western patterns, 83;
students *see* university students;
trading activities, 25, 40;
traditional marriage rituals observed
  by, 92
questionnaires:
  consistency checks in, 17;
  primary school children, 310;
  professionals, 307-10, 323-32;
  students, 306-7, 314-23
racial prejudice, 47
railways, iii, 26, 27
reference groups, 33-4
references, 333-9
relatives:
  assisting with education, 43-4, 207,
    209;
  as source of marital conflict, 208,
    223, 224, 234-40;
  care of aged, 79-80;
  children, keeping, 215;
  obligations to:
    escaping from, 217-8;
    for education, 207, 209;
    gifts to, 216;
    hospitality to, 216;
    monies paid to, 208, *215*, 218;

Provincial couples' concern for, 207, 217;
wife's, 215-6;
young, 214;
responsibility to, 210;
role in marriage, 173-4;
settling disputes, 81, 234-40, 244;
stereotypes of relationships with, 79-81;
traditional attitude to, 207;
see also, children, family, parents
religion *see* Christianity, Muslim
religious:
affiliation:
as prestige factor, 52;
in choice of marriage partner, 161;
of professional group, 39-40;
discrimination against illegitimate children, 139
roads, iii, 29
ruling families:
defined, 28n4;
membership of, as prestige factor, 51, 52, 53;
professionals and students from, 50
rural:
background of university students, 9-10;
population, iii;
society, traditional character of, 13
sample, significance and size of, 12-13
sampling frame, 12-13
Sande, 157n2
school chillren:
essays by secondary, 310;
questionnaire to primary, 310;
responses on conjugal roles, 204-5;
stereotypes of:
bridewealth, 68-9;
care of the aged, 79-80;
child-family relationship, 76-8;
choice of marriage partner, 67-8;
marital relationships, 71-5;
married couples and relatives, 79-81;
role of the wife, 75-6;
sexual fidelity, 74
secret societies:
enthusiasm for, 166-7;
membership of:
as prestige factor, 51, 52, 53;
professional, 166-7;

promoting cultural syncretism, 62;
Provincial professional and student attitudes to, 166-7;
see also Bundu, Poro
Selection Trust, 30
sentimental model:
of family life, 11;
of monogamous companionate marriage, 15
separation:
as preferable to divorce, 98;
extent of, 99;
judicial:
attitudes to, 98-9;
provision for, 98;
methods of arranging, 98;
wife deemed to have left home, 105
servants in African households, 198
settlers:
African, 22;
white, 23
sex:
attitudes towards family limitation and, 250-78;
conjugal relationships and, 250, 270, 271
sexual:
fidelity:
attitudes to, 75, 142, 268;
stereotypes of, 74-5;
intercourse:
beliefs about, 265-6;
gratification from, 277;
traditional rules about, 266n15;
relations, extra-marital *see* extra-marital;
relations in marriage, 153, 154-5, 255, 268-70, 271, 277;
relations, premarital:
age of, 169-70;
attitudes to, 168-9;
freedom and, 195;
female viewpoint, 167-9;
male viewpoint, 167, 168, 169;
marriage intentions and, 168;
use of contraceptives in, 170;
standards, double, 268n20, 269
sexuality:
attitudes to, 264-70;
attitudes of men to, 270-6
Sierra Leone:
history of, 21-34;

particularities of situation in, 6-7
Sierra Leone People's Party:
  as the government, 29, 30;
  defeat of, 31
slaves, freed, 22
slave trade, 21
social:
  background:
    of professional group, 48-60;
    of university students, 16;
  behaviour, Creoles as reference group
    for, 33-4;
  change:
    beliefs and, 125, 154;
    concepts of tradition and modern-
      ity, 63-5;
    education and, 5-6;
    predicting trends in, 6;
  development, standard-setting and,
    33-4;
  environment, marital roles and, 2-3;
  equality of Creoles and British, 28;
  importance of Christianity, educa-
    tion, and statutory marriage, 54-5;
  independence of women, 174, 175;
  mobility, educational qualifications
    and, 5, 6-7;
  relations, traditional, 13;
  situation, totality of, 3-4;
  status, *see* status;
  stratification, and education, 6
society:
  family and, 2, 288-95;
  marital relationships and, 2-3, 279,
    294-5;
  structure of colonial, 22;
  the individual and, 2-3
Southern Province:
  average number of persons per house-
    hold, 57;
  education in, 33
Spanish Traders, 21
standard-setting role:
  and the professionals, 9-10;
  of elite, 6, 8-9;
  of sub-elite, 6;
  of the Creoles, 29, 33-4
statistical procedures, 13
status:
  assigned to university degree, 5;
  dual systems of, 51-3, 286;
  education and, 5-6;

marriage partners and, 38;
of children born out of wedlock, the,
  124-56;
of professional wives and monogamous marriage, 17;
social:
  age and, 51, 52;
  as problem in traditional and ur-
    ban marriage, 249;
  factors determining, 51-2, *52*;
  impact of western urban ideas, 51;
  in village and town, 51-3;
  monogamy and, 54-6;
  methods of evaluating, 51-2;
  occupation and, 48-50;
  Provincial and Creole views, con-
    vergence and divergence, 51-2,
    52;
  rating, in urban values, 52-3;
standard-setting role of Creoles, 34;
symbols, colonialism and emergence
  of, 1
step-children, inheritance and, 148
stereotypes:
  concepts of tradition and modernity,
    63-5;
  Creole cultural affinities, 62-3;
  defined, 14;
  of:
    child-family relationship, 76-8;
    choice of marriage partner, 67-8;
    courtship, 67;
    economic independence of women,
      76, 83;
    equality of women, 76, 83;
    expression of affection, 72;
    household duties shared by hus-
      band, 74;
    marriage relationships, 70-5;
    marriage rites, 69-70;
    married couples and relatives, 79-
      81;
    role of the wife, 75-6;
    sexual fidelity, 74-5;
    stability of, 15, 66-7;
  sources of, 15, 56-7;
  summary of: 81-3:
    areas of divided opinion, 83;
    traditional attributes favoured,
      82-3;
    western attributes favoured, 82
sterility:

and use of contraceptives, 259;
attitudes to:
    native, 264n13;
    sterile or impotent people, 260-2;
    wife's adultery excusable in cases of, 262-3;
    see also impotence
Stevens, Siaka, 30
stores:
    distinction between buying in market and, 198n4;
    shopping in:
      husband, *201*, 203;
      wife, 198, 199
sub-elite, 6
superiority, Creole attitude of, 24, 28, 58, 279
Syrians:
    attitudes to, 280;
    encouraged to immigrate, 28, 280;
    trading activities of, 27
table manners, as source of conflict, 224, 243
teaching, Creoles in, 28
Temne, the:
    attitude to Creoles, 34;
    Creole manipulation of, 34;
    early relations with Creoles, 24;
    -Mende antagonisms, 34;
    -Mende uniformity of culture, 61-2;
    northern, support of APC, 30;
    percentage of professional group, 35
tensions:
    between indigenous people and Creoles, 28-9;
    between indigenous people and settlers, 22n1, 24;
    ethnic, among professional group, 34
Thai family life, 174
towns:
    heterogeneity of, 62;
    professionals born in, 36, 37;
    size of, iii;
    social status in village and, 51-3
traders' children, 21
trading activities:
    as basis of economy, 25;
    British, 27, 28;
    by indigenous people, 25;
    by Provincials, 25, 40;
    by Syrians, 27-8, 280;
    Creole, 23, 24, 25, 27, 28, 58, 62,

174, 280;
Creole women, 174, 206;
early European, 21;
education acquired for, 21;
extended in the Protectorate, 26, 40-1, 280;
in the hinterland, 24;
realization of potential for, 27-8
tradition, concepts of modernity and, 63-5
traditional:
    as part of indigenous culture, 14;
    attitudes:
      defined, 13;
      influence on married professionals, 13;
      persistence among university students, 10;
    background of university students, 9-10;
    culture, appreciation of intrinsic value of, 10;
    defined, 13, 14;
    dichotomy between western and, 14;
    household, expenditure in, 206-7;
    practices:
      defined, 13
    influences on married couples, 13
tribal:
    affiliations and politics, 30-1;
    antagonisms, Creole manipulation of, 32, 34;
    composition of professional group, 35-6;
    composition of Sierra Leone, complexity of, iiin6;
    composition of university students, 35;
    legal systems, 19;
    migration, iiin6, 25;
    migration into peninsula, efforts to limit, 25;
    practices, Creole attitudes to, 29
tribe(s):
    absence of territorial distinction, 87;
    cultural uniformity among, 61-2;
    defined, 61n2;
    indigenous, ii, 61;
    migrant, iiin6;
    number of, living in Sierra Leone, 84-5;
    represented in professional group,

35, 61
United Democratic Party, 31
university education and degrees:
  Creole's preference for overseas, 36;
  economic position associated with, 7;
  percentage of professionals with Sierra Leone degrees, 36;
  preference for study abroad, 36;
  prestige of degree, 7, 8;
  professionals and, 5-6;
  professional wives with, percentage of, 163;
  sacrifices made to achieve, 7-8;
  standard-setting and possession of, 6;
  social mobility and, 5, 6-7;
  status and, 5
university students:
  as predictors for future, 35-6;
  as the new professionals, 9-10, 16, 35;
  attitudes to:
    bridewealth, 68;
    equal division of inheritance, *152*;
    having a family quickly, 263;
    marriage, 16;
    marriage age, 39;
    polygamy, 91;
    proof of woman's fertility before marriage, 262;
    secret societies, 167;
    sexual fidelity, 142;
  birthplace, 37;
  career aspirations, 36;
  collection of data from, 16;
  Creole, percentage of, 35;
  education:
    at home, 44;
    away from home, 44-5;
    boarding school, 44-5;
    early, 9-10;
    financial obligations, 46-7;
    of parents, 41, *41, 42*;
    present-day and future trends, 59-60;
    Provincial, 44-5;
    remittances to home, 46;
    sacrifices made for, 45-6;
    study abroad, 47;
    working to meet costs of, 43;
  expectations of, 16;
  expectations of children supporting old age, *211*, 211-2;

father's occupation, 50;
half-brothers and sisters, 55;
marital relationships, expectations and trends in, 16;
marriage partner, criteria for choice of:
  education of women, 163n8;
  family approval, 171-4, *172*;
  family background, 161;
  importance of virginity, 167-9;
  love, 159, *172*, 173;
  physical attractiveness, 159;
  religious affiliation, 161;
  tribal background, 170-1;
  wealth, 161;
married, 46;
married with children, 46;
Muslim, 9;
parents of:
  attributes of, 53, *53*;
  polygamy among, 55;
  separated, 98;
  type of marriage of, *54*, 54-5;
preferences, 10;
questionnaire to, 306-7, 314-23;
religious affiliation, 40;
responses on:
  care of children, 205;
  conjugal roles, 205;
  ideal number of children, 250, *251*;
  social status, 51-3;
self-confidence of, 10;
sexual relations, 163-4;
social background of, 16, 59-60;
stereotypes of:
  child-family relationships, 78;
  choice of marriage partner, 68;
  equality for women, 76;
  expression of affection, 73;
  physical violence, 72;
  settling disputes, 81;
  sexual fidelity, 74-5;
survey of, i;
traditional background of, 9-10;
traditional values held by, 10;
tribal composition of, 35;
under ward system, 45
unmarried:
  relations between the:
    adolescence as a new problem, 177-8;
    assumption about, 175-6;

attitudes to employed women and men, 175;
economic and social independence of women and, 174-5;
marriage viewed as a career, 177;
question of morality, 176-7;
problems faced by Sierra Leonean, 177-8;
young men:
  and marriage partners, 157-95;
  attitudes to girl's behaviour, 161;
  attitudes to girl's educational standard, 162-4;
  judged on personal achievement, 161, 195;
  length of educational process changing relationships, 157;
young women:
  and marriage partners, 157-95;
  attitudes to wealth and education, 161;
  aspirations of, and professional men, 141, 158;
  behaviour of:
    absence of guidelines in traditional society, 157, 195;
    Creole rules for, 158, 179-81;
    family background and circumspect, 161;
    patterns and marriage with professionals, 158, 161;
    standards of, 161-2;
  boy-friends:
    mature, 163-4;
    number of, 162;
    question of morality, 176-7;
  Bundu society, role of, 157-8;
  favoured position of, 195;
  liaison without intention of marriage, 158n6;
  preferring to be mistresses, 158n6
unwed mothers:
  awareness of rights, 115, 130;
  chances of marrying, 131, 133;
  education and the position of, 130;
  female attitudes to, 131;
  impaired status of, 131, 132;
  social stigma attaching, question of, 115, 130-1;
  suing for maintenance, 128, 278
urbanism, effects of, 1-2
urbanization, polygamy and, 92

values:
  attitudes and, 16-17;
  behaviour and, 16,17;
  husbands place on marriage, 197
villages:
  heterogeneity of population, 62;
  professionals born in, 37;
  social status in town and, 51-3;
  students born in, 37
violence, aversion to, 95, 97;
virginity:
  and *Bundu* practices, 157, 164-5, 167;
  attitudes to:
    parental, 165-6;
    traditional, 164-5;
  protection of girl's, as mother's duty, 204;
  students' views on importance of, 167-9, 283;
  see also sexual relations, premarital
wage-earning: emergence of class, 4
ward system:
  as type of adoption, 119;
  Christian influence on, 9;
  duties in household, 198;
  education and, 45;
  numbers involved, 45;
  operation of, 24, 34, 45;
  passing as Creole, 88;
  social significance of, 34;
  treatment of wards, 45, 46
wealth:
  as a prestige factor, 51, 52, 53;
  choice of marriage partner and, 161;
  traditional signs of, 207
weddings:
  as status symbols, 123;
  bachelor's party, 192;
  church, 95;
  churching the bride, 194;
  civil, 95;
  costs of, 192, 239;
  Creole, 192;
  described, 192-3;
  drop in number of, in, 9, 67-68, 95, 97;
  honeymoon, 194;
  parties following, 193-4;
  reception, 193;
  social significance of, 192;
  stereotypes of, 69-70;
  the *ashobe*, 193-4

western:
  as progressive and modern, 14;
  defined, 13-14;
  dichotomy between traditional and,
    14;
  type of education, 9;
  values:
    and the colonial situation, 9;
    Sierra Leoneans' view of, 14;
    university students' attitudes, 10
Western Area:
  age structure of households, *58*;
  average number of persons per house-
    hold, 57, *58*;
  educational opportunities in, 45;
  legal system, 85, 86;
  professionals born in, 36, 37;
  registration of births in, 126;
  university students born in, 37
Western province, education in, 33
widow inheritance, 90-1, 93
wife:
  authority of husband and role of,
    241-2;
  dual role of educated, 241;
  role of:
    and marital conflict, 240-3;
    conflict between traditional and
      western values in, 118;
    stereotypes of, 75-6;
    see also wives
witchbird, belief in, 260-1
witchcraft, 63
wives:
  careers and earning:
    as source of marital conflict, 224;
    attitudes to:
      school children, 204-5;
      university students, 205;
    male attitudes to, 49-50;
    methods of earning, 49;
    rearing of children and, 204;
  curse, 264-5;
  infidelity of, 75, 224;
  inherited, 90-1, 93, 109-10, 111;
  in the household:
    concepts of conjugal roles, 197;
    cooking, 198, 199, 201;
    domestic responsibilities, 198-200;
    responsibilities for children, 204-5;
    supervision of children, 201;
    tasks not delegated by, 200-1;
  of professionals:
    education of husbands, 47;
    educational qualifications of, 48,
      163;
    need to make success of marriage,
      17;
    occupations of, 48, 49;
    periods worked before and after
      marriage, 49;
    status and monogamous marriage,
      17;
    'unemployed', 49;
  opposition to illegitimacy bill, 151-2;
  position of divorced, 107
woman damage, 101-2, 268
women:
  attitudes to:
    polygamy, 91;
    relatives supporting education, 44;
  belief in:
    promiscuity of, 268-9;
    supernatural powers of, 264-5;
  educational opportunities for, 7, 26;
  importance of child-bearing to, 131n3,
    143, 144;
  influence over men, 264-70;
  in professional group:
    age, 36;
    birthplace, 36-7;
    estranged, 50;
    marital status, 37;
    married, percentage of, 50;
    non-Sierra Leonean, 37;
    occupations of, 48;
    percentage with Sierra Leone de-
      grees, 36
  National Federation of Women's Or-
    ganizations, 152;
  sexuality of, 264-70;
  stereotypes of, 70;
  see also mothers, unmarried, wives
young men, women, *see* unmarried